CQ GUIDE TO

CURRENT AMERICAN GOVERNMENT

Spring 2007

CQ PRESS

A Division of Congressional Quarterly Inc.

Washington, D.C.

Congressional Quarterly Inc.

Congressional Quarterly Inc., a publishing and information services company, is the recognized national leader in political journalism. CQ Inc. serves clients in the fields of business, government, news and education with complete, timely and nonpartisan information on Congress, politics and national issues. CQ Press is a division of Congressional Quarterly Inc. The Library Reference imprint of CQ Press publishes this work and hundreds of others on the institutions, processes and policies of government to serve the needs of librarians, researchers, students, scholars and interested citizens. Other titles include the *Guide to the Presidency,* the *Guide to Congress,* the *Guide to the U.S. Supreme Court,* the *Guide to U.S. Elections* and *Politics in America.* CQ Press's American Government A to Z Series is a reference collection that provides essential information about the U.S. Constitution, Congress, the presidency, the Supreme Court and the electoral process. *Congress and the Nation,* a record of government for each presidential term, is published every four years. CQ Press also publishes the *CQ Researcher,* a weekly print periodical and online reference database covering today's most debated social and political issues. Visit www.cqpress.com to learn more about these and other publications of CQ Press.

CQ Press
1255 22nd Street, NW, Suite 400
Washington, DC 20037

Phone: 202-729-1900; toll-free, 1-866-4CQ-PRESS (1-866-427-7737)

Web: www.cqpress.com

Cover photos: Scott J. Ferrell, (Congressional Quarterly) and Department of Defense
Cover design: Paul P. Pressau

♾ The paper used in this publication exceeds the requirements of the American National Standard for Information Sciences—Permanence of Paper for Printed Library Materials, ANSI Z39.48-1992.

Printed and bound in the United States of America
10 09 08 07 06   1 2 3 4 5

ISBN 10: 0-87289-349-9
ISBN 13: 978-0-87289-349-8
ISSN 0196-612-X

Contents

CONTENTS

Introduction

Guide to Current American Government is a collection of articles from *CQ Weekly*, a trusted source for in-depth, nonpartisan reporting on and analyses of congressional action, presidential activities, policy debates and other news and developments in Washington, D.C. *CQ Weekly* also covers the intersection of government and commerce. The articles, selected to complement introductory U.S. government texts with up-to-date examinations of current issues and controversies, are divided into four sections: Foundations of American Government, Political Participation, Government Institutions, and Politics and Public Policy.

Foundations of American Government. This section examines issues and events that involve interpretation of the U.S. Constitution, such foundational principles as federalism and democracy and political ideologies and political culture in the United States. This edition of the *Guide* includes articles that look at the "fair use" doctrine and copyright law in the case of a project by Google to digitize library collections, problems the government is encountering in electronically protecting the privacy rights of citizens, attempts to rein in the video game industry's dissemination of graphic content and the congressional practice of earmarking money in the federal budget.

Political Participation. The articles in this section examine current issues in electoral and party politics, voting behavior and public opinion. The articles selected for this edition examine the run-up to the 2006 midterm elections, focusing on Democratic prospects for regaining one or both houses of Congress, and Republican attempts to hold onto power for the foreseeable future, especially in light of President George W. Bush's lame-duck status and declining poll numbers.

Government Institutions. This section explores the inner workings of Congress, the presidency and the federal courts. Included here are articles that examine tensions between Congress and the executive branch, the Bush administration's conduct of Middle East policy and the "war on terror" and current issues involving the Supreme Court and the federal judiciary.

Politics and Public Policy. The articles in this section profile major policy issues on the national agenda. This edition features articles that examine policies pertaining to federally funded student loans, the U.S. Army's high-tech transformation, the future of the United States' Cuban policy, and the politics of embryonic stem cell research, high-speed Internet access and race in formulating drug policy.

Foundations of American Government

This section highlights current issues in American politics that involve the core principles of democracy—individual rights and liberties, the role of government, the limits of federalism and American political ideologies and political culture. These foundations frame the attitudes, interests and institutions that dictate political choices and outcomes.

The first three articles in this section are explorations of the fundamental challenges posed by technological advances in our digital age. The doctrine of "fair use" in copyright law protects free speech by allowing the use of otherwise protected materials in a number of situations. But the technological advances that make the much-anticipated Google Library Project possible were unanticipated when the 1976 Copyright Act was written. The first article looks at how the right of free speech collides with the economic rights of book publishers in the Association of American Publishers' landmark lawsuit against Google over its ambitious and unprecedented plan to digitize and make searchable the collections of five major libraries.

The second article in this section contemplates the government's responsibility to protect the privacy rights of its citizens. When a Department of Veterans Affairs analyst's laptop and external hard drive were stolen recently, sensitive personal information belonging to more than 26 million veterans and active duty military personnel was compromised. The article chronicles not only this example but a number of other cases in which rights considered fundamental to the American conception of individual liberty were at risk due to governmental inability to keep up with the ever-evolving challenges of cybersecurity.

The video game industry is under increasing pressure to police itself for graphically sexual and violent content. The Entertainment Software Ratings Board (ESRB) is the self-regulating group charged with this responsibility, but critics are calling for more government involvement in monitoring the industry. So far the industry has successfully fought numerous statutes aimed at codifying video game ratings at the local and state level, and it is prepared to do the same at the federal level. The third article examines the debate between those who assert that video games, as works of artistic expression, fall under the rubric of constitutionally free speech and those who wish to protect children from inappropriate graphic images.

The manner in which power is shared between a centralized authority and its component parts has been a persistently thorny issue throughout American history, often dividing people into two camps—federalists and anti-federalists. Though the meaning of the term *federalism* has changed over time in our political culture, the fundamental tension remains. The relationship between federal and state power is complex, however, and surfaces in ways that sometimes obscure the battle lines. The last article in this section considers the congressional practice of earmarks, known pejoratively as "pork barrel spending," whereby lawmakers set aside money in the federal budget for pet projects back home. Though this custom is often reviled and has been a recurring feature of several high-profile ethics investigations, this article demonstrates that the benefits to recipients of earmarks—and the help members of Congress receive in return to secure reelection—outweigh the forces opposed to this practice. The balance of power is thus preserved, as both local and federal power holders get what they want.

Data Drip

Americans' personal information is leaking from federal agencies, going astray or being stolen with alarming frequency. Experts say the government's vulnerability is deep and its safeguards are flimsy.

CHRIS CAMPBELL RECALLS BEING STUNNED, then muttering "Oh, that's not good" when a shamefaced U.S. Department of Agriculture official called in January to ask that he return a computer disk full of personal data about farmers who had taken part in a $10 billion federal buyout of tobacco crops.

Campbell, a data analyst for the nonprofit Environmental Working Group, normally lives for this sort of juicy information — he has documented waste and irregularities in federal farm programs for years. But when he filed a routine request with the agency for expenditures on the buyout, he got a lot more than he bargained for. The department forwarded Campbell a data-rich computer disk that contained not only a list of program payments but also the names, addresses and Social Security numbers of the 350,000 buyout recipients.

What's more, Campbell wasn't the only office jockey plunged into this vast trove of information. Eight banks and financial institutions that sought information about the buyout in the hope of generating business also received the information. It took department officials in Washington three weeks to recognize the scope of the problem and request that Campbell and the banks mail back the disks.

"I'd never gotten Social Security numbers in the mail before," said Campbell. "Let's just say I was surprised."

A string of data security breaches in recent months has compromised the personal information of millions of Americans, leading privacy experts to question the government's ability to protect citizens' personal information in the information age. Security experts say lax controls and bureaucratic mix-ups are leaving electronic records precariously exposed. In some instances, government auditors say, federal officials are ignoring privacy laws specifically designed to protect sensitive data. (*Privacy laws, p. 6*)

One security leak gained nationwide attention recently after a laptop computer and external hard drive belonging to a Department of Veterans Affairs analyst were stolen in May from the analyst's suburban Maryland home. The equipment contained Social Security numbers and other personal information belonging to at least 26.5 million veterans and active-duty military personnel. VA officials recovered the laptop and drive on June 29 and said that it appeared that the thief had not been able to gain access to the data. The Bush administration has requested $160.5 million to monitor the credit ratings of the affected individuals for a year.

The case of the VA's missing laptop drew national attention because of the sheer amount of data it contained, in addition to the fact that it involved active-duty military personnel. But experts say it also reveals the vulnerabilities in the federal government's vast stores of personal data and the immense potential for more problems. Millions of Americans reveal their financial status to qualify for housing subsidies, student loans and other types of federal aid. Senior citizens submit information about their medication needs in order to use the new Medicare drug benefit. And nearly 135 million individuals and

Leaky Data Raises Privacy Concerns

During the past four months, federal agencies have reported a series of incidents in which vast amounts of citizens' personal information was compromised due to unintended releases of government records, computer hacking or other circumstances. Some of the most notable incidents, starting with the one most recently made public:

AGENCY / DATE DISCLOSED	RECORDS AFFECTED	SECURITY BREACH
Navy June 23	28,000	The Navy said a civilian Web site disclosed the names, birth dates, and Social Security numbers of some personnel and their dependents.
Federal Trade Commission June 22	110	Two laptops were stolen from an employee's vehicle. The hard drives contained names, addresses, Social Security numbers, birth dates and financial account numbers gathered in law enforcement investigations.
Agriculture Department June 21	26,000	A hacker broke into the computer system containing names, Social Security numbers, and photographs of current and former employees and contractors.
Energy Department June 13	4,000	Police found a 1996 list containing personal information of workers at a former nuclear weapons complex, known as the Hanford Site, in a private home that was raided in a drug case.
Energy Department June 12	1,502	Names, Social Security numbers, and other data for National Nuclear Security Administration contractors and others were compromised when a hacker gained entry in November 2005 to an agency computer system in Albuquerque.
Social Security Administration June 8	200	An employee's laptop containing names, Social Security numbers and other personal data was stolen while he attended a conference in Virginia.
Internal Revenue Service June 5	291	An IRS laptop containing personal information of employees and job applicants — including fingerprints, names, Social Security numbers and birth dates — was lost during an airline flight.
Centers for Medicare and Medicaid Services June 1	268	Humana Inc., a contractor to the government, reported the theft of Medicare enrollment forms.
Veterans Affairs Department May 22	26,500,000	An analyst's laptop and external drive containing detailed data on all veterans discharged since 1975, as well as more than 2 million active-duty personnel and reservists, was stolen from his Maryland home. The equipment was recovered June 29.
Centers for Medicare and Medicaid Services May 19	17,000	Personal health information was left on a hotel computer in Baltimore.
Defense Department April 5	14,000	An intruder gained access to a Pentagon computer server containing confidential health care insurance information.
Marine Corps March 30	207,750	A portable drive was lost containing personal information used for research on re-enlistment bonuses.

SOURCE: Individual agency reports, Privacy Rights Clearinghouse

businesses each year submit highly detailed tax and employment information to the IRS.

Yet the defenses around data at most federal agencies have been vulnerable for years and continue to fall below acceptable standards, according to security experts and government auditors. Even in the aftermath of the high-profile incident at the VA, the Government Accountability Office on June 20 repeated warnings that the federal bureaucracy is riddled with "weaknesses in almost all areas of information security controls."

The government "has an overwhelming amount of data, which is why they ought to be leading by example," said Alan Paller, a data security expert at the SANS Institute, a computer security training center in Bethesda, Md. "It's worth getting mad about."

Cabinet-level agencies including the Agriculture Department, the VA and the Department of Defense have been unable to control security breaches for years, according to government reports. And most agencies do not give their top information security officials the authority to oversee all of their computer systems, restrict access to sensitive data, and reprimand or fire employees who compromise data. Government officials who have studied the situation describe a frequently splintered and leaderless environment in which departments spend tens of millions of dollars studying problems and preparing reports that then go unread. In March, the House Government Reform Committee, which has jurisdiction over federal records, issued a report card that gave the government's data security efforts a grade of D+.

THEFT AND HUMAN ERROR

The recent string of disclosures bears out the assessment that many departments suffer from inertia. Government agencies remain vulnerable to human error — the culprit in the Agriculture Department's unintended leak of tobacco buyout recipients — as well as hacking and other malicious intrusions from outside.

"What we know is that in most agencies, the necessary security controls are not in place," said Bruce Brody, a consultant who was the Energy Department's chief information security officer until January and who served in a similar role at the VA from 2001 to 2004.

Four months after the Agriculture Department accidentally released the tobacco buyout information, a hacker tapped into department computer systems containing the names, Social Security numbers and photos of 26,000 of its Washington area employees

LEAKY DATA: VA Secretary Jim Nicholson, tells lawmakers at a June 29 House Veterans' Affairs hearing that a stolen laptop containing the personal information of at least 26.5 million veterans and active-duty personnel has been recovered. The theft focused nationwide attention on the vulnerability of personal data in the government's hands.

and contractors. The department is paying to monitor the credit ratings of the affected individuals for one year.

Hackers also penetrated the Department of Energy's computers. Officials in June disclosed a series of security breaches, including an instance in which a hacker gained access to the personal records of 1,500 employees and contractors of the National Nuclear Security Administration, which oversees the nuclear weapons stockpile. Although the incident took place last September, mid-level agency officials did not tell Energy Secretary Samuel W. Bodman until mid-June, saying they believed he had been informed through other channels. The agency also acknowledged that records including the Social Security numbers, birth dates and work assignments of more than 4,000 contract employees at the Hanford Site in Washington state turned up on June 2 in a private house that had been converted into an illegal drug lab. Hanford is a former nuclear weapons complex with nine nuclear reactors.

Energy Department data also has gone missing in a series of computer thefts. Ten laptops containing personal information about approximately 30 employees were stolen from a Germantown, Md., payroll office in June, and another computer thought to have held personal data was stolen from a contractor at the Oak Ridge nuclear site in Tennessee. A former employee whose security badge was not confiscated is suspected of stealing the computer in Tennessee, officials said.

Even the Federal Trade Commission, which is responsible for, among other things, investigating fraud and identity theft on the Internet, has been victimized by a security breach. The agency disclosed in June that one of its employees lost a laptop containing the personal records of 110 people.

Some incidents are coming to light by pure happenstance. An individual conducting a search on an Internet search engine unexpectedly discovered that his medical records had been posted on a Web site maintained by the Indian Health Service, a division of the Department of Health and Human Services (HHS), according to HHS data security officials familiar with the case.

Indian Health Service officials, alerted to the problem in late January, quickly removed the records but say they cannot explain how the mishap occurred or know for sure how long the information was posted. The incident, which has not been publicly disclosed, may be a violation of the 1996 Health Insurance Portability and Accountability Act, or HIPAA, that HHS is in charge of enforcing. Officials say that no disciplinary action was taken against anyone involved in the incident.

HHS, a sprawling agency that holds tens of millions of Americans' health records, says its employees and contractors have accidentally lost or released personal data five times this year, which is not unusual for large government agencies. Only four of the 16 major agencies contacted for this story — the departments of Labor, Interior, Housing and Urban Development, and Transportation — say they had no security breaches this year. Some agencies, like the departments of Agriculture, Homeland Security and Justice, refuse to say how many times personal data has been compromised at their agencies.

The government says there is no evidence that information compromised in the recent incidents has been used to commit identity theft. But it could take a year or longer to assess the fallout because many individuals listed in the electronic records are unaware that their information was exposed and might not notice something suspicious.

There is no law requiring the government to notify individuals whose personal information was compromised. Those who can prove they were defrauded or otherwise victimized by a security breach could collect $1,000 per incident under the 1974 Privacy Act, a law that gave citizens access to personal information the government collects about them.

Bush administration officials acknowledge the recently disclosed incidents point to the need for a culture change that puts a higher premium on security. Clay Johnson III, deputy director for management of the White House Office of Management and Budget (OMB), ordered agencies on June 23 to take more control over personal data by encrypting all sensitive data on computers and wireless devices and installing a feature on laptop computers that automatically requires user re-authentication after a half-hour of inactivity.

"The question is, What assurances can we give the American people?" Johnson said shortly before issuing the directive. "We need to give them a greater level of assurance than they have now, obviously."

HEIGHTENED AWARENESS

Despite the recent breaches, experts say some federal agencies are taking necessary precautions to safeguard sensitive data. The experts give particularly high marks to departments with years of experience safeguarding private information, such as the Social Security Administration (SSA) and the U.S. Postal Service. The SSA, for example, uses armored trucks to carry backup computer tapes to secure, off-site storage facilities. And both of the agencies have centralized their electronic operations so that a single office has oversight over all computer systems. The Department of Labor also gets generally high marks among Cabinet-level agencies for the way it has put one official in charge of overseeing security efforts and buying necessary software.

Experts add that federal agencies have become more adept at responding to new electronic incursions that rely on deception or cutting-edge technologies. Agencies are training workers how to recognize a practice known as "spearphishing," in which electronic intruders send e-mails that appear to be from the secretary or other top officials. The messages sometimes direct workers to Web sites that mimic the agency's own site so well that even employees may not be able to tell the difference. Opening an e-mail or clicking on links on the Web site could unleash viruses or worms that disable the department's system or capture keystrokes or other sensitive data.

Agency security officials also are training employees to recognize the perils of using some new technologies. One concern is the advent of tiny, high-capacity "flash drives" that can be used to copy huge volumes of information from desktop computers, but also can be easily lost or misplaced. Officials are instructing workers when it is appropriate to use the drives — and also how to recognize instances in which unscrupulous workers or contractors might

Security Built on a Patchwork of Standards

Federal agencies are legally required to protect certain types of sensitive personal information. In large measure, the obligation stems from federal privacy laws dealing with financial services, health care, government and the Internet. However, standards are spottily enforced, and there are variations in how closely the agencies adhere to the laws. Some of the most prominent laws dealing with personal identification:

2002 "E-Government Act"
- Authorized creation of a federal chief information officer in the Office of Management and Budget (OMB) to oversee the development, application and management of electronic information within the federal government.
- Targeted $45 million for information technology to link agencies and facilitate information-sharing.
- Required federal agencies to adhere to uniform information security standards.
- Directed OMB to establish an interagency committee on government information and issue guidelines for agency Web sites.
- Required OMB to submit an annual report to Congress on the state of e-government.

1999 Gramm-Leach-Bliley Act
- The Federal Trade Commission, in rules to implement provisions in the banking overhaul law, has required financial institutions to have an information security plan that includes administrative, technical and physical safeguards to ensure the confidentiality of consumer information, and to protect against hazards, such as hacking.

1996 Health Insurance Portability and Accountability Act
- Required the Department of Health and Human Services (HHS) to issue rules for protecting the confidentiality of health information. The security standards, which HHS finalized in 2003, mandate that health care providers to keep administrative, technical and physical safeguards to ensure the confidentiality of electronic health records, and to protect against hacking and other hazards to the security of that information.

1914 Federal Trade Commission Act
- A series of updates to the law have empowered FTC to prevent unfair competition or deceptive acts affecting commerce. As part of its mandate, the agency enforces the promises in companies' privacy statements, including promises about the security of customers' personal information.

use the devices to surreptitiously download millions of bits of information.

"Data security was hardly a blip on the radar as late as 1999 and has become a higher priority since then," said Peter Swire, former chief counselor for privacy at OMB in the Clinton administration. Swire noted that the federal government has a strong record in protecting the approximately 10 percent of government data that is categorized as classified through safeguards such as forbidding employees and contractors from accessing classified records via an Internet connection. But he added that officials only recently have turned their attention to protecting non-classified data.

The increased awareness is partly due to a 2002 law known as the Federal Information Security Management Act, or FISMA, that required agencies to assess how well they are protecting privacy and step up the training of their employees and contractors.

"Agencies stop a lot of bad things from happening all the time," said Dan Chenok, a former Bush administration security official, who serves as the chairman of the federal Informa-

tion Security and Privacy Advisory Board. "Security officers set up detection systems so that thousands of potential incidents don't become the virus that makes the front page."

The precautions mirror those being taken in the private sector, which also has a mixed record safeguarding personal information. The Privacy Rights Clearinghouse, a California-based organization that tracks personal data losses, estimates that more than 85 million records in the private and public sectors may have been compromised nationwide since February 2005, when a major data broker, Choice Point, unknowingly sold the personal data of about 145,000 Americans to criminals posing as legitimate buyers of information.

But experts say the federal government faces special challenges because of the variety of sensitive information it keeps, the increasingly mobile nature of the federal workforce and the pervasive use of contractors, which allow thousands of individuals with varying levels of security clearance to access government databases from remote sites. A 2004 government survey on the work practices of 1.8 million federal workers found that more than 140,000 had clearance to connect with government computer systems from home. The IRS says 50,000 of its employees have laptops allowing them to access personal and business tax information from anywhere. And 133 Education Department personnel can access more than 10,000 records containing student loan recipients' personal information.

Government departments that detect security breaches also face special hurdles ensuring that the problems don't recur. Requests for additional money to bolster cybersecurity must compete with other needs and sometimes languish for weeks or months. Agency officials often need to win unofficial support from congressional appropriators to reprogram money for more security.

PROBLEM AGENCIES

Although the government may be more aware of how vulnerable its data has become, experts say a number of federal agencies have been particularly slow to bolster their electronic defenses and remain at serious risk of compromising or losing sensitive information

The VA, HHS and Energy departments have been blamed for not taking a top-down approach to securing sensitive information in regional offices, leaving officials in Washington unable to gauge which employees or contractors can access what information.

After the VA laptop was stolen, the agency said it would assemble an "access inventory" to identify what kind of data each employee can access. Officials at other agencies say this kind of laborious process is extremely rare. But several security experts and former government officials say more departments should follow the VA's lead to better understand what their employees are doing.

"Almost all big agencies have large and powerful field operations with their own . . . congressional interests [sponsors] across 50 states, and decentralized management doesn't work in security," said Brody, the former Energy Department and VA official. "You need centralization and the need to hold people accountable."

Lack of controls over contractors has been a particular concern, as evidenced by an incident reported in June involving Humana Inc., a health insurer that administers Medicare benefits for HHS. A Humana analyst accidentally left a copy of a file containing the personal information of 17,000 Medicare recipients on a public computer terminal in the business

center of a Baltimore hotel. The breach was discovered when an auditor from the HHS inspector general's office, who was coincidentally working at the hotel, logged in on the same computer and found the copy of the stored file.

The slip-up appears to be in violation of HIPAA, which was intended to protect confi-

> **"The question is, What assurances can we give the American people? We need to give them a greater level of assurance than they have now."**
>
> — Clay Johnson, deputy director of the Office of Management and Budget

dential patient records. HHS officials said that they are watching Humana closely and have ordered the company to monitor the credit records of individuals whose information was on the computer. The agency also told Humana to devise a plan to prevent similar breaches in the future.

The VA ran into trouble tracking the activity of contractors hired to prepare electronic records of doctor office visits for the Veterans Health Administration. Some contractors outsourced the work to subcontractors in India and Pakistan, leaving VA officials "incapable of controlling or detecting where the information was transcribed [from doctors voice

recordings], or who had access to it," according to an audit released last month by the agency's inspector general.

One subcontractor threatened the VA last year when a dispute arose over $28,000 in payments that the subcontractor said the agency owed him. The subcontractor threatened to publish about 30,000 medical records of veterans on the Internet unless the VA paid. The VA agreed to pay the full amount, and the subcontractor promised to destroy the records. But the inspector general's office concluded there is no way of validating whether the subcontractor followed through or whether other patient information was compromised.

VA officials told lawmakers at a June 21 hearing of the House Veterans Affairs' Subcommittee on Health that they are no longer using contractors to transcribe medical records. But the lack of more-centralized controls continues to be the subject of concern.

"The more we learn about the awful results of decentralization, in contrast to the bright promises offered by some VA officials, the more we see that the system has no departmental standards," said House Veterans' Affairs Committee Chairman Steve Buyer, an Indiana Republican. "More important, the system . . . doesn't identify who is in charge of developing policy, implementing policy or enforcing policy."

The 2002 federal data law requires agencies to take full responsibility for the activities of contractors, who are supposed to undergo the same training as agency employees. Contractors also are expected to test their systems to ensure they comply with federal standards.

But the inspectors general of six agencies have reported that their departments "rarely" or only "sometimes" checked contractors' activities for compliance. Agencies that checked rarely included the departments of Defense, Homeland Security and State. Those that checked sometimes included Agriculture, HHS and NASA.

Agencies also have been victimized by contractors' reluctance to report security slip-ups in a timely fashion. Humana, the HHS contractor, waited about a month before telling officials in Washington that an employee's laptop was stolen from his car, resulting in the loss of 268 applications for Medicare coverage that contained personal health data.

Moreover, experts say, some agencies have been generally slow to embrace low-cost, common-sense strategies to securing sensitive data that do not require elaborate new policies or training. The Veterans Health Administration until recently did not have a mechanism for limiting the amount of time patient records could be viewed on computer screens, which meant that electronic medical charts might sit for hours on desktops, in full view of visitors to clinics. After the theft of the VA analyst's laptop, the agency announced it would install screensavers that automatically come on after five minutes of inactivity.

OTHER FIXES ELUSIVE

Security experts and government officials say a long-term solution to the government will require a reassessment of existing laws and a stronger commitment to security from the executive and legislative branches. Experts predict that without more vigorous enforcement, vulnerabilities will be difficult to fix in anything but a scattershot fashion.

One subject under discussion is the role of an agency's chief information officer, or CIO, a position that many agencies strengthened after enactment of the 2002 federal data law. The CIO is supposed to buy computer technology, direct the response to security breaches and oversee privacy officers who set limits on how the agency collects and protects data. Although the job description confers considerable authority, many CIOs in reality face resistance from other bureaucrats within their departments, who fear additional security measures could impose new rules or drain budgets.

Officials say CIOs need support from department secretaries or other higher-ups to make and enforce changes. Some skeptics joke the CIO's primary responsibility is to make sure the secretary's BlackBerry wireless device works.

"You have to have buy-in . . . from the agency head on down, so that it becomes part of the culture and not just a requirement you're going to meet," said Tonya Manning, chief security officer at the Department of Labor, an agency many say does a good job protecting data.

The VA general counsel's office underscored the information officers' tenuous authority in a pair of rulings from 2003 and 2004, stating the CIO could not actually order or enforce security or privacy policies but only request that the secretary take action.

Brody said in an interview that he wanted to add protective measures in 2003 in the face of cybersecurity

threats but faced resistance from some within the Veterans Health Administration. He asked the general counsel to clarify his authority. The response was that Brody could issue policies but could not oversee daily security operations, which remained under the purview of other VA officials.

After a hacker attack damaged VA computer operations, Brody sought further clarifications and was told in early 2004 that he only could complain to the secretary if his security requests were not followed. The reason was that the 2002 law stated that agencies should "ensure" compliance with requirements that secure the sys-

> # Government officials have **"**an overwhelming amount of data, which is why they ought to be leading by example. It's worth getting mad about.**"**
>
> — **Alan Paller,** security expert, SANS Institute

tems, as opposed to enforcing compliance. The VA has since moved slowly to centralize authority over its electronic operations.

The 2002 law itself has been criticized for contributing to some of the current security problems.

Skeptics say the law emphasizes the need for studies and audits at the expense of hands-on

> # **"**The federal government has a strong record in protecting the approximately 10 percent of government data that is categorized as classified through safeguards such as forbidding employees and contractors from accessing classified records via an Internet connection. **"**
>
> — **Peter Swire,** former chief counselor for privacy at OMB

troubleshooting. Security experts estimate that at least $1 billion has been spent to date on certification reports that often go unread. The government spends about $5 billion a year on security software and other technology to protect its computer systems.

STRENGTHENING CURRENT LAW?

Many agencies see the law's requirements as nothing more than a "paperwork exercise," according to House Government Reform Chairman Thomas M. Davis III, a Virginia Republican.

"It's not obvious that this law makes the systems more secure," added Frank Reeder, a privacy expert and past chairman of the federal Information Security and Privacy Advisory Board. "The fact that there's a law doesn't change behavior but may create more processes that people just ignore. If you have a paper process, you can create a false sense of security."

Reeder and others note the law requires agencies to test their computer systems annually. But instead, some agencies do superficial checks, then ask their security officers whether any new problems have become apparent. "Agencies can say they have done an annual review without knowing the vulnerabilities and configuration weaknesses of their systems," said Paller of the SANS Institute.

Some agencies also rely on contractors such as KPMG or PricewaterhouseCoopers to audit the performance of their systems using one-size-fits-all criteria that do not take into account in the audit individual agency's particular needs. The results of the audits are rarely read by systems administrators, and problems in the audits are not always fixed.

Agencies also are failing to comply with a requirement in the law that they report electronic security incursions — ranging from attempts to knock an agency's computer system off-line to a cyberespionage plot. Johnson and other OMB officials say reporting by some agencies is "sporadic."

Those reports that are compiled are sent to a division of the Department of Homeland Security for review. The division, known as the U.S. Computer Emergency Readiness Team (US-CERT), was created in 2003 to coordinate defense against and responses to cyberattacks across the nation as part of a broader post Sept. 11 effort to fortify critical infrastructure. But experts say the division cannot compel other government agencies to provide accounts of unreported incidents.

Further complicating matters, government CIOs, privacy officers and cybersecurity officials disagree among themselves about how much technology is enough to safeguard the government's data — and to what degree the government should curb the amount of information it gathers in order to reduce the amount of data it has to protect.

The GAO recommends that agencies restrict the collection of personal information in order to prevent privacy breaches. Agencies also should keep personal data for only as long as necessary and should encrypt more data using a process that scrambles electronic information. Computer users can only unscramble the information with special electronic "keys" or passwords.

Many agencies, including the VA, encrypt data primarily when it is transmitted outside of the organization but usually not when it is sent within the department.

Johnson, the OMB deputy director, told the House Government Reform Committee last month that some agencies have ignored the directives from OMB and National Institute of Standards and Technology that were developed in response to the 2002 legislation, including policies encouraging encryption.

After the VA breach, CIOs and privacy officers at other agencies in June openly debated whether agencies should add more encryption at a privacy workshop sponsored by the Department of Homeland Security. Many said adding more controls is too costly and time-consuming.

"There is a whole discussion about how much encryption is needed," said Zoe Strickland, the chief privacy officer at the U.S. Postal Service. "You can decide at great expense to encrypt the whole thing ... but encryption is not a magic bullet."

On June 23, OMB tried to settle some questions when Johnson demanded that data on laptops or wireless devices such as BlackBerries be encrypted. But at many agencies, officials are still discussing how much encryption is needed for desktop computers or transmissions within a department.

Agencies also are in disagreement over whether they should abandon the longstanding practice of identifying citizens with their Social Security numbers. Decades ago, agencies like the Defense Department created unique identification numbers, but practices changed

Agency Security Efforts Yield Mixed Results

The 2002 Federal Information Security Management Act requires agencies to review their data security efforts and report findings annually to the Office of Management and Budget. The 2005 results reveal significant disparities in the way certain agencies track problems and secure personal information. Below are excerpts from the reports of several agencies regularly cited as having particularly strong or weak security efforts. The evaluations were conducted by agencies' inspectors general and chief information officers.

Agencies cited for having data-security problems include:

Department of Agriculture
- 62 percent of the agency's 117,128 employees received data security training.
- The agency has not documented special procedures for using emerging technologies and countering new threats to data.
- Agency's inspector general and chief information officer do not agree on the number of agency-owned data systems or on the number of systems used or operated by contractors or other organizations on behalf of the agency.

Department of Defense
- The agency's inventory of major information systems is 50 percent or less complete.
- Inspector general findings on data security are rarely incorporated into corrective plans of action.
- The agency rarely ensures that information systems operated by contractors need federal security requirements.

Department of Interior
- Inspector general rated the quality of the agency's information systems certification and accreditation processes as poor.
- OMB determined the agency had an ineffective plan of action to remedy security weaknesses.
- 66 percent of agency employees with significant responsibilities had received security training.

Agencies credited with above-average performance include:

Social Security Administration
- The agency's inventory of major information systems and oversight efforts to ensure the systems comply with federal standards are 96 percent to 100 percent complete.
- Corrective plans of action are almost always an agencywide process, incorporating all known information security weaknesses.
- No internal security incidents were reported in 2005.

Department of Labor
- 94 percent of the department's 17,160 employees received data security training.
- 100 percent of the department's security controls and contingency plans were tested.
- The agency's inventory of major security systems is 96 percent to 100 percent complete.

SOURCE: Office of Management and Budget

as the population grew.

Security experts worry the lingering disagreements will preclude agencies from collaborating on a comprehensive set of safeguards, leaving the government responding to individual security breaches on an ad hoc basis. Substantive change, they predict, will only arrive when the government adopts a fear of failure.

Federal laws serve as encouragement to "agencies that want to do the right thing. But those that don't, have no oversight. There's no penalty for doing the wrong thing," said Ari Schwartz, an attorney for the Center for Democracy and Technology, a Washington privacy advocacy group.

The concern is echoed by former Bush administration officials, who say the government needs to promote a change in bureaucratic culture.

"At the highest level, you need better executive stewardship and emphasis of IT security issues, pretty much across the board," said Amit Yoran, the former cybersecurity chief for the Department of Homeland Security. Agency officials often "don't understand how much they rely on IT and how critical it is to their success until they do have a breach, whether it is a high visibility event like the VA or whether it is a lower profile but potentially even more damaging problem." ∎

Limits of 'Fair Use' Tested By Google Library Project

Landmark copyright lawsuit pits publishers against plan to make major book collections searchable online

To listen to Michael Holdsworth, managing director of Cambridge University Press, Internet company Google might be the publishing industry's savior. Cambridge and Google, archetypes of old and new media, are partners in Google's new book search feature: Cambridge provides copies of its works, Google makes the books searchable, provides limited access to the text and links to sites where interested readers can buy the actual books.

Across the publishing industry, Google's book search has boosted sales of older "back list" books that cannot hope to compete with the sales posted by John Grisham or Dan Brown. "We've had a fantastic boom," Holdsworth says.

But ask Holdsworth about Google's more ambitious project to digitize the collections of five major libraries and make all that material searchable as well, and his tone changes. "We see these two projects as absolutely separate," he says.

As well they might, since American publishers are mounting a landmark lawsuit against the Google Library Project. One way or another, the suit, brought by the Association of American Publishers last October, should sort out the book business's mixed feelings about the miracle of Google's searchable Internet technology.

Ultimately, it's a question of money. The publishers want to sell books and the rights to their texts; Google wants to provide searchable online texts at the lowest possible cost — free if possible — and add its own advertising.

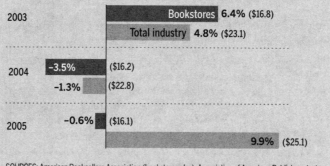

Book Sales Up, but Not From Stores

While net sales for the publishing industry grew almost 10 percent in 2005, bookstores have seen sales fall off for two consecutive years as more people — prompted by services like Google — turn to the Internet to do their browsing and shopping for new titles.

Percent change in net sales from previous year (sales, in billions)

2003	Bookstores **6.4%** ($16.8)
	Total industry **4.8%** ($23.1)
2004	**–3.5%** ($16.2)
	–1.3% ($22.8)
2005	**–0.6%** ($16.1)
	9.9% ($25.1)

SOURCES: American Booksellers Association (bookstore sales), Association of American Publishers (net industry data)

How the two work out their relationship, or how the courts define it for them, will help determine the shape of copyright law in the digital age.

"The issues in the Google case are unprecedented," says Peter S. Menell, a law professor at the University of California at Berkeley and an authority on intellectual property law. "It's a case that the copyright system was never designed to deal with," because the governing law — the 1976 Copyright Act — was written long before technologies for indexing information on the Internet were even imagined.

TRANSFORMATIVE USES

The Association of American Publishers — a trade association that counts Congressional Quarterly's publishing arm, CQ Press, among its members — sued Google in U.S. District Court in Manhattan, contending that its "library project" to digitize millions of volumes at Harvard, Oxford, Stanford, the University of Michigan and the New York Public Library is depriving writers and publishers of royalties due them for duplication of their work. The Authors Guild, a professional group for writers, made similar claims in a suit filed in the same federal court last September.

The case hinges on a doctrine in copyright law allowing for the "fair use" of protected material in ways that allow free speech — in book reviews, for instance, or news stories, parodies, teaching and academic research. To meet the fair use standard, the party using the material has to show it has made a "transformative" use of the work — i.e., putting the work to a use that is not commercially competitive with the work's originally intended purpose.

Google contends that the application of search technology to a vast body of copyrighted works is itself transformative. The company also argues that it's logistically impossible to sort out the copyright standing of all the works in its library project, since most existing books do not have a clearly enforceable copyright.

Publishers insist that Google is simply seeking to profit from their copyrighted work, much as marketers of pirated DVDs and MP3 files do.

Google refuses to release details of most of its library agreements; the one that has been made public, with the University of Michigan, allows Google to copy the school's entire collection. Three other collections being digitized — at Harvard, Oxford and the New York Public Library — are allowing Google only to digitize works already in the public domain. The details of Stanford's agreement are not fully known.

The publishers don't dispute Google's central economic claim: That like the books being made available on Google's book search function, the library collection will probably be a great boon to the back lists, by allowing readers to track down titles long considered dead. Presumably some of those readers will buy books they never knew existed. That's a publisher's dream, right?

Yes and no, says Allan Adler, vice president of legal and government affairs at the Association of American Publishers. "Google is fond of saying they don't see any harm to publishers because they aren't making the full text available," Adler says. "They don't seem to realize that they are depriving publishers and authors of using the valuable content they have created in precisely the way Google has found to use it."

In other words, says Adler, Google is making big money — via advertisements on its site — thanks to the searchability of the library books and the additional eyeballs they draw, and it's not paying the publishers and authors a penny. Sure, they might pick up some more book sales. But what if publishers themselves wanted to set up a site to search books — or team with another company to do so, taking all the advertising dollars for themselves? The Google project would render any such business plan a sure loser.

Google, for its part, acknowledges the core legal charge that it is copying the library books without permission. But many legal experts think that, in the face of recent digital test cases, it's the publishers who have the more difficult burden of proof.

BURDENS OF PROOF

When and if the case gets to trial, the District court will probably consult three major precedents in recent copyright law, two of which would seem to bolster Google's position in the library dispute and one of which Google itself lost.

In 2003, the U.S. 9th Circuit Court of Appeals in San Francisco ruled that a Web search company called Arriba Soft had not violated the copyright of photographer Leslie A. Kelly when it reproduced thumbnail versions of her work in response to searches.

Arriba Soft said the image search was a transformative use, and the court largely agreed. The essence of the case, legal experts

say, favors Google, since it, like Arriba Soft, is copying full works into its database, making them searchable, and allowing viewers to see only a limited portion.

In another case just decided, the 2nd Circuit Court of Appeals in New York ruled that it was fair use for Dorling Kindersley Publishing to include small unlicensed reproductions of Grateful Dead posters in a book about the band. The court cited the Arriba Soft case in agreeing with the publisher.

As a result, says Jonathan Band, a Washington lawyer who specializes in copyright law, "any effort by the publishers to say the Arriba Soft decision was a crazy West Coast misinterpretation of the law is unsustainable now that the 2nd Circuit has relied on it. Google had a strong argument before, but now it's much stronger."

But the third recent copyright case runs counter to the Arriba findings — and it's a case that Google lost in pursuing much the same line of argument it's likely to follow in the library suit.

The case pitted Google against Perfect 10, a Beverly Hills, Calif., publisher of nude photos of women. In February, a Los Angeles federal district court judge ruled in favor of Perfect 10, which argued that Google's image search function harmed its business by permitting Web surfers to look at thumbnail-sized images from Perfect 10's site.

Unlike the plaintiff in the Arriba Soft case, Perfect 10 was able to show that it had been financially harmed by Google, since it had previously signed a licensing agreement to sell thumbnail images for use on cell phones.

AAP's Adler says the publishers, too, plan to stress the loss of potential profits. In the Perfect 10 case, he says, the attractions of Google's search function as a "cool, neat, very useful" digital tool "didn't trump the court's reasoned analysis of fair use."

SLIVER OF THE MARKET

If the Google Library Project is such a threat to publishers' business, what's to keep them from simply opting out of it? After all, Google has promised to remove any books that a copyright holder requests it to remove.

Publishers argue that such a demand also runs counter to copyright law: The copier should be the seeker of permissions, not the originator of a copyrighted work.

And this is precisely why the stakes in the suit are so high for Google. A blizzard of copyright requests would effectively kill the library project,

argues Google senior product counsel Alexander Macgillivray. "Part of the issue here is that this isn't just about books that the publishers control, which is a tiny sliver of the whole."

That sliver represents just 3 to 5 percent of existing published work, Macgillivray says, while another 20 percent are easily proven to be in the public domain. That leaves the remaining 75 percent — 25 million or so titles — in a state of copyright purgatory, with rights not clearly in the possession of either creator or publisher.

Congress is preparing to act on new legislation approved by a House Judiciary subcommittee last month that would expedite use of this largest category of works "orphaned" under the terms of the 1976 copyright law. These tend to be works copyrighted after 1923 — the year when copyrights lapse into the public domain under current law — but before 1970, when new tracking technologies made it easier to verify a work's copyright status.

Publishers tried convincing Google that it could adopt a similar clearinghouse remedy, together with a large across-the-board royalties settlement, but the company deemed such a deal unworkable.

Unless Google gains a freer hand to duplicate library collections, Macgillivray argues, both the public and the publishers will lose. "What will be lost is the wealth of books that can't be found any other way. Instead of being able to search the entire text, we would be left with the old card catalogue."

This is the case's main technological conundrum: Open-sourced online access involves cannibalizing earlier canons of intellectual property, whether the work in question is "Ulysses" or photos of Brad Pitt and Angelina Jolie's baby.

Google clearly is betting that the New York court will build on the Arriba Soft case and conclude that a comprehensive database of published works — a 21st-century version of a globally accessible card catalogue — is sufficiently transformative to qualify as a fair use application.

The case may also be resolved on a decidedly Older Economy basis: a pretrial cash settlement. Many legal experts, among them David Leichtman, a partner with Morgan, Lewis & Bockius in New York, expect that all the publishers really want out of Google is a royalty payment. After all, the publishers spent several months trying to work out an arrangement with the company before filing suit, and then did not ask for an injunction. ■

Video Game Ratings: A Hot-Button Issue

Legislators fielding complaints about graphic content seek some control over this self-regulating industry

BATTLE CRY: Some lawmakers want to impose new rules on gamemakers, saying self-regulation is not working.

FOR THE PAST YEAR, Congress has tried to work out an effective way to regulate the objectionable, graphic content of many video games that are popular among children. Lawmakers' interest in the issue was sparked by the news last summer that fans of the top-selling "Grand Theft Auto: San Andreas" had successfully decoded hidden sexual scenes embedded in the game but not intended to be played.

That was shocking enough, given the outlaw cachet the game — which casts its users as urban criminals who rob banks, murder pedestrians and solicit prostitutes — has among teens. But legislators in both parties were more astonished to learn that the game's publisher, Rockstar Games, had not disclosed the hidden content to the Entertainment Software Rating Board

(ESRB), the industry group that issues ratings for just about every game sold in the United States.

The ESRB moved to change the rating on "Grand Theft Auto: San Andreas" from Mature (suitable for those 17 and older) to Adults Only (intended for those 18 and older). But critics contend that this measure was just another instance of the gaming industry doing too little, too late — and further evidence that the existing scheme of industry self-regulation isn't working.

Advocates who want the government more involved in game regulation gained ammunition in June, when the Federal Trade Commission (FTC) concluded its yearlong inquiry into the "Grand Theft Auto" affair. The FTC announced a settlement with Rockstar that prohibits the gamemaker from misrepresenting the content of its games or its game ratings in the future, but it levied no fines on the company.

Frustration over such seemingly cosmetic arrangements is fueling calls for the government to take a more active role to keep violent games out of the hands of children. "We've got a Congress full of angry parents," said Fred Upton, R-Mich., a senior member of the House Energy and Commerce Committee. "And as parents, we want trust and integrity in the system."

Upton is preparing a bill that would give the FTC the authority to fine gamemakers that deliberately mislead consumers with ratings labels, including those that make games with hidden content. His message for the industry: "If you're not going to do it yourself, get out of the way."

For a dozen years, the game industry has operated under the voluntary ESRB system, which assigns age-appropriate ratings and "content descriptors" warning of everything from blood and gore to sexual themes and profanity. Retailers and parents are supposed to consult the system to ensure that inappropriate games are kept away from kids.

But as the $7 billion game industry continues to attract young players, more and more legislators contend that the ratings are inconsistent and undependable and that retailers are too lax in enforcing them. Congress held hearings this spring, with lawmakers in both parties sponsoring bills that would use the ESRB system to regulate game sales. And a half-dozen states have passed laws over the past two years that restrict sales of violent games to minors.

The industry has so far fought the state statutes and several local laws in court, winning a string of legal decisions that found that government regulation of video game sales violates the First Amendment. And gamemakers are prepared to mount a similar battle against federal legislation if they have to.

RATINGS COMPLAINTS

The debate over video game violence has been simmering since the 1999 Columbine High School massacre, which some say was inspired by "Doom." The gory game helped popularize the "first-person shooter" format, which puts the player into the action with a 360-degree, first-person view of a virtual world. But the tipping point came last year with "Grand Theft Auto."

That case dramatized a central complaint among parents and industry watchdogs: The ratings cannot convey the level of violence in many games today. "If a video game allows me to earn points by murdering police officers and shooting a woman in the knee — and as she is writhing in pain on the ground, I can urinate on her and douse her with gasoline and swing a shovel and chop off her head — all of those things do not come through by putting a sticker on the side of a box that says Mature," said Tim Winter, executive director of the Parents Television Council.

In addition, ESRB ratings strike many as unreliable. Professor Kimberly Thompson, director of the Kids Risk Project at the Harvard School of Public Health, has compared ratings and content descriptors to actual game play. Among her findings: Many games considered suitable for children contain significant violence, and titles targeted at older audiences often lack descriptors for content that some parents might find objectionable.

The trouble, Thompson says, is that the ESRB assigns its ratings without ever playing most games. Instead, it requires publishers to provide video footage and extensive information about story lines, scripts, lyrics and graphics, including the most extreme content.

Because the ESRB relies on the self-reporting of its members, it occasionally has to revise its own ratings, as it did recently with a game called "The Elder Scrolls IV: Oblivion." The board had originally rated the game Teen — i.e., suitable for kids 13 and older — but changed it to Mature after finding that "Oblivion" contained more blood and gore than was originally disclosed, as well as its own locked-out file that lets users play with topless female characters.

"The fundamental problem is that the video game industry is not accountable to anyone

outside the video game industry," said Dennis McCauley, publisher of the Web site GamePolitics.com, who nonetheless believes that ESRB ratings work pretty well as a guide for parents.

Late last month, Florida Republican Cliff Stearns introduced legislation that would bar gamemakers from hiding game content from the ratings board, prohibit the ESRB from issuing misleading ratings and require the ESRB to play a game through before issuing a rating.

But ESRB President Patricia Vance argues that it is impractical for the organization to play all 1,100-plus games it rates each year — some of which can take up to 100 hours to complete. What's more, she said, playing a game may not provide a complete picture of its content, because a game — unlike, say, a movie — may unfold differently each time it's played.

The only way to ensure a consistent, comprehensive ratings system, Vance insists, is to rely on the cooperation of gamemakers. The true measure of success, she added, is whether parents find ESRB ratings useful. And according to an industry-commissioned study in March, 91 percent of parents surveyed said the ratings accurately describe game content.

Yet parents aren't always the first adults screening games for young players — retailers often are. And that leads to the second major criticism of the ESRB regime: spotty marketplace enforcement. Although most big retailers won't carry unrated games — and many won't carry Adults Only games — compliance is voluntary.

The FTC's latest "secret shopper" survey found that 42 percent of children ages 13 to 16 unaccompanied by an adult were able to purchase Mature-rated video games in 2005. That's down from 85 percent in 2000 but is still considered too high by many critics.

Gamemakers want to preserve the existing system "because it says falsely to the public that they have a ratings system that keeps these games out of the hands of kids, even as they continue to sell to kids," said Florida attorney Jack Thompson, an industry critic.

Bo Andersen, president of the Entertainment Merchants Association, which represents retailers, emphasized that most big chains train clerks to check identification — often to placate parents. Indeed, a number of the nation's leading game retailers, including Wal-Mart, Blockbuster and Best Buy, joined the ESRB in June in a pledge to beef up ratings enforcement and educate customers about the ratings system.

But Jeff Brown, a vice president for gamemaker Electronic Arts, acknowledged that "commitment to the system is only as strong as the guy behind the cash register." And given the high rate of turnover in many retail jobs, he said, retailers must constantly "rededicate" themselves to enforcing ratings.

A ROLE FOR CONGRESS

That's why some in Congress want to put the force of law behind the ESRB ratings system. A Senate bill sponsored by Hillary Rodham Clinton of New York and other Democrats, and a counterpart House bill introduced in May by Utah Democrat Jim Matheson, would impose penalties on retailers that don't enforce ESRB ratings.

As Matheson sees it, his proposal is no different from rules requiring retailers to check the age of anyone buying alcohol or cigarettes. "Asking for an ID in a store is something that's done all the time in this country," he said.

Winter added that gamemakers should support this approach because it's based on their own ratings system. "If they intended for their rules to be abided by, they would have no opposition to this," Winter said.

But gamemakers contend that codifying a private ratings system into law would violate the First Amendment. For Douglas Lowenstein, head of the Entertainment Software Association, which represents gamemakers, the bottom line is simple: Video games are constitutionally protected speech. "Video games are animation, graphics, music, story boards and scripts, all tied together with software engineering," he said. "For someone to say that games aren't artistic expression is simply not true."

Mindful that state courts have so far reached much the same conclusion, Rep. Joe Baca, a California Democrat, is trying a different tack: He is sponsoring a bill that would require the FTC to study how closely ESRB ratings reflect actual game content.

The Clinton and Stearns bills would also require studies of the ratings system. But Clinton believes that restrictions on game sales also could eventually withstand constitutional scrutiny, justified by research showing that interactive games that reward players for injuring or killing opponents can lead to aggressive behavior. "The government has a compelling interest in protecting the well-being of children," she said. "This is about protecting kids, not censorship." ∎

Budget Villain, Local Hero

The much-reviled appropriations 'earmark' has a longevity secret: Folks back home think it's a fine way to get things done, and their representatives on the Hill are glad to help

CONGRESSIONAL earmarking, or "pork-barrel spending" to its detractors, is as vilified these days in Washington as it is pervasive.

The practice of allowing individual lawmakers to set aside money in the federal budget for pet projects back home is a thread that runs through several ethics investigations, including the bribery case against former Rep. Randy "Duke" Cunningham of California. Budget hawks regularly take to the House or Senate floors to condemn earmarks as wasteful and irresponsible and try to strip them out of legislation. Other critics of the practice say the pursuit of money for highway projects, museums and hospitals back home has come to consume congressional offices at the expense of broader policy questions facing the nation.

But for all that, Congress is almost sure to leave earmarking alone because the forces that benefit from it outweigh those opposing it. Recipients of earmarks, such as cities and colleges, count on the money and solicit their lawmakers for more. Members of Congress have found it a way to help their states and districts while helping ensure their own re-election. And a growing number of lobbyists seek new earmarking opportunities while enlisting new clients to take advantage of them. Some lobby shops make earmarking a specialty.

CQ Weekly June 12, 2006

EARMARK, OHIO: With septic tanks seeping into yards, the village of Corning sought and received a special $1 million appropriation to help build a new sewer system.

To see all these forces at work, consider just one comparatively small earmark in an appropriations bill under consideration this year: $1 million from the budget of the Appalachian Regional Commission for a sewer system in the village of Corning, Ohio, population 621.

A Republican congressman, David L. Hobson, earmarked that money for Corning, which is in his southern Ohio district. A coal mining community, Corning is struggling economically. People there know full well that Congress has been handing out earmarks to many other communities like theirs; who's to say Corning's needs are not as great as the others who have come before?

A SAMPLING OF 2005 EARMARKS: AGRICULTURE

Alternative salmon products **$1,099,000** ■ Berry research **$1,300,000** ■ Appalachian Fruit Laboratory in Kearneysville, W.Va. **$2,045,000** ■ Center for Grape Genetics in Geneva, N.Y. **$3,625,000** ■ Management of beaver, Mississippi **$539,000** ■ Control of feral hogs, Missouri **$50,000** ■ Noxious weeds account **$1,920,000** ■ Farmers' Market Promotion Program **$1,000,000** ■ Plant pests **$100,217,000** ■ Fruit fly exclusion and detection **$59,976,000** ■ Income Enhancement

Though Congress has been earmarking money for as long as there has been a Congress the practice has become more prevalent in the past two decades as it has evolved from a privilege exercised by a handful of influential lawmakers on behalf of favored constituents to almost an adjunct of the regular appropriations process.

The town's request seems reasonable: Local septic tanks have failed, and according to town attorney Frank Lavelle, untreated human waste is pooling in places on the ground and running into a local creek.

Corning might get a grant for its sewer system from the Appalachian commission, which was created 40 years ago to help lift Appalachia out of poverty. But the current limit on such grants is $250,000. By going straight to Hobson, who is chairman of the Appropriations subcommittee that funds the Appalachian commission's budget, the town has secured a promise for four times that much, without having to tangle with the bureaucracy.

Hobson, for his part, has been more than happy to oblige. He gets to bring dollars home to voters in his district — and divert some money from an agency he would just as soon eliminate in the first place. As he sees it, filtering federal money for poor communities through layers of bureaucracy is wasteful and inefficient — particularly, he says, when members of Congress know better than any government official in Washington what the people back home need.

In fact, after cutting the commission's budget nearly in half, Hobson inserted 15 earmarks worth just over $9 million for Corning and other communities.

Those earmarks, in turn, caught the attention of at least one lobbyist: Michael Fulton of GolinHarris, a public relations, marketing and communications firm. Fulton has a client who he thinks could make as good an argument for a share of the spending. So he contacted staff members in the Senate, which is now considering its own version of the Energy and Water Development spending bill, to let them know that the House had opened the Appalachian commission's budget to earmarks. He asked them to consider adding one for his own client, whose identity he declined to share publicly.

"You know the Senate is going to add more," Fulton said later. "And in conference, it may expand further."

This is the cycle of earmarking that members of Congress have set in motion and would be hard-pressed now to stop even if they want-ed to. Despite proposals to limit or even eliminate earmarks, the main thing that Congress seems to be gathering itself to do legislatively — listing members' names next to their earmarks in each piece of legislation — would have the least effect.

In fact, public disclosure might have the opposite effect of what the sponsors intend: With everyone's earmarks so visible, lawmakers will compete even more intensely to impress constituents with their influence. Many already boast of their earmarks in hometown news releases.

As Scott Lilly, a former staff director of the House Appropriations Committee, puts it, "Have you ever met a politician who wouldn't accept responsibility for sending other people's tax money to the folks back home?"

BRIDGES TO SOMEWHERE

The folks back home, by most accounts, love it. The local demand for earmarks, which are a shortcut to federal aid with few strings attached, is the main source of pressure on Congress to preserve the current system.

There was a good deal of clucking when Alaska lawmakers put line items in last year's highway bill for two "bridges to nowhere," but that won't stop anyone from seeking bridges for themselves. A bridge in your district, after all, is never a bridge to nowhere.

"It may not sound very palatable here," explained Ed Rosado, legislative director for the National Association of Counties, "but it sure sounds palatable back home."

Though Congress has been earmarking money for as long as there has been a Congress, the practice has become more prevalent in the past two decades as it has evolved from a privilege exercised by a handful of influential lawmakers on behalf of favored constituents to almost an adjunct of the regular appropriations process.

It's difficult to know exactly how prevalent the practice is now because there is no consensus about the number of earmarks in the

---

A SAMPLING OF 2005 EARMARKS: AGRICULTURE

Demonstration, Ohio **$1,247,000** ■ National Wild Turkey Federation **$234,000** ■ Tropical and Subtropical Research program for Florida and Hawaii **$9,548,000**

■ Alabama Beef Connection **$850,000** ■ Iowa Vitality Center **$248,000** ■ Ohio-Israel Agriculture Initiative **$593,000** ■ Wood Biomass as an Alternative Farm Product,

New York **$188,000** ■ Pseudorabies **$391,000** ■ Jointed Goatgrass Research in Washington and Idaho **$355,000** ■ Russian Wheat Aphid Research in Colorado **$306,000**

budget, the amounts of money involved or even how an earmark is defined. *(Counting earmarks, p. 20)*

Most everyone does agree, though, that earmarking has grown greatly in recent years, and that states, counties, municipalities and colleges are increasingly dependent on the practice and strongly opposed to giving it up. As Corning's leaders found, the system often works to their advantage because they can get more money faster than if they waited in line for grants or formula allocations from federal agencies. They also have greater freedom to tailor an earmarked program or project as they see fit, since they don't have to conform to the parameters of a grant program.

"Expectations are becoming even higher," said Rosado. "Members are being asked more often by local government officials for help through the earmarking process rather than

> ❝ **I said, 'I want to be the guru of earmarks. I want to bring federal dollars back to my community.'** ❞
>
> — **Rep. Emanuel Cleaver II,**
> Democrat of Missouri

through the grants process and other normal federal programs."

The biggest concern for all these groups is not that Congress will foreswear earmarking, but rather that the increasing competition for limited dollars is driving down everyone's cut.

Rep. Emanuel Cleaver II of Kansas City, now in his second year in Congress, is receiving nearly four times the number of requests for earmarks from officials back home: 136, compared with 35 in 2005. He has consequently asked for more earmarks — $217 million in all — from Appropriations subcommittees, including $450,000 for a "mobile command post" for a local sheriff's department and $3.5 million for a social-services group called Partnership for Children. His list also includes $40 million for ammunition requested by the Marine Corps that will be made at a factory in his district.

Part of what's going on is that more people in his district have realized they can ask Cleaver for money now that he's been in Washington a while. But government agencies at home also need more help, particularly since the state of

Missouri has been cutting spending.

And he, like Hobson and many other members of Congress, wants to respond. In fact, Cleaver told a visiting delegation from the Kansas City Chamber of Commerce a few weeks ago that securing money for his district is an important part of his job. "I said, 'I want to be the guru of earmarks. I want to bring federal dollars back to my community.'" Cleaver recounted. "And the Chamber types were nodding their heads. They were saying, 'That's what we want you to do.'"

"Local communities understand this process," he said. "They're not going to abandon it. They are going to be advocates for earmarking."

Donovan Mouton, director of urban affairs for Kansas City, describes earmarks as one of the four legs of the city's funding, along with federal formula grants, competitive grants and local revenue.

Cleaver, who was mayor of Kansas City before winning a seat in Congress, recalls that earmarks were critical during his tenure in city

Do Not Pass Go, Head Directly to K Street

Most local governments seeking earmarked appropriations deal directly with their local members of Congress. But with budgets tightening and competition for federal dollars growing, more cities, counties and colleges are hiring lobbyists to make their cases.

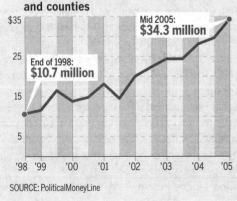

Spending on lobbying by cities and counties

Mid 2005: **$34.3 million**

End of 1998: **$10.7 million**

'98 '99 '00 '01 '02 '03 '04 '05

SOURCE: PoliticalMoneyLine

A SAMPLING OF 2005 EARMARKS: COMMERCE, JUSTICE AND SCIENCE

Maryland Institute for Dexterous Space Robotics at the University of Maryland, College Park **$3,500,000** ■ Ultra-Long-Duration Balloon Program at New Mexico State University **$1,750,000** ■ Laser Dry Cleaning Capability at the Goddard Space Flight Center **$2,500,000** ■ Autonomous Rendezvous and Docking Center of Excellence **$5,000,000** ■ Ball State University, Indiana, Human Performance Laboratory **$1,000,000** ■ Innocent Images National Initiative **$2,690,000** ■ Advanced Virtual

hall for such things as affordable housing and the renovation of historic areas that attract visitors to the city. Local officials can only go to local taxpayers for more revenue so many times.

"You just can't go back to the well again and again," Cleaver said. "And No. 2, we pay significant federal taxes. Millions and millions of dollars leave Kansas City and go to the federal coffers. All we're saying is we want some of those dollars to be spent back where they came from."

CONSUMING OCCUPATION?

Members of Congress have created the earmark system as it is today for the benefit of their states and districts, and for themselves. They have a direct interest in keeping it going.

"It works. It helps people get elected," said Republican Rep. Ray LaHood, who is now serving his sixth term from western Illinois.

Cleaver was more blunt: "If earmarks are eliminated, it will place members of Congress in political jeopardy."

Often, he said, people who grouse about the evils of earmarks in general will rate their members of Congress by how many federal dollars they bring home.

And lawmakers make it very clear that they want their earmarks. Last year, appropriators in charge of the bill that funds the departments of Labor, Health and Human Services, and Education, the largest of the domestic spending measures, put a moratorium on special appropriations — a deal to make more money available in a tight year for major education and health programs. But lawmakers said they wanted their earmarks back, and they got them this year: the amount of money earmarked is expected to be about the same as previous years, a bit more than $1 billion.

Because of pressure from fiscal conservatives, appropriators say they are getting a better grip on earmarking within their committees, for instance by limiting the number of requests they will consider from each member or by requiring local recipients to put up matching money.

The House Appropriations Committee this year put a limit on the number of earmark requests it would consider from any one member and, as a consequence, reported that requests had dropped by 37 percent since last year. But the committee may not be counting all the requests: The electronic forms that congressional offices are supposed to use to submit their earmarks will not allow them to go over the limit, but that does not keep them from submitting other requests by letter, which may not be included in the overall tally, said committee spokesman John Scofield.

The committee also says it will add member earmarks to its bills when they are up for House consideration — and there is time for scrutiny — but not during conference negotiations, as some bills have been handled in the past. But once the conferences start, that plan might go by the board depending on what the Senate wants to do. That chamber has placed no limit on earmark requests.

Such measures might slow the procession of earmarks, but they won't make much difference over the long haul. The tighter the budget becomes, the more states have to cut back on spending and the more pressure there will be on Congress to help states and districts via the shortcut approach of earmarks.

That is the foremost criticism of earmarks: Each of the projects might be worthy of support, but not through a system that circumvents the regular appropriations process of request, justification, hearing and markup. In earmarking, money flows according to influence rather than considered policy, critics say. Research that might not stand up to peer review gets funded simply because a lawmaker wants it in his home state.

For example, communities in Ohio would benefit from 11 of the 15 earmarks Hobson put into the Appalachian commission's budget. But the Ohio governor's representative to the commission, T.J. Justice, wants lawmakers to get out of the business of distributing the money themselves. He says the commission works carefully, with input from local, state and federal agencies, to direct money to projects with the needs of the larger region and the commission's founding mission in mind.

"As a resident of Appalachia Ohio, I have found this to be one of the most effective programs the federal government offers," Justice said. By earmarking the money, Congress short-circuits that process, he says.

Earmarking also has too often become a consuming and distracting occupation for congressional offices that already are short of workers, critics say. All of those requests must be processed and shepherded by someone.

HELPING HAND: Hobson says he carefully checks earmark requests 'to make sure that they pass the laugh test and the smell test.'

A SAMPLING OF 2005 EARMARKS: COMMERCE, JUSTICE AND SCIENCE

Engine Test Cell, Springfield, Ohio **$2,000,000** ▪ Mentally ill jail diversion program, Pinellas County, Fla. **$500,000** ▪ National Institute of Justice's Cyberscience Laboratory, Rome, N.Y. **$1,500,000** ▪ NASA Virtual Teams Collaboration Pilot at Glenn Research Center **$900,000** ▪ Northern Utah Fiber Redundancy Project **$250,000** ▪ Chesapeake Bay Interpretive Buoys **$500,000** ▪ Blue Crab Advanced Research Consortium **$500,000** ▪ Hawaiian Sea Turtles **$7,800,000**

Waste 'Watchdog' Barks for Donors

WHO IS WATCHING the budget watchdogs? Citizens Against Government Waste is best known for its annual "Pig Book" ridiculing millions of dollars in earmarks that members of Congress add to legislation. Yet this avowed watchdog group has a sideline in lobbying Congress on behalf of its contributors.

Two years ago, for instance, the organization plunged into an obscure agricultural dispute over avocados. It issued press releases and prodded its members to support avocados from Mexico. Tom Bellamore, whose California Avocado Commission was fighting the Mexican imports, was puzzled. "I don't think avocados have much to do with government waste," he said.

Indeed, Citizens Against Government Waste did not reveal what motivated the aggressive campaign: It had received about $100,000 from Mexican avocado growers.

That's just one of many instances in which CAGW has traded on its watchdog reputation by taking money from companies and trade associations and then conducting lobbying and public relations campaigns in their behalf — without revealing that money changed

hands. The campaigns show how Washington lobbying often is done under disguise. When companies and trade associations want to give the appearance of public support, they pay front groups to create "grass roots" lobbying campaigns.

The campaigns work best if the watchdog appears to be independent, so CAGW has not revealed who bankrolled its work:

CAGW took at least $245,000 from tobacco companies while urging the federal government not to regulate tobacco and to drop a lawsuit against the industry.

It received thousands from a health club association while promoting a bill that would give tax breaks for health club memberships.

CAGW took money from Diageo North America, a major liquor company, and wrote letters to Congress opposing government regulation of flavored malt beverages, which Diageo makes.

Despite such campaigns, CAGW is still referred to by major news outlets as "a public interest group" or "a taxpayer watchdog." Matt Myers, the president of the Campaign for Tobacco-Free Kids, an anti-tobacco group, said CAGW is neither. "They are nothing but a voice of industry," he said.

SEEKING OUT WASTE

CAGW was founded in 1984 to continue the work of the Grace Commission, which President Ronald Reagan created to identify waste in government. CAGW describes itself as "a nonpartisan, nonprofit organization dedicated to eliminating waste, fraud, abuse, and mismanagement in government."

"That's my biggest concern about earmarks," said Lilly, who left Congress in 2004 after 31 years to become a senior fellow at the liberal-leaning Center for American Progress in Washington. "What we have now is a Congress that pays so much attention to 2 percent of the spending that it ignores the other 98 percent. And that suits the executive branch just fine."

For their part, appropriators complain that the earmarks in spending bills are unfairly singled out for criticism. Authorization committees put earmarks in their bills, such as billions of dollars for local projects crammed into last year's highway law.

Congressional tax writers give special breaks to particular industry groups, and those, too, are earmarks — the most expensive of all in the long run, appropriators say.

Meanwhile, the White House pursues earmarks of its own.

But appropriators such as Hobson and many rank-and-file lawmakers also vigorously defend earmarks in principle, though acknowledging that the system has at times been abused. It's the job of Congress to direct federal spending, and no one knows the needs of their districts better than lawmakers elected to represent them, said Rep. Mike Simpson, an Idaho Republican and member of Hobson's Energy and Water Appropriations Subcommittee.

"Congress has ceded too much authority to the executive branch already," Simpson said.

And eliminating earmarks will not save money, Simpson and others say. The dollars will just be spent by federal agencies.

Hobson said he and his staff carefully vet the earmarks he puts into his bill. In the case

of Corning, for example, his field representative in the area visited the village and talked through its project. Hobson himself is in and out of Corning regularly, so he knows the community.

"What I try to do with my earmarks is make sure that they pass the laugh test and the smell test," Hobson said.

HIRING ADVOCATES

Where there are laws being made, there are lobbyists, and these advocates have been moving into the appropriations earmark process and helping it grow.

Congressional aides say most earmarks, like Corning's, are handled directly by local officials without a lobbyist. Lawmakers, they say, are sometimes offended if local people send a lobbyist to make their pitch. But the increase

---

A SAMPLING OF 2005 EARMARKS: ENERGY AND WATER

Yazoo Basin Backwater Pumping Plant **$20,000,000** ■ Mohave Bird Study **$250,000** ■ Mind Institute in New Mexico **$11,000,000** ■ Wastewater Pollution and Incinerator Plant in Auburn, N.Y. **$250,000** ■ St. Johns Bayou and New Madrid Floodway **$4,950,000** ■ Nuclear Survivability Campaign **$22,386,000** ■ High-energy Petawatt Laser Development **$35,000,000** ■ High Explosives Readiness/Assembly Campaign **$17,097,000** ■ Weatherization Assistance **$240,400,000**

Tom Schatz, CAGW's president, often testifies before congressional committees, and the group is widely quoted.

"Americans everywhere should thank Citizens Against Government Waste for its tireless efforts to terminate waste and pork from the federal budget," Sen. John McCain, the Arizona Republican, said in 2001. He often quotes from the Pig Book.

The group portrays its Pig Book as the product of unbiased research, but in at least one case, CAGW used it to help a contributor. The International Health, Racquet and Sportsclub Association, which has given at least $5,000 to CAGW in the past year, has long been critical of YMCAs because they are tax-exempt and they occasionally receive federal grants, giving them an advantage over privately owned clubs.

In the past four Pig Books, CAGW's list of wasteful programs mentioned federal grants to YMCAs. Also, CAGW singled out the YMCA money in its "awards" for frivolous spending. Schatz, the president of CAGW, said the book's mention of YMCAs was not influenced by the money CAGW has received from the health club association. He said, "The Ys are there because they qualify as pork. Period."

As a nonprofit group, CAGW is not required to reveal its contributors, and Schatz would not provide a complete list. He confirmed several that were discovered through independent research, but said many others did not want to be identified. "If somebody wants to support an organization and remain anonymous," he said, "that's their right."

He acknowledged that his organization had taken money from groups such as the avocado growers for lobbying campaigns, but he characterized it as a small part of CAGW's work and said it fits within the group's principles. "We have always opposed increased taxes and increased regulations on all kinds of issues," he said.

Ron Campbell, a lobbyist representing the Mexican avocado growers, said he had no qualms about hiring CAGW. "Hey, that's the way Washington works, right? Nothing is for free, and it's very expensive to do a mailing," he said. In the end, Campbell's side won.

Schatz said his group had become more dependent on money from corporations and foundations because of shrinking individual contributions. The corporate/foundation money accounted for less than 10 percent of the group's revenue in the past but now accounts for about 22 percent.

However, Schatz said that in his group's lobbying work, "we think we are still representing our members and their interests." CAGW has sometimes declined to work on some issues for clients, he said. "We have not worked on issues that didn't fit with our mission."

A FRONT GROUP

Congressional records show that the group's lobbying arm, the Council for Citizens Against Government Waste, has written hundreds of letters to members of the House and Senate on issues that have no apparent connection to the group's stated mission.

John Stauber, executive director of the Center for Media & Democracy, which tracks public relations campaigns, said CAGW is a front group that lets corporate interests such as tobacco companies stay in the shadows. "The basic idea is to put your words in the mouth of somebody the public is going to trust," said Stauber.

Stauber said groups such as CAGW should be forced to disclose their donors. "If they were up-front about the fact that they are hired guns for the tobacco industry or big powerful corporations like Philip Morris, people would really be skeptical of what they are doing and what they have to say."

But he admires their well-chosen name.

"What a fabulous name!" Stauber said. "Who is for government waste? It sounds like a wonderful organization of patriotic people who are trying to make government better."

---

in earmark lobbying has been noticeable. A decade or so ago, "appropriations was not a particular target of the lobbying industry," said Lilly, the former appropriations aide. Most well-paid lobbyists were doing tax or regulatory work, he said.

"That has changed dramatically," Lilly said. "My observation is that most firms have a major proportion — and a great deal have more than half — of their business wrapped up in appropriations."

Lobbyists have also been central to the scandals and investigations that have drawn more scrutiny down on the practice. Federal investigators reportedly are examining the relationship between House Appropriations Chairman Jerry Lewis of California and

K Street's Top Earmarkers

Firms reporting the most lobbying business under the "budget and appropriations" public disclosure category during the first six months of 2005, the most recent period with complete data on file.

		REVENUE	CLIENTS
1	Van Scoyoc Associates	$9,140,000	173
2	Cassidy & Associates	7,640,000	79
3	Ferguson Group	4,450,000	107
4	Patton Boggs	3,850,000	60
5	Copeland Lowery Jacquez Denton & White	3,060,000	75

SOURCE: Senate Office of Public Records

a former appropriator-turned-lobbyist named Bill Lowery. It is an extension of the investigation into the activities of Cunningham, who went to jail earlier this year after pleading guilty to taking bribes for steering earmarks to

defense contractors.

Lobbyists, of course, contribute, sometimes generously, to the campaigns of members of Congress. But they say they contribute something else of value to the process: They often make lawmakers aware of worthy projects, and they help clients locate the best place in the budget to find the money.

The source of money for earmarks inside the federal budget is constantly shifting, based on many different factors: the policies or priorities of the chairmen of the various subcommittees, or external events. The Sept. 11 terrorist attacks provided an opening for earmarks for fire departments, hospitals and other emergency responders. The devastation of Hurricane Katrina last year opened the door for

---

A SAMPLING OF 2005 EARMARKS: INTERIOR

Alaska Western Arctic National Parklands **$12,733,000** ■ Repairs for the Sala Burton Maritime Museum Building in San Francisco **$4,350,000** ■ Old Faithful Inn

at Yellowstone National Park **$11,118,000** ■ Bering Sea Fishermen's Association **$450,000** ■ Eider and Sea Otter Recovery **$1,200,000** ■ Northern Aplomado Falcon

Recovery Activities **$150,000** ■ Fish Screens at the Northwest Power Planning Area **$2,000,000** ■ Erosion protection for Middle and Buckley islands, West Virginia **$435,000**

A Project by Any Other Name

FINDING AND COUNTING EARMARKS in the complex and densely worded federal budget is hard, especially since there is so little agreement on what an earmark is.

When the Congressional Research Service was asked by members of Congress to total up earmarks for the past eight fiscal years, it chose to follow a different definition for each appropriations bill, explaining that there was just too much variation to add them all up. In the agriculture spending bill, for example, the agency counts as an earmark any discretionary appropriation for a specific project, location or institution. In the Defense budget, an earmark means allocating money "at a level of specificity below the normal line item level."

The CRS reports suggest that earmarking by Congress and the administration increased in the past year from $52 billion to $67 billion. By contrast, the House Appropriators Committee, using a narrower definition of earmarks, says they have declined from $19.8 billion in fiscal 2005 to $17 billion in fiscal 2006.

Appropriators say the CRS definition of earmarks is so broad that it's dead wrong, including, for example, financial support for the Andean Counternarcotics Initiative because the Foreign Operations Appropriations bill directs dollars to certain countries. According to the CRS, nearly 75 percent of the foreign operations bill is earmarked.

The Appropriations Committee has software that tracks member requests as they move through the system, and uses a "know it when you see it" standard for identifying earmarks, said committee spokesman John Scofield.

"No one knows better what an earmark is than the Appropriations Committee," he said.

In the agriculture bill, for instance, there's about $70 million in earmarks in "federal facility accounts" — money for things such as an agriculture research facility at a specific university, Scofield said.

Another group, Citizens for Government Waste, well known for its annual "Pig Book" highlighting earmarks it views as wasteful, falls in between CRS and appropriators in its tally of earmarks. Using a narrower definition than CRS, that group says there were fewer earmarks this year than last but that more money is being earmarked — $29 billion this year vs. $27.3 billion the previous year.

But Citizens Against Government Waste also lobbies Congress on some issues, raising questions about its independence. (*Watchdog or front group? p. 18*)

ENTITLEMENT IN THE MAKING

The budget watchdog group Taxpayers for Common Sense, which considers an earmark anything itemized in a way that goes to a specific district or state, said that earmarking declined a bit, from a record $32.9 billion in fiscal 2005 to $31.9 billion this year. One of the main reasons for the decline, said Keith Ashdown, the group's vice president for public policy, was that appropriators put a one-year moratorium on earmarks in the Labor-HHS bill — something they have now reversed.

"You have to give them a little credit for the progress they've made, but now we have to get much more ambitious," he said.

Ashdown said he doesn't envy appropriators. Earmarks "are now considered an entitlement by a lot of powerful people."

Congressional aides feel the burden of dealing with all the requests. Recently, Scott Lilly, a former staff director for the House Appropriations Committee, spoke to a colleague still working on Capitol Hill who told him just how heavy the flow of requests continued to be despite all the bad publicity about the practice. Local governments looking at earmarks, the aide told him, are "beating down the doors."

earmarks in Gulf states trying to rebuild.

The best lobbyists do what Fulton was doing when he came across Hobson's earmarks: They scan appropriations bills looking for opportunities, said lobbyist David Gogol, a former GOP Senate aide who now works for Baker & Daniels in Washington.

"Each year appropriation strategies shift as opportunities shift," Gogol said.

Fulton says he wouldn't be bankrupted personally if earmarking were scaled back — he provides public relations and other services to clients. But helping schools and others get earmarks and grants is what he's best at and

what he loves.

"Even if they reduce earmarks to next to nothing, it's not going to stop me from having clients come to Congress with their good ideas," he said.

GROWING COMPETITION

He and other lobbyists say they do spend a good bit of time these days lowering the expectations of groups seeking earmarks, in large part because there is less money available for almost everything.

Municipalities, counties and others can expect increasing competition for earmarked

dollars, and it's for that reason that projects will be scrutinized more carefully and lawmakers will be looking more often for communities to put up local matching money.

Earmarks are generally smaller than in the days when fewer groups were competing for them, so communities more often will have to view earmarks as one piece of a larger package of funding for projects, said Roger Gwinn, a lobbyist with the Ferguson Group in Washington, which represents local communities seeking earmarks.

But no one expects the current scrutiny on earmarks to cause any big shifts in the kinds

---

A SAMPLING OF 2005 EARMARKS: DEFENSE

Repair and Improvement of Existing Windows and Doors **$1,000,000** ■ Future Tactical Truck System **$7,000,000** ■ Hickam Air Force Base Alternative Fuel Vehicle Program **$3,400,000** ■ Flame Contaminant Detection System **$1,000,000** ■ Digitization of Department of Defense Manuals **$17,000,000** ■ Knowledge Management and Decision Support System **$3,500,000** ■ Stainless Steel Sanitary Space **$1,050,000** ■ Hawaii Wireless Interoperability Network **$500,000**

HERE'S WALDO: Earmarks helped save the old Waldo hotel in West Virginia, but critics question the propriety of such projects.

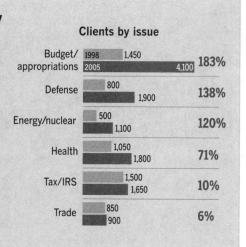

A Growth Industry

Spending on lobbying is on the rise overall, but the number of companies, schools, local governments and others that have paid money for help with budget and appropriations matters nearly tripled in the eight years since lobbyists started filing their semi-annual reports electronically. *(Lobbyists are required to identify their clients' interests in one of 77 categories.)*

SOURCE: Senate Office of Public Records

NOTE: Data for the first six months in each year

Clients by issue

Issue	1998	2005	Change
Budget/appropriations	1,450	4,100	183%
Defense	800	1,900	138%
Energy/nuclear	500	1,100	120%
Health	1,050	1,800	71%
Tax/IRS	1,500	1,650	10%
Trade	850	900	6%

that Congress hands out. That's in large measure because everyone believes their own earmarks are justified.

National League of Cities President Jim Hunt, a city councilman in Clarksburg, West Virginia, has seen a project close to home caught up in questions about the propriety of earmarking. The local congressman, Democrat Alan B. Mollohan, had to step down from the House ethics committee amid questions about earmarks he had used to fund three nonprofit groups he had established.

One of those groups used earmarks to help purchase a historic hotel in downtown Clarksburg for renovation that private developers would not touch. The whole affair might look bad from the outside, but folks in Clarksburg see renovating the hotel, the Waldo, as a vital economic development project, Hunt said.

"I'm not going to say it would be a national tragedy if they tore that building down," Hunt said. "But in our small community in West Virginia, that building is key to development of our downtown."

Back in the village of Corning, local officials say they have been knocking on every door, and also expect to receive grants for their sewer system from the state. The town also will take out a loan of $2 million or more that it will have to repay, said Bob Allen, the local representative of a nonprofit helping Corning. Residents are already paying an extra $18-a-month sewer surcharge for design costs for the project; that charge will go to $24 in January and eventually could go as high as $60.

But the federal dollars earmarked by Hobson, local representative say, are critical to finally getting the project under way, to help open the way to those other sources of funding, officials said. With any less, Corning would have to take on more debt — and risk driving its residents away with even higher fees to repay the loans, Allen said.

And as long as Congress is handing out earmarks, Allen said, communities such as Corning will pursue them. ■

A SAMPLING OF 2005 EARMARKS: TRANSPORTATION, TREASURY AND HUD

Public Safety and Transportation Improvements at the St. Louis Zoo **$5,000,000** ■ Museum of Glass in Tacoma, Wash. **$550,000** ■ Fort Dupont Ice Arena **$495,000** ■ Capitol Hill Baseball and Softball League **$50,000** ■ Washington State Ferries Wireless Over Water Project **$1,000,000** ■ Missouri Soybean Association **$500,000** ■ Demolition of Dangerous Structures in Detroit **$500,000** ■ Trail Improvements to Shiawassee Park in Michigan **$150,000**

Political Participation

Political participation is the lifeblood of U.S. democracy. This section is devoted to the groups and individuals who help choose the country's leaders and set its course. The articles in this section all focus on a range of electoral issues on the eve of the midterm elections of 2006.

As George W. Bush enters the last two years of his presidency, Democrats are increasingly hopeful of a return to power as Republicans are trying to retain it. The first article in this section explores a recent landmark Supreme Court decision centering on a controversial mid-decade redistricting scheme in Texas. Engineered by the then House majority leader, Tom Delay of Texas, whose efforts eventually led to his tumble from power, the redrawn boundaries were upheld by the Court with one notable exception involving the protection of ethnic minority voting rights. The Court thus determined that how electoral lines are drawn is essentially a political matter to be left up to the states. How this will affect future redistricting efforts will be an important development to watch in future congressional elections.

With President Bush's approval numbers continuing to sag, many congressional Republicans are distancing themselves from the White House as they seek to retain power. The second article shows that some of the most intense political action is within the Republican Party itself, where the infighting can get quite intense. The article looks at the case of the Club for Growth, a group whose mission is to target Republican congressional incumbents at the primary level who it views as insufficiently conservative.

The next article is an in-depth exploration of Democratic Party prospects of getting back into power, not just for the midterm elections in 2006 but also the race for the presidency in 2008 and beyond. The tide of the current events and the prevailing national mood has been working against the president and his party lately, but Republicans continue to hold major advantages in the key areas of fundraising and redistricting; the power of incumbency will not be easily overcome.

Less than two years after the GOP leadership tried to intervene in a Florida family's fight over euthanizing a comatose woman that prompted a national debate on the issue, most Republicans are now distancing themselves from this polarizing incident. The third article in this section details how a majority of Americans view the Terri Schiavo case as an example of overreaching by lawmakers with a pro-life agenda and how both Republicans and Democrats are staying largely silent on what is a volatile and politically divisive subject.

The last article in this section once again demonstrates Republicans showing an increasing willingness to assert their independence from President Bush. The article follows Rep. Heather A. Wilson (R-N.M.), normally a reliable supporter of the president, sponsoring legislation to overhaul the Foreign Intelligence Surveillance Act (FISA), one of the important weapons in Bush's war on terror, in the midst of her difficult reelection bid.

Supreme Court OKs Texas Redistricting
Majority says Constitution doesn't prohibit mid-decade remap

THE SUPREME COURT has upheld the extraordinary mid-decade congressional redistricting of Texas nearly in its entirety, rejecting all but one of the arguments that the mapmakers had violated the Constitution and federal voting rights law.

There were three principal outcomes of the six opinions issued in the case, *League of United Latin American Citizens v. Perry*, which stands as the most closely watched voting rights case of the past decade.

Seven of the justices essentially provided vindication of the audacious effort by the majority Republicans in the state Legislature — who were spurred on by Texan Tom DeLay during the height of his power as House majority leader — to break with four decades of precedent and redraw boundaries that had been in effect for just one election. The consequences for the balance of political power in Washington were profound: In 2004 the GOP won six more seats in the state than it had in 2002; without those gains, the party would have lost House seats overall in the last election. *(2003 Almanac, p. 14-6; 2004 Almanac, p. 18-17)*

By rejecting the argument that such mid-decade redistricting is unconstitutional, the justices left some lawmakers and "good government" activists envisioning a worrisome contagion of similar efforts in other states — spurred on whenever one party takes control of state government away from the other.

Finally, the court underscored that the protection of ethnic minority voting rights remains one of the few criteria it sees as justification for entering the fundamentally political matter of drawing electoral lines. A 5-4 majority ruled that one district — the expansive 23rd, which runs from the suburbs of El Paso 800 miles along the Rio Grande to Laredo, then up to San Antonio and west again through the Hill Country — was altered to dilute the political power of Mexican-Americans in violation of the Voting Rights Act.

The Supreme Court's June 28 ruling sent the case back to a three-judge federal panel in Austin. The next day, U.S. District Judge T. John Ward asked parties in the lawsuits to submit new proposals for configuring the 23rd District — and, of necessity, at least one other adjacent district — by July 14. Oral arguments will be held Aug. 3. That is five months after the state's primary.

The One District Held Invalid

The Supreme Court's June 28 decision blessed the 2003 Texas congressional map with one exception: It ruled that the reconfiguration of the 23rd District so diluted the voting power of Hispanics that it violated the Voting Rights Act. The mapmakers reduced the district's Hispanic voting age population to 51 percent, from 63 percent, by shifting about 100,000 Hispanics from the Laredo area into the adjacent 28th District and adding mostly Anglo voters from the Hill Country northwest of San Antonio. The result was that Republican Henry Bonilla, who won with just 52 percent in 2002, won with 69 percent in 2004. A federal court will now decide how the map is to be redrawn for a third time this decade.

The situation echoes what happened on a much larger scale in Texas a decade ago, when the Supreme Court invalidated three Texas districts as unconstitutional racial gerrymanders. That August, a federal court issued a map that complied with the court's decision by altering 13 districts' boundaries. A compact calendar of candidate filings, primaries and runoffs was set that resulted in congressional elections being finalized in December. *(1996 Almanac, p. 548)*

PRECEDENT BROKEN

Since the court set the "one person, one vote" standard for drawing House districts in 1964, states have generally made maps once a decade, after the census has yielded the data to use in apportionment, unless ordered back to the drawing board because their handiwork is rejected by the courts. But the court held that the Texas Legislature did nothing wrong in breaking that precedent.

"With respect to a mid-decade redistricting to change districts drawn earlier in conformance with a decennial census, the Constitution and Congress state no explicit prohibition," Justice Anthony M. Kennedy wrote.

Republicans argued that their action in 2003 was justified because the new map better reflects the strong Republican voting trends in Texas than had the map used in the 2002 election, which federal judges drew because the Legislature, which was politically divided at the time, couldn't get the job done on its own. The Legislature moved to redo the map after it won total control in Austin in 2002, and the

map worked nearly to perfection: Republicans had won only 15 of the state's 32 House seats in 2002; two years later, they won 21.

Rep. Chet Edwards, the only Texas Democrat targeted for defeat by the remap who won re-election anyway, said he would introduce legislation to prohibit multiple redrawings of congressional lines within a decade.

"The court has essentially ceded the field for the judiciary, and state legislatures have largely been given a free hand to do what they will with Congressional districts," said J. Gerald Hebert, a lawyer for Texas congressional Democrats. "Let the redistricting festivals begin."

But other political analysts said they were skeptical that such a festival would open. Electoral cartography can be grueling: The Texas GOP effort took three special sessions of the Legislature and several rounds of litigation, for example. And so far only Georgia has followed Texas' lead; its House map was redrawn by a newly unified GOP legislative majority last year in hope of gaining the party two seats this fall. *(Background, 2005 CQ Weekly, pp. 3399, 500)*

But Democrats have not moved to retaliate in states where they are in control. After taking control of the Illinois General Assembly in 2004, for example, party officials could not come to a compromise on how to fashion a map that could increase the party's 10-9 edge in that state's House delegation.

If nothing else, the high court's ruling stands as a victorious coda for the career of DeLay, whose redistricting quest — starting with his efforts to raise money for GOP state legislative candidates in 2002 — led to the legal troubles that accelerated his path out of power during the past year. (*2006 CQ Weekly, p. 976*)

For what amounted to four different reasons, the court also rejected the Democrats' argument that the Texas map amounted to an unconstitutionally partisan gerrymander, again disappointing those who hoped the justices would use the case to set a standard for deciding when political considerations receive too much weight in the drawing of election lines. The court deadlocked on that question just two years ago in a challenge to Pennsylvania's map. (*2004 Almanac, p. 18-21*)

SINGLING OUT THE 23RD

The one victory for the Democrats — the invalidation of the 23rd District — was based on a portion of the Voting Rights Act (PL 89-110) that says minorities must be allowed to "participate in the electoral process and to elect representatives of their choice." That language is not subject to alteration in the reauthorization of the law that has stalled in Congress in recent weeks. (*2006 CQ Weekly, p. 1793*)

Republicans redrew the district because the GOP incumbent, Henry Bonilla, prevailed by only 6,500 votes in 2002. The new map shifted about 100,000 Hispanics — and the home of Bonilla's 2002 opponent, Democrat Henry Cuellar — into an adjacent district, which was already predominantly Hispanic. Bonilla won easily in 2004, and Cuellar took the adjacent seat.

Plaintiffs successfully argued that by reducing the Hispanic voting-age population of the 23rd District from 63 percent to 51 percent, the Legislature had made it impossible for Mexican-Americans to effectively control elections because of their below-average voting participation. "In essence, the state took away the Latinos' opportunity because Latinos were about to exercise it," Justice Kennedy wrote.

The unsuccessful Republican counterargument was that the party had acted without racial bias — and was motivated entirely by the desire to shore up Bonilla.

The court also rejected a challenge to the way the new map dispersed among several districts the territory that was long represented as the 24th District by Democrat Martin Frost, who is white. The court said there was insufficient evidence that African-American voters, who accounted for 21 percent of the old 24th's voting age population, preferred Frost and effectively controlled elections in that area. Running in new territory, he lost in 2004. ■

Fiscal 2007 Coast Guard Bill Catches Up With Its Predecessor

CONGRESS CLEARED the long-delayed fiscal 2006 legislation authorizing the Coast Guard on June 28 — the same day that a House panel approved a bill authorizing the agency for fiscal 2007.

Nearly three months after conferees agreed to a report on the fiscal 2006 legislation (HR 889), lawmakers sent the $8.7 billion measure to President Bush on June 28. That same day, the House Transportation and Infrastructure Committee by voice vote approved legislation (HR 5681) authorizing $9 billion for the Coast Guard in fiscal 2007.

The panel gave next year's bill the green light after adopting two amendments by voice vote. One, by Frank A. LoBiondo, R-N.J., Coast Guard and Maritime Transportation Subcommittee chairman, would accelerate the program known as Deepwater to modernize aging ships, airplanes and communications systems by ordering completion of the program in 15 years. The amendment would increase Deepwater's funding to about $1.7 billion, from $1.1 billion in the original bill.

LoBiondo incorporated into his amendment changes to the legislation sought by his colleagues on both sides of the aisle, including a provision that would make the Coast Guard the primary federal entity responsible for providing maritime security for nuclear facilities located on navigable waters.

Sue W. Kelly, R-N.Y., who represents an area of the Hudson Valley just north of New York City that includes the Indian Point nuclear power facility, sought the provision. Kelly said current efforts to protect nuclear facilities from terrorist attacks are inadequate.

Earlier this month, Kelly introduced similar stand-alone legislation (HR 5614) that formed the basis of the amendment. She said that "a tugboat with no fixed armament and a weekly flyover do not adequately address the threat to a nuclear facility in the middle of the nation's top terror target."

The manager's amendment also included a provision sought by Juanita Millender-McDonald, D-Calif., that would direct the superintendent of the Coast Guard Academy to prescribe a sexual harassment policy for the school's personnel.

The underlying legislation would make permanent a 500-person increase in the number of authorized Coast Guard officers, to 6,700. The agency was granted a temporary increase after the Sept. 11 terrorist attacks.

As was the case with the fiscal 2006 Coast Guard authorization legislation, which stalled over a dispute about a wind farm off the Massachusetts coast, the devil may very well be in the details of the 2007 bill.

Debate about the merits of narrowly tailored exemptions to the Jones Act — a 1920 law requiring that U.S. companies build, own and operate ships that carry cargo exclusively between domestic ports — dominated much of the panel's discussion.

The panel adopted an amendment by Gene Taylor, D-Miss., that deleted a section in the bill creating a permanent exemption for Nabors Industries, a drilling company that recently moved its headquarters to Bermuda for tax purposes. Taylor said the waiver, which Congress granted in 2004 but which expires next August, allows Nabors to maintain a large presence and many employees in the United States while avoiding much of the federal tax burden it would otherwise owe.

The 2006 bill would authorize $1.6 billion for Deepwater and includes several provisions designed to help the Coast Guard deal with the aftermath of Hurricane Katrina, including $300 million for operations and fuel costs. ■

Conservative 'Club' Wins With a Broader Battle Plan

Strategy shift from incumbent races to open seats pays off in Club for Growth's fight against GOP moderates

CONSERVATIVE FIREBRAND Patrick J. Toomey and the Club for Growth, the fundraising phenomenon that he now runs, are going RINO hunting again this year: stalking what they call "Republicans in Name Only" and targeting a pair of these centrists for extinction in GOP primaries.

He's pressing hard to achieve one of the group's still-unfulfilled goals: replacing incumbent members of Congress it views as too liberal with people who adhere to what the group describes as the inviolable conservative tenets of lower taxes and unbending fiscal discipline. This strategy will get its next test next week in the Republican primary in Michigan, where Rep. Joe Schwarz faces a serious challenge in his bid for a second term from Club-backed Tim Walberg, a former state representative who finished behind Schwarz in the primary when the south-central 7th District seat was open two years ago.

Toomey himself represents the high-water mark in the Club for Growth's effort to get rid of insufficiently conservative Republicans at the Capitol. Two years ago, he gave up his own congressional seat to take on Sen. Arlen Specter in Pennsylvania's GOP primary and came within a percentage point of victory. And in his new role, he has sought to broaden the scope of the group — expanding the roster of races in which it has gotten involved and even finding a Democrat to endorse for the first time ever.

Stephen Moore, the departed co-founder of the group, became famous — and controversial — in political circles for coming up with the idea of going after a few moderate Republican incumbents starting in 2000, which spurred accusations from GOP regulars that he was risking seats held by the party by exacerbating divisions within its voter base. Pennsylvania in 2004 was a prime case in

point: After barely surviving the primary, Specter won his fifth term in the fall by 11 percentage points.

Yet despite the splash that it's made with unsuccessful challenges such as those, the Club has actually had some significant success in pushing conservatives to primary victories in reliably Republican congressional districts. And in his first election cycle at the helm of the Club for Growth, Toomey sought to expand upon this strategy in hopes of growing the Club's beachhead of influence within the ranks of congressional Republicans.

OPEN-SEAT EMPHASIS

The group this year has had much more success with, and has deployed the greater share of its resources to, much lower-profile Republican primaries in which there are no incumbent RINOs. One Club ally already in Congress is John Campbell, who won the December special election for the Southern California seat that veteran Republican Christopher Cox vacated to head the Securities and Exchange Commission.

This spring, three more Club candidates have won open-seat primaries in Republican bastions, virtually guaranteeing them seats when the 110th Congress convenes in January.

The Club, under Toomey, also endorsed freshman Democratic Rep. Henry Cuellar of Texas. Cuellar won the March 7 Democratic primary with the help of $17,800 from the Club for Growth's political action committee and $171,000 in bundled contributions from individual donors.

Toomey said he was "delighted" to be the first chairman to endorse a Democrat he felt was sufficiently committed to the organization's ideals, a development he said was good for the Club for Growth.

There's one race, though, where Toomey is going for broke — and is hearing echoes of the complaints fired at Moore of putting a GOP

Senate seat at serious risk. He's gone RINO hunting in Rhode Island by pouring Club for Growth funds into Cranston Mayor Steve Laffey's competitive challenge to Lincoln Chafee, the most liberal Republican senator. Their primary contest is Sept. 12.

A chorus of GOP strategists and officials — and Moore himself — have condemned the Club's involvement in the race on grounds that a primary upset would surely mean the Republicans would lose the seat in Rhode Island, normally a Democratic stronghold. "If I were running the Club, we wouldn't be doing that race," Moore said in an interview. "I don't know what was behind the thinking of getting behind Laffey, but all I can say is, I think it could backfire."

Toomey admitted the Club is willing to brook potential losses in pursuit of its goals. "We've taken risks. We've supported some underdogs already," he said, but "the guys who are front-runners don't need our support."

But he said Club members could stomach such losses — and in fact expected the Club to take on risky races — because it would encourage more candidates allied with their message to run in the future.

MONEY IN, MONEY OUT

Toomey has continued Moore's practice of using the organization's multiple organs for funding endorsed candidates.

Those include the Club for Growth's PAC, which is limited by federal campaign finance law in the amount it can give directly to candidates; a "527" organization, regulated under Section 527 of the IRS code, which can accept unlimited contributions and make unlimited expenditures on behalf of its favored candidates as long as that spending is not coordinated with the candidates' campaigns; and "bundling," a practice in which the Club, like many activist groups, collects and distributes individual donations made out to specific candidates.

The PAC pumped $152,000 into Campbell's victory, for example, while Club members designated another $120,000 for the candidate.

The three primary winners so far this year in safely Republican open seats have been the biggest recipients of Club largess, including its PAC's $860,000 in expenditures. The PAC spent $106,000 in behalf of state Sen. Jim Jordan, who has locked up the Ohio seat from which Michael G. Oxley is retiring, and the Club channeled $86,000 to him in bundled contributions. It directed $92,000 in PAC money and $317,000 in bundled funds to state Sen. Adrian Smith, who has effectively secured the Nebraska seat being vacated by Tom Osborne. And its PAC spent $172,000 while the Club bundled another $347,000 for state Rep. Bill Sali, who seems certain to succeed C.L. "Butch" Otter in Idaho.

The organization also is supporting three other open-seat candidates who have not yet had their primaries: Sharron Angle, who will be facing even-money general election odds if she survives the Aug. 15 GOP primary in the sprawling Nevada district that has been held by Jim Gibbons; Doug Lamborn, who is a viable candidate in the Aug. 8 primary for the nomination to succeed Joel Hefley in a district centered on Colorado Springs; and Rick O'Donnell, who is unchallenged for the GOP nomination in the highly competitive suburban Denver swath being vacated by Bob Beauprez.

The Club for Growth has not sunk much PAC money into these races, but as of June 30, Angle was the second-highest recipient of bundled funds of any Club-supported candidate, with $509,000 from donors. Lamborn made the top 10 with $114,000, while O'Donnell lagged with $19,000. Winning any of these races would be a coup for the organization, given the minimal output from the Club for Growth itself.

SOUTH DAKOTA COUP

The Club for Growth counts 39 members of Congress as recipients of its campaign aid since its founding seven years ago. Its crowning achievement, according to former director Moore, was its backing of John Thune in his bid to unseat Senate Minority Leader Tom

Recent Club Winners

Since its founding in 1999, the low-tax, small-government Club for Growth has been known best for a string of so-far unsuccessful efforts to defeat Republican congressional incumbents it views as insufficiently conservative. (Freshman Rep. Joe Schwarz in Michigan, whose primary is next week, is the group's next target.) But, increasingly, the club has been putting money and organizational muscle into electing conservatives to open and reliably Republican seats. Its biggest recent successes:

2004

Spent $182,000 from its political action committee to help **Patrick T. McHenry** win a four-candidate primary in western North Carolina by 85 votes, assuring his election, at age 29, as the youngest member of this Congress.

Spent $176,000 to defeat moderate primary front-runner Curt Bromm in eastern Nebraska, assuring the election of **Jeff Fortenberry**, who the Club found sympathetic even though it endorsed a third person.

Spent $174,000 to help Rep. **Jim DeMint** score a come-from-behind primary victory over former Gov. David Beasley in South Carolina's Senate primary. DeMint went on to win the general election by 10 percentage points.

2005

Spent $152,000 to help **John Campbell** survive a 10-way primary and win the southern Orange County seat vacated when Christopher Cox became SEC chairman.

2006

Spent $106,000 on state Sen. **Jim Jordan**, who took 51 percent against five opponents in the May 2 primary in the rock-ribbed Republican part of west-central Ohio that Michael G. Oxley represented since 1981.

Spent $92,000 to help state Sen. **Adrian Smith** win a three-way May 9 primary with 39 percent in the rural, solidly Republican western Nebraska district that Tom Osborne gave up to make a bid for governorship.

Spent $172,000 to help state Rep. **Bill Sali** take 26 percent to win the six-way May 23 primary in western Idaho for the reliably Republican seat that C.L. "Butch" Otter, the GOP nominee for governor, held for three terms.

Daschle in South Dakota two years ago.

But other Republicans not associated with the Toomey-led Club are less impressed with its victories than they are worried about its setbacks.

The Club is taking a rare leap by getting involved in one of the nation's most competitive House races: backing O'Donnell, a former Col-

orado higher education commissioner, for the seat that Beauprez is giving up to run for governor. The Democratic candidate will be either former state Sen. Ed Perlmutter or former state Rep. Peggy Lamm.

Two of the Club's favorites already have lost this year. State Rep. Phil Krinkie, its candidate in the Minneapolis suburbs to succeed Mark Kennedy, who is running for the senate, dropped out after the local Republican organization gave its backing to state Sen. Michele Bachmann. And Kevin Calvey, who had the Club's endorsement, finished fourth in the crowded primary last week in the Oklahoma City district that Ernest Istook relinquished to run for governor.

Now all GOP eyes are on Rhode Island.

Although Chafee has established himself as a maverick within Senate Republican ranks, the party establishment has taken the pragmatic route and stuck with the incumbent. They have done so on the grounds that a center-left Republican is the only kind who could win in Rhode Island, especially against the strong takeover effort expected by state Attorney General Sheldon Whitehouse, the prohibitive Democratic primary favorite.

Most GOP officials brand Laffey's challenge as an unnecessary threat to a Republican-held seat in a year when the party's Senate majority is under a Democratic siege. The Club for Growth is "working against our efforts to maintain the majority through what they're doing in Rhode Island," said Brian Nick, a spokesman for the National Republican Senatorial Committee.

But Toomey has stood behind the decision. "At the end of the day, we're not a subsidiary of the Republican Party," he said. "Our mission is not to worry so much about the number of Republicans in office at any point in time. It's to make sure that the right people are getting elected."

Danielle Doan, director of House relations at the conservative Heritage Foundation, summed up the Club's current role in the political universe.

"Their goal is not entirely to get conservatives into Congress," said Doan. "The Club is there to shake up the system and to shake up the status quo. So even though, yes, when they get people elected, it's very good for them and they are happy with that, they're also happy when they change the dynamics within the structure." ∎

JUSTIN BILICKI

Blue State Special

Democrats expect an Election Day feast, but they still can't be confident about the size of the banquet

AS EVERY weatherman knows, it's hard to make an accurate forecast more than a couple of days out. To say what's coming your way three months down the road is well nigh impossible.

Electoral politics is no different. If the 2006 midterm election were held today, tomorrow or even next week, it would be safe to say that Republicans would hold on — barely, but with just enough room to spare — to their majorities in both the House and Senate. They retain all the advantages of incumbency, fundraising and redistricting, and the Democrats would still need a net gain of at least 15 seats to take over the House and a net of six to retake the Senate. Those are not impossible numbers to achieve, to be sure, and the minority has picked up that many seats, and more, in midterms past. But not often, and certainly not in recent years.

But the elections to fill all 435 House seats and 33 Senate seats are still a dozen weeks away. So many things can happen between now and then to turn one race, or several, in a different

direction. It would be a fool's errand to say with any degree of confidence that the forecast for today will hold beyond tomorrow.

All you can do, really, is figure out which way the wind is blowing. And the wind that's blowing today has the GOP running, not walking, for protective cover. All current indicators suggest that the Big One — hurricane, tidal wave, tsunami or tornado; pick your own catastrophic metaphor — is gathering in the middle distance.

U.S. forces continue to confront sectarian violence in Iraq and, according to generals there, the increasing possibility of civil war. Israel is battling the Shi'ite Hezbollah in Lebanon while Iran builds its nuclear capabilities. The thwarted airline bombing plot in Britain spurs Republicans to take credit for being tougher in the War on Terror, and Democrats to blame the party in power for failing to interdict the world's terrorist masterminds in the five years since the Sept. 11 attacks.

At home, Congress continues to wrangle with immigration, taxes, the minimum wage, rising gas prices and lobbying scandals with unending gridlock — within the GOP itself. The House and Senate plan to be in recess

between the end of September and the middle of November — meaning the Republican majorities will probably go home to face the voters with few newly minted legislative trophies to brag about.

As a result, Republicans find themselves particularly vulnerable in the Midwest and Northeast, and they even have cause for worry in their geographic strongholds of the South and West. The only thing the GOP appears to have going for it right now is the fact that most voters have yet to tune in to the details of their upcoming electoral choices. So if the Republicans can just keep their heads down, they might avert a fatal storm.

"There's just no doubt it's going to be a Democratic year," said Norman Ornstein, a resident scholar at the American Enterprise Institute and one of the nation's most veteran observers of congressional politics. "The difficulty we have in making any predictions is, we're trying to gauge the strength of the wind."

A POSSIBLE POLITICAL SHIFT

But change is definitely in the air, said Thomas Mann, a senior fellow at the Brookings Institution and author, with Ornstein, of "The Broken Branch: How Congress is Failing

America and How to Get it Back on Track." "This appears to be one of those midterm elections that happens once a decade. Strong negative feelings in the public toward the party in power leads to substantial swing — and with it a substantial swing of seats away from the party."

Great political shifts can arise and culminate over a very short period of time. Hardly anyone saw the "GOP Revolution" coming before October in 1994, and then most political professionals discounted the notion that 40 years of Democratic hegemony in the House was about to come to an end. A similar sea change occurred almost without warning in the last two elections of the 1960s, when the Vietnam War, the Cold War with the Soviet Union and racial tensions in the cities contributed an atmosphere of political turmoil and ultimately cost the Democrats the presidency and a combined 51 seats in the House and eight seats in the Senate.

But megatrends are rarely seen from 40,000 feet. More often they are foretold in the parochial storylines of individual contests. Last week's primary in Connecticut, where Joseph I. Lieberman was denied the Democratic nomination for a fourth Senate term by Ned Lamont, a millionaire businessman and vitriolic critic of the Iraq War, demonstrated how fast the landscape can change on even the most entrenched incumbent.

Just three months ago — roughly the amount of time between now and Election Day — Lamont was a virtual unknown; only 9 percent of respondents to a Quinnipiac University poll in May knew enough about him to state any opinion, and the respected survey organization reported that Lieberman's support for President Bush's conduct of the war was no threat to his re-election.

By early June, Lamont had taken a big step forward, to 40 percent support in the polls, but most political analysts assumed that Lieberman would survive merely by reminding voters why they had liked him in the first place. But by late July, with Lamont investing heavily in his campaign and liberal activists maintaining a drumbeat of criticism against Lieberman, the challenger had edged ahead.

Lamont's victory has sparked debate over what it means for the party's bid for control of Congress — especially if Lieberman, the party's nominee for vice president just six years ago, continues to run as an independent — and beyond that for its 2008 presidential nomina-

"As the Lieberman race shows, a growing number of voters are looking for ways to send signals to the president and for representatives who are willing to check executive power."

— Bruce E. Cain, University of California political scientist

tion contest. Republicans and even some centrist Democrats see it as evidence that the party is in thrall to its most liberal elements. Many Democrats see it as liberating the party from fear of speaking out against the war.

But the Connecticut primary is a political allegory that has to give pause to incumbents in both parties, given the unstable political climate — perhaps mostly to Republicans, who have so much running against them this year.

"As the Lieberman race shows, a growing number of voters are looking for ways to send signals to the president and for representatives who are willing to check executive power," said Bruce E. Cain, a University of California political scientist who runs the school's operation in Washington.

Forecasting the outcome Nov. 7 is made enormously difficult by the fact that so much is happening, on so many fronts, that could move the national mood or at least sway undecideds in bellwether races.

Consider just a few of the unanticipated events that have made headlines in the past month. There was the raid on Israel by Hezbollah forces, precipitating a Middle East crisis. There was the testimony before the Senate Armed Services Committee by top generals, who previously had been generally optimistic, warning that an outright sectarian civil war is getting closer in Iraq. There was the Senate's rejection of the get-out-for-the-summer legislative deal promoted by the GOP leadership, which married an increase of the minimum wage — popular with Democrats and GOP moderates — to a cut in the estate tax that's popular with Republicans and some Democratic moderates.

Then, last week, Republican Bob Ney gave in to pressure from GOP leaders and abandoned his bid for a seventh term in what had been a safe Ohio House seat for him — until he became a focus of the federal influence-peddling investigation spawned by lobbyist Jack Abramoff. And

British authorities announced that they had broken up an advanced plot to blow up several passenger airliners on their way to the United States.

Republicans were in a defensive crouch before these recent developments, none of which gave them inarguable reason for further optimism. The realists among them are bracing for the worst.

"I think we're in for the toughest election we've had since we've been in the majority. So I expect this to be hard-fought, intense and close," said Rep. Tom Cole of Oklahoma, who came to the House in 2003 after running the staffs of both the National Republican Congressional Committee and the Republican National Committee. "I think we ought to recognize that we're in a very difficult election, and that it could go either way."

THE HOUSE PROJECTION

So far this year, the trend lines have gone almost exclusively in favor of the Democrats, and as a consequence the party's candidates have become more competitive in seats across the country in recent months.

As a result, the Republicans are currently on course to win only 220 House seats in the 110th Congress — and that's if they take every one of the races that CQ currently rates as safe, favored or leaning in their favor. That total, of course, is just two seats more than the number required to claim a majority in the House.

There are also 13 contests — 12 for seats held by Republicans and one by a Democrat — rated as too close to call. The campaigns for these tossup seats, by definition, can as readily go to the Republicans as to the Democrats. So if the GOP picks up half of them, it can expect to go into 2007 with no more than 227 seats — or the smallest majority the party has had since 2001, when it held 221 seats and counted on one GOP-voting independent.

But the bulk of the tossups could slip away from the Republicans if the trends continue to blow strongly against them this fall. In the big swing years of the recent past, including the Republican upsurge in the 1994 "Contract With America" election and the Democrats' rout in 1974 just after Watergate forced President Richard M. Nixon's resignation, nearly all of the most hotly contested races broke in favor of the victorious party.

Just as worrisome for Republicans, they hardly have a lock on the 220 races now tilted in their favor. In 20 of them, the Republican has only a slight edge because of incumbency, fundraising

CQ's Projection at a Glance

Based on its assessments of all 468 congressional races this year, CQ currently projects that Republicans will hold both the House and Senate in November — but with just two seats to spare in each — assuming they win every race in which they now have the edge and lose everything else. But most races where the dynamic is changing have trended the Democrats' way in the past three months.

HOUSE

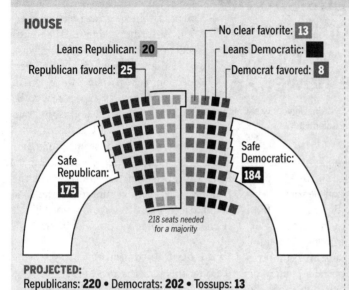

Leans Republican: **20**
Republican favored: **25**
No clear favorite: **13**
Leans Democratic: ■
Democrat favored: **8**
Safe Republican: **175**
Safe Democratic: **184**

218 seats needed for a majority

PROJECTED:
Republicans: **220** • Democrats: **202** • Tossups: **13**

SENATE

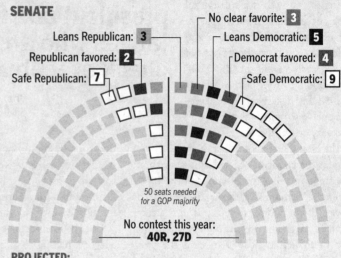

Leans Republican: **3**
Republican favored: **2**
Safe Republican: **7**
No clear favorite: **3**
Leans Democratic: **5**
Democrat favored: **4**
Safe Democratic: **9**

50 seats needed for a GOP majority

No contest this year:
40R, 27D

PROJECTED:
Republicans: **52** • Democrats: **45** • Tossups: **3**

Congressional Quarterly defines its rankings this way: **No clear favorite:** A true tossup in which neither party has established a definite lead. **Leans:** One party has a slight edge, but the contest remains highly competitive, and an upset is a viable possibility. **Favored:** One party has a strong lead and appears likely to win, but an upset cannot be completely ruled out. **Safe:** One party is such a heavy favorite that its losing is virtually impossible.

---

advantages or political demographics. And so the Democrats could win any or all of them if their candidates' strengths gain a bit of traction — or if the voters' mood shifts much more against the GOP, or against incumbents in general.

Only 10 seats now held by Democrats, by contrast, are that closely competitive.

Beyond these races that are tossups or "leaning" to one party or the other is a third category: contests in which the front-running candidate has serious advantages that make election likely, but where other factors make an upset plausible. And here is where the partisan imbalance is greatest of all: There are 25 seats where Republicans are favored — pretty solid, but not quite safe — but only eight seats where Democrats are similarly vulnerable to an upset.

Beyond that, almost all the races that have become more competitive in recent weeks have tilted toward the Democrats. Since *CQ Weekly*'s last overview of the campaign, on April 24, the political staff's ratings of 26 House races and six Senate races have changed — in favor of the Democrats in 25 of the House races and four of the Senate races. Most have been Republican-held seats that appear increasingly vulnerable to Democratic takeovers; the others have mainly been Democratic-held seats where the threat of a

Republican challenge has faded.

Add all that up and it's clear why Republicans have so much to fear. Of the year's most closely contested House races, 32 are in Republican-held districts, compared with 11 in Democratic-held districts. When you include the long-shot challenges, a total of 57 GOP seats — one-quarter of the seats they now hold — are currently in play, to just 19, or 10 percent, for the Democrats.

Those 76 competitive and still-kicking races give the Democrats a surprising advantage for November when you consider what they take with them going in: Democrats hold 184 safe seats, which they are virtually guaranteed to keep. To reach the magic number of 218, they need to win only 34 of the 76 competitive contests, or fewer than half.

THE SENATE PROJECTION

The math is considerably more favorable for the Republicans in their bid to keep hold of the Senate, where they occupy 55 of the 100 seats today. They will still have 52 next year if you start with the 40 GOP senators whose seats aren't on the ballot this year and add the dozen contests in which the Republicans are favored or the races are at least leaning their way.

But in the past month, the number of races

in which Republicans are favored has dropped by two, and in both cases the campaigns have become too close to call. One is in Montana, where Republican Conrad Burns' bid for a fourth term has drawn intense opposition because he was the leading recipient of campaign contributions from Abramoff and his associates. The other is in Democratic-leaning Rhode Island, where the centrist Lincoln Chafee will probably be challenged by former state Attorney General Sheldon Whitehouse, the favorite in the Sept. 12 Democratic primary — that is, if Chafee staves off aggressive opposition in his own primary from Mayor Steve Laffey of Cranston, who is being pushed hard by fellow conservatives. (Primary defeats are hardly a factor in Congress this year. Just one senator and two House members have been denied renomination, all last week, and there's almost no chance that number will grow.)

Democrats are the incumbent party in just one state where the Senate seat is now a tossup: Minnesota, where Mark Dayton is retiring.

Only one Senate seat currently is more at risk of partisan turnover than the three tossups — in the bellwether state of Pennsylvania, where conservative two-term Republican Rick Santorum has been running behind Democratic state Treasurer Bob Casey for months. Though a

The Electoral Signposts: An Update

The CQ political team has been tracking these eight indicators, or "signposts," as a means of comparing the Republicans' advantages en route to taking over Congress in 1994 with this campaign's situation for the Democrats. This latest evaluation has some slightly improved news for the GOP, but in the main the party continues to face a situation at least as sour as the one the Democrats confronted a dozen years ago.

Congressional polls

A July 21-25 CBS News/New York Times poll found only 28 percent approving of the job Congress is doing — in between 25 percent and 36 percent in other, similar polls taken last month. While an uptick from this spring, and higher than the ratings of the 1994 Congress, it's not something for the Republican majority to brag about. The solace is that the CBS poll showed a traditional disparity, with 57 percent approving of their own House members.

Presidential polls

President Bush, too, has edged back a bit from career lows — as little as 31 percent — in job approval polls this spring: Three recent polls put him at 40 percent. But that is still slightly below where President Bill Clinton stood three months before the Democrats' 1994 debacle. Just as worrisome for Republicans are polls finding that three-fifths or more of the public describes the nation as on the wrong track.

President's policies

A slight uptick in positive news from Iraq led Republicans to reject calls for a Bush exit strategy and accuse Democrats of wanting to "cut and run." But continued violence and the administration's indefinite time frame for withdrawal make the war a big problem for the GOP. High gas prices, Bush's moribund Social Security initiative and the aftermath of Hurricane Katrina are also clear negatives, and his veto of the stem cell research bill angered part of the electorate. Confirmation of two Supreme Court justices is among the few victories of Bush's second term. His situation is at least comparable to that of Clinton, who in 1994 was singed by his failed health care overhaul and anger over tax increases.

Recruitment

Republicans scoff at the Democrats' "B-list" challengers, but the minority party has put enough seats into play to make serious gains in both chambers if the tide runs hard against the GOP. They haven't, however, matched the Republican recruiting success of 1994. Republicans are mostly playing defense this year and don't have many top recruits to tout, but they don't need to take over many seats to thwart the Democrats' efforts to win control.

Ethics

Investigations of Jack Abramoff's influence-buying and past ties to the now-convicted lobbyist have put several GOP seats in play that otherwise wouldn't be. Democrats, who were badly damaged in 1994 by a series of scandals, now accuse the GOP of fostering a "culture of corruption." But the difficulty of making that stick was evident in June, when Republicans held the California seat that Randy "Duke" Cunningham vacated to go to prison for bribery. A bribery probe of Democratic Rep. William J. Jefferson of New Orleans hasn't helped the Democrats' effort.

Economy

The expansion that took hold three years ago hasn't run out of gas. But gasoline price spikes, rising interest rates, increases in health care, housing and tuition costs, foreign competition, concerns about immigration and high debt have many voters worried about the economy, dampening its benefits to the majority party. The 1994 Democrats had a different woe: The economy hadn't completely emerged from a recession.

Retirements

Unlike the 1994 Democrats, the 2006 Republicans haven't seen a major incumbent exodus leaving a long list of vulnerable open seats. But the short list has nonetheless had an impact on competition. Of the 19 House seats left open by the GOP, 12 are competitive — to five of 11 for Democrats. But Democrats have three open Senate seats to defend, compared with one Republican seat. And all are in play.

Pre-election jolt

Democrats pushed hard to win a momentum-claiming victory in June in the San Diego-area House seat that Cunningham left — but they fell 7,200 votes short. They had another near-miss in a special House election in Ohio last August. In contrast, two Republican special-election takeovers in 1994 were omens for that November's tsunami.

recent poll suggests that an aggressive ad campaign has enabled Santorum to cut into Casey's once-gaping lead, he remains the only undisputed underdog congressional incumbent.

Still, the competitive balance in the national Senate campaign is closer than in the House campaign: Nine Democratic seats and eight Republican seats are at least moderately competitive. So to win the majority, Senate Democrats will have to win a higher share of the close ones than their House counterparts.

But recent Senate election history suggests a burgeoning trend that has to be worrisome for Republicans: One party ends up dominating the closest contests. In 2000, the Democrats gained four seats to pull into a 50-50 tie with the GOP by triumphing in five of the seven contests decided by margins of 5 percentage points or less. Two years later, Republicans won back control by taking five of the seven closest races, and they expanded their majority in 2004 by winning five of the six closest campaigns.

Still, retaking the Senate should prove difficult for the Democrats, who will be operating with little margin for error. Because of their success six years ago, they are defending more seats now: 18 to the Republicans' 15. For the six-seat net gain they need to grab control, Democrats must win 40 percent of all GOP seats that are up this year, and that's only if the Democrats manage to hold all of their own seats. Losing any of those would move the Democrats' chance of a takeover to an implausible level.

The quest is even more problematic because the Senate campaign is being staged mainly on territory that is difficult for the Democrats. Only three of the Republican seats are in states that John Kerry carried in the 2004 presidential election: Pennsylvania, Rhode Island and Maine. And although the first two are very much in play, the best challenger the Democrats could

Does 'Majority Of the Majority' Have a Future?

ALL OF THE TALK in political circles is about whether the country is preparing to sweep the Republicans out of power in the House and hand control over to the Democrats. But there is less talk of another scenario that, for now at least, is just as plausible: a near-miss that would leave Republicans in charge again, but just barely.

If the GOP hangs on to win all the races that are at least leaning its way at the moment — and loses all the tossups and the contests where the Democrats are maintaining an edge — they would go into the 110th Congress with 220 seats, just two more than the minimal majority. (Of course, which party has the advantage in which contests could change significantly in the next dozen weeks, either strengthening the Republicans' hand or tipping the odds solidly in favor of a Democratic takeover.)

But the fact that the Republicans' hold on power is so precarious right now raises the possibility that it could be just as shaky after Election Day. Republicans could find themselves in a scenario that in some ways is almost as bad as losing the House: holding on to power and the attendant responsibility but with diminished leverage for carrying it out. And Speaker J. Dennis Hastert of Illinois, whose often-stated goal is to "please the majority of the majority," would have to decide whether that would still be a viable strategy for running the House.

"It becomes very, very hard to get much done if you try to hold that majority together for every vote, every day," said Robert S. Walker, a lobbyist who as a Pennsylvania congressman was a close ally of Newt Gingrich when Republicans won control of the House in 1994.

If Republicans end up with a deeply diminished majority, "there's going to be a recognition by the leadership that you can't just please the majority of the majority," said Rep. Michael N. Castle of Delaware, one of a shrinking group of House GOP moderates. "You're going to have to please every segment of the Republican majority to get things done."

Hastert has managed thin majorities before. In 2001 and 2002, there were just 221 House Republicans, the closest margin of control since the GOP ran the chamber in 1953 and 1954. But he had two sig-

HASTERT'S DOCTRINE: He will be hard-pressed to move only bills that can command most GOP votes if he returns next year as Speaker of a House that's just barely Republican.

nificant advantages at the time. President Bush was new and extraordinarily popular after the Sept. 11 attacks, and Republicans were willing to rally around his agenda with few exceptions. And whenever that was not enough, Hastert had the strong-arm whip operation of Tom DeLay to help keep rank-and-file Republicans in line.

Both advantages are gone. Bush is no longer a politically strong commander in chief, but an unpopular president who will be entering his final, lame-duck two years in office. And DeLay is out of office, his operation replaced by a newer leadership team that doesn't have as strong a track record in holding Republican votes together.

"In a way, the worst of all nightmares into '08 and on would be for the Republican majority to come out of the '06 elections greatly diminished but not extinguished — control the gavel but not the majority," said Michael Franc, vice president of government relations at the conservative Heritage Foundation.

Even with the 231-seat majority Republicans have now, Hastert's job got harder last year after the most conservative members of his caucus — members of the Republican Study Committee — became fed up with the compromises they felt they had made in behalf of

---

find for Olympia J. Snowe is Jean Hay Bright, an organic farmer and frequent candidate.

The remaining top-tier Democratic targets are all in states that voted twice for Bush, and where the current Republican lean may yet prove sufficient to counter formidable Democratic challengers: Tennessee, where Bob Corker, a former Chattanooga mayor, won the GOP primary this month to oppose Democratic Rep. Harold E. Ford Jr. for the seat left open by retiring Majority Leader Bill Frist; Missouri, where Republican Jim Talent is seeking his

second term against state Auditor Claire McCaskill; and Ohio, where Republican Mike DeWine is running for a third term against Democratic Rep. Sherrod Brown.

For a true shot at the majority, the Democrats may have to boost their chances significantly in two states where their candidates are currently long shots: Arizona, where developer Jim Pederson is challenging two-term incumbent Jon Kyl; and Virginia, where author and former Navy Secretary Jim Webb is opposing George Allen's quest for a second term.

THE LOCAL BASE

The Republicans' national campaign effort is undergirded by a well-honed organization, engineered by master strategist Karl Rove and his protégé Ken Mehlman, now chairman of the Republican National Committee. This political machine proved its talent for turning out sympathetic voters during the 2002 election, which gave Republicans the Senate majority, and the 2004 election, when Bush won re-election.

"Republicans have put together a superior

Bush's first-term agenda, such as expanding Medicare to cover prescription drugs and expanding the federal role in education with the No Child Left Behind law. Meanwhile, moderates have flexed their muscles this year by fighting cuts in social spending and forcing the leadership to embrace a minimum wage increase it opposed.

If Republicans end up with a thinner House majority and no popular presidential agenda to rally around, Hastert and his leadership team will have even less leverage to contain conservative rebellions, or even moderate rebellions, than they do now. "They've got the machinery. They've governed with narrow majorities before. They know how to do it," said Ronald M. Peters Jr., a political science professor at the University of Oklahoma who studies the House. "But all of that assumed there would be incentives to maintain party loyalty, and I just don't think that will be the case this time."

A wafer-thin margin of control, of course, means less in the Senate, especially in an era when both sides have decided to use their parliamentary powers to set 60 votes as the threshold for doing anything remotely controversial — meaning that the majority leader must find help from at least a few minority party members almost daily.

WHAT'S THE LESSON?

In the House, the first post-election decision the leadership would have to make is what lesson to draw if the Republicans suffer significant but not majority-ending losses. Their governing strategy could depend on how they settle a debate already starting in the GOP ranks: Is their majority in trouble because they have moved too far to the right, or because they have made too many compromises that undermine basic conservative principles?

Many of the members most vulnerable to defeat are Northeastern moderates — among them Christopher Shays, Rob Simmons and Nancy L. Johnson of Connecticut — and lawmakers and political analysts generally agree that such moderates, many of whom represent areas with a Democratic lean, will take a disproportionate share of the losses Nov. 7. If so, the Republicans that remain in the House will be, on balance, even more conservative than they are now.

In some ways, that might make it easier for Hastert and Majority Leader John A. Boehner of Ohio to hold the conference together on tough votes such as spending cuts, since there would be fewer moderates to raise concerns. "You'd end up with the Republican Study Committee being more of the majority than they are today," just as liberals have come to dominate the Democratic Party as their moderate ranks have thinned, said Franc.

And many of the conservatives who were left would argue that the losses happened because the base was demoralized. They'd say the solution is a back-to-the-basics approach that stresses tax cuts and spending restraint and rejects departures from conservative doctrine. "I think you become more united. You don't try to do as many exotic things, and you stick to your principles," said Rep. Tom Feeney of Florida, a member of the Republican Study Committee. "I don't think a Medicare bill could pass today on the House floor."

"The base is not upset with conservative congressmen. The base may sit on its hands for the moderates," he said. "That's not something I wish for, but it may happen."

But there are plenty of conservatives in competitive races too, such as John Hostettler in Indiana and J.D. Hayworth in Arizona. And moderates aren't buying the argument that a smaller majority would mean the party has sold out its conservative base too often. If anything, they'd tell Hastert the party needs to broaden its appeal. "There are just not enough conservative districts to make a majority party," said Castle. "If we go further to the right, we'll be a minority party for sure."

The key to the Republicans' majority status is not the districts that voted solidly for Bush, he said, but the districts that voted against Bush but still returned Republican incumbents to Congress. "Moderates have to run far ahead of the president to get re-elected, in some cases 20 to 25 points ahead. And they do it," said Castle. "That says to me that there's some appeal to the country."

Even the most conservative House Republicans don't argue the point, and they say they're doing everything they can to make sure the moderates keep their seats. "While we may have our disagreements with Chris Shays and Ray LaHood and Rob Simmons, everyone in the conference is dedicated to making sure they get re-elected," said Jeb Hensarling of Texas, who chairs the Republican Study Committee's budget task force.

Still, it is Hastert who will have to referee the family fights if Republicans hold on to the House by only a small margin. As Republicans begin to make the transition from Bush to searching for their next leader in 2008, they may have less of a reason to close ranks on tough votes and even less of an agenda to pull them together. "I think it's going to be much more difficult to find any one person who sets the agenda for the party," said Feeney.

That reality isn't likely to diminish the Republicans' energy in fighting to save their majority. But it is likely to diminish their energy if they succeed. The Democrats know what they want out of this election: power. The Republicans already have it, and even if they hang on, they may end up wondering if the fight was really worth it.

---

ground organization that will allow them to get their record to their past supporters while continuing to woo new recruits," said Lawrence Jacobs, a political scientist at the University of Minnesota. "Republicans are quite effective at micro-targeting its slices of the electorate."

Republicans, in fact, are staking their fortune on a focus on issues specific to their own states and districts — and their arguments about why their particular candidates are best suited to address those issues — to thwart the Democrats' efforts to turn this midterm into a national referendum on Bush and unified GOP control in Washington.

"The prospects of holding the majority are excellent," said Republican Phil English, who is a prohibitive favorite in his own bid for a seventh House term in northwestern Pennsylvania. "That's because it's coming down to a series of local races, which are breaking very well and are ultimately local in character. . . . It comes down to each individual Republican candidate offering their positive vision and where they're headed."

Or as Rep. Thomas M. Reynolds of New York, the blunt-spoken chairman of the National Republican Congressional Committee, recently put it: "House contests are like horse races — local horse races. And right now, I like the horses I've got."

In pursuing this strategy, however, Republicans are counting on one of the oldest truisms about American politics staying true: Voters may hate Congress, but they like their own senators and representatives well enough.

Recent polling reflects that. Public approval

of Congress has languished below 30 percent in some surveys, a level that for the GOP majority is uncomfortably close to the mark given the Democratic-controlled Congress of 1994. And a Washington Post/ABC News poll published Aug. 8 found 55 percent approving of their own House members' job performance, but a 36 percent approval for Congress as a whole.

Those same numbers come with yet another worrisome caveat for the GOP. The 55 percent approval rating for incumbents was the lowest since the eve of the 1994 election.

These numbers only mirror voter discontent that has been emerging throughout the year:

• Bush's job approval sank as low as 31 percent this spring. Even with an uptick to as high as 40 percent in some recent surveys, his standing is worse than President Bill Clinton's prior to his party's congressional drubbing a dozen years ago.

• Generic polls, which ask respondents to express a preference for the parties without mentioning any candidates, are of limited utility in determining the outcomes of individual elections. Still, they have consistently shown a substantial preference for the Democrats, as have polls asking respondents which party they would prefer controlling Congress.

• Nearly all polls on specific domestic issues, including such kitchen-table topics as the overall economy, jobs and health care, show that public opinion now favors the Democrats — and the party is even challenging the Republicans' traditionally solid advantages on security-related issues such as national defense and preventing terrorism.

DEMOCRATS ON THE OFFENSE

In the end, the decision for many voters on whom to elect to the 110th Congress may come down to their views on the stewardship provided by the Republican majority in the 109th. And Democrats aren't waiting to provide their epitaph until Congress goes home to campaign. Although the GOP has already promised a lame-duck session

More Coverage
Updated election forecasts, along with daily coverage of House, Senate and gubernatorial campaigns, are at www.CQPolitics.com. You can also sign up for a daily political e-mail alert. Both services are free to the public.

SENATE HOT SPOTS: From top: Rhode Island's Chafee is in trouble with conservatives in his GOP primary next month—and liberals if he gets past that; Tennessee's Ford is bidding to become the first popularly elected African-American senator from the South.

after the election, no matter what the outcome, the party out of power has started branding this as a "do-nothing" Congress.

In their view, the Republican majority is culpable for policy failures across a broad spectrum of issues, including lack of oversight of

the Bush administration's handling of the wars in Iraq and Afghanistan and its foreign policy in general; a long-stalled investigation into intelligence failures leading up to the Iraq conflict; a tepid response to revelations that Bush has invoked presumed presidential powers to greatly expand domestic surveillance in the name of fighting terrorism; the failed effort to tie a minimum wage increase to yet another "tax break for the rich"; a lack of relief for the short-term pain of rising energy prices; and failing to override the first veto of the Bush presidency, by which he stopped a bill that would have loosened restrictions on federal funding of embryonic stem cell research.

In the Republican view, the criticism is a histrionic effort to obscure their considerable top-tier accomplishments of the past two years, which they describe as laws that limit class-action lawsuits, crack down on consumers seeking to slough off personal debts by heading to bankruptcy court, update federal highway and mass transit programs and overhaul energy policy; and most recently the bill Bush has promised to sign aimed at shoring up the nation's decaying pension system.

This is, to be sure, a rather modest record when compared with the standards the Republican majority set for itself. With Bush declaring that he'd won a mandate along with his re-election two years ago, the Republican leadership signaled their willingness to move on his top domestic priorities at the time: reconfiguring the Social Security program to include personal savings accounts and extend-

ing indefinitely the tax cuts he won in his first term. Both have failed emphatically.

And the marquee domestic initiative the president added to the legislative agenda this year — reducing illegal immigration and offering millions of people already here illegally a path to citizenship — is mired in discord that is most noticeable within the GOP majority's ranks.

All told, it would be accurate to say that, by historical standards, the record of the 109th Congress is middling — and that, politically, few of the laws enacted have the sort of broad popular appeal that would permit incumbents to brag about them effectively on the campaign trail.

Republican leaders have sought to address that by at least arranging votes on several items loudly championed by the party's conservative base, including one constitutional amendment to ban desecration of the American flag and another to prohibit marriages of same-sex couples. None were passed, but many Republicans will brandish their support as proof of continued allegiance to conservative values.

"The average voter doesn't appreciate how high the bar is on passage of anything," said Michael Franc, vice president of government relations for the conservative Heritage Foundation. "The Republicans' challenge is to show

that any reason why their ideas aren't going through is because of the obstructionism and the 'just say no' characteristic of the Democratic leadership in Congress."

But Franc noted that it may not be as easy as in the recent past for the GOP to get its allies to the voting booth this November. Polls have shown a growing restiveness among the Republican base — though in most cases, it's not because they view this Congress as too conservative, but rather as not conservative enough.

A sizable segment of the base has chastised the party's leaders for failing to reduce the deficit further and for buying into the culture of "earmarking," or dedicating millions in appropriations to parochial projects. There is even a small but growing chorus on the right expressing concern that the United States is now engaged in an overly long and too costly nation-building exercise in Iraq.

Whatever voters' impression of Congress is now, when the Capitol is as empty as it ever gets, Republican leaders contend that they have an excellent chance to improve their standing once they return after Labor Day. But given that they have at most 18 workdays before their scheduled pre-election departure, the potential for any further major accomplishments for Republicans to tout looks slim. ∎

A Life Line Drawn In Political Sand

Range of opinion on questions posed by the Schiavo case is problematic for both parties in election year

IT SEEMS INCREDIBLE now how consumed Washington was for about two weeks in spring 2005 with the case of Terri Schiavo — and how convinced Republicans seemed to be that here was an issue that would last and play to their political advantage long-term, particularly with religious and social conservatives who were urging them on.

GOP leaders interrupted their spring recess to get involved in the Schiavo family fight over whether to withdraw a feeding tube from the brain-damaged Florida woman. Senate Majority Leader Bill Frist of Tennessee, a physician, took to the floor after watching a videotape of Schiavo to question other doctors' diagnosis that she was in a persistent vegetative state. House Majority Leader Tom DeLay of Texas all but called Schiavo's husband a murderer for trying to take his wife off life support.

Democrats, meanwhile, were divided. They stood aside as the Senate and House passed legislation — which ultimately proved futile — that was intended to overturn a state court decision and keep Schiavo on life support.

A year and a half later, with the midterm election approaching, if any politician is still talking about Terri Schiavo, it's most likely to be a Democrat. Republicans have mostly shut up about an episode that, far from helping them politically, became an embarrassment. It put them at odds with much of the public, hurt their credibility, and even upset some elements of their party — conservatives whose aim is to limit the reach of government, not

TALKING REVENGE: Michael Schiavo, shown here campaigning for Lamont in July, wants to defeat lawmakers who tried to keep his wife alive.

expand it into cases like Schiavo's.

The Republicans' silence is all the more striking because of the importance to the party of religious and social conservatives. Midterm elections, in which the turnout is lower than in presidential years, are normally decided by such loyal and ideologically motivated voters.

Instead, for the Republican Party nationally, Schiavo has come to define a limit to the "pro-life agenda" — a political line past which it will be difficult for anyone to lead the party again. That line runs across the thresholds of the hospital rooms where families and their

doctors decide how far to go to keep brain-damaged and comatose patients alive and how aggressively to treat the aged and the terminally ill.

In the Schiavo case, the Republican Congress overreached into a realm of personal decisions about medical treatment and the end of life that many Americans believe should be private, said a former House Republican leadership aide who is now a lobbyist. In so doing, he said, "we lost the middle."

"For the average Joe, it became a question of, is this really someplace where we want the government involved," said this former aide, who asked not to be named because the issue is so divisive for his party.

GOP pollster Whit Ayres says people clearly think that the best place for such decisions to be made "is with the people who love the patient dearly, in consultation with their physicians and religious authorities."

Ayres expects that if the issue is raised in campaigns this fall, it will most likely be against Republicans running in Democratic-leaning territory.

The polling that showed the public opposed to Congress getting involved with the Schiavo case has encouraged Democrats to talk about the episode as part of a broader message about privacy and Republicans' willingness to meddle in the personal lives of Americans. They pair the Schiavo case with the Bush administration's domestic surveillance policy, among other issues.

"The religious right so overplayed its hand, it gave us running room," said Democratic consultant Mike Lux. "It gave us confidence.

Half of effective communication in politics is just having confidence."

But the issue is tricky for Democrats. In the House, nearly half the Democrats who came back to town when the Schiavo legislation was put on the floor — on the first Monday of what was supposed to be a two-week recess — voted in favor of intervening in the case. Even now, Democrats in conservative states run a risk in criticizing Congress' role in the Schiavo case.

They also could run afoul of some disability advocates, such as members of the Chicago-based group Not Dead Yet, who made common cause with social conservatives on the Schiavo case. Those activists worry that Democrats, in embracing privacy rights, are becoming too laissez-faire about what may go on behind closed hospital doors when patients can no longer speak for themselves.

So far, Democrats have used Schiavo most prominently against one of their own: Sen. Joseph I. Lieberman of Connecticut, who supported congressional intervention in the case and lost his bid for renomination last month. Schiavo's husband, Michael, campaigned for the winner of that primary, Ned Lamont.

Michael Schiavo has formed a political action committee, TerriPAC, in an attempt to defeat politicians who supported intervening in his case. Celebrating Lieberman's defeat, he linked the senator to DeLay, who resigned from Congress this year while under indictment in Texas for alleged campaign finance violations. "They share a common arrogance and contempt for Americans," Schiavo said in a statement.

COMPLICATED AND PERSONAL

What's problematic for both parties is the range of opinion on the life-and-death questions posed by the Schiavo debate and how those opinions cut jaggedly across the ideological spectrum. In January, the Pew Research Center for the People and the Press found that attitudes about death and dying are extraordinarily complicated. Three-quarters of those polled said that family members should be left to make decisions about treatment for terminally ill loved ones, and almost four in five supported "right to die" laws. About three in five said that "mercy killing" of a suffering, terminally ill spouse is sometimes or always jus-

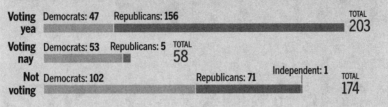

How the House Voted on Schiavo

When Congress intervened in the Terri Schiavo case last year, half its members did not go on record. Interrupting the start of a scheduled recess, the Senate passed the bill by voice vote on Sunday, March 20, and just after midnight 40 percent of House members missed the vote to clear it — including almost the entire California delegation and half those from New York and Texas.

Voting yea	Democrats: 47	Republicans: 156		**TOTAL** 203
Voting nay	Democrats: 53	Republicans: 5		**TOTAL** 58
Not voting	Democrats: 102	Republicans: 71	Independent: 1	**TOTAL** 174

tifiable. But at the same time, the public was deeply divided over the idea of physician-assisted suicide.

Conservative Christians generally were opposed to allowing Schiavo's feeding tube to be removed. But as Janice Shaw Crouse of the conservative group Concerned Women for America explains, some of them also did not like the idea of government intruding into decisions made by one spouse for another, since they believe the bond between husband and wife is sacred and biblically sanctioned.

That aspect of the Schiavo case troubled them, even though Schiavo's husband, who was living with another woman and had fathered two children with her, was not a sympathetic figure for them.

For conservatives, as well as groups such as Not Dead Yet, what was at stake was the sanctity of human life and the moral imperative to provide patients with food and water — basic care, as they saw it — whatever the judgment of others about their quality of life. Some conservatives say they still believe Republicans are standing behind their position in the Schiavo case.

As evidence, Richard Land, who runs the public policy arm of the Southern Baptist Convention, points out that when Frist was asked about the Schiavo case on NBC's "Meet the Press" in January, he defended Congress' attempt to intervene and his own role in that effort. But that interview cut both ways. Asked what lessons he learned from the episode, Frist said, "Well, I'll tell you what I learned from it, which is obvious, is that the American people don't want you involved in these decisions."

Indeed, many Republicans seem to have concluded that they lost the rhetorical battle over Schiavo and that "it's too dangerous to go there," said an aide to one social conservative in the House.

Other conservatives outside Congress say

they feel abandoned by the GOP on this issue. Crouse said that many Republicans seem happy to have the case behind them and "will steer as far from this as they possibly can."

HANDLE WITH CARE

After congressional action failed to move the courts and Schiavo died, the fight moved to the state level, with a flurry of bills inspired by the case introduced in state legislatures around the country. Many were modeled on language written by the group National Right to Life that would forbid anyone from withdrawing food and water from an incapacitated patient unless the patient had clearly ordered it beforehand.

But the movement has not gotten much traction, said Charles Sabatino, director of the American Bar Association's Commission on Law and Aging. "Legislators have been more circumspect about changing the laws radically," he said.

So far, only one state, Louisiana, has passed any such legislation post-Schiavo, and the law there is narrow and qualified. It says a spouse may not speak as a "surrogate" for an incapacitated husband or wife if that spouse is cohabiting with someone else — an oblique reference to Schiavo's husband.

In Tennessee's Senate Republican primary to replace Frist, who is retiring, the Schiavo case did not come up even though the race was all about which candidate was the more conservative. "Not even Frist himself is talking about it," said political scientist Anthony Nownes of the University of Tennessee in Knoxville.

Neither are Democrats, he said, because however much the GOP overreached on the Schiavo case, Democrats think it is too dangerous an issue in such a conservative state.

If any candidate of either party raises the issue this fall, it will probably be late in the campaigns and targeted narrowly to a particular constituency, said Kelly Patterson, a political scientist at Brigham Young University in Utah, who studies political direct-mail advertising.

The issue is so volatile and complicated that politicians, no matter what their party, would be wise to handle it with care, political analysts say. "It's not a third rail like Social Security," said Curtis Decker, executive director of the National Disability Rights Network. "But this is full of electricity." ■

Wilson Takes a Risk By Taking a Stand

Challenge to presidential power becoming key issue in New Mexico Republican's tough re-election race

As President Bush's popularity sags, congressional Republicans are distancing themselves from him in various ways. Some have attempted to localize their races by focusing on economic issues, for example. Others have registered their displeasure over the war in Iraq by going after Defense Secretary Donald H. Rumsfeld.

Then there is Rep. Heather A. Wilson. The New Mexico Republican, who is in her most difficult re-election race since taking office eight years ago, is challenging Bush and his war on terrorism not around the edges but at its very center — the power of the executive branch in conducting it.

Wilson is now the lead sponsor of legislation that would overhaul the Foreign Intelligence Surveillance Act (FISA), the 1978 law that governs wiretaps, and would set new rules for domestic surveillance. The bill, cosponsored by the chairmen of the Judiciary and Select Intelligence panels, is expected to form the basis of wiretapping legislation that will go to the floor this month.

Her bill would expand the president's authority to conduct the wiretapping, but would put restrictions on the number of days the surveillance could take place without a court order and require that Congress receive additional reports from the administration on its surveillance operations.

But her approach is stricter than a Senate compromise brokered between the White House

HEATHER ANN WILSON

Path to Congress: Elected with 45 percent in June 1998 special election in New Mexico's 1st District (Central — Albuquerque) to succeed Republican Steven H. Schiff, who died; re-elected four times with 55 percent or less.

Hometown: Albuquerque

Born: December 30, 1960, in Keene, N.H.

Religion: Methodist

Family: Husband, Jay R. Hone; two sons, one daughter

Education: Air Force Academy, B.S. 1982 (international politics); Oxford U., M.Phil. 1984 (Rhodes scholar), D.Phil. 1985 (international relations)

Military Service: Air Force, 1978-89

Subsequent Career: National Security Council staff, 1989-91; president of Keystone International Inc. management consulting firm, 1991-95; New Mexico secretary of children, youth & families, 1995-98

Committees: Energy & Commerce; Select Intelligence (Technical & Tactical Intelligence — chairwoman)

and Senate Judiciary Chairman Arlen Specter, R-Pa., that is widely seen as giving Bush almost everything he wanted. That puts her in conflict with the administration, but also with committee Democrats and some conservatives who argue that it would diminish civil liberties.

At the same time, Wilson has not backed down in her support for the war in Iraq. In other words, she is attempting to thread a difficult needle by separating herself from the administration's surveillance program while not putting her law-and-order bona fides at risk. That is important because her opponent, Patricia Madrid, is the state's attorney general.

GOING AGAINST TYPE

Wilson would seem a natural ally for the Bush administration on matters of national security. The four-term Republican was among the first female graduates of the U.S. Air Force Academy and was the first female military veteran to serve in Congress. She speaks in the precise and unadorned manner of a former military officer, and she took to drafting her legislation with the meticulousness of a battlefield planner. It went through 60 drafts, she said.

But her big break from Bush came last February, when she called a reporter at *The New York Times* to say publicly that she was troubled by a warrantless wiretapping program at the National Security Agency that Bush signed off on shortly after the Sept. 11 attacks — a program that Wilson, as chairwoman of the Intelligence subcommittee with jurisdiction over the NSA, did not learn of until the Times disclosed it in December.

"My concern is, we want to spy on our enemies and protect our Americans," she said in her trademark monotone, a quality that observers of her career said goes hand in hand with a steady, hard-working demeanor and an ability to remain unflappable under pressure. (When reflecting on how the administration gave her more information on the wiretapping program after she went public with her complaints, Wilson said of the maneuver, in her understated fashion, "It had the desired effect.")

Her military background, combined with a stint with the National Security Council and her current perch atop the Intelligence Technical and Tactical Intelligence Subcommittee, give her the standing to tackle the warrantless wiretapping issue.

"It's an issue she has a lot of credibility on," said Lonna Atkeson, a professor of political science at the University of New Mexico.

A PASS FROM HER PARTY

The question is how real this departure is, and how much of it is an attempt by her and her party to demonstrate independence at a time when Republican lawmakers need to demonstrate their independence from Bush.

Democrats, but also some independent observers, think she would not be as visible during this debate if not for her political vulnerability in the fall elections. The Wilson-Madrid race is one of the most pitched battles this fall. Her district could easily go Democratic; John Kerry won the majority of the vote there in 2004. Brian Sanderoff, president of the independent Albuquerque firm Research and Polling Inc., said Republicans make up only 40 percent of the district's voter registrations, compared with Democrats' 46 percent.

The president's low approval ratings helped Democrats to recruit better in Wilson's district than they had in the past, Sanderoff said. With Madrid, the party found a Hispanic in a state where that group represents a significant voting bloc.

Madrid has repeatedly accused Wilson of being an unquestioning ally of the president, sometimes on intelligence matters. In November, she put out a news release about Wilson's resistance to the House Intelligence panel conducting a review of how intelligence was used or misused in the run-up to the Iraq War.

Wilson's stance on the warrantless wiretapping program, then, from her February complaint to the *Times* to her sponsorship of the leading House bill on the topic, has given her a platform to draw attention to how she is not in lock step with the president.

"It's a smart way of portraying herself as independent," said Sanderoff. Whether she is truly independent or not, Sanderoff said, "I can only say that is how she's trying to present herself."

ALLIES, MOSTLY: The president came to Albuquerque in June to raise money for Wilson's re-election bid.

Sanderoff and other New Mexico political observers took note of a line from a campaign advertisement that hit the air recently; "Sometimes I'm working with people in my party; sometimes they're not in my party," Wilson says in the ad. She is quick to note that she did not consult the White House when writing her measure.

In 2005, she took a sharp turn away from Bush in her voting. She voted with the president 70 percent of the time, down from her previous low support percentage of 88.

The shift came with a rise in her profile on intelligence issues. "She has achieved a pretty prominent position on this for a relatively junior member of the committee," said Thomas Mann, a senior fellow at the Brookings Institution.

That prominent position arouses Madrid's suspicion in part, she said, because Wilson was so quiet for so long despite her subcommittee chairmanship.

Wilson, for her part, said her previous quietness can be traced to the nature of her work. "I spend about a third of my time working on intelligence matters that nobody knows about or would understand," she said.

Also, she said, this year she became particularly disturbed by the revelation of the NSA program, which was reported in *The New York Times* and caught many lawmakers by surprise.

"I saw the newspaper in the box at 1st and C Street, SE, at 9 a.m.," she said. "Before I finished my coffee, I called the [Intelligence] chairman [Peter Hoekstra, R-Mich.]. On Saturday, the administration acknowledged [the program's] existence. On Sunday afternoon, a letter I drafted was hand-delivered to the attorney general asking to be fully briefed."

"For the next 51 days, we did not get a response from the administration." After that, she went public with her concerns.

Wilson said politics did not factor into her recent actions on intelligence issues. "I've been working on these issues my entire adult life," she said. "There is nothing new about that."

THE REACH OF POWER

Whatever her motives, the issue puts Wilson now fully in the thick of one of the stickiest problems of the post-Sept. 11 world: how much power the president should have to wage war against an unconventional enemy, and how those powers are balanced against the value the nation places on civil liberties.

It is a complicated constitutional issue, and one that cuts to the heart of the Bush presidency. In other words, there would be easier and more obvious ways to demonstrate one's political independence to voters.

"It's a difficult subject, and it's a politically tricky one," said Mann. "It's not a gimme. It's not an easy shot."

Wilson's legislation, drafted at the request of Hoekstra, reflects her attempt to find a middle ground between the values of civil liberties and national security. Her bill would offer the president tiered limits on the amount of time he could conduct warrantless surveillance, with those tiers based on whether there had been a recent terrorist attack or other emergencies. It would also require additional congressional notification about intelligence operations.

At a Sept. 6 hearing of a House Judiciary subcommittee, an administration official weighed in on her approach for the first time. Steve Bradbury, the acting assistant attorney general in the Department of Justice's office of legal counsel, said the bill showed "promise" because it would strengthen the president's hand by changing the definition of "electronic surveillance" to exclude international communications in which the target was not a person in the United States.

But Bradbury said some of the bill's provisions are overly restrictive, such as those requiring a terrorist attack to trigger expanded surveillance powers. "The president cannot and should not wait for thousands of Americans to die before initiating vital intelligence collection, and we urge that this provision be amended to allow for a program when the intelligence indicates a severe threat of attack," he said.

Hoekstra's cosponsorship of Wilson's bill is noteworthy, not only for the weight it lends her legislation but also because there are seeming disconnects between their views on the wiretapping program. Hoekstra has demonstrated little outrage over either the wiretapping itself or the level of congressional notification — the default reaction for most congressional Republicans.

Hoekstra called Wilson's bill an "important base for our deliberations as the committee moves ahead with the process."

In an interview, Wilson tried to downplay any differences between her and her chairman — she noted his cosponsorship when asked about them, then added that she also considers the bill a starting point — but eventually agreed that she has been more concerned than Hoekstra about the scope of the program.

Aides to Intelligence committee Democrats privately said Hoekstra's willingness to hold public hearings on a topic that could aid Wilson's re-election battle smelled of politics.

Perhaps that played a role in the partisan tenor of a July 27 Intelligence hearing at which Wilson and other lawmakers presented their legislative proposals for addressing the NSA program. But Democrats well before the hearing had aligned themselves with legislation sponsored by Rep. Jane Harman of California, the ranking Democrat on the panel, that re-established the existing FISA law as the means by which surveillance must be conducted.

"To the point, Ms. Wilson, your bill scares me," said Rep. Alcee L. Hastings, D-Fla., who added that Wilson's bill would expand the president's surveillance powers to e-mails and give future presidents a "blank check" to conduct surveillance.

Democrats hardly asked a question of Wilson as they took turns criticizing her legislation as a sop to Bush. If ever the stakes of the debate, either on a political or policy front, might have overwhelmed Wilson, it would have been that day. But just a few hours later, she chuckled about it.

"I found it a little amusing," she said. "In some ways, it was flattering." ∎

Candidates Invade MySpace

WHATEVER ELSE it turns into, the 2006 election will be the first MySpace race.

The social networking Web domain, which commands fierce loyalty among the nation's teenagers, is all — well, mostly — grown up. It now boasts 96.5 million users, 80 percent of whom are of voting age. It draws more traffic than such online mainstays as Yahoo, Google and Hotmail have pulled down in recent years.

Those kind of numbers guarantee that politicians will tag along, to target likely voters, to identify issues, and of course to raise money — not least because the service is itself free. "I don't think there's any doubt that technology is changing the entire structure of the midterm elections," says **Joe Trippi**, who managed the

Howard Dean Democratic presidential campaign of 2004.

Among the more prominent "official" MySpace sites are those belonging to Senate candidates **Ned Lamont** of Connecticut, **Allan Lichtman** of Maryland and **Ford Bell** of Minnesota, all Democrats. Pundits watching this week's primary between Lamont and incumbent **Joseph I. Lieberman** consider it an ideological bellwether — but it may prove to be a technological one as well. (Lichtman and Bell are also-rans in their Sept. 12 primaries.)

"The biggest payoff of having set up a MySpace site," says Lamont's director of Internet communications, **Tim Tagaris**, "is that we did it before anyone else could." So far, their page has garnered 177 affiliated "friend" pages and more than 10,000 page views.

Virtually every nationally known politician has a MySpace presence — although most are featured on "tribute" sites established by supporters and fans. There are also, inevitably, parody sites, professing to belong to prominent figures such as President Bush and Senate Commerce Committee Chairman **Ted Stevens.** The Alaska Republican in June proclaimed that

"The Internet is a series of tubes," making him an online laughingstock.

Still, the number of office-hungry voluntary MySpace users is growing. Indeed, **Joe Ford Jr.** — who last week lost a shoestring Democratic primary bid to succeed his cousin **Harold E. Ford Jr.**, who's bidding for the Senate, as Memphis' congressman — used a free MySpace page as his official campaign Web site.

The political traffic on MySpace is now brisk enough that the domain plans to launch a designated channel for politicians and service groups. And come September, the rival Facebook service will start selling political advertising.

Still, the freewheeling networking world will always contain hidden costs. Shortly after Republican **Brian P. Bilbray** won the special election to replace the imprisoned Randy "Duke" Cunningham in California, links to a MySpace page sporting photographs of the new congressman's underage kids in gleeful states of inebriation began caroming around the Internet. "Their mother is not real happy," Bilbray tersely announced to the press.

Government Institutions

The articles in this section provide insight into the workings of the three branches of the U.S. government, focusing in turn on Congress, the presidency and the federal judiciary and Supreme Court. The two articles on Congress are explorations of the sometimes uneasy balance of power between the legislative and executive branches of government. The first article notes Congress's furor over the FBI's May 20, 2006, raid on the office of Rep. William J. Jefferson (D-La.) as part of a Justice Department bribery investigation. It examines the separation of powers implications of this issue and explores the constitutional clause that protects members of Congress from politically motivated investigations by officers of the executive branch. The next article is a detailed examination of the inspector general (IG) system. Lawmakers are increasingly frustrated by IGs that are neither established nor empowered by Congress but directly appointed instead by the very agencies and bureaus they are investigating. Critics contend that such arrangements are end runs around congressional oversight responsibility and lack independence. The article examines in detail the categories of inspector generals, whom they serve and how they function.

The next three articles, on the executive branch, look at the Bush administration and its conduct of foreign policy and the war on terror. The first article is an in-depth assessment of the Department of Homeland Security. In the aftermath of the attacks of September 11, 2001, the Bush administration and Congress made the historic step of combining 22 government agencies into a single department to handle domestic security. But, frustrated with bureaucratic missteps and unpopular decisions, some congressional critics are wondering if there may come a day when the department may be significantly reduced or even dismantled. The next article evaluates President Bush's foreign policy leadership, specifically with regard to the recent crisis in Lebanon brought on by fighting between Islamic resistance movement Hezbollah and Israel. Whereas past presidents have employed diplomacy to quell Middle Eastern flare-ups, the Bush administration prefers instead to give Israel its blanket support. The article goes on to demonstrate how, after six decades, the United States no longer wants or is able to be the Middle Eastern mediator. The final article in this section takes the five-year anniversary of 9/11 as an opportunity to address the accomplishments and failures of the Bush administration's war on terror. The article tries to determine what effect the White House's preference for military power over a diplomatic approach has had.

The first article on the Supreme Court and the judiciary explores the impact that the Bush administration has had on the federal judiciary and how much the scales have been tilted in the conservative direction by Bush appointees. The second article considers the implications of the use of cell phones as tracking devices, the reaction of the federal courts and the larger implications of the Fourth Amendment right against unreasonable search and seizure. A recent series of federal court decisions has stymied law enforcement in its effort to obtain data from mobile phone companies in its efforts to track the location of subscribers. The third article looks at administration efforts to work with Congress to create a new policy following Supreme Court rejection of Bush's position that the Geneva Conventions do not apply to enemy combatants detained around the world. The White House is in the process of crafting a new strategy to deal with such prisoners, one that will maintain many features of its predecessor yet survive judicial scrutiny. The fourth article examines the courts' reliance on the doctrine of judicial restraint in favor of legislative consensus to reject the right to same-sex marriage. Having suffered recent judicial setbacks in two states, gay rights supporters are questioning the wisdom of relying on the courts to establish new civil rights.

Lawmakers Blast FBI's Hill Raid

Seizure of documents from Rep. Jefferson's office causes leaders of both parties to challenge executive branch

AN FBI RAID on the office of Rep. William J. Jefferson, D-La., drew little attention on a quiet weekend when the Rayburn House Office Building was largely vacant.

By waiting until the early evening of May 20, when millions were watching the Preakness horse race on television, the FBI ensured that the first-ever search of a lawmaker's office would not disrupt Congress. And at first, congressional leaders had only a muted response to the latest episode in a trail of ethical woes that has beset the 109th Congress. *(Ethical problems, 2006 CQ Weekly, p. 174)*

But as members studied details of the raid, they questioned why the Justice Department had kept secret a signed search warrant for 50 hours and then served it without notifying Speaker J. Dennis Hastert, R-Ill., and other congressional leaders.

Hastert responded with uncharacteristic fury, openly challenging the administration's decision to violate a longstanding tenet of the separation of powers doctrine. As most members of Congress view it, a clause in the Constitution holds that law enforcement officers of the executive branch do not take criminal investigations into the halls of Congress or other congressional workplaces. *(Clause history, p. 43)*

Hastert questioned why the FBI had slipped into the office "when no one was around" and had not notified him well in advance. "I would have told them 'no' if I would have known about it," he said.

And in a rare public display of cooperation with the opposition party, Hastert joined Minority Leader Nancy Pelosi, D-Calif., to demand that the Justice Department return documents seized in the raid.

For his part, Jefferson filed a motion in federal court May 24, also seeking return of the documents.

Attorney General Alberto R. Gonzales responded that investigators repeatedly had been denied access to materials they sought in their investigation of Jefferson. "We have an obligation to pursue the evidence wherever it

Hastert discusses the FBI raid at a news conference May 25, in which he raised questions about whether the search violated the separation of powers doctrine.

exists," he said at a news conference May 23. "At the end of the day, a decision was made that this was absolutely essential to move forward with that investigation."

As the confrontation between the two branches escalated, Bush stepped in on May 25 and sealed the seized records for use by either side for 45 days. He wanted to impose a cooling off period to allow lawmakers and the Justice Department to work out a compromise that will let investigators pursue their case against Jefferson while safeguarding constitutional principles that House and Senate leaders say were violated.

Bush's action did not settle the conflict, Hastert said, "but it gives us some time to step back and take a breath and then work out the problems."

Jefferson called Bush's order "a step in the right direction," but said, "There are other things that should be done to truly correct this, which I think would involve returning the documents to the office from which they were taken."

Jefferson is the subject of a 15-month-long

federal probe into allegations that he demanded and accepted bribes from business associates in exchange for his help establishing telecommunications deals in Africa. Two of those associates — one a former aide — have pleaded guilty to bribery and have implicated Jefferson in sworn statements. *(Jefferson, p. 44)*

In searching his Rayburn office, investigators said they were looking for evidence of official actions taken by Jefferson to promote business projects in Africa in return for cash from a Kentucky telecommunications executive.

Neither party defended Jefferson's conduct, and Hastert's rank and file made it clear in a May 25 meeting that they were not happy to see their most prominent leader giving the impression that congressional offices can be used as safe houses for hiding evidence of criminal conduct.

HISTORIC REACTION

The outrage over the raid, which started with the presentation of the warrant at 6:20 p.m. on May 20 and continued until 1 p.m. the next day, echoed the congressional reaction to the Abscam sting investigations of 1980 that resulted in convictions of Sen. Harrison A. Williams, D-N.J., and five House members on bribery and conspiracy charges. A Senate select committee later exonerated the Justice Department of charges that it unfairly used undercover activities to target lawmakers. *(1980 Almanac, p. 513)*

After hearing about the search of Jefferson's office, an enraged former Speaker Newt Gingrich, R-Ga. (1977-99), accused the Justice Department of an "abuse of power" in an e-mail he circulated May 21.

Hastert spent the week pressing Bush and Gonzales in private to make concessions. He spoke with the president about the matter three times in two days, including once on Air Force

'Speech or Debate,' A Thin Case History

THOSE LOOKING TO constitutional precedent as a guide for how to view the raid on Louisiana Democratic Rep. William J. Jefferson's office may not find much to build an un-rebuttable case.

Article 1, Section 6 of the Constitution says that members of Congress "shall in all cases except treason, felony and breach of the peace be privileged from arrest during their attendance at the session of their respective houses, and in going to and returning from the same; and for any speech or debate in either house, they shall not be questioned in any other place."

The language was intended to protect members of Congress from politically motivated criminal and civil harassment while performing legitimate functions of their office. Historians say there's no evidence that the Founders anticipated a situation like the FBI's execution of a search warrant in Room 2113 of the Rayburn House Office Building on May 20-21, a Saturday night and Sunday morning when the House was not in session.

Since no congressional office has ever been searched by an executive branch authority, there is no defining precedent to which either side can point.

Aware of the legal protection generally afforded members of Congress while they are at work in the Capitol, Rep. Adam Clayton Powell (1945-67, 1967-71) for a time avoided public appearances in his district to keep from being arrested for civil contempt convictions related to a defamation lawsuit.

In 1972, the Supreme Court ruled in *U.S. v. Brewster* that the "speech or debate" clause protects members of Congress from prosecution for their legislative actions per se, but not from prosecution for crimes that might be related to their legislative roles — such as taking a bribe to cast a certain vote. The "shield" of legislative immunity "does not extend beyond what is necessary to preserve the integrity of the legislative process," the court ruled.

The clause was invoked unsuccessfully in the defense of Rep. Joseph M. McDade, R-Pa. (1963-99), who was charged in 1992 with taking more than $100,000 worth of illegal gratuities, bribes and extorted favors from defense firms. McDade, who was the Appropriations Committee's top Republican at the time, and House lawyers argued that his status as a committee leader so permeated the indictment that it violated the speech or debate clause. U.S. District Judge Robert S. Gawthrop III refused to throw out the indictment, saying such an interpretation would create "the impression that members of Congress are immune from prosecution merely because they are members of Congress." McDade was eventually acquitted. *(1996 Almanac, p. 1-35)*

In the the Iran-Contra criminal trial, former White House aide Oliver L. North subpoenaed records from the House Select Intelligence, International Relations and Armed Services committees, as well as members of Congress and staff members. The House general counsel resisted the effort, calling it an invitation to "wholesale rummaging" through privileged documents collected by the various committees during their investigation of the Iran-Contra affair. U.S. District Judge Gerhard A. Gesell rejected North's request.

Sen. William Proxmire, D-Wis. (1957-89), lost a libel suit filed by a recipient of one of his "Golden Fleece" awards. Proxmire's comments were protected on the Senate floor, but not in a subsequent press release and newsletter, the Supreme Court ruled.

The 1970s FBI sting operation known as Abscam did not involve actions inside members' offices. President Richard Nixon had ordered wiretaps of some congressional offices on his infamous "enemies list" in 1971, but that was an effort to find political dirt on his opponents.

Through the 19th century, the only workspace a member of Congress had was a desk in the chamber. "Offices didn't exist until the Cannon Building was built in 1908," Deputy House Historian Fred W. Beuttler noted, describing the question posed by the Jefferson raid as a gray constitutional area. "Is an office like a 19th century member's desk? Or is it like his apartment?"

One during a trip from Illinois to Washington.

"We think those materials ought to be returned," he said after a two-hour closed-door meeting with Republican House members May 24. "And we also think those people involved in that issue ought to be frozen out of it just for the sake of the constitutional aspect of it."

"The Speaker sees this and the members see this as an important constitutional question," added House Majority Whip Roy Blunt, R-Mo. "The Speaker is vigorous in this."

Hastert was joined in his concern by his Senate counterpart, Majority Leader Bill Frist, R-Tenn. Frist met with Gonzales on May 26 to discuss the matter.

He also instructed Rules and Administration Committee Chairman Trent Lott, R-Miss., to search for any precedents that could provide guidance. In a two-page memo, Lott said he thought the FBI should be required to notify the sergeant at arms and the leader before initiating a raid on the Capitol grounds.

"We need to be sure we don't allow a situation where some future administration could use it for intimidation, pilfering through our papers and such," said Lott. "You may say that it wouldn't happen, but you never know."

Lott said he would develop a Senate protocol, with the intention of instructing the Justice Department to follow those rules in the future. "We can say 'comply with this or we will see you in the Supreme Court,' " Lott said.

House Judiciary Committee Chairman F. James Sensenbrenner Jr., R-Wis., plans to hold a hearing on what he called the "profoundly disturbing constitutional questions" raised by the seizure of documents from a congressional office. He took the unusual step of scheduling the hearing during a recess, on May 30, and for added emphasis listed as its topic, "Reckless Justice: Did the Saturday Night Raid of Congress Trample the Constitution?"

Hastert left open the question of how the incident would affect negotiations in another ongoing dispute over breaching the separation of powers.

The House general counsel has been negotiating with Carol C. Lam, the U.S. Attorney for Southern California, over the prosecutor's request in connection with the investigation that led former Rep. Randy "Duke" Cunningham, R-Calif. (1991-2005), to plead guilty to bribery and tax evasion. *(Cunningham case, 2006 CQ Weekly, p. 611)*

In March, Lam requested a large number of documents from three House committees and interviews with nine current and former aides to two panels. She has refused a request by House officials for an outline of the information she is seeking from the aides, and has yet to reach agreement on another demand by the chairmen of the three committees that she narrow her request for documents.

Legal experts in both parties are urging Hastert to shut the door on Lam. Lawmakers are mindful that throwing open the doors of the legislative branch to the Justice Department in order to minimize the political damage of recent scandals could establish precedents Congress would later regret.

But with House members in both parties under scrutiny, defying Justice Department requests for information could put House leaders in the awkward position of appearing to be stonewalling.

The raid on the Rayburn office opened up a debate over how far to interpret the constitutional clause in question: Article 1, Section 6.

Donald A. Ritchie, associate Senate historian, noted that modern congressional offices contain constituent mail, exchanges of correspondence with federal employees, including whistleblowers, and other documents that are not intended to be shared with the prying eyes of the executive branch. "A lot of freedoms are violated when you cross into a member's office," he said.

In expressing his anger over the Rayburn office raid, Gingrich said that Hastert would be well within historical tradition if he took dramatic steps to protect legislative privilege. "The protection of the legislative branch from the executive branch's policing powers is a fundamental principle which goes all the way back to the English Civil War," Gingrich said.

He referred to a celebrated case in 1642, when the Speaker of the House of Commons, William Lenthall, refused a command from King Charles I to help locate five members of Parliament. "May it please Your Majesty, I have neither eyes to see, nor tongue to speak in this place, but as the House is pleased to direct me, whose servant I am here," Lenthall replied.

And some have tried to assert special privileges using the clause. For instance, in 1999, Sen. Robert C. Byrd, D-W.Va., used text from the clause — directing that members, except in the case of "treason, felony and breach of the peace, be privileged from arrest" — to persuade authorities in northern Virginia not to write him a traffic ticket.

New Details in Jefferson Case

THE FBI AFFIDAVIT filed to obtain the warrant to search the office of Rep. William J. Jefferson last week provided new detail of the evidence investigators already have as they consider whether the Louisiana Democrat may have accepted bribes and committed wire fraud when he attempted to help set up some telecommunications deals in Africa for a Kentucky-based company called iGate Inc.

The 95-page document, which was heavily redacted, maintains that investigators have video images made July 30, 2005, of Jefferson accepting $100,000 stuffed in a briefcase as a bribe from an iGate investor who was working as an FBI informant. The informant, identified in the affidavit as "CW-1," first tipped the FBI in March 2005 that Jefferson might be involved in a bribery scheme. All but $10,000 of the money delivered by the informant later was recovered in an FBI search of Jefferson's Washington home on Aug. 3, the affidavit said. It was found in his freezer, wrapped in aluminum foil and placed in frozen-food containers.

According to the affidavit, authorities also have recordings of the lawmaker talking about taking official action as a member of Congress to help facilitate business deals in exchange for payments and evidence linking Jefferson to eight so-called schemes in which he "sought things of value in return for his performance of official acts."

Vernon L. Jackson, a former iGate chairman, said as part of a plea agreement that Jefferson demanded and collected more than $400,000 in exchange for helping to secure the African telecommunications deals. Brett Pfeffer, a former Jefferson aide, was sentenced May 26 to 96 months in prison in the case. The House ethics committee has announced it is starting an inquiry into the Jefferson case. *(2006 CQ Weekly, pp. 1403, 1242)*

"There are two sides to the story and . . . we'll get our chance to make our side in the proper forum, but this isn't it," Jefferson said at a Capitol Hill news conference May 22. He said he has been "extraordinarily effective" in representing his New Orleans constituents since 1991 and said he had no plans to resign or to drop his bid for a ninth term.

But already, several prominent Democrats have been approached about running for the seat, among them the New Orleans city council president, Oliver M. Thomas Jr., state Sen. Derrick Shepherd and state Rep. Karen Carter. GOP attorney Joe Lavigne is mounting a vigorous campaign against Jefferson at the moment, but the 2nd District is overwhelmingly Democratic.

In a clear signal that the Democratic leadership has lost faith in Jefferson, Minority Leader Nancy Pelosi of California told him May 24 that she wanted him to resign from his seat on the Ways and Means Committee. Jefferson refused.

More recently, questions of preferential treatment arose when Rep. Patrick J. Kennedy, D-R.I., was involved in a traffic accident at about 3 a.m. on May 4 near the Capitol. Capitol Police officers reported that Kennedy appeared to be intoxicated but said they did not give him a sobriety test after he claimed that he was on his way to vote in the House, which had adjourned hours earlier. Kennedy blamed the incident on sleep medication and arranged to receive treatment for an addiction to painkillers. *(2006 CQ Weekly, p. 1252)*

Some lawmakers said Congress should not have the ability to thwart criminal investigators.

"I certainly think they had a right, with the probable cause that they had, but whether they did it right or not I don't know," said Rep. Joel Hefley, R-Colo., who is the former chairman of the House ethics committee. "The office isn't a sanctuary." ∎

Where's the Bite?

Watchdog IGs have become the last line of oversight.
Some even have teeth — independence and power
to serve two masters.

FOR NEARLY TWO months after the National Security Agency's domestic surveillance program was disclosed, most members of Congress had to sit on the sidelines, learning about it through news reports and administration press conferences. Only a handful of lawmakers had known about it before, and they couldn't talk about it. Finally, on Feb. 6, the Senate Judiciary Committee had a chance to get some of its questions answered.

How do we know, Chairman Arlen Specter, R-Pa., asked, that the agency is monitoring only terrorists and not snooping on the phone calls of innocent Americans? Attorney General Alberto R. Gonzales had a ready answer, one he would give several times that day. There are numerous checks and balances in the program, he said, and one of them was that the

NSA's inspector general provided "rigorous oversight" over it. Indeed, he told Specter, the inspector general "has been involved in this program from its early stages."

Gonzales' assurances suggested that NSA Inspector General Joel F. Brenner was a watchdog with all of the legal powers to examine records and conduct investigations usually associated with government inspectors general. But that's not the case. Brenner's office was not established and empowered by Congress, as most inspectors general are. Nor was he appointed by the president. Brenner was hired by the director of the NSA, has no authority beyond what the director gives him and, indeed, can be dismissed by the director.

And yet, the lawmakers who tried to get another watchdog on the case found themselves blocked at every turn. In December, Rep. Zoe Lofgren of California, the ranking Democrat on the Homeland Security Com-

mittee's Intelligence Subcommittee, and a group of party colleagues wrote to the inspectors general of the Defense and Justice departments asking if they would investigate the NSA surveillance program. Both have statutory authority and presidential appointments.

Both declined. Thomas F. Gimble, the acting inspector general for the Defense Department, reasoned that the NSA inspector general was already looking at the program, so there was no need for him to get involved. Glenn Fine, the Justice Department inspector general – who has produced scathing reports on other subjects, such as the U.S. government's treatment of detainees – told the lawmakers that he had no jurisdiction over the NSA program. Any questions on the legality of warrantless surveillance, he said, would have to be handled by a separate entity at Justice called the Office of Professional Responsibility, which looks into questions about the conduct of

Three Tiers of Inspectors General

Inspectors general fall into three major categories, depending on how their offices were established. Congress created the first two IGs in 1976 and 1977 and has created 60 more since. Several agencies have set up internal oversight officers on their own. Those authorized by federal law — 30 confirmed by the Senate and 32 picked by agency heads — have the most independence. Below is a description of each type and a list of which agencies employ them. There is no comprehensive list of non-statutory IGs.

	PRESIDENTIALLY APPOINTED	AGENCY APPOINTED	NON-STATUTORY
Number	30, including one for each of the 15 Cabinet-level agencies	32, including such agencies as the Library of Congress and the Federal Election Commission	No comprehensive list available, but includes the military service branches and several agencies
How They Are Appointed	Nominated by the president, confirmed by the Senate	Selected by the head of the agency	
Who Can Fire Them	Only the president. If he does so, he must explain his reasons to Congress	The head of the agency, with an explanation to Congress	At the agency head's discretion
Budget	Separate line item in appropriations bills, which prevents the agency from cutting or raiding their budgets	No separate line item in the appropriation bill	
What They Can Do	Conduct audits and investigations on topics of their own choosing; subpoena information and documents; request the help of other federal, state and local government agencies		Fewer powers than statutory IGs

PRESIDENTIALLY APPOINTED (30)

Departments
Agriculture
Commerce
Defense
Education
Energy
Health and Human Services
Homeland Security
Housing and Urban Development
Interior
Justice
Labor
State
Transportation
Treasury
Veterans Affairs

Agencies
Agency for International Development
Central Intelligence Agency
Corporation for National and Community Service
Environmental Protection Agency
Export-Import Bank
Federal Deposit Insurance Corporation
General Services Administration
NASA
Nuclear Regulatory Commission
Office of Personnel Management
Railroad Retirement Board
Small Business Administration

Social Security Administration
Tennessee Valley Authority
Treasury Inspector General for Tax Administration

AGENCY APPOINTED (32)
Amtrak
Appalachian Regional Commission
Commodity Futures Trading Commission
Consumer Product Safety Commission
Corporation for Public Broadcasting
Equal Employment Opportunity Commission
Farm Credit Administration
Federal Communications Commission
Federal Election Commission
Federal Housing Finance Board
Federal Labor Relations Authority
Federal Maritime Commission
Federal Reserve
Federal Trade Commission
Government Printing Office
Legal Services Corporation
Library of Congress
National Archives and Records Administration
National Credit Union Administration
National Endowment for the Arts
National Endowment for the Humanities
National Labor Relations Board
National Science Foundation
Office of the Director of National Intelligence
Peace Corps
Pension Benefit Guaranty Corporation

Securities and Exchange Commission
Smithsonian Institution
Special Inspector General for Iraq Reconstruction
United States Capitol Police
United States International Trade Commission
United States Postal Service

NON-STATUTORY (EXAMPLES)
Army
Navy
Air Force
National Security Agency
Defense Intelligence Agency
National Reconnaissance Office
Army Corps of Engineers

NOTE: Does not include IGs for agencies that are now defunct or have been incorporated into other agencies

SOURCE: Congressional Research Service, Defense Council on Integrity and Efficiency

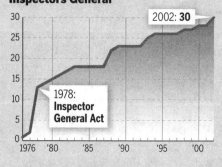

Number of Presidentially Appointed Inspectors General

2002: **30**

1978: **Inspector General Act**

Justice officials.

So that office took up the case. In May, its executives reported back to the Hill. Sorry, they said — we can't get the security clearances to investigate the surveillance program.

This exercise in frustration and dead ends illustrates the weaknesses of the inspector general system that Congress created in 1978, later expanded and has increasingly relied on to monitor executive branch agencies. At a time of one-party government, when most congressional oversight has withered away to symbolic efforts, inspectors general have become a last line of supervision, what Tennessee Democrat Jim Cooper calls a "vital safeguard" for Congress and the public.

Yet not all inspectors general were created equal. Congress has authorized 62 inspectors general for executive agencies, but only 30 have their own line-item budgets that guarantee some independence. Many more have been appointed ad hoc by agencies and bureaus, like Brenner at the NSA, and have only the authority the agency grants them.

The result is a wildly inconsistent, hodge-podge system. "Inspector general" does not mean the same thing in one agency as in another. Some of the watchdogs can brag about significant oversight accomplishments. But there are enough weak ones to throw their overall effectiveness in doubt. The best of the inspectors general take political risks and publish reports that expose deep, embarrassing problems at their agencies, such as waste in the program to rebuild Iraq or fraud in the hurricane relief program from the Gulf Coast. The weakest ones are inspectors general in name only, appointees used as excuses to avoid tougher oversight — just as the NSA inspector general (IG) was used to dodge potential inquiries by Defense and Justice investigators.

That worries lawmakers of both parties who try to keep watch on the watchdogs. Sen. Susan Collins of Maine, the Republican chairwoman of the Senate Homeland Security and Governmental Affairs Committee, says she has found an "uneven level in terms of the quality of the inspectors general and their independence from the agencies that they oversee."

She and the committee's ranking Democrat, Joseph I. Lieberman of Connecticut, have asked the Government Accountability Office (GAO) to assess a range of suggestions for strengthening the inspector general system. Collins expects the report in September, and legislation might follow next year.

Cooper, meanwhile, has promoted legislation to make the IGs more independent of the agencies where they work, and more able to take on difficult and politically sensitive cases.

The independence of inspectors general is the central issue of any debate about their effectiveness because in practice they serve two masters — Congress and the executive branch.

Unlike the GAO, which is an auditing office run by Congress, the inspectors general are based within executive branch agencies. That was a deliberate decision when Congress created the system because "there was serious concern that we not create a second GAO," said Gregory H. Friedman, the Department of Energy inspector general.

As a result, inspectors general can do more detailed investigations and inspections than the GAO, which tends to focus on more general issues that cross different agencies.

But the practical consequence of placing the inspectors general within the executive branch is that they've become professional split personalities. They have to report to the

agency heads as well as Congress. They have to work every day with the people they're supposed to oversee, including the heads of their departments and agencies.

"Inspectors general don't have enough independence to be a legitimate, credible check and balance against agency leaders," said Tom Devine, legal director of the Government Accountability Project, which defends government whistleblowers. They can be effective when the agency heads are interested in hearing about mismanagement within their ranks, Devine said, but their effectiveness will always be limited by how open the agency heads themselves are to hearing bad news. "That's an inherent and serious qualifier," he said.

Some inspectors general have made their own suggestions for strengthening the system, such as setting fixed terms in office and permitting them to be fired only for specific reasons, and the GAO is evaluating those as part of Collins and Lieberman's request.

But even lawmakers who support changes in the system say that many inspectors general are not using the power they already have.

"There's a great deal of pressure within any bureaucracy to go along to get along," said Senate Finance Committee Chairman Charles

E. Grassley, R-Iowa, who does a lot of oversight work and has paid close attention to the inspector general community.

"The inspectors general have a law that gives them independence," Grassley said. "In many cases, they have that independence, but they don't exercise it. And maybe there's some political pressure on them not to."

STIRRING THE STATUS QUO

At their best, inspectors general can shake up the government. When Stuart Bowen arrived in Baghdad in February 2004 to begin his new job as inspector general of the Iraq reconstruction effort, he overheard a sliver of a conversation in the hallway of the Coalition Provisional Authority headquarters. "You can't do that," a woman was saying about some

Stuart Bowen
Inspector General,
Iraq Reconstruction

Bowen, a Texas lawyer and former aide to President Bush, has won near-universal praise for his efforts to audit the U.S. reconstruction program in Iraq, including his finding that $8.8 billion was essentially missing because of sloppy bookkeeping.

action. "There's an IG now."

That statement speaks to the potential power inspectors general have to deter wrongdoing in government. Just showing up, it seems, is a good part of the job — as long as the government workers believe you're truly independent.

The most widely respected inspectors general are the ones who tackle important themes and are willing to speak frankly to those in power. It was Fine's office, for example, that disclosed that hundreds of immigrants were held under harsh conditions and without charges after the Sept. 11 attacks. And it was Bowen who found that $8.8 billion in Iraqi funds overseen by the Coalition Provisional Authority had such sloppy controls that no one could say for certain how it was spent.

When they stick to the basics of waste, fraud and abuse, the inspectors general can point to a long list of measurable accomplishments. In their fiscal 2004 report to the president — the most recent one published — the statutory inspectors general estimated their work had saved the government $18 billion, through better management of programs and money recovered in criminal and civil cases.

They have also been closely watching the reconstruction of the Gulf Coast after Katrina. It was Richard L. Skinner, the Department of Homeland Security inspector general, who revealed that nearly 11,000 unused mobile homes were sitting in Hope, Ark., while Katrina survivors continued to struggle with basic housing needs. Overall, inspectors general have secured 174 indictments, made 152 arrests, and won 48 convictions for abuses like theft fraud, overbilling and false claims.

"I'm very proud of our accomplishments as a community," said Friedman, who also serves as vice chairman of the President's Council on Integrity and Efficiency, which sets standards for presidentially appointed inspectors general and helps to coordinate their work.

One of the largest operations is the Department of Health and Human Services inspector general office, which was the prototype for the modern inspector general when it was created by Congress in 1976. Run now by Daniel R. Levinson, the office has nearly 1,600 employees and focuses on the routine search for fraud, waste and abuse in the health care system — especially fraud. It also is under con-

Gregory Friedman
Inspector General, Energy
A career federal auditor, Friedman is vice chairman of the President's Council on Integrity and Efficiency, which represents inspectors general at major agencies. "If you look at the hard-hitting reports that we produce every day, it's hard to argue that we don't have a great deal of independence," he says.

stant demand to take on new assignments.

In 1996, Congress funded a major expansion of the office so it could put more focus on health care fraud. But the office already had a broad portfolio, with numerous programs in need of basic oversight. Besides Medicare and Medicaid, HHS runs the State Children's Health Insurance Program, Temporary Assistance for Needy Families, and the foster care and child support enforcement programs, as well as public health agencies such as the National Institutes of Health, the Food and Drug Administration, and the Centers for Disease Control and Prevention.

Levinson says his office is gearing up to monitor the Medicare prescription drug program as it gets going. But it will always place one of its highest priorities on Medicaid, because that program is run by the states with a combination of federal and state financing; any fraud the states don't catch costs the federal government money. He has visited U.S. attorneys in cities from Miami to Chicago to Los Angeles to send the message that they're

partners and that "we all need to be working from essentially the same script to protect these dollars."

One of the most widely praised watchdog offices is the Iraq inspector general. Created by legislation sponsored by Democratic Sen. Russ Feingold of Wisconsin, the Iraq inspector general reports jointly to two departments: Defense and State. Technically, Bowen was chosen by the Defense Department, with the State Department's sign-off. But the fact that he answers exclusively to neither one, and has the ability to report quickly to both department heads and Congress if he is denied access to any documents, has given him the political strength to overcome occasional friction such as grumbling from other inspectors general who had designs on the funds that Congress gave to his office.

"We've run into resistance, but the provisions of our law are good," said Jim Mitchell, a spokesman for Bowen's office, which is called the Special Inspector General for Iraq Reconstruction. "We've got the kind of independence you need to be able to investigate things and establish accountability."

Bowen's success in monitoring an obviously difficult program is evidence for others that inspectors general have significant authority and can operate effectively within government agencies.

"If you look at the hard-hitting reports that we produce every day, it's hard to argue that we don't have a great deal of independence," said Friedman, who is considered by some private watchdog groups to be one of the more aggressive inspectors general in the Bush administration. "I have a good relationship with my department managers, but I also feel a great deal of independence."

CAUGHT IN THE WEEDS

But there also are inspectors general who focus on more trivial issues, such as relatively unimportant rule violations by low-level employees. One November 2004 report by the Amtrak inspector general, for example, faulted Amtrak Technologies for contracting with a consultant "without providing the Procurement Department with a copy of the signed contract."

Impartiality Called Into Question

FEDERAL INSPECTORS GENERAL are supposed to be chosen in a non-partisan manner and solely on the basis of their auditing or investigative skills, but some lawmakers and watchdog groups say the Bush administration has been using the inspector general offices to give jobs to political supporters and allies.

Indeed, some inspectors general have clear political ties to the administration or the Republican Party. Gregory A. Brower, the inspector general at the Government Printing Office, is a former Republican state assemblyman in Nevada; NASA inspector general Robert W. Cobb was an associate counsel to President Bush. But inspectors general in office now come from a variety of backgrounds. At least six are former Secret Service agents; at least that many have spent their careers in the agencies they now keep an eye on. A few are former prosecutors or officials in the Justice Department.

The staff of Rep. Henry A. Waxman of California, the ranking Democrat on the House Government Reform Committee, conducted one study that tried to measure the qualifications of Bush appointees. It found that only 18 percent of Bush's inspector general appointees had previous experience working in inspector general offices, at the Government Accountability Office or at private auditing firms, while 66 percent of President Bill Clinton's appointees had that kind of experience. By contrast, the report found, nearly two-thirds of Bush's appointees had political experience of some kind, while fewer than a quarter of Clinton's had political backgrounds.

CHECKING UP: Waxman says Bush picks IGs based on politics.

"Congress didn't intend for the IGs to be treated like political appointees, but that's what's happening," said Beth Daley, director of investigations at the private Project on Government Oversight (POGO), which is working on its own study of how well the inspector general system is working.

Daniel R. Levinson, the inspector general at the Department of Health and Human Services, takes issue with that argument. Inspectors general have always been political appointees, he says, even though their jobs are not political. Over the years, he says, there have been shifts in the kinds of people who have been selected. In the 1980s, most were investigators, in keeping with President Ronald Reagan's determination to eliminate waste in government. By the 1990s, most of the candidates came from auditing backgrounds, to help programs work better.

Now, Levinson says, most are lawyers — not necessarily specialists in any one issue, but experts in the government process. "The fact that we're looking more toward lawyers means we may be finding more people with political backgrounds," said Levinson. "Lawyers who have worked for Capitol Hill or the White House bring valuable experience to the job."

Levinson himself epitomizes the mixture of professional experience and politics. He is a lawyer and a certified fraud investigator. He also has strong Republican connections, having held political appointments in the Reagan administration and the first Bush administration, and serving as chief of staff for then-Rep. Bob Barr, a conservative Republican from Georgia, from 1995 to 1998.

Even critics of the Bush administration's appointments, however, concede that an inspector general with a political background isn't necessarily going to be a pushover.

One of Waxman's favorite inspectors general, for example, is Stuart Bowen, who oversees the Iraq reconstruction effort. Bowen had previously held several positions in the Bush White House and was involved in the Florida recount for Bush's team during the 2000 presidential election.

WATCHDOG TROUBLE

Still, serious questions have been raised about the conduct of a few of the Bush administration inspectors general with political backgrounds.

As inspector general of HHS, Janet Rehnquist, the daughter of former Supreme Court Chief Justice William H. Rehnquist and a former associate counsel to Bush's father, delayed an audit of the Florida pension system in 2002 at the request of the chief of staff for Republican Gov. Jeb Bush, who was up for re-election that year. In addition, her intervention in negotiations on a Medicare billing case helped a Pennsylvania hospital get a better settlement.

She kept a gun in her office. Longtime senior managers quit or were reassigned. After less than two years on the job, Rehnquist resigned in 2003 under heavy criticism.

And last year, Joseph E. Schmitz, the Defense Department's inspector general who once worked in the Reagan administration as an assistant to Attorney General Edwin Meese III, resigned as Senate Finance Committee Chairman Charles E. Grassley of Iowa prepared to launch a congressional investigation of whether he had blocked two criminal probes of senior Bush administration officials. Grassley also warned Schmitz that his heavily redacted report on the Air Force's controversial effort to lease unneeded tankers from the Boeing Co. "raises questions about your independence as IG."

That's not exactly the kind of issue that would catch the eye of a busy lawmaker. "Too often, some IGs get caught up in various weeds, such as, 'Did Mary fill out her paperwork?' That's not so useful to Congress," said an aide to Grassley.

And in the worst cases, inspectors general provide the fiction of independent oversight without the reality of it, which prevents tougher investigations from taking place. Sometimes they simply don't have enough power to be taken seriously, like the NSA inspector general. But in a few cases, they've actually thrown investigators off the trail and raised questions about their own political motives. For instance, when Janet Rehnquist was inspector general of HHS in 2002, she delayed an audit of the Florida pension system at the request of the chief of staff to Gov. Jeb Bush, who was up for re-election that year.

Inspectors general also draw complaints from government whistleblowers, even though the two might seem to be natural allies. In one case, former FBI undercover agent Mike German said the Justice Department's inspector general office downplayed his complaint about the mishandling of a terrorism investigation and allowed FBI officials to correct some of their misstatements about the case. German said he was frozen out of anti-terrorism work in retaliation for his complaint.

Tom Fitton, president of Judicial Watch, a conservative, nonpartisan organization that uses open records requests to uncover evidence of government misconduct, says his organization never has gotten much useful information from the inspectors general.

"In terms of combating and fighting corruption, they're largely irrelevant," Fitton said. "They're creatures of the agency. They don't help whistleblowers."

The bottom line is, when big public policy breakdowns happen — the controversy over the NSA surveillance program, the federal government's response to Katrina, the intelligence failures before Sept. 11 and in Iraq — the inspectors general don't have the staff or the stamina to substitute for active congressional oversight.

"When you look at the major meltdowns of the last 25 years, you can always find that the IGs were writing reports about them before the scandals blew open, but they were not in the lead in producing legislation or launching a full-blown investigation," said Paul C. Light, a professor of public service at New York University and author of "Monitoring Government," a 1993 book about inspectors general. "I can't think of a single investigation, other than Medicare fraud, in which the IG was the primary driver."

The weakest links, those who study the system say, are inspectors general whose offices are created, appointed and paid for within a particular agency. They have neither the authority nor the resources of colleagues in statutory jobs. The NSA inspector general, for instance, has about 60 investigators, auditors and support personnel. The Department of Defense inspector general has more than 1,400.

"There were instances where the NSA inspector general would call me and ask the Defense Department to investigate some program because the NSA inspector general felt awkward because they didn't have the independence to do it," said Eleanor Hill, who served as the Department of Defense inspector general under President Bill Clinton. "It's not very big. It doesn't have a lot of resources. The Department of Defense inspector general should have been looking at this all along."

In addition, Brenner himself doesn't appear to have an extensive national security background for the NSA job. Before the Sept. 11 attacks, he was a partner in a general law practice in Washington. One of his claims to fame was his work on the Prudential Securities case in the early 1990s, in which tens of thousands of investors won restitution for being defrauded by the firm in the 1980s.

After the terrorist attacks, Brenner felt a need to reach beyond securities law. "After

9/11, Joel wanted to do something for the good of the country," said Laurence Storch, a senior counsel at Fulbright & Jaworski and Brenner's former law partner in the firm of Storch & Brenner.

Another example of a non-statutory inspector general office is the Army Corps of Engineers. In a scathing report, the corps recently accepted blame for the failure of the levees during Katrina — but the inspector general had nothing to do with it. The report was sponsored by the corps but prepared largely by outside engineers.

Why would the corps' own inspector general not participate in the report? Because, according to corps spokesman Wayne Stroupe, the agency wanted to make sure the report looked independent. "We didn't want it to be seen as a rubber-stamped Army Corps report," he said.

SERVING DIFFERENT BOSSES

Being creatures of Congress and the executive branch, inspectors general have the tricky task of figuring out who their primary audience is. Those who have done the job say it can be handled by reminding everyone of their good-government role and sticking to it.

"You shoot straight. That's what your job is," said Kenneth M. Mead, a former inspector general at the Department of Transportation. A successful inspector general will find ways to make sure Congress pays attention to his work, Mead said, but the most important priority is that "you're not going to play politics. You really have to run true to that compass. Otherwise, you're going to get into trouble."

Levinson says the dual audiences make the inspector general's job "unique," but he insists he doesn't struggle for independence and doesn't find it uncomfortable to be based in the executive branch while also reporting to Congress. "If you view the Congress as the board of directors and the president as the chief of the management team, the structure makes sense from a corporate model standpoint," he said.

Sometimes, though, the politics can be forced on them. Nikki Tinsley, a longtime auditor who stepped down in March as inspector general at the EPA, said her office got little interest from Republicans in control of Congress, and the interest it got from Democrats was usually in the form of politically loaded requests for investigations. "They tended to be things like, 'Did the assistant administrator lie when he said X?'" she recalled.

Tinsley handled it, she said, by working with their offices to rephrase the questions into a

neutral form — such as determining whether an agency's actions followed its normal procedures. "We actually got to some of the questions the members were interested in," Tinsley said, "but we didn't do it with a bias."

Even if they make administration officials mad, most inspectors general don't have to fear for their jobs. President Ronald Reagan fired all of the inspectors general after taking office in 1981 so he could hire his own people; his action prompted such a backlash that it has never been repeated. "The Reagan administration was a unique situation, which I think everyone recognizes in hindsight was a big mistake," said Friedman.

Inspectors general don't have to be fired outright, though. They can be eased out, or simply cut out of the loop in more subtle ways. President Bush appointed Clark Kent Ervin to be the first inspector general at the Department of Homeland Security, but after he issued a series of scathing reports that he publicized heavily — disclosing weaknesses in airport screening, port inspections and the record of border inspectors who are supposed to reject foreigners with stolen passports — Ervin says he was called in for a scolding by then-Homeland Security Secretary Tom Ridge.

"Are you my Inspector General?" Ridge asked, according to an account in Ervin's book, "Open Target." "When I was Governor of Pennsylvania, I had an Inspector General, but he wasn't out there like you constantly criticizing and embarrassing us." Ridge has disputed Ervin's account of that meeting, but the way Ervin's career as an inspector general ended is undeniable: Ervin had been appointed during a congressional recess, and the administration stopped pushing his nomination; the appointment quietly expired with the next Congress.

Some Democrats think the Bush administration is trying to quietly circumvent Bowen's office for Iraq reconstruction by providing $1.6 billion in the last supplemental spending bill but routing it through accounts in the jurisdiction of the State Department inspector general's office.

"There are a thousand ways to disrespect the inspector general without crossing the line," said Tennessee's Cooper. "The most common way of doing it is the 'freeze-out' — the office in the basement, you don't get the memos, etc."

GETTING IT FROM ALL SIDES

If anyone illustrates how even the most respected inspectors general can find them-

selves caught between competing political pressures, it is Fine, the Justice Department inspector general who has been in the middle of numerous cases related to the war on terror.

The test of a good inspector general, according to Danielle Bryan, executive director of the Project on Government Oversight, or POGO, is, "Are they interested in investigating only low-level employees who commit petty crimes, or are they interested in institutional problems that really get to the core of an agency?" By that standard, most watchdog groups agree, Fine has shown more courage than most. It was his office, for example, that disclosed that 762 foreign detainees had been held without charges after the Sept. 11 attacks, at a time when their exact number and the nature of their plight was a mystery.

He also documented the abuse of detainees at the Metropolitan Detention Center in Brooklyn after the attacks. More recently, his office disclosed that the FBI had committed 108 possible violations of procedures, including wiretapping, in its intelligence work, such as intercepting communications they weren't supposed to hear and continuing investigations after their authority had expired.

Fine sidestepped the NSA investigation, though, in essence handing it off to the Office of Professional Responsibility because he said it involved the conduct of Justice Department officials.

Fine's decision on the NSA case did not impress the House Democrats who asked for the investigation. They fired back a letter arguing that he was the one responsible for reporting to Congress on "abuses and deficiencies" in the department's programs and that he was the sole contact for complaints about civil liberties violations.

"The IG system is good in theory, but it can't stand up to an administration that's determined to stage a massive coverup," said Lofgren. The only thing that can work in such a case, she said, is for Congress to use its subpoena power.

Fine, who declined to be interviewed for this article, also doesn't win unanimous raves for his treatment of whistleblowers.

German, the former FBI agent who complained to Fine's office about mistakes in a terrorism investigation in Orlando, Fla., in 2002, said the inspector general's office passed on to the FBI the fact that he had a transcript of an informant's tape recording that the bureau had denied existed. That gave FBI officials a chance to revise their statement about the recording. "It was clear to me that they were trying to manage the situation rather than truly investigate it," said German.

The inspector general's report on the case last year substantiated most of German's allegations about the Orlando case. But Cynthia Schnedar, a spokeswoman for Fine, said German had initially blamed the Office of Professional Responsibility for passing on the information that he had the transcript, and that the inspector general's office found no evidence to back up his claim.

In testimony at a House subcommittee hearing on whistleblowers in February, Fine acknowledged that the FBI had "mishandled" the investigation and that an FBI official had retaliated against German for reporting the problem with the recording.

SEEKING MORE PROTECTION

The power of an inspector general's office is tied closely to the individuals who run it, and most don't seem to be crying out for major changes. But the report that GAO is working on could shed some light on the prospects for changes that have been proposed for years.

One of the changes in Cooper's bill, for example, would give inspectors general fixed terms of seven years and allow them to be removed only in cases of "permanent disability, malfeasance, inefficiency, neglect of duty, conviction of a felony or conduct involving moral turpitude." Right now, most of the inspectors general don't serve for any set length of time; only the Postal Service and Capitol Police inspectors general, which were added separately, have fixed terms.

Taking the firing decisions out of the hands of the president and agency heads, Cooper says, would make the inspectors general more independent. Collins proposed a similar measure in 1999, and in a survey provided to Collins and Lieberman by a committee of inspectors general, 58 percent of the statutory inspectors general who responded said fixed terms and specific conditions for firing would strengthen their independence. A few reported past cases in which their jobs had been threatened by political pressure.

Another Cooper proposal that's likely to gain more support among the inspectors general is to allow them to submit their budget requests directly to Congress, rather than going through their agencies. Even though the funds for presidentially appointed inspectors general are protected once Congress appropriates them, their budget requests still have to be negotiated with their departments and the White House's Office of Management and Budget.

Such a change would be a particular help to the agency-appointed inspectors general, who don't have protected budgets, said Debra Ritt, a former inspector general at the Smithsonian Institution. She resigned recently because her budget had been cut so much that she believed she could no longer do her job effectively. She now works in the inspector general office at the Small Business Administration.

"I do think my budget was competing with several other high priorities at the Smithsonian," said Ritt. "The combination of an understaffed audit shop and the cutbacks of funding for other monitoring was not a good situation."

Another rewrite that's needed for those inspectors general, she said, is to place the hiring decisions in the hands of agency governing boards whenever possible, not the agency directors. Such a change would "really enhance the independence" of those offices, she said.

The GAO report also is likely to recommend consolidating some of the smaller inspector general offices and converting some inspector general offices that agencies have created into presidentially appointed posts. Collins said she proposed consolidations in the past, but the idea has been opposed by many of the agency-appointed inspector general offices, which argue that such mergers would not help and might even hurt their oversight efforts.

Getting any such changes through Congress will be difficult, especially since Collins' House counterpart, Government Reform Committee Chairman Thomas M. Davis III, a Virginia Republican, doesn't see much need for changes. He believes the Cooper legislation "may be trying to fix things that aren't broken," according to spokeswoman Andrea LeBlanc.

And Henry A. Waxman of California, the ranking Democrat on the Government Reform Committee, says the real problem is that the Bush administration isn't paying enough attention to the law's provisions to protect the inspectors general from political pressure.

"Maybe Congress has to be more prescriptive in spelling out exactly what it expects," said Waxman, but "I don't know if it's going to work if the administration isn't going to follow the law as it exists now."

In the long run, though, inspectors general will always have to negotiate a balance between Congress and the executive branch — and face the fact that the biggest scandals will never be averted unless Congress pays attention itself. But that doesn't mean they need to limit their sights to cleaning up messes after the fact, those who have done the job say. They can do more to help their agencies prevent them, too.

"I don't think the real question is capability or knowledge or background. I think the real question is your ability to exercise your independence," said Hill, the former Department of Defense inspector general.

For watchdogs who have to work every day with the people they oversee, proving that independence will always be their biggest challenge. As Tinsley, the former EPA inspector general, put it: "If you don't look independent, it doesn't matter if you are." ∎

Revisiting

HOMELAND SECURITY

Lawmakers with second thoughts about their creation have moved from criticizing the troubled department to chipping away at it

THE HOMELAND Security Department's announcement last month that it was cutting counterterrorism aid to New York and Washington and giving more to small cities such as Ft. Lauderdale and Memphis set lawmakers' teeth on edge. Like the color-coded threat levels and ordering old ladies to take their shoes off at the airport, it seemed to the politicians like just another bureaucracy-driven decision that had little regard for common sense and even less for political realities.

And in a way, it was an insult added to injury: It came just at a time when Congress was trying to figure out how to funnel more money — not less — to the metropolitan areas that are considered the most threatened, especially after Sept. 11, 2001.

"As far as I'm concerned, the Department of Homeland Security and the administration have declared war on New York," railed Rep. Peter T. King, the New York Republican who oversees the department as chairman of the Homeland Security Committee.

"It's a knife in the back to New York," said King, who lost friends, neighbors and constituents in the 2001 attacks, "and I'm going to do everything I can to make them very sorry they made this decision."

Members of Congress have spoken harshly before about the Homeland Security Department, complaining about its response to Hurricane Katrina, for instance, and its inability to control illegal immigration. But for the first time, lawmakers are going beyond talk to action, actively promoting legislation to remove pieces of the department.

This could lead, in time, to a wholesale dismantling of the department that was created

with such urgency more than three years ago. No one is going that far yet, but members of Congress are increasingly asking themselves whether they and the Bush administration made a mistake in agglomerating 22 government agencies, bureaus and offices into one department to handle domestic security.

"What we're now seeing is the kind of rethinking of the organization that should have taken place before it was created," said Norm Ornstein, a resident scholar at the American Enterprise Institute, a conservative think tank. "First of all, there should have been a recognition that pulling together any kind of disparate agencies is an enormously difficult task that can take years to do, sometimes decades."

The forced merger of these various agencies is one of the main reasons that Homeland Security is not working as Congress intended. Each agency brought with it a distinct culture and, in some cases, its own problems. FEMA had been a government backwater, and sometimes a dumping ground for unwanted political appointees, long before Sept. 11. The Coast Guard had for decades struggled to find the resources to handle its various missions.

Once created, the department was put in the hands of a former state governor — Pennsylvania Republican Tom Ridge — who some critics said was a better politician than he was a manager. His successor, Michael Chertoff, is a former judge with no experience running a major agency.

Finally, some critics say that the Bush administration and Congress were not prepared to give the new department the level of resources it needed to fulfill such an ambitious mandate.

The result has been more a confederation of agencies than a cohesive department, leaving little wonder that members of Congress have proposed removing some of those agencies and letting them operate on their own.

In May, two House committees approved legislation to pull FEMA out of the Homeland Security Department and let it operate on its own. Committee members thought an independent FEMA could devote more effort to disaster recovery.

That is much the same reason other lawmakers think the Coast Guard should be removed, too. Its civilian responsibilities, such as search and rescue, they say, are not inherently related to homeland security. And a House committee in May approved a bill to take away some of the department's responsibilities for medical response to disasters.

Such views are not widely held in Congress; the consensus seems to be that it is too soon or would be unwise to make such changes. The administration opposes removing any agencies. For one thing, it might threaten the entire structure.

"Once you start tearing this thing apart, it's all open for consideration," said Paul C. Light, a New York University professor who specializes in the federal bureaucracy. "Congress should be very careful about taking things out. It could be a house of cards."

It is also not clear that those who want to remove certain agencies are driven by policy alone. Creation of the department scrambled congressional committee jurisdictions and left some chairmen with less power than they previously had. A reorganization could give some of it back. (*Turf wars, p. 56*)

But never before have the congressional complaints about the department been so insistent. Even the chairman of the House Appropriations subcommittee that funds the department, Kentucky Republican Harold Rogers, indicated recently that there may come a day when he would favor dismantling it.

"I'm not quite there yet," Rogers said, though his subcommittee's fiscal 2007 bill withholds $1.3 billion until the department produces strategies, planning documents and other material Rogers has asked for.

EARLY WARNINGS

Once, and not that long ago, a Homeland Security Department was a shiny new idea about good government. In February of 2001, the U.S. Commission on National Security/21st Century predicted that a terror attack on U.S. soil was likely within the next 25 years. If that happened, the commission warned, it would decimate lives and wreak destruction that would damage U.S. pre-eminence in the world. And the

Homeland Uncertainty

If Congress changes the structure of the Homeland Security Department, the most likely targets will be the Federal Emergency Management Agency (FEMA), which has been plagued by mistakes, and the Coast Guard, an agency Congress dotes on and had misgivings about adding to Homeland Security in the first place. So far, lawmakers have done little more than talk about altering the department, but action is likely if the problems persist. Here's a rundown on some of the proposals:

FEMA Lawmakers were so upset by FEMA's fumbled response to Hurricane Katrina and with Homeland Security's management of the agency that 11 bills to do something about it have been introduced. Eight would yank FEMA out of the department altogether. Alaska Republican Don Young's bill to make FEMA its own agency with Cabinet status has been approved by his Transportation and Infrastructure Committee and by Government Reform. The administration opposes the idea and GOP congressional leaders have not gotten involved. The House Homeland Security Committee has approved a competing bill to give FEMA more responsibility and clout but leave it where it is.

Coast Guard When Congress created the department some members, such as Young, worried that the Coast Guard's traditional maritime roles, such as search and rescue, would get short shrift in a department primarily dedicated to counterterrorism and border security. Their concerns have only increased as the Coast Guard tries to handle multiple roles with limited resources. Lawmakers probably won't try to move the Coast Guard anytime soon, but Alaska Republican Ted Stevens, chairman of the Senate Commerce, Science and Transportation Committee, is considering legislation on the subject.

National Disaster Medical System When Congress created the department it incorporated teams that coordinate the medical response to disasters. These teams, which had been under the Department of Health and Human Services (HHS), were attached to FEMA. Last month, the House Energy and Commerce Committee approved legislation to move them back, saying they could operate better as part of HHS. "Unless we want these agencies to suffer the fate of FEMA, we will need to remain vigilant," said John D. Dingell of Michigan, the committee's ranking Democrat. Both the administration and the Homeland Security Committee oppose the move.

government would not be ready.

"In the face of this threat, our nation has no coherent or integrated governmental structures," said the members of the panel, nicknamed the Hart-Rudman Commission, in their final report. "We therefore recommend the creation of an independent National Homeland Security Agency (NHSA) with responsibility for planning, coordinating and integrating various U.S. government activities involved in homeland security."

The expected attack came months, not years, later. Sept. 11 drove President Bush to appoint a homeland security czar to oversee the agencies, bureaus and operations spread out across the federal government that had any responsibility for defending the country against such attacks. This adviser would operate from the White House in the Office of Homeland Security.

Tom Ridge was not in the job long before reports began to surface of agencies that did not want to take his direction. Congress became angry when Ridge, citing executive privilege, refused to testify at committee hearings. Rep. Jane Harman, a California Democrat, brandished a chart demonstrating how complicated, dissolute and uncoordinated federal homeland security was. Lawmakers began discussing in earnest the work of Hart-Rudman.

Bush resisted the idea, pushed mostly by Democrats, of a Homeland Security Department. But when revelations of intelligence failures made headlines in the spring of 2002, he proposed his own plan for a department. Republicans got on board. Very few members of Congress voted against the final bill, approved late the same year.

Department supporters point to accomplishments since. "Their track record, outside of Katrina, is pretty good," said Adam H. Putnam of Florida, chairman of the House Republican Policy Committee. "There have been no terrorist attacks inside the U.S. since 9/11."

In the early days of the department, the focus was on vision and strategy. Retired Coast Guard Adm. James Loy, who served as deputy secretary and in other capacities, said one of Ridge's great accomplishments was setting forth the key operational principles of the department: awareness, prevention, preparedness, response and recovery. A similar iteration of those principles still guides the department.

The department, said current deputy secretary Michael Jackson, has increasingly focused on "systemic discipline." An anthrax scare at the Pentagon led the department to develop specific lists of actions for each kind of attack, listed in a book that Jackson can flip through to find recommended responses and tasks for, say, a "chlorine tank explosion."

Each secretary can claim responsibility for reducing a variety of vulnerabilities. Both Loy and Jackson praised the department's progress on the difficult task of guarding critical infrastructure — the chemical plants, computer networks and other structures that pose tempting terror targets. The overdue National Infrastructure Protection Plan is ready for release this week, Jackson said.

Under Ridge, the department went from executive order to interim plan, Loy said. Under Chertoff, it has begun to expand on that work, not only finalizing the plan but completing an inventory of all critical infrastructure, prioritizing it and recommending action for some of the higher-risk chemical plants in the nation.

In several ways, the department also has consolidated its operations — under Ridge, it cut the number of bill-paying centers from 19 to six — and benefited from synergy among its agencies that its creators envisioned. The department's grants and training division, which distributes aid to states and first-responders, has called upon the expertise of the Transportation Security Administration, FEMA and other agencies for information about vulnerabilities and needs in such areas as mass transit and disaster preparedness.

However fragmentary those achievements are, they are close to the way government agencies in general grow and evolve. Experts warned when the department was created, and still caution today, that building an effective structure could take years, even decades.

As such, Jackson said, Congress' impatience is healthy and expected; the country cannot afford to wait 10 years to have a fully functioning department when the threat of terrorism still looms. But it is not a reason to do something drastic. The department must be given time to mature.

"We had the right vision," he said. "We ought to have the courage of our convictions to stand by what we created."

In Light's view, "Congress just has to be patient and avoid the temptation to undo the merger with continued bad news from the department."

BAG AND BAGGAGE

And yet, there is general agreement that the department is a mess — more so than members

POLITICAL SAVVY: In 2003, Tom Ridge, then director of Homeland Security, was elevated to the Cabinet.

of Congress expected it would be at this point.

At least part of that is because of the merging of agencies with vastly different cultures and missions. Some of the agencies had only a small connection to security. The Coast Guard was primarily focused on search and rescue and fisheries, and devoted just 25 percent of its efforts to homeland security. Likewise, FEMA was not a protective agency like the Secret Service — it had always focused on natural disasters.

After three and a half years, Homeland still has a split personality. According to the administration's fiscal 2007 budget request, 40 percent of the department's spending would be for activities not related to homeland security.

And plenty of the government's homeland security spending is in agencies outside the department, such as the FBI. Another Bush budget document places the total federal homeland security budget at $58.3 billion, of which nearly half is for the Homeland Security Department.

Some agencies also brought baggage as well. At the time, the Immigration and Naturalization Service was referred to as the most dysfunctional agency in the federal government. The Coast Guard was a good agency but historically starved of needed funding, said Elaine Kamarck, a Harvard University Kennedy School of Government Professor who managed Clinton's "reinventing government" initiative.

Combine that with the stress of any reor-

Three Years On, Turf Wars Persist

CONGRESS MAY HAVE CREATED the Department of Homeland Security, but it has done no better than the department itself in coming to grips with the disparate and interwoven missions of the various agencies it oversees.

Legislation on the protection of seaports and railroads and the security of airline cargo has been left hanging because lawmakers cannot agree on solutions, cannot find the money to pay for solutions or refuse to compromise on committee jurisdictions. Lawmakers have not even been able to reauthorize the department they built.

After it created the department, the House created a Homeland Security Committee to oversee these issues. The Senate more recently gave its Senate Governmental Affairs Committee jurisdiction over domestic security issues. But given the department's vast and disparate responsibilities, congressional oversight of its operations remains diffuse — spread across no fewer than 65 committees and subcommittees.

That has left the new committees feeling a little like the new kid on the block, with veteran chairmen from other panels balking at attempts to consolidate oversight of the Homeland Security Department.

For example, Don Young, the Alaska Republican who chairs the Transportation and Infrastructure Committee, has refused to share much jurisdiction over the Coast Guard even though it is part of the Homeland Security Department. Wisconsin Republican F. James Sensenbrenner Jr., chairman of the Judiciary Committee, has been unwilling to give up much oversight of immigration, which also is under the control of Homeland Security. The House Energy and Commerce Committee, meanwhile, has tried to maintain control of technology issues such as the emergency radio spectrum.

John Gannon, a former staff director for the House Homeland Security Committee, says that while he was there he spent much of his time battling over jurisdiction. "We got clobbered by the other committee chairmen," he says. "There was a dismissive attitude."

Turf also has been an issue on port security, which Congress has been arguing about for years. Last year, Senate Commerce, Science and Transportation Committee Chairman Ted Stevens, an Alaska Republican, guided a bill through the panel to authorize $729 million over three years for port security. This spring, Maine Republican Susan Collins persuaded her Homeland Security and Governmental Affairs Committee to approve a similar port security bill that calls for spending $835 million a year.

There has been no progress in merging the two. "That's just a jurisdictional fight," Stevens said after the Collins bill was approved. Just because Collins has homeland security as part of her panel's jurisdiction, Stevens said, "that doesn't mean they have control over ports."

CONTROLLING THE SPENDING

The usual struggles between appropriators and the authorizing committees also plague homeland security oversight. The tough task of investigations has been overshadowed by the lure of Homeland Security appropriations, which allow members of Congress to send anti-terrorism money back to their home districts.

Kentucky Republican Harold Rogers, chairman of the House Homeland Security Appropriations Subcommittee, has come under fire for steering homeland security business to companies in his district, including language that helped a business in Corbin, Ky., win federal work making identification cards for transportation workers.

Bringing appropriations home is nothing new, but critics say the power that appropriators have over homeland security far outweighs that of the authorizing committees, making it hard to have an impact on spending levels or formulas for anti-terrorism grants. For instance, appropriators, especially those from rural or small-town districts, have opposed homeland security grant formulas that would benefit high-threat areas such as New York, Washington or Los Angeles.

House Homeland Security Committee Chairman Peter T. King, R-N.Y., says a department authorization bill modeled after the annual defense authorization — in which authorizers set a Pentagon spending blueprint, but the appropriators make specific funding decisions

ganization, and ineffectualness was bound to reign. "The simple act of moving something is extremely disruptive and distracting to the core mission," said Michael O'Hanlon of the Brookings Institution.

Kamarck said some of the decisions made during the merger compounded the woes of the department. Customs was combined with the INS, then split into three units — Customs and Border Protection, Immigration and Customs Enforcement, and Citizenship and Immigration Services.

That led to problems for all three agencies, according to the department's inspector gen-

eral, such as the detention and removal of aliens and a lack of coordination in intelligence-gathering and investigations.

Furthermore, the initial merger of the 22 agencies was not the last shakeup. Last summer, after months of review, Chertoff ordered a department-wide reorganization that merged several divisions and created new ones. "They've been reorganizing internally at a relatively rapid pace," Light said. "The department has been in turmoil since the beginning."

Jackson, though, said Chertoff's reorganization was designed at least in part to chop away at internal dysfunction, some of it inherent to

the foundation of the department. For instance, Congress mandated the creation of an Information Analysis and Infrastructure Protection Directorate. For a while, it was considered the most dysfunctional portion of the department, and the different divisions of the directorate, with different kinds of expertise and goals, did not always see eye to eye. Chertoff separated them, creating a special intelligence office and putting infrastructure protection into a Preparedness Directorate — a better fit for the respective tasks, Jackson said.

"There was a profound operational dysfunction in the way that was glommed togeth-

House Homeland Security Chairman Peter T. King

House Homeland Security ranking Democrat Bennie Thompson

in a pretty bipartisan way, and we are the prime committee of jurisdiction," the chairman says. But none of this legislation has passed Congress. "Legislatively, there's not a lot of successes to look at," says James Jay Carafano, a homeland security and defense analyst at the Heritage Foundation, a conservative think tank. "Jurisdiction is a problem . . . and it just isn't getting any better."

It is not that Homeland Security officials have avoided Capitol Hill. Since its inception in 2003, the department has participated in 601 congressional hearings and provided nearly 6,000 congressional briefings. The department's two secretaries, Tom Ridge and Michael Chertoff, have testified 38 times.

—would give Congress a firmer hold over programs, funding levels and priorities for the far-flung department. "In the ideal world it would send a message to the department and would set a structural base for the department," King says. "And it's important to establish credibility for the committee." But he isn't holding out hope.

King is hoping to have his committee take a stab at an authorization bill again this summer. The House last year passed a fiscal 2006 reauthorization, but the Senate did not take it up, and this year again it has no plans to mark up a Homeland Security authorization.

'TAKING A WHILE TO SHAKE OUT'

Collins says that with a department as large as Homeland Security, "it's no surprise this [jurisdiction] is taking a while to shake out." Her committee has marked up bills dealing with chemical plant security, grant formulas and port security.

The House panel has been more active since King took over. In the past year it has held a dozen markups on bills ranging from the handling of ammonium nitrate to port security. "We are working

But while all of these hearings show that House and Senate committees are interested in homeland security issues such as port security and the federal response to Hurricane Katrina, the diffuse mission of the committees means that one panel is not there to hold the new department accountable. And the turf wars further complicate the problem, experts say. "Congress has tragically failed in its oversight," says Timothy J. Roemer, a member of the Sept. 11 commission and a former Democratic House member from Indiana. "Congress needs to do less finger-pointing at the agency and look in the mirror."

Rep. Bennie Thompson of Mississippi, the ranking Democrat on House Homeland Security, scoffs when asked about congressional oversight of the biggest government reorganization since World War II. "You mean the lack of congressional oversight," he says.

Gannon, a former CIA deputy director who is now an executive at the aerospace firm BAE Systems, says that if the department fails, it is ultimately a reflection on Congress. "The department," he said, "needs focused, strong congressional oversight."

er," he said. "Now they're aligned and doing a good job."

MANAGING CHANGE

The Hart-Rudman Commission assumed that a department devoted to homeland security was not the only answer to protecting the country. "There is no perfect organizational design, no flawless managerial fix," the members wrote. "The reason is that organizations are made up of people, and people invariably devise informal means of dealing with one another in accord with the accidents of personality and temperament. Even excellent orga-

nizational structure cannot make impetuous or mistaken leaders patient or wise, but poor organizational design can make good leaders less effective."

Ridge and Chertoff, the two secretaries of the department, have each received mixed reviews on their management. Ridge, a capable politician, proved most adept in front of the camera, communicating to the public. Internally, he engendered loyalty among aides.

Chertoff, an admired intellectual, brought the regimented thinking of an attorney from his time as a judge and top official in the Department of Justice.

But their strengths have also sometimes been a detriment. And in the views of their critics, each also brought a similar flaw.

"They are not operations guys. You need a heavy-duty operations guy in there," Kamarck said. Chertoff , she said, is a "brilliant lawyer and brilliant judge, and he's never run a major operation involving thousands of people. Frankly, Tom Ridge wasn't much better, either. He was a politician. They've had two inadequate directors."

Ridge, insiders said, had a tendency to let internal disputes drag on too long, a result of his politician's instinct not to displease anyone. He also gained a reputation for letting other departments tread on his turf, such as in 2003 when he signed a memorandum with the Department of Justice that granted them lead authority for terrorism finance investigations, much to the dismay of investigators in his own department.

Chertoff has a tendency toward frankness, for instance saying repeatedly that not everyone and everything in the country can be protected, a message that often offends lawmakers.

And more than a few insiders quietly wished Chertoff had half of Ridge's political savvy when Hurricane Katrina hit. His unwillingness to take control of the situation when FEMA Director Michael D. Brown was floundering was a setback for his department, said Kamarck.

Democrats began calling on him to resign as early as last summer. But during the fury over the fiscal 2006 state grants, for the first time a Republican, Rep. John E. Sweeney of New York, joined the chorus. Some of Chertoff's early supporters have begun to abandon him.

"I've lost a lot of confidence in Secretary Chertoff," said King. "It's getting more and more difficult to defend him."

Neither Ridge nor Chertoff granted interview requests last week, but their deputies, Loy and Jackson, defended them in a similar fashion: The secretaries may not have been former chief operating officers, but they brought their own skills to bear in the job and surrounded themselves with people who possessed the skills they lacked.

The department's management problems extend far below the secretary's office. The department has had trouble finding candidates for management jobs who are both capable and willing. Only three of the more than 20 top managers in the department today served under Ridge for more than a day.

"Sometimes you'll find people who just don't want the grief," said Jackson. Testifying before Congress "is not always a lovefest, and there's a risk to your career if you leave after getting beat up on things."

A survey last year ranked the Department of Homeland Security the second-worst place to work among large agencies. The worst was the Small Business Administration.

When Homeland Security sought a replacement for Brown, several candidates rejected the offer flat out. Critics say the department has not often enough taken responsibility for finding top managers. The result is that those who are brave enough to stay sometimes end up taking on added responsibilities, serving as "acting" director of an agency while maintaining their old jobs as well.

"The joke on our side is that we could really start a local at DHS for the Screen Actors' Guild, there are so many people 'acting,' " said Rep. Bennie Thompson of Mississippi, ranking Democrat on the Homeland Security Committee.

The appointment process also stalled last year during Chertoff's reorganization review, when it was not clear what the department's deck chairs would look like, and the administration declined to appoint leaders to agencies that might not exist once the review was through.

Some of those who have been willing to come work at the agency have had their qualifications questioned. Most prominent is Julie L. Myers, head of Immigration and Customs Enforcement, who had limited experience with most of the agency's work, but was the wife of John F. Wood, Chertoff's chief of staff, and is the niece of Air Force Gen. Richard B. Myers, the departing chairman of the Joint Chiefs of Staff.

"Maybe we should fix the appointment process and make changes in how we select top officers at homeland security," Light said, citing the Myers appointment.

Jackson said the department has had success finding capable job candidates with its pitch to prospective employees: "There's no more exciting place to be in government than the Department of Homeland Security. And nothing exceeds the importance of what we're doing."

FINDING THE MONEY

The importance of that mission has led President Bush to declare that only two department budgets should be protected from cuts: Defense and Homeland Security. Given that the president originally opposed creating Homeland Security, that would be something of a turnaround.

But the funding numbers are somewhat deceptive. While the fiscal 2007 budget request for Homeland Security did recommend an increase, some of it was predicated on Congress enacting fees that the administration knew lawmakers would almost certainly reject. Not counting fees, the department's budget would increase by just 1 percent.

That budget has hovered just above $30 billion since the department's inception. Democrats say that's not enough to shore up an infinite list of vulnerabilities and get the department's management in order.

"Money would fix some obvious things, like if you had more people on the border," said Thompson. "Money would fix some of the interoperability problems" for incompatible first-responder radio equipment, he said.

That unwillingness to spend the significant amounts of money that would have helped first-responders from different jurisdictions communicate with one another during Katrina "is scandalous," said Ornstein.

On the other hand, Homeland Security has often spent its money wastefully. A contract with Boeing to install bomb-detection machines in airports, worth a little more than $500 million originally, mushroomed to $1.2 billion over the span of 18 months. According to former inspector general Clark Kent Ervin, the contract structure allowed the company to profit from its costs and its subcontractors' costs, for a total of $82 million. Ervin documented $500,000 spent on artwork and silk plants for an operations center at the Transportation Security Administration.

Problems keeping track of money persist. Immigration and Customs Enforcement has been so beset by money woes that it once instituted a hiring freeze and cut back on expenses such as cell phone calls and gasoline. This month, the Government Accountability Office concluded an investigation at the direction of the House Homeland Security Committee that found about $1 billion worth of waste, fraud and abuse in Katrina disaster aid, with some of the money being spent on items such as a sex-change operation and some being spent by people in jail.

Congress has itself to blame for some of the department's resource problems, because it often cuts money from management accounts to pay for other priorities. Last year, negotiators on the annual Homeland Security spending bill agreed to give the administration a little more than half of what it wanted for a new personnel system.

Some aspects of that personnel system are unpopular in Congress because government employee unions allege that it would strip them of basic rights. But in a department trying to unify its pay system, thereby better integrating the department as a whole, the funding reduction hurt.

BOILING OVER

Nothing is likely to change in fiscal 2007. During House debate of the latest Homeland Security spending bill, more than $100 million was pulled from the $255 million for the Management Directorate, the secretary's office and related programs, which was already $51 million less than the president sought.

An Evolving Bureaucracy

The Bush administration's original plan was to build the Homeland Security Department by reorganizing 22 existing agencies and offices into four divisions — dedicated to border and transportation security, emergency preparedness, defense against weapons of mass destruction, and information analysis — and adding the Secret Service (formerly in the Treasury). Some components, such as FEMA, stayed much as they had been when the department was created in a 2002 law (PL 107-296). Others, such as the FBI's domestic preparedness office, disappeared. A few became hybrids — the Animal and Plant Health Inspection Service is run jointly by the Homeland Security and Agriculture departments. Congress, meanwhile, specified that the Coast Guard and Secret Service would be part of DHS while retaining their own identities. A reorganization last summer changed the original lineup. How the agencies drawn into Homeland Security are arranged now:

THE 22 AGENCIES BEFORE SEPT. 11

	Bush's fiscal 2003 budget
Border & Transportation Security	
INS/Border Patrol (part of the Justice Department)	$6.4 billion
Customs Service (Treasury)	$3.8 billion
Animal and Plant Healthy Inspection Service (Agriculture)	$1.1 billion
Transportation Security Administration (Transportation)	$4.8 billion
Coast Guard (Transportation)	$7.3 billion
Federal Protective Service (General Services Administration)	$418 million
Federal Law Enforcement Training Center (Treasury)	not available
Office for Domestic Preparedness (Justice)	not available
Emergency Preparedness & Response	
Federal Emergency Management Agency (Independent agency)	$6.2 billion
Strategic National Stockpile of Vaccines and the National Disaster Medical System (Health and Human Services)	$2.1 billion
Nuclear Incident Response Team (Energy)	not available
National Domestic Preparedness Office (FBI)	$2 million
Chemical, Biological, Radiological & Nuclear Countermeasures	
Civilian Bio-Defense Research Programs (HHS)	$2 billion
Lawrence Livermore Lab (Energy)	$1.2 billion
National Biological Warfare Defense Analysis Center (Defense)	$420 million
Plum Island Animal Disease Center (Agriculture)	$25 million
Information Analysis & Infrastructure Protection	
Critical Infrastructure Assurance Office (Commerce)	$27 million
Federal Computer Incident Response Center (GSA)	$11 million
National Communications System (Defense)	$155 million
National Infrastructure Protection Center (FBI)	$151 million
Energy Security and Assurance Program (Energy)	$20 million
Secret Service	$1.2 billion

THE DEPARTMENT TODAY

Preparedness Directorate: Primarily makes grants to state and local agencies, and helps them identify risks and train workers. (Fiscal 2006 appropriation: $4 billion)

Science & Technology Directorate: Research and development on counterterrorism. ($1.5 billion)

Management Directorate: Includes an intelligence analysis office that was downgraded after the department lost turf battles with the CIA and the Pentagon. ($946 million)

FEMA: Prepares for and coordinates federal response to natural disasters and terrorist attacks. ($2.6 billion)

TSA: Largely unchanged since it was created by Congress in 2001 to protect airports and planes. ($3.9 billion)

Customs & Border Protection: A marriage of the Customs Service's inspection system and the Border Patrol. ($5.9 billion)

Immigration and Customs Enforcement: The combined investigative functions of the former Immigration and Naturalization Service and the Customs Service. ($3.2 billion)

Citizenship and Immigration Services: The part of the old INS that deals with naturalization, visas and policy. ($114 million)

Federal Law Enforcement Training Center: The Georgia training base for law enforcement personnel. ($280 million)

Coast Guard: Combines border security with maritime services such as search and rescue. ($7.7 billion)

Secret Service: Protects the president and other officials and investigates financial crimes. ($1.2 billion)

SHARE OF FY2006 BUDGET
TOTAL: $31.6 billion

- Coast Guard: 24.4%
- Customs and Border Protection: 18.7%
- Preparedness Directorate: 12.7%
- TSA: 12.3%
- Immigration and Customs Enforcement: 10.1%
- FEMA: 8.2%
- Science and Technology: 4.8%
- Secret Service: 3.8%
- Management Directorate: 3.0%
- Less than 1% each: Federal Law Enforcement Training Center; Citizenship and Immigration Services; Other

---

"Why not help them get the resources they need to succeed?" Light asked of Congress. "They still don't want to spend any money. They still don't want to fix the personnel system."

Among the lawmakers starting to reconsider the Homeland Security Department's structure, no two better illustrate that movement than Sen. Trent Lott of Mississippi and Rep. Thomas M. Davis III of Virginia, both Republicans.

Each played a role in creating the department in 2002: Lott was Senate Republican leader and Davis was a subcommittee chairman of House Government Reform, which reviewed the legislation. Last summer, though, the department's response to Katrina gave them second thoughts about the wisdom of putting FEMA into Homeland Security.

"Preliminarily, my opinion is absolutely that was a mistake," Lott said after the storm. "You can't blame that on anybody but us."

Both Lott and Davis have now cosponsored bills to make FEMA an independent agency, and the House version might come to the floor this week.

FEMA would lose one of its own agencies under a bill approved in May by the House Energy and Commerce Committee. It would return the National Disaster Medical System to the Health and Human Services Department. Under the bill, HHS would become the primary agency in charge of coordinating federal assistance to state, local and tribal governments in preparing for or responding to bioterrorist attacks or public health or medical emergencies.

"Unless we want these agencies to suffer the fate of FEMA, we will need to remain vigilant," warned ranking Democrat John D. Dingell of Michigan.

Even though the Coast Guard performed heroically during Katrina as part of Homeland Security, there are some who still believe it, too, does not belong in the department.

Senate Commerce, Science and Transportation Chairman Ted Stevens, R-Alaska, said he was preparing legislation to remove the Coast Guard from the Homeland Department. "That's a very burdensome overlay of supervision it doesn't need, and we're devoting some of the money that could be used to modernize the Coast Guard to provide it with more supervision that it doesn't need," Stevens said.

Others simply argue that the department is a hopeless affair, what Massachusetts Democrat Jim McGovern called "a bureaucratic nightmare." For them, it is up to Congress to reconsider a number of aspects of the 2002 legislation.

At a Rules Committee hearing in May, Putnam asked Rogers, the Appropriations subcommittee chairman, whether he thought the department should be broken up, eliciting Rogers' comment that he was "not quite there."

"The point of my questioning that particular day was not to lob grenades at the DHS," Putnam said, "but to ask the question of myself and my colleagues, because we are the ones who created this.

"Isn't it time for us to take a long hard look at what we have done and determine whether we accomplished what we have set out to? Aren't we the best ones to ask that question, since we're the ones that created it? The longer it exists, the less likely we'll be able to make the big decisions, the tough decisions to reform it." ■

Taking Sides

America's support for Israel is longstanding, but now even the semblance of U.S. even-handedness in the Middle East evaporates as the White House lines up squarely with its ally in the war on Hezbollah

THE OPEN MICROPHONE incident at the G-8 summit last week, in which President Bush expressed his frustrations about the explosion of violence in the Middle East to British Prime Minister Tony Blair, exposed the raw side of the president — a tough talker who can be a bit crude in his choice of words.

"What they need to do is get Syria to get Hezbollah to stop this doing this shit, and it's over," the president told Blair, referring to the United Nations and its secretary general, Kofi Annan.

Cable news shows couldn't stop replaying the tape, as commentators tittered over Bush's unpresidential language. But Middle East watchers were struck by something else. What they saw was a president who is no longer willing to deal directly with countries such as Syria, which Bush regards as a supporter of terrorism and an implacable foe of Israel, the administration's chief ally in the region in the war on terror.

The notion that the United States would be dependent on the U.N.'s Annan to get the Syr-

ians to take action shows the extent to which the United States has dealt itself out of any multilateral effort to broker peace in the region, these experts say. "That is not a particularly effective way to deal with the Syrians in this situation," said Martin Indyk, a former Middle East adviser to President Bill Clinton.

But that is exactly how Bush prefers things. His approach to the crisis in Lebanon is the latest expression of the post-Sept. 11 shift in U.S. policy that paved the way for the U.S. invasion of Iraq three years ago. Dismissing the diplomacy that previous administrations used to tamp down repeated flare-ups along the Israel-Lebanon border, Bush has opted for a far more direct approach: He has given Israeli Prime Minister Ehud Olmert the green light to crush the Hezbollah, the radical, Shi'ite Muslim militia that incited the new round of violence. In the process, he has abandoned any pretense of even-handedness in the Arab-Israeli conflict, essentially turning the conflict in Lebanon into a proxy confrontation between Israel and the United States, on one side, and Hezbollah's patrons, Syria and Iran, on the other.

Confident that Israel can accomplish the job, Bush believes his policy will produce a

promising new reality in which Lebanon finally will be able to extend its sovereign control over the border region with Israel, where Hezbollah effectively had operated as a state within a state. In addition to bolstering Lebanon's fragile democracy, Hezbollah's defeat would represent a severe setback for Shi'ite Iran and its aspirations for broader influence in the Middle East.

"Sometimes it requires tragic situations to help bring clarity in the international community," Bush said on July 18. "I want the world to address the root causes of the problem. And the root cause of the problem is Hezbollah."

But Bush's strategy is a dangerous gamble reminiscent of Israel's 1982 invasion of Lebanon, when the Reagan administration tacitly supported Israel's use of force to crush Palestinian guerrillas and reorder Lebanon's fractious political landscape. That adventure prompted Iran to found Hezbollah, which subsequently blew up the barracks of U.S. Marine peacekeepers in Beirut a year later and eventually forced the Israelis to withdraw unceremoniously from the country in 2000. Today, the dangers are different but no less daunting.

POLICY SHIFT: Bush explains his Mideast strategy to top aides and congressional leaders July 18. He favors giving Israel enough time to destroy Hezbollah gueril-las in Lebanon to pave the way for a U.S. diplomatic initiative.

One is that the longer Israel's campaign in Lebanon lasts, the greater the risk it could draw in Syria and Iran and turn into a full-blown regional war. Even without such a night-mare scenario, experts say, it is not clear that Israel can entirely destroy Hezbollah.

Bush's policy also puts the United States' moderate Arab allies in Egypt, Jordan and Saudi Arabia in a difficult spot. While many Arab lead-ers blame Hezbollah for provoking the current fighting – thus hewing to their moderate approach toward Israel – ordinary Arabs praise the militants for fighting the Israelis and are outraged over the mayhem and destruction they have inflicted on Lebanon. This gap between ruler and ruled, and the growing appeal of the Shi'ite militia and its Iranian supporters, threat-ens the stability of these moderate Sunni Arab countries.

By extension, the administration's approach also makes it much more difficult for the Unit-ed States to act as an honest broker for any res-olution of an Arab-Israeli conflict. That, of course, assumes that the Israelis and Arabs are willing to negotiate, which is not at all clear.

"For the first time in a long time, there are people talking about a much wider war in the Middle East," said Kenneth M. Pollack, a for-mer Middle East specialist on Clinton's National Security Council.

'A NEW MIDDLE EAST'

In previous administrations, the typical U.S. response to Arab-Israeli fighting was immediate intervention: calling the parties, appealing for calm, even dispatching senior-level diplomats to the region to conduct shut-tle diplomacy. The object of such exercises was to preserve the region's stability, and they usually succeeded in preventing a wider con-flict.

But in Bush's view, the temporary cease-fires of yesteryear are no longer the answer because they would leave Hezbollah intact, with its missiles still pointed at Israel. At any time, Iran could encourage the group to pro-voke another crisis, diverting attention away from, say, Bush efforts to rein in Tehran's nuclear programs.

In the current crisis, Bush's reliance on Israel to destroy Hezbollah's military capacity repre-sents another major shift in U.S. Middle East policy. Previous administrations always sought to strike a delicate balance in their dealings with the Israelis and the Arab states in order to be seen as a credible mediator for their dis-putes.

But now, with Iran and Islamic groups such as al Qaeda, Hezbollah and Hamas posing the biggest threat to U.S. interests, Bush sees Israel as a valuable ally in his larger war against ter-

rorism – especially with U.S. forces tied down in Iraq.

Israeli commanders say they have destroyed about half of Hezbollah's military capacity in Lebanon and will need another one or two weeks to finish the job.

In the meantime, Secretary of State Con-doleezza Rice planned to travel to Israel on July 23 and then to Rome, where she will meet with Arab and Western officials to fash-ion a long-term solution, involving what she called a "robust" international force that would prevent further Hezbollah attacks on Israel. She has ruled out any quick cease-fire as a "false promise" and rejected compar-isons to the situation in 1982.

What is different from that time, she said at a July 21 news conference, is that "you have a circumstance in which a young, democratic government . . . is trying to assert its authori-ty over Lebanese territory . . . and those extrem-ists want to strangle it in its crib . . . much as the extremists want to strangle other new demo-cratic governments in the region. So this is a different Middle East, and its a new Middle East."

Meanwhile, U.S. lawmakers have lined up behind Bush's argument that a cease-fire can work only after Hezbollah has been smashed.

On July 18, the Senate adopted a resolu-

Small Clashes Ignite Big Conflict in Radioactive Region

1. On June 9, an explosion at a crowded beach in the northern Gaza Strip killed a family of five. Palestinian officials blamed Israel. Four days later, the Israeli military struck a van containing two Palestinian militants in Gaza City. Nine civilians died in the process.

2. Palestinian gunmen snuck across the border with Israel through an underground tunnel on June 25, killing two Israeli soldiers and taking a third captive. Over the next week, Israeli forces moved into northern and central Gaza in unsuccessful attempts to rescue the soldier. Hamas retaliated with missile strikes into a southern Israeli town.

3. On July 12, as the fighting continued in the Gaza Strip and southern Israel, Hezbollah launched missiles at military posts in northern Israel. Hezbollah fighters also crossed the border, capturing two Israeli soldiers and killing eight others. Israel responded with airstrikes in Southern Lebanon. Several dozen Palestinian and Lebanese civilians were killed as the fighting escalated into the next day.

Since then, the fighting has continued unabated as both sides continue sending missiles across the border and the death toll mounts. Many foreign citizens in Lebanon have evacuated, and European and American leaders are considering sending peacekeeping forces into the region.

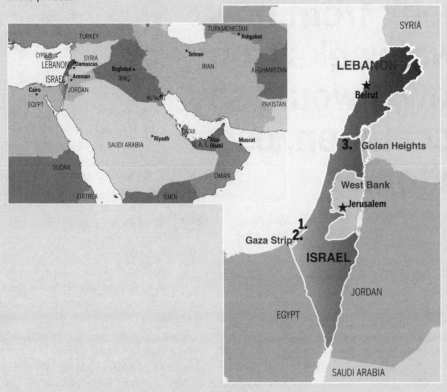

	POPULATION _in millions_	HEAD OF GOVERNMENT		MAJOR RELIGIONS	ESTIMATED U.S. AID _(in millions, fiscal 2006)_		
					ECONOMIC	MILITARY	TOTAL
Israel	6.4		Prime Minister Ehud Olmert	Jewish **77%** Muslim **16%** Arab Christians **2%**	$238.1	$2,257.2	**$2,495.3**
Jordan	5.9		Prime Minister Marouf Suleiman Bakhit	Sunni Muslim **92%** Christian **6%**	254.0	207.9	**461.9**
Lebanon	3.9		Prime Minister Fuad Siniora	Muslim (Shi'ite majority) **60%** Christian **39%**	41.3	1.0	**42.3**
Iran	68.7		President Mahmoud Ahmadinejad	Shi'ite Muslim **89%** Sunni Muslim **9%**	6.5*	none	**6.5***
Syria	18.9		Prime Minister Muhammad Naji al-Utri	Sunni Muslim **74%** Other Muslim sects **16%** Christian **10%**	—	none	—
PALESTINIAN AUTHORITY							
West Bank	2.5	President Mahmoud Abbas (Fatah)	Prime Minister Ismail Haniya (Hamas)	Muslim (Sunni majority) **75%** Jewish **17%**	148.5	none	**148.5**
Gaza	1.4			Muslim (Sunni majority) **99%**			

*Includes Syria

SOURCE: U.S. Agency for International Development (U.S. assistance), CIA (country information)

tion that defends Israel's actions and condemns Hezbollah, its "state sponsors," Iran and Syria, and Hamas militants in Gaza. Two days later, the House overwhelmingly approved a similar resolution.

"These acts of aggression deserve the rapid and decisive response they received," said House Majority Leader John A. Boehner of Ohio.

DANGER OF ESCALATION

Bush's policy of letting the Israelis stamp out the Hezbollah threats across their border has brought considerable destruction to Lebanon. The good news so far is that the fighting has not spiraled into a full-scale regional war. But Middle East experts warn that such local conflicts can swiftly spin out of control.

Indeed, the 1967 Middle East war was touched off by a Palestinian guerrilla attack on Israel out of Syria, according to Michael B. Oren, an Israeli expert on the conflict with the Arabs and author of "Six Days of War: June 1967 and the Making of the Modern Middle East."

Wary of retaliating against Syrians, who enjoyed the support of the Soviet Union, Israel responded instead by striking at guerrilla bases in Jordan, which then blamed Egypt for ignoring Israel's aggression, Oren writes in his book. To restore his reputation as the leader of the Arab world, Gamal Abdel Nasser, president of the United Arab Republic evicted U.N. peacekeepers and moved Egyptian troops up to Israel's border.

He also closed the Red Sea's Tiran Straits, blockading the Israeli port of Eilat, and signed military pacts with Syria and Jordan. Rather than wait for the combined Arab onslaught, Israel struck first.

Oren, a senior fellow at the right-wing Shalem Center in Jerusalem, argues that as long as Syria remains untouched in the current battle with Hezbollah, Damascus will facilitate Iran's rearming of the group, setting the stage for continued cross-border rocket attacks. In a July 17 commentary on *The New Republic*'s Web site, he calls for Israel to deliver an "unequivocal blow" to Syrian forces to deter them from further support for Hezbollah. Israel says it is keeping all of its options open.

But an Israeli move against Syria would probably draw in its close ally, Iran, which has warned that it will join the battle if Syria is attacked.

"If you ask me what is the most likely outcome a week from now, two weeks from now, I would say escalation, escalation."

— Shibley Telhami, a Middle East scholar at the University of Maryland

For now, the Bush administration is counting on Israel to keep its military campaign confined to Lebanon. Moreover, Bush has emphasized that he doesn't want the Israeli military campaign to weaken the Lebanese government of President Fuad Siniora to the point where it can't fill the power vacuum left by Hezbollah's destruction.

"We're also mindful . . . about the need to make sure the government of Lebanon does not collapse," Bush said July 18. "It's in our interests that Lebanon be free and the Siniora government succeed."

The problem for Bush, say a number of regional experts, is that a concentrated Israeli campaign against Hezbollah inside Lebanon is unlikely to eradicate the group. If anything, Israel's U.S.-supported bombardment will probably drive Hezbollah underground, where it has proved to be skillful at conducting spectacular attacks on U.S. and Israeli targets.

During the 1980's, the group took a number of Westerners hostage, including several Americans, and carried out the 1983 bombing that destroyed the U.S. barracks in Beirut and killed 241 American servicemen. In 1992, Hezbollah bombed the Israeli embassy in Argentina, killing 29 people, and then two years later bombed a Jewish community center in Buenos Aires, killing 95.

Because of its record of resistance, analysts also note, Hezbollah enjoys widespread support among Lebanese Shi'ites, as well as strong backing from Iran, which regards the group's willingness to take on Israel as a potent card in Tehran's bid to challenge the United States in the Middle East, as well as its moderate Sunni allies in Saudi Arabia, Egypt and Jordan. Meanwhile, Syria, which depends on Hezbollah to protect its interests in Lebanon, is unlikely to abandon the group.

At some point, these experts say, Hezbollah will rearm and resume its attacks across the border, possibly hitting Tel Aviv or a major installation. And at that point, Israel will have to escalate its response.

Meanwhile, protracted fighting in Lebanon also could affect the situation in Iraq. Moqtada al Sadr, the head of the Iranian-backed Mahdi Army in Iraq, already has warned that he will not "sit by with folded hands" in the face of U.S. support for Israel in the Lebanon conflict, indicating that his militia may launch attacks on U.S. soldiers in retaliation.

"If you ask me what is the most likely outcome a week from now, two weeks from now, I would say escalation, escalation," said Shibley Telhami, a Middle East scholar at the University of Maryland. And, he added, "escalation, by definition, is unpredictable. You cannot control it, especially when you don't know what the other side can do."

JITTERS IN MODERATE STATES

At a emergency meeting of the Arab League in Cairo on July 15, Saudi Arabia, Egypt, Jordan and several Persian Gulf states publicly castigated Hezbollah for provoking the crisis in Lebanon, condemning what they called the group's "unexpected, inappropriate and irresponsible acts."

Their statement stunned many Middle East watchers. In the past, Sunni Arab governments always reflexively condemned Israel when any fighting with an Arab group erupted. But their willingness to criticize fellow Arabs in the midst of a battle with Israeli forces underscores their fears about the growing influence of Shi'ite Iran in the region in the wake of the Iraq War. Among their biggest concerns are Iran's ability to incite their own Shi'ite populations against them and Tehran's efforts to develop nuclear weapons.

Some Middle East watchers suspect that Tehran may have engineered the Lebanese crisis to derail Bush's agenda at the G-8 summit to push for U.N. sanctions against Iran for its nuclear programs. Bush acknowledged that the Lebanon crisis took up most of the summiteers' time.

But with Iran's July 17 call for a cease-fire and prisoner exchange, these analysts say Iran is making a broader power play.

"I would not rule out the possibility that the Iranians, who I believe — I can't prove it —decided that it was convenient to start this crisis at this particular moment, and will want to show themselves as capable of ending the crisis as well, and in that way demonstrate that they are a player across the Middle East," said Indyk, now director of the Brookings Institution's Saban Center for Middle East Policy.

Bush's policy, of course, precludes any role for Iran in resolving the Lebanon crisis, but experts point out that Tehran's support for Hezbollah and Hamas militants has already broadened its appeal and influence among ordinary Arabs.

Hisham Milhem, a journalist for the Lebanese daily An-Nahar and host of a call-in program broadcast on the Al Arabiya satellite television network, says that as TV images of the Israeli destruction in Lebanon are beamed into Arab homes, many Arabs now see Iran and its Islamic allies as the alternative to Washington's secular Arab allies who have failed to deliver on their promises of democratic change, economic development and help for the Palestinians.

"The sense that is prevailing in the region today is that George Bush's moment in the Middle East is over, or is going to be over soon, that the Americans are drowning in Iraq's quicksand, and that the American project to spread democracy in the Middle East has reached a dead end," Milhem said at a July 17 symposium at the Brookings Institution in Washington. He added that Hezbollah's "culture of resistance is now being projected as the alternative to this

NO END IN SIGHT: Israel's bombardment of Hezbollah strongholds in Beirut's southern suburbs has caused widespread destruction, prompting international calls for an immediate ceasefire.

failed approach."

The University of Maryland's Telhami, who monitors online discussions about the Lebanon crisis in Arabic-language chat rooms, said: "No question, the vast majority of Arabs, whether they are Saudi or Egyptian or Moroccan or Jordanian, are very much rooting for Hezbollah and blaming Israel."

Referring to the Hezbollah raid and its continued resistance to the Israeli onslaught, he added: "It revived a sense of pride in the Arab world. Some of the Saudis say, 'You have raised our heads.' So people are looking at this as Hezbollah doing something honorable."

According to Arab diplomats, the reason Rice is holding her principle discussions in

Rome is that Sunni Arab leaders, fearful that her arrival would inflame anti-American sentiment and destabilize their own regimes, refused to host her.

"The events have intensified public opposition to these governments and put them in a place where they simply cannot be indifferent to the level of civilian casualties," said Telhami.

ROUGH SLEDDING FOR RICE

Ever since modern Israel was born in 1948, U.S. diplomats have played the role of trusted mediators in the Jewish state's disputes with its Arab neighbors. Indeed, some of the greatest achievements in Arab-Israeli peacemaking — the disengagement agreements among Israel, Egypt and Syria after the 1973 war, the 1979 Israel-Egypt peace treaty — were midwifed by American diplomats.

Washington's ability to play that role has always rested with the close relations and trust that it has fostered with all parties to the conflict.

But as Bush's unguarded comments to Blair suggest, that is no longer the case. If previous U.S. diplomacy in the region were based on preserving the status quo in Arab countries as a foundation for broader peace efforts, Bush saw such an approach as a mistake because, he argued, it ultimately produced the Sept. 11 terrorist attacks. Instead, Bush has embraced a policy of regime change, zero tolerance for terrorism, and the spread of democracy as cure to the region's militant Islamic impulses.

Practically, however, this policy has backfired in several important hot spots. Elections in the Palestinian territories last January brought to power Hamas militants, whom the administration has branded terrorists and will not talk to. In last year's elections in Lebanon, a Shi'ite coalition headed by Hezbollah won 23 seats in the 128-member parliament and secured two ministries in the government. The Bush administration also regards Hezbollah as a terrorist organization. And according to Joseph R. Biden Jr. of Delaware, the ranking Democrat on the Senate Foreign Relations Committee, the White House never took the preventive step of assisting the new Beirut government in disarming the group.

"We didn't do anything to help them," he said on NBC's "Meet The Press" on July 16. "We didn't do anything at the time to give any attention to it."

Now, amid the current crisis, Bush's goal is

IRAN'S PROXY: Hezbollah Chief Hassan Nasrallah is helping Tehran broaden its influence into the Arab-Israeli dispute.

Hezbollah's disarmament. But the administration barely speaks to the Syrians these days, and it is locked into a growing confrontation with Iran over its nuclear program.

"You have a big problem when you cannot talk to the Iranians, when you cannot talk to Hamas, when you cannot talk to Hezbollah, and you have minimal contacts with the Syrians," said Milhem. "How are you going to influence their behavior?"

According to Indyk, the only remaining source of leverage that the White House has to disarm Hezbollah is Israel's use of force. "And that is why the administration is holding back the demands for a cease-fire," he said.

It is far too soon to say if Bush's gamble will work. On July 21, Israel called up army reservists for a possible major ground assault against Hezbollah, suggesting that its air and artillery, punctuated by small-scale commando raids into Lebanon, have not removed the threat. In the meantime, many analysts agree, televised images of a rising civilian casualty toll in Lebanon will make it increasingly difficult for Bush to continuing resisting international demands for a cease-fire.

One thing is likely, however, experts say. In any future negotiations to ease tensions between Israel and its Arab enemies, the United States will not be playing the role of honest broker, at least not while Bush remains in office. His pro-Israel policy may have won him bipartisan support here at home, but in the Arab world, his administration is now deeply distrusted, and that will become clearer as Secretary of State Rice holds discussions in Rome this week.

After nearly six decades in U.S. hands, the job of Middle East mediator will probably fall to someone such as European Union Foreign Minister Javier Solana. Or, as Bush himself suggested, it may go to Kofi Annan. ∎

STRATEGIC PARTNERS: Bush has given Olmert, shown during a recent visit to Washington, a free hand in Lebanon.

9.11.01
9.11.06 ←

THE WAR ON TERROR

Since 9/11, the White House has banked on military power over diplomacy and global cooperation. A growing number of critics say that strategy has failed.

INE DAYS AFTER Islamic extremists used hijacked airliners to destroy the World Trade Center in New York and damage the Pentagon in Washington, President Bush stood before a joint session of Congress and committed the nation to a global "war on terror" to restore its security. Bush's strategy for waging this war, as it developed over the succeeding months, and indeed has continued to evolve, has been to project U.S. power and influence abroad as a way to protect U.S. interests at home — in the president's words, to "fight the terrorists overseas so we do not have to fight them here at home."

Known terrorist leaders such as Osama bin Laden would be hunted down remorselessly and their networks disrupted or destroyed. Countries that harbored or supported terrorists would be treated as enemies. "Either you are with us," Bush famously said, "or you are with the terrorists." Allies would be welcomed and indeed encouraged to help, but Bush made it clear to the world that he would act alone and attack pre-emptively if he thought it was necessary.

The peaceful side of Bush's strategy was to prevent the proliferation of weapons of mass destruction that could arm terrorists and to encourage the spread of democracy in all areas of the world, and especially the Middle East, as a way to undermine the appeal of extremists.

This war on terror would be long, the president cautioned Congress and the watching nation on that September evening. But he promised perseverance. "Our war on terror begins with al Qaeda, but it does not end there," Bush said. "It will not end until every terrorist group of global reach has been found, stopped and defeated."

After five years, that goal appears just as distant and difficult — perhaps more so. Osama bin Laden remains at large and is still trying to acquire weapons of mass destruction. Iran's leaders most recently have refused to give up their nuclear program. Foreign policy and terrorism experts say that the war in Iraq and the Bush administration's uncom-

TOUGH STANCE: 'We're on the offense against the terrorists on every battle front,' Bush said 'and we'll accept nothing less than complete victory.'

promising approach to Middle East policy — refusing to negotiate with militant groups such as Hezbollah and Hamas, for instance — have actually helped terrorist networks recruit and train followers. Mostly because of the Iraq War, international support or at least sympathy for the U.S. campaign has largely evaporated. In Afghanistan, the extremist Taliban, which was ousted from power five years ago, has begun to regain authority over parts of the country.

The issue now is whether the Bush administration's strategy can ever win the war against terror or whether the strategy must be radically altered.

Foreign policy scholars and defense experts generally agree that the administration has put too much reliance on military power and too little on diplomacy, with the result that the effectiveness of both has

AFGHAN INSECURITY: A deadly bomb blast Sept. 8 near the U.S. Embassy in Kabul showed that peace is tenuous five years after the Taliban was ousted.

been compromised. What is needed, they say, is a more pragmatic approach to the Middle East and the diplomatic side of the war on terror.

"It's been primarily a military enterprise," said James Dobbins, who was Bush's special envoy to Afghanistan immediately after Sept. 11. He is now at the Rand Corp.

"At some point," Dobbins said, "this or some administration is going to have to establish a better balance between the kind of rhetoric which secures domestic support and the kind of rhetoric which could secure much greater international support."

The mounting disaffection with the war on terror was perhaps articulated most clearly last week by Prime Minister Dominique de Villepin of France, a country that, for all its criticism of the Iraq invasion, remains one of America's most valuable allies in the covert war against jihadist bombers. "Against terrorism," Villepin said, "what's needed is not a war. It is, as France has done for many years, a determined fight based on vigilance at all times and effective cooperation with our partners. But we will only end this curse if we also fight against injustice, violence and these crises" in the Middle East.

His comments followed the release by the Bush administration of a revised strategy to counter terrorism that was mainly a restatement of the main pillars of Bush's plan: preemptive force and the spread of democracy.

An exception was the omission from the new document of the need to resolve the Israeli-Palestinian conflict, and those who have studied the region for years say the omission is notable and hazardous. That conflict has poisoned the climate of the Middle East for decades and nurtured extremist groups and terrorists. Resolving it, or at least tamping it down so that it doesn't flare into the kind of open war that engulfed Lebanon in July, is crucial to any peace in the region. Bush's unqualified backing of Israel's military campaign against Hezbollah removed any vestige of U.S. impartiality in the region's politics.

At home, the administration's response to the approaching congressional election has been to adopt ever-harsher rhetoric about terrorist groups, calling them "Islamo-fascists," and ever darker intimations that Democrats would not protect the country as Bush has done — that they would, in fact, appease terrorists as British Prime Minister Neville Cham-

berlain did Hitler before World War II.

Arguing about what words to use in describing terrorists makes no sense to Brian Michael Jenkins, an internationally respected terrorist expert who considers himself "ferociously" nonpartisan.

"Five years after 9/11, to be having this kind of stupid debate is evidence of an absence of strategy and understanding of the foes we have faced from the beginning," said Jenkins, who in 1972 started Rand's counterterrorism program. Without criticizing anyone in particular, Jenkins said the kind of partisanship currently evident in the United States on the subject of fighting terrorism is a "disservice" to the nation.

Such experts worry now that far from winning the war on terror, the administration's strategy and ways of carrying it out are making the conflict worse.

According to Jenkins, the fighting in Iraq is creating problems for the United States, rather than preventing them, as Bush envisioned.

"Not only is there another cohort or generation of jihadist veterans being created in Iraq, but they are significantly improving their skills," he said. "We are going to be confronting jihadists in the future that are technically more adept than those we face now."

The administration's strategy of defeating the terrorist ideology by "spreading the hope of freedom across the Middle East," as Bush put it in a speech this month, has been contradicted by the administration's continued support for autocratic regimes such as Saudi Arabia; its refusal to talk to Hamas, the elected leadership of the Palestinians; and its depiction of Hezbollah as a terrorist organization in the likeness of al Qaeda. Hezbollah enjoys widespread support in Lebanon and forms a core part of the country's new government, whose leadership is backed by the administration.

Saad Eddin Ibrahim, an Egyptian democracy activist and professor of political sociology at American University in Cairo, wrote a scathing analysis of the administration's reaction to Islamists who are increasingly entering the political structures of his home region. "The rest of the Western world must come to grips with the new reality, even if the U.S. president and his secretary of State continue to reject the new offspring of their own policies," he wrote.

What a number of foreign policy experts say is needed in the U.S. approach to the Middle East is more realism that would perhaps allow negotiation. As it is now, all sides are dug into ideological or religious positions that permit no retreat.

Jeffrey Sachs, an economics professor and director of Columbia University's Earth Institute, says that ordinary, moderate people could help now by demanding an end to violence and "tragic illusions" that a final victory over terrorism can be achieved.

"Crass tribalism now threatens to overwhelm all that unites us in our common care for our children, our planet and our future," he said. Jenkins wrote in his book "Unconquer-

"This or some administration is going to have to establish a better balance between the kind of rhetoric which secures domestic support and the kind of rhetoric which could secure much greater international support."

— James Dobbins, special envoy to Afghanistan

able Nation" that with a more sober approach to foreign relations, "the less fear, the less public clamor there will be for responses that could threaten our liberties and destroy our hard-won reputation as a beacon of justice and freedom."

STAYING THE COURSE

Bush and his top aides see no such concern in their war on terror, and in fact they say they have had major successes, starting with the 2001 overthrow of the Taliban that denied al Qaeda terrorists a haven in Afghanistan.

Bush's war has significantly weakened the al Qaeda network around the world. The administration claims to have captured or killed most of those responsible for the Sept. 11 attacks — with the glaring exception of Osama bin Laden and deputy Ayman al-Zawahiri. U.S. forces killed Abu Musab al-Zarqawi, the leader of al Qaeda in Iraq who led deadly attacks against American forces and Iraqi civilians.

In Iraq, Bush says, a U.S.-led coalition of nations is fighting side-by-side with Iraqi national forces against terrorism to secure a unified, stable and democratic country in the heart of the Middle East. And nearby countries

such as Saudi Arabia and Pakistan, which tolerated and often stoked Islamic radicalism, have now joined in the war on terror, providing the United States and its allies with valuable intelligence on radical groups and individuals, U.S. officials say.

Meanwhile, the United States, together with other friendly countries, have cracked down on terrorist financing, making it harder for extremists groups such as al Qaeda, Hezbollah and Hamas to receive money and move it to their members.

"America and her allies are fighting this war with relentless determination across the world," Bush said in a Sept. 5 speech to the Military Officers Association. "Together with our coalition partners, we've removed terrorist sanctuaries, disrupted their finances, killed and captured key operatives, broken up terrorist cells in America and other nations, and stopped new attacks before they're carried out."

In the administration's updated "National Strategy for Combatting Terrorism," released Sept. 5, the White House also claims "a broad and growing global consensus that the targeting of innocents is never justified by any calling or cause."

And Bush has focused on the use of this tactic by various Middle Eastern groups — al Qaeda, Hezbollah and Hamas — to portray them as parts of what he calls "a single movement, a worldwide network of radicals that use terror to kill those who stand in the way of their totalitarian ideology."

In addition to taking the war to the terrorists' home turf, Bush says he has strengthened the nation's homeland defenses. He cites the 2003 creation of the Homeland Security Department, the 2004 overhaul of the nation's intelligence community to facilitate greater information sharing, and the 2001 passage of the anti-terror law known as the Patriot Act,

"Not only is there another cohort or generation of jihadist veterans being created in Iraq, but they are significantly improving their skills. We are going to be confronting jihadists in the future that are technically more adept than those we face now."

— Brian Michael Jenkins, terrorism expert

CHOOSING SIDES: Experts warn that U.S. support for Israel's campaign against Hezbollah in Lebanon, which was bombed repeatedly this summer, has deepened Muslim hatred for the United States.

which expanded the powers of law enforcement to deal with terrorist threats.

At the same time, however, the administration acknowledges that major challenges remain in the war on terrorism. The strategy document cites the dispersal and decentralization of terrorist networks, their continued use of the Internet to communicate, train and sign up new recruits, and unaddressed holes in the nation's homeland defenses.

"Five years after our nation was attacked, the terrorist danger remains," Bush warned in his Sept. 5 speech. "We're a nation at war."

ONE SIZE DOES NOT FIT ALL

Experts say the United States' ability to prevail in that war depends largely on how it approaches problems in the Middle East, the fountainhead of animosity toward the United States. And that, they say, will require a willingness to address each of the region's conflicts on its own terms.

Until now, they note, the administration's emphasis on the tactics of terrorism has caused it to gloss over the specific issues and irritants that feed the region's most stubborn conflicts, leaving the United States unprepared for the problems that inevitably come to the surface.

"There is a problem with terrorism, but we've made a mistake in trying to turn every problem into a problem of terrorism," said Kenneth Pollack, a former Middle East analyst at the CIA. In Iraq, for example, the adminis-

tration decided its opponents in Iraq were part of the war on terror and "completely missed the growing sectarian violence" between Sunnis and Shi'ites that now defines the war there, he said.

Similarly, experts note, when fighting erupted between Israel and Hezbollah in Lebanon this past summer, the administration abandoned its traditional role as an honest broker and sided with Israel because of the perception of Hezbollah as a purely terrorist organization. "We're treating the symptoms instead of the disease and often prescribing medicine for the wrong disease, and in some cases making the patient sicker," Pollack said.

And experts say that by siding with Israel in its refusal to deal with Hamas, the fundamentalist Islamic party that won Palestinian elections in January but which both Israel and Washington consider to be a terrorist group, the administration has all but abandoned the Middle East peace process. "Neglect of the peace process is what is biting us in the ass right now," said Pollack, citing the spiraling violence in Gaza and the threat of another explosion in Lebanon.

Vali Nasr, a national security and Middle East expert at the Naval Postgraduate School, says all the groups at the center of the violence in the Middle East are different and must be treated as such. Hezbollah and Hamas, for example, are fighting for concrete political gains in Lebanon and the Palestinian territories and do not directly threaten U.S. security, while

al Qaeda represents a far more dangerous threat. "We are actually confusing ourselves and blunting what might be a much more effective way of dealing with this," he said.

Analysts from inside the Middle East also stress that a key to a Western victory in the war against terrorism lies with the United States showing a willingness to accept the results of the democracy that Bush prescribes as the antidote to the region's problems.

Saad Eddin Ibrahim, the Egyptian democracy activist, notes that for the first time in decades, hopes for democracy flowered in the region last year as Lebanon's so-called Cedar Revolution drove out Syrian occupation troops and produced a new independent government in Beirut, and as elections went forward in Iraq, Egypt and the Palestinian territories. But he noted that a "sudden chill" fell over Washington when Hamas won the Palestinian vote and Hezbollah and Egypt's Muslim Brotherhood scored major election gains.

"Instead of welcoming these particular elected officials into the newly emerging democratic fold, Washington began a cold war on Muslim democrats," Ibrahim said. "Even the tepid pressure on autocratic allies of the United States to democratize in 2005 had all but disappeared by 2006."

Flynt Leverett, once a senior adviser to Bush on the Middle East, says the Bush doctrine has produced what he calls "devastating" results in the Middle East.

"Over the last five years, U.S. policy in the Middle East has emboldened radicals and weakened moderates," he noted. As illustrations for this grim assertion, he cites Iraq's deepening instability, Iran's growing influence in the region, and Syria's undiminished support for both Hamas and Hezbollah.

What the United States needs to add to its toolbox for the war on terror, other former Bush administration officials suggest, is more high-level diplomatic involvement and, above all, patience.

Richard Armitage, the former deputy secretary of State, was asked if he subscribed to the view that Bush should be more personally involved in Middle East diplomacy. "Who doesn't?" he replied with characteristic bluntness.

"The feeling is if you speak and no one listens, then you've lost prestige," Armitage said, describing what many see as the administration's reluctance to jump into the Mid-

SHOW OF DEFIANCE: Iraqi militiamen loyal to Shi'ite cleric Moqtada al-Sadr carry mock coffins.

dle East peace process. "My own view is that you're always better to be on the side of the angels."

Richard N. Haass, Bush's former policy planning chief at the State Department, said U.S. officials and the American public would be well advised to accept the reality that winning the war against terrorism is going to require a lot of time and must be able to withstand major setbacks. As an example, he cited the appearance in Britain of home-grown Islamic suicide bombers despite that country's long history of democracy.

"Building a true democracy requires decades, or even generations," Haass noted.

But he also cautions against viewing democracy as the panacea to the region's woes, as Bush suggests. Democracy, he notes, is "irrelevant" to committed terrorists who seek to re-create a 7th century caliphate or restore Sunni domination in Iraq. For such enemies, many experts say, blunt force is the only answer.

A FRACTURED COALITION

Immediately after the Sept. 11 attacks, dozens of nations rallied to the side of the United States to cooperate with Bush in the fight against terrorism. As the war in Afghanistan continues into its fifth year, many of the countries that came together in solidarity remain part of the international anti-terror coalition.

But experts agree that the war in Iraq has severely tested some of those allegiances. European nations such as France and Germany still support operations in Afghanistan, but they do not participate in Bush's "coalition of the willing" in Iraq. China and Russia, which supported the war in Afghanistan, also stayed out of Iraq. More important, the two big powers are now major thorns in Bush's side at the United Nations Security Council as the administration tries to persuade that body to impose punitive sanctions against Iran in response to its refusal to halt its nuclear enrichment program.

In some cases, terrorism and popular political pressure at home have driven U.S. allies to withdraw their forces from Iraq. After suspected al Qaeda terrorists blew up several trains in Madrid in March 2004, Spaniards elected a new, less-pro-American government that swiftly withdrew Spanish forces from Iraq. Italy's new left-wing prime minister, Romano Prodi, withdrew much of his country's military contingent from Iraq in June.

The rift between the Bush administration and the rest of the world over the way it is pursuing the war against terrorism has also affected Washington's ability to stabilize the situation in Lebanon in the wake of the fighting this summer. Because of its strong support for Israel in the conflict, the administration has decided it would not be advisable to contribute any U.S. forces to a U.N.-sanctioned international peacekeeping force that is being called upon to help the Beirut government reassert its sovereignty over south Lebanon, where Hezbollah ruled. But as a result, other countries are not rushing in to join the peacekeepers in an area that Bush has portrayed as another front in the war on terrorism.

The prospects for mending the rifts and rebuilding an international coalition to fight the war on terrorism do not look promising, at least as long as Bush remains in office. This month, a survey of Europeans and Americans found their relations deteriorating and portrayed a worrying picture of decreasing willingness to cooperate on security issues that would benefit the United States.

The poll, conducted by the German Marshall Fund, concluded that despite a shared fear of terrorism on both sides of the Atlantic, only Britain, the Netherlands and Romania

Federal Response in Retrospect

THE SEPT. 11 ATTACKS of five years ago prompted the most comprehensive overhaul of the nation's domestic security apparatus since World War II and spawned a host of expensive initiatives designed to secure borders and strengthen law enforcement's ability to track terror suspects.

The Bush administration persuaded Congress to quickly enact an anti-terrorism law — which Republicans dubbed the Patriot Act — that has since become a crucible for debates over national security and civil liberties. It also presided over an oft-criticized consolidation of 22 different government agencies into a new Department of Homeland Security.

The initiatives have yielded a mixed bag of successes and failures. While the government has improved the way it screens cargo and met benchmarks it set for airport security, it has fallen woefully short in efforts to equip emergency responders with interoperable radios and met only half of its goals of building a computer network to track foreign visitors. Last year's bungled federal response to Hurricane Katrina, moreover, cast lingering doubts on the government's ability to respond to future crises.

How the domestic federal response has held up in the past five years:

• **Reshaping the bureaucracy** Five years after it was created, the Homeland Security Department continues to iron out bureaucratic and operational problems stemming from the merger of nearly two dozen federal agencies. Critics cite the Federal Emergency Management Agency's performance in Katrina's aftermath as proof the department has placed domestic security above disaster relief, and predict that it could take years to properly prioritize the agencies' many missions.

"The department has problems that will only be resolved over maybe a decade — problems of different cultures, different agencies being thrown together," said James A. Thurber, director of American University's Center for Congressional and Presidential Studies. He

SECURING PORTS: Since the attacks, the government has tightened what had been a porous shipping security system. Today, every manifest is checked, and about one in 20 containers gets a thorough search.

says Congress is partly to blame for failing to effectively reorganize the jurisdictions of committees that oversee the department.

• **Enhancing investigations** The Patriot Act, which Congress passed overwhelmingly within two months of the attacks, has also been the focus of much criticism and scrutiny. Critics, from civil liberties groups on the political left to libertarians on the right, used the expiration of 16 provisions in the law this year to launch a barrage of criticism, focusing on prosecutorial powers conferred by the law and the rights of individuals targeted in investigations.

Congress wound up clearing a compromise reauthorization that made several changes. Lawmakers decided to permit recipients of government requests for business records to challenge a gag order, although they would have to wait one year to overturn it and prove that the government acted in bad faith. They also ended a requirement that recipients of national security letters, which are used to request records related to a terror suspect and do not require court approval, disclose the name of any attorney they consult or intend to consult. And they clarified language in the 2001 law to ensure that

had positive views of U.S. leadership in world affairs. Most Europeans prefer a more independent approach to security and diplomatic affairs, the survey showed, and only 45 percent of Americans seek closer relations with Europe, a drop of 15 points from a similar poll last year.

INTELLIGENCE PROBLEMS

"Five years after Sept. 11, 2001, the image of the United States in the world has not recov-

ered from its steep decline after the war in Iraq," the poll said.

Intelligence work has helped the government break up some terrorist networks and plots, but it remains a troubled sector of the war on terror largely because of bureaucratic tensions between the CIA and military spy agencies and because of the difficulty such agencies have in penetrating Islamic extremist groups.

The CIA was widely criticized for not uncov-

ering the Sept. 11 plot in time and for lacking accurate intelligence on Iraq's alleged weapons of mass destruction. Bush replaced George J. Tenet, the CIA director at the time of the Sept. 11 attacks, with Republican Congressman Porter J. Goss of Florida, who was unpopular enough at the agency to drive away a number of senior officials and career employees. Goss was replaced this spring by Air Force Gen. Michael V. Hayden, who had previously run the

libraries that operate in traditional roles and not as Internet service providers would not be subject to national security letters.

President Bush signed the legislation revising the law on March 9, a day before the old provisions were to expire.

• **Securing the skies** The Transportation Security Agency (TSA), created two months after the attacks, replaced contract baggage screeners with federally trained screeners in U.S. commercial airports and deployed equipment to screen for explosives in all checked baggage.

In less than six months, about 1,000 explosive detection system machines and 6,000 tabletop explosive trace detection machines were installed at commercial airports. And more than 25,000 individuals were trained to be federal screeners.

But since the beginning of 2003, the TSA has been grappling to deal with more passenger traffic while minimizing staffing requirements by deploying automated in-line baggage screening, which uses conveyor belts to transport bags to explosive detection devices.

Twenty-three airports now have full in-line explosive detection systems, and 287 more have partial systems. Other airports continue to screen checked bags with devices installed in lobbies and other spaces in terminals.

> **"The department has problems that will only be resolved over maybe a decade—problems of different cultures, different agencies being thrown together."**
>
> — James A. Thurber, director of American University's Center for Congressional and Presidential Studies

Though the majority of baggage screeners are employed by TSA, five airports are enrolled in a partnership allowing them to hire private screeners who work under federal oversight.

The government has had much more limited success checking prospective airline passengers against terrorist watch lists. In 2004 it scrapped CAPPS II, a computerized system that collected names and other personal identifiers at the time a flight reservation was made. The system aroused privacy concerns, with groups such as the American Civil Liberties Union and Electronic Privacy Information Center questioning how the information was used and what redress people have if they are mistakenly put on no-fly lists. The Government Accountability Office also found that CAPPS II failed to meet seven of eight criteria Congress established, such as ensuring privacy and demonstrating efficacy.

CAPPS II was replaced with a system called Secure Flight, which continues to be a source of privacy concerns. Airlines and the government also have had operational problems using the system. The program is being overhauled.

• **Securing the ports** A more successful transportation security initiative is the screening of containerized cargo at American ports. U.S. Customs and Border Protection, an agency that has become part of the Homeland Security Department, now physically inspects or scans 100 percent of cargo it considers high-risk, which makes up 5 percent to 7 percent of all cargo. The agency uses a so-called 24-hour rule requiring that shippers provide manifests before containers are loaded at a foreign port. Officials then use an automated risk-assessment system to identify which U.S.-bound containers are a potential threat.

Customs officials say it's impossible to inspect all of the approximately 11 million ocean-going containers arriving at U.S. ports each year without seriously disrupting trade.

• **Tracking visitors** Another trouble-plagued computerized security effort has been a $340 million system designed to track the entry and exit of all foreign visitors. The so-called US-VISIT program collects digital finger scans, photos and biographical information on most foreign visitors, excluding Canadians. The program has data on more than 60 million individuals.

The program is in place at at least 115 U.S. airports and 15 seaports with international arrivals, and in the secondary inspection areas of 154 overland ports of entry. But exit tracking is not as widespread, and the system cannot monitor which foreigners remain in the country and who has overstayed a visa. Tracking the time visa holders spent in the country was the program's original purpose, which was inspired by disclosures that some of the Sept. 11 hijackers were in the country on expired visas.

The exit portion of the program is now being tested at 12 airports and two seaports, with no dates set for further expansion. Meanwhile, five land ports are testing radio frequency identification systems at both entry and exit.

• **Keeping one watch list** Responding to calls from Congress to consolidate multiple terrorist watch lists, President Bush in 2003 issued a directive to create a comprehensive list maintained by the Terrorist Screening Center within the Department of Justice. Officials say that despite early complications, they have combined information from 10 of 12 databases and are connected to the two remaining ones.

military's super-secret National Security Agency, which was controversial itself because it had been eavesdropping on some U.S. domestic phone calls in its pursuit of terrorists. In the meantime, Bush appointed John D. Negroponte to a newly created post as director of national intelligence, in which he was to coordinate the jobs of the CIA and other intelligence agencies.

Critics say that revamping the spy system has failed to unify the covert activities of the multiple members of the community. They say that though the intelligence community clearly needs to focus its efforts on terrorism, the administration itself undermined the community's credibility before the Iraq War by ignoring advice that did not support its case for going to war.

A Government Accountability Office report this year found that the government had yet to establish processes for sharing terrorism-related information among agencies, even though such coordination was a key recommendation of the commission that investigated the Sept. 11 attacks.

Paul Pillar, who was national intelligence officer for the Near East and South Asia from 2000 to 2005 said the intelligence community had "no input" in the policy process on Iraq. He compared it unfavorably with the Vietnam era, when

Defense Secretary Robert S. McNamara was "continually asking for assessments." He added, "With Iraq, there was nothing like that."

There are signs of progress. Haass wrote in an op-ed in August that "improved and better coordinated intelligence, law enforcement and homeland security efforts at both the national and international levels" had made it harder for terrorists to succeed.

But he added, "It is also possible that the desire of some terrorists to accomplish something more dramatic than the 9/11 attacks may have complicated their ability to implement their plans and increased the prospect that they will be detected."

Yet gaps remain in the United States' knowledge of the Mideast. "Critical information needed for analysts to make many of their judgments with confidence about Iran" is missing, according to a report released last month by the staff of the House Intelligence Committee.

The now widely reported practice of CIA "renditions," in which suspects are plucked from European countries and spirited off to secret detention centers, are a public relations problem for the administration and a strain on relations with countries where the camps have been located, and their willingness to

> **"Improved and better coordinated intelligence, law enforcement and homeland security efforts at both the national and international levels" had made it harder for terrorists to succeed.**
>
> — **Richard N. Haas,** former policy chief at the State Department

cooperate in the future. Bush acknowledged the existence of the camps for the first time last week and announced the transfer of prisoners to Guantánamo Bay in Cuba.

NUCLEAR THREATS

Integral to the war on terror because of the danger that it seeks to avert is Bush's campaign to prevent the spread of nuclear arms and other mega-weapons. In his 2002 State of the Union address, Bush described an "axis of evil" among Iraq, Iran and North Korea and warned that if any of the three developed nuclear weapons, "they could provide these arms to terrorists, giving them the means to

match their hatred. We will work closely with our coalition to deny terrorists and their state sponsors the materials, technology and expertise to make and deliver weapons of mass destruction."

U.S. officials had been working with European allies on negotiations with Iran about its nuclear program, but the fighting in Lebanon, in which Iran supported Hezbollah and the United States strongly sided with Israel, made such talks more difficult.

Six-party talks aimed at halting North Korea's nuclear program have been on ice for months, even though that country's nuclear capability is more developed than anyone else's on the list of rogue regimes. North Korea refuses to return to the table until the United States lifts financial restrictions imposed because of Pyongyang's alleged counterfeiting of U.S. currency and trade in illegal drugs.

Nor are efforts to avoid nuclear materials reaching terrorist hands proceeding quickly enough, experts say. "A dangerous gap remains between the urgency of the threat of nuclear terrorism and the scope and pace of the U.S. and world response," wrote Matthew Bunn and Anthony Wier at Harvard University in a study released in July. "The most fundamental missing ingredient of the U.S. and global response to the nuclear terrorism threat to date is sustained high-level leadership." ∎

The Bush Bench

GOP majorities on most appellate courts show that the president's judicial agenda is doing just fine, thank you

TO HEAR PRESIDENT BUSH tell it, you would think he's been stymied in his efforts to put a conservative imprint on the federal judiciary, what with the constant "obstructionism" from Senate Democrats. But in fact, Bush-appointed judges already have made their mark on the courts, and before he's through in 2008, they could unleash a groundswell of conservative jurisprudence that we have not seen in nearly a century.

So far, the Senate has confirmed 39 Bush nominees to federal courts of appeal around the country, helping to create or solidify Republican majorities on all but three of the 12 regional courts. And evidence shows that Bush's judges already are tilting the scales significantly in a conservative direction.

A new study by nonpartisan academics indicates that Bush's judges turn out to be more conservative on civil rights, civil liberties, and worker and consumer protections when compared not only with Democratic appointees but also with judges named by previous Republican presidents.

Robert Carp, a professor at the University of Houston, and co-authors Ronald Stidham of Appalachian State University and Kenneth Manning of the University of Massachusetts at Dartmouth, used the common definition of liberals as more protective of individual rights (and conservatives as less so) in their analysis of more than 75,000 opinions published from federal courts since 1933.

With two Bush-appointed justices, the Supreme Court may be shifting to the right — giving lower-court judges that much more room to move in the same direction.

By their count, Bush's judges issued liberal rulings or opinions in 33 percent of their nearly 800 decisions in the study. That was predictably lower than the figures for judges named by Democratic presidents Lyndon B. Johnson, Jimmy Carter or Bill Clinton. But it was also lower than the scores for judges named by Richard M. Nixon (38 percent), Ronald Reagan (36 percent) or the elder George Bush (37 percent).

"There's been a quiet, silent revolution going on," Carp said in an interview. "If you're a conservative, you're going to say, 'Thank God.' If you're a liberal, you're going to put your hands over your head and say it's a nightmare."

Conservative activists discount this kind of analysis. "There's no evidence that the current president's judges are more politically conservative," says Sean Rushton, executive director of the pro-Bush Committee for Justice. Bush's judges may be more "legally conserva-tive," he says. But he and other conservatives maintain that protecting individual rights too often amounts to activism instead of the judicial restraint and deference that most Americans favor.

Rushton slides over some examples of hard-line conservatives Bush has named to the federal bench. As Alabama attorney general, William H. Pryor Jr. was an outspoken opponent of abortion rights and gay rights before being appointed to the 11th Circuit Court of Appeals in 2004 (he was confirmed last June). Former White House lawyer Jay Bybee wrote the now disavowed memorandum claiming a presidential power to authorize torture before his confirmation to a seat on the 9th Circuit in 2003.

LEGISLATIVE GRAVEYARD?

Too often, Bush's judges display a political slant in deciding when to exercise judicial restraint and when not. Bybee, for example, voted in dissent in 2004 to strike down a "living wage" ordinance enacted by the city of Berkeley, Calif. Two Bush appointees on the 5th Circuit voted, also in dissent, to limit the scope of the Endangered Species Act. With more Bush judges, dissenting opinions like those could become majority rulings, making federal courts a graveyard for legislative initiatives as they were in the early 20th century.

As seen in reports by the liberal group People for the American Way, Bush's appellate judges often vote to make it harder for people claiming the protection of federal anti-discrimination laws to get their cases before a jury. Bush's judges, the group believes, "are already threatening the rights of ordinary Americans." And with more Bush appointees, women, minorities, people with disabilities and others could become victims of judges actively working to restrain the enforcement of federal civil rights laws.

Bush campaigned even more explicitly than previous GOP presidential candidates on a platform of trying to remake the federal bench. He pursued his strategy by turning over the screening of judicial candidates to the conservative Federalist Society and other like-minded interest groups. He also eliminated the American Bar Association's decades-long role in prescreening nominees — a bugaboo for conservatives ever since the group's mixed verdict on failed Supreme Court nominee Robert H. Bork in 1987.

Carp says his study has no political motive. "I'm just calling it the way the data calls it," he says. He also has no fault with the Bush judges' qualifications. "These are polished judges who've gotten good ratings from the ABA," he says.

But make no mistake, Carp suggests, about the direction of the federal bench. With two Bush-appointed justices, the Supreme Court may be shifting to the right — giving lower-court judges that much more room to move in the same direction. "If the Supreme Court starts to change," Carp says, "I think you've got a lot of district court judges who are chomping at the bit."

Privacy Battle Shaping Up Over Cell Phone Tracking

Federal magistrates have begun to say probable cause must accompany requests for tracking information

THE REQUESTS FROM law enforcement officials trickle into federal courthouses every day, seeking orders compelling mobile phone companies to turn over electronic data about the location of subscribers suspected of committing crimes.

For more than a decade, federal magistrates signed off on the requests in an almost pro forma fashion, reasoning that the tracking information can help police locate fugitives, break up drug deals and find abduction victims. But at least some of the magistrates have harbored misgivings that these court orders do not protect against unreasonable searches and seizures — a right guaranteed by the Fourth Amendment — by requiring that law enforcement agents demonstrate probable cause in their applications, as they do when they seek search warrants.

Those concerns have burst into public view in recent months in an unprecedented series of decisions to deny access to the tracking data. Since last August, nine magistrates across the country have turned down government requests to obtain the data without showing probable cause. Because Congress has never explicitly established what legal standards must be met to access tracking information, the judges have questioned whether the Justice Department is interpreting existing privacy and surveillance laws in ways that were never intended.

The rulings have added a new twist to the ongoing controversy over how the government collects phone records and have sparked intense debate among privacy advocates, prosecutors and jurists about the circumstances in which cell phones can be used as tracking devices. A number of magistrates — who are selected for fixed terms to help United States District Court judges administer their dockets — have urged that law enforcement officials seek further guidance from appellate courts on establishing a legal standard for the requests.

> ## "While the cell phone was not originally conceived as a tracking device, law enforcement converts it to that purpose by monitoring cell site data."
>
> — Federal Magistrate **Stephen W. Smith** of Houston

Privacy experts, however, hope Congress might yet step in and set definitive rules.

"Location information is a fairly new issue, and the law doesn't deal well with new technology," said Michael Altschul, general counsel of CTIA, a trade group representing the wireless phone industry. "This is a huge gray area."

BIG BROTHER?

Government officials and privacy experts say there is no reliable estimate of how many requests are made for tracking information. The case files are sealed, and magistrates are not required to publish an opinion when approving or denying a request. Wireless carriers comply with the court orders, but in doing so are wary of compromising subscribers' privacy.

"People don't want to feel their cell phone is big brother," said John Morris, an attorney with the Center for Democracy and Technology, a Washington-based privacy group.

The federal court system's concerns first surfaced last August when James Orenstein, a magistrate based on Long Island for the Eastern District of New York, rejected a request for tracking information. Then, in October, Stephen W. Smith of Houston, a magistrate in the District Court for the Southern District of Texas, denied a similar request and issued a 31-page opinion outlining his rationale. His primary concern is establishing a straightforward legal standard for issuing the orders. He wrote that there are serious privacy concerns because cell phones leave electronic trails that lead into private places.

"While the cell phone was not originally conceived as a tracking device, law enforcement converts it to that purpose by monitoring cell site data," Smith wrote. "Permitting surreptitious conversion . . . without probable cause raises serious Fourth Amendment concerns."

Smith and other magistrates say wireless phones make an inviting target for law enforcement because the devices communicate with cell phone towers whenever they are on, regardless of whether calls are being made. The towers record subscribers' approximate whereabouts on registers that are updated about every 15 minutes. But wireless companies keep the data when a call is placed for billing and troubleshooting. This information can reveal a subscriber's movements within an accuracy of several city blocks.

A Justice Department official, who agreed to outline the government's rationale for pursuing the records on the condition of anonymity because of agency policy, said that law enforcement and government agents are cur-

Pinpointing People by Cell Phone

Wireless phone companies, responding to an FCC directive, have developed new technologies to pinpoint the location of a cell phone subscriber in the event of an emergency. Privacy advocates worry that law enforcement might yet try to obtain location information from such enhanced services without having to show cause.

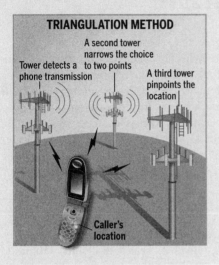

TRIANGULATION METHOD

A second tower narrows the choice to two points

Tower detects a phone transmission

A third tower pinpoints the location

Caller's location

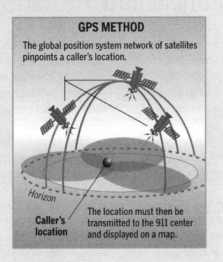

GPS METHOD

The global position system network of satellites pinpoints a caller's location.

Horizon

Caller's location

The location must then be transmitted to the 911 center and displayed on a map.

rently seeking access to this type of tower data and, sometimes, more specific information about which face of a tower is receiving a signal from a wireless phone to better narrow down a suspect's location.

But Albert Gidari, a partner with the law firm Perkins Coie who represents a number of wireless carriers, said law enforcement officials want location information that is as precise as possible. He noted that the government in the past sought more detailed information using data from multiple cell towers before encountering resistance from the courts.

And privacy advocates fear that law enforcement may yet set its sights on even more accurate tracking information that wireless companies are capable of supplying. To comply with a Federal Communications Commission requirement, carriers must provide "enhanced" 911 service, which can automatically deliver highly detailed information about a subscriber's whereabouts to emergency operators. Carriers are also using global positioning system capabilities to sell location-based offerings for the consumer market. Sprint Nextel, for example, recently launched its "Family Locator" service, which allows parents to track the movements of a child's cell phone, and its "TeleNav" service, which provides turn-by-turn driving directions based on a user's location.

PINPOINTING SUBSCRIBERS

Privacy advocates acknowledge that the government has valid reasons for obtaining track-

ing information: Location data could help find a fugitive on the run, or give clues about the location of an illegal transaction involving drugs or weapons. But the advocates fear that the government can glean far more information about a subject's contacts and habits without having to legally justify the request.

"Cell phone location data can provide a complete map of your comings and goings, the political and religious meetings you attend, whom you are doing business with, and all the other people and places you associate with," said Kevin Bankston, an attorney with the Electronic Frontier Foundation, a San Francisco civil liberties group.

However, few agree on what standards law enforcement should meet to access the data. The FCC requires telecommunications carriers to protect the privacy of customer data, including location information, but makes an exception for law enforcement. And Congress has not directly addressed the issue.

The government uses a multipronged argument when it requests tracking information.

Justice contends that tracking information is data captured in real time that accompanies a message but does not include the actual contents of a conversation. This call identifying — or "pen register" — data is protected by a lower legal standard than the actual contents of a conversation, meaning law enforcement can use a simple court order to access it. The standard was established in the 1986 Electronic Communications Privacy Act, the first major

privacy law in the digital age.

By the 1990s, concern about location tracking prompted Congress to erect more barriers to such surveillance in a 1994 law, the Communications Assistance for Law Enforcement Act, which requires phone companies to build wiretapping capabilities into their networks. This law states that law enforcement cannot rely only on court orders for pen register data to track a suspect's location. However, the 1994 law does not define a higher legal standard for this kind of surveillance.

A 'HYBRID' ARGUMENT

To surmount the extra hurdle, the Justice Department relies on another provision in the 1986 law that sets rules for government access to "non-content" records stored with a communications provider. Government agents can obtain these records with a court order by demonstrating that the information sought is relevant to an investigation.

One Justice Department official said the government has relied on this argument to address the 1994 restriction for more than a decade. "We think the rules are relatively clear on what authority is needed to obtain location information," he said.

But Susan Freiwald, a law professor at the University of San Francisco, believes the government is simply combining parts of the 1986 law dealing with different types of data in order to get access to what it wants. "Zero plus zero still equals zero," she said.

Some magistrate judges have reached the same conclusion. Smith argues that law enforcement agents must obtain a probable-cause warrant to access cell phone location data in order to satisfy Fourth Amendment concerns. The Supreme Court has ruled that while government agents do not need a search warrant to track a suspect in a public place, they do where there is a reasonable expectation of privacy.

Smith, who estimates that he gets at least one request for location information a day when he is on duty, adds that until Congress sets an explicit standard for access to such data, the standard should be a full warrant.

So far, the Justice Department has yet to appeal any of the magistrate judges' denials. But some observers speculate that the government may be waiting for the right case.

That would be fine with privacy advocates and the magistrates, who believe the issue needs to be hashed out promptly.

"We're trying to avoid an Orwellian state," Freiwald said. ■

Better Late Than Never

Geneva Convention compliance remains in the best interests of detainees and the nation alike

As JUSTICE FELIX FRANKFURTER once wrote, "Wisdom too often never comes, and so one ought not to reject it merely because it comes late." So now is not the time to criticize President Bush for insisting, for more than four years, that the Geneva Conventions did not apply to the hundreds of suspected enemy combatants held at Guantánamo Bay, Cuba, and elsewhere in the world. Nor is it the time to rue the years wasted as the administration defended that position until the Supreme Court rejected it last month in *Hamdan v. Rumsfeld*.

Instead, now is a time to commend the Bush administration for promising to comply with the Geneva Conventions, thus taking a first step toward regaining some of the prestige and respect lost at home and abroad because of its decision to thumb its nose at international law. And it is also time to recall that, through more than two centuries, the United States generally has worked to promote international law — not out of mushy-headed idealism, but because of a hard-headed judgment that advancing the rule of law worldwide serves the national interest.

The Geneva Conventions — a package of four treaties signed in 1949 to govern the treatment of wartime captives — reflect that understanding of international law. Few Americans know the details of those treaties, but most probably recognize them as generally embodying humanitarian policies that the United States itself can invoke to safeguard U.S. service members held abroad as wartime captives.

> The president was wrong on legal and policy grounds alike that the treaties did not bind the United States in the conflict with al Qaeda.

Secretary of State John Foster Dulles made that point in urging the Senate to ratify the treaties in 1955. More recently, Sen. John McCain, the Arizona Republican who spent five-and-a-half years in a North Vietnamese prisoner-of-war camp, told a Red Cross audience in 1999 that he and his colleagues in the Hanoi Hilton would have been "a lot worse off" without the Geneva Conventions.

Bush and others are right, of course, that al Qaeda is not a party to the treaties and that its terrorist tactics — targeting civilians, taking hostages and so forth — mock the treaties' provisions and its aspirations. But the president was wrong on legal and policy grounds alike that the treaties did not bind the United States in the conflict with al Qaeda.

As a matter of law, the treaties were written — with World War II atrocities fresh in mind — to strengthen the protections for captured combatants. Most provisions deal with warfare between nation-states. As Justice John Paul Stevens explained, however, the so-called Common Article 3 — common, that is, to all four treaties — was written precisely to require signatory nations to extend minimal protections to combatants in other types of wars.

The list is short, but hardly controversial. Most notably, Article 3 prohibits "humiliating or degrading treatment" and requires the use of "regularly constituted" courts that afford "all the judicial guarantees which are recognized as indispensable by civilized peoples."

WHAT THE JUSTICES FOUND

As a matter of policy, the administration has not furthered U.S. interests nor honored American values by claiming a right to circumvent those obligations. "Al Qaeda does all sorts of things that we don't do," says John Murphy, an international law expert at Villanova University Law School. "But these protections are based on humanitarian considerations that the civilized world thinks are necessary."

Moreover, on the most practical grounds, the legal fight over the military commissions Bush established has contributed to protracted delays in bringing any of the detainees to trial. Even acknowledging the difficulties in compiling evidence and preparing charges, it's astounding that no detainee has been brought to trial more than four-and-a-half years after Guantánamo was opened.

The administration may not have learned its lesson, however. The Justice and Defense Department lawyers who testified before Congress last week signaled the administration's intention to try to preserve many or most of the features of the military tribunals that the justices faulted as likely violations of either the Geneva Conventions or the Uniform Code of Military Justice, or both.

Among the defects Stevens cited were excluding the accused and their civilian counsel from some parts of proceedings and allowing use of hearsay and even coerced testimony. Justice Anthony M. Kennedy also noted that the tribunals — unlike regular courts-martial — were not to be independent and their members not necessarily military lawyers.

With their general provisions, the Geneva Conventions and the military justice code give Bush and Congress some flexibility in designing new tribunals. Taking their cue from the high court itself, administration officials are saying that the *Hamdan* decision provides "an opportunity" for the political branches to work together on crafting the best policy.

The opportunity had been there since 2001 if the administration had only wanted. "Collaboration is better than unilateral action," GOP Sen. Lindsey Graham of South Carolina told the administration witnesses last week. With the Supreme Court's help, perhaps Bush can now recognize the wisdom of that view — and act on it.

Restraint vs. Rationality

Under the guise of judicial restraint, recent rulings on same-sex marriage safeguard societal prejudices

A FEW YEARS BACK, the city of Cincinnati tried to reduce on-street litter by prohibiting the distribution of "commercial handbills" from sidewalk news racks. The city allowed the coin-operated news racks to remain, however, on the theory that people were more likely to discard free commercial shoppers than bought-and-paid-for newspapers.

The policy seemed sensible, but not sensible enough for the Supreme Court, which turned its attention to the commercial publishers' First Amendment rights. The justices in 1993 ruled the policy unconstitutional on the ground that Cincinnati had failed to show a "reasonable fit" between its anti-litter goal and the selective enforcement scheme adopted to further the goal.

The decision illustrates in an unremarkable way the courts' well-established role in critically examining the rationality of legislative or executive branch policies that affect constitutional rights. As important as the First Amendment is to our society, one might think that courts would be at least as rigorous in scrutinizing the basis of laws affecting more personal liberty interests, including the right to select a life partner.

Last month, however, the highest courts in two states — New York and Washington — were far less than rigorous in finding a "rational basis" for laws denying same-sex couples the right to marriage. The two blue-state rulings — which leave Massachusetts alone in recognizing marriage for same-sex couples — have forced gay rights supporters to reconsider litigation as a strategy for achieving marriage equality for gay men and lesbians.

> **Courts in New York and Washington in effect said gay couples are so virtuous they don't need the binding ties of marriage, but opposite-sex couples do.**

The judicial setbacks for gay rights supporters reinforce a growing body of thought among liberals against using courts instead of legislative bodies to establish new civil rights and liberties. Jeffrey Rosen, a professor at George Washington University Law School and frequent legal commentator, provides the most extended recent version of this thesis in his new book, "The Most Democratic Branch: How the Courts Serve America."

Rosen argues that courts can reliably safeguard individual rights only if they already are recognized for the most part by a "constitutional consensus" among Congress, the president and the public. In his view, *Brown v. Board of Education* survived because the public was ready to bury racial segregation. *Roe v. Wade* became a battleground because Americans were not — and still are not — ready to accept what opponents call "abortion on demand."

Rosen cites the Massachusetts decision on gay marriage along with *Roe* as examples of "judicial unilateralism." He calls instead for "judicial restraint," which he depicts as a "venerable tradition" under siege from activists of the left and the right.

The New York and Washington decisions on gay marriage, however, represent restraint at the expense of reason. The two grounds that both courts cited as providing a rational basis for limiting marriage to opposite-sex couples fall apart under even the slightest degree of critical scrutiny.

THE TIES THAT BIND SOME

Most provocatively, the courts argued that legislators had good reason for limiting marriage to opposite-sex couples because they are all too prone to producing babies "by accident or impulse." For the sake of these casually conceived children, the courts reasoned, legislatures give opposite-sex couples an incentive to stay together: marriage, with its attendant legal and financial benefits.

Gay couples with children don't need the same incentive to stay together, both courts reasoned, because they have to think and work harder before they can have kids. As any number of gay commentators remarked, the courts in effect said that gay couples — far from being instinctively promiscuous — are so virtuous that they don't need the binding ties of marriage, but opposite-sex couples do.

In addition, the New York and Washington courts both said that legislators could have believed that children fare better in families with both a mother and a father as role models. Neither court had research to prove the point: There is none. Instead, as the New York court said in the main opinion, the supposed advantage was a "common sense premise" supported by "intuition and experience."

Whatever quibbles one might raise about each of the points, both courts were guilty of an overriding lapse of logic. The issue in both cases was not whether marriage for opposite-sex couples is a good thing, but whether legislators had some reason — other than ignorance or prejudice — to deny those benefits to same-sex couples. As Chief Judge Judith Kaye wrote in dissent in the New York case, "There are enough marriage licenses to go around for everyone."

Far from being under siege, judicial restraint appears to be very much in vogue these days — endorsed by no less a figure than Chief Justice John G. Roberts Jr. Despite Rosen's reconstruction of history, however, the United States would have fewer freedoms and less justice today if courts always had waited for a constitutional consensus before safeguarding individual rights. And, when restraint does no more than provide cover for societal prejudice, courts dishonor their proper role by going along.

Politics and Public Policy

This section focuses on political issues that directly affect the everyday lives of the American people. The articles examine the changing student loan market, the United States' policy toward Cuba, the U.S. Army's attempted high-tech transformation, the polarizing issue of embryonic stem cell research, the state of competition in the high-speed Internet access market and congressional response to the growing methamphetamine epidemic.

Over the past 10 years, the Republican-led Congress has incrementally changed the rules that govern federally funded student loans, shifting the system of direct government loans to students to one that favors private lenders. The second article in this section questions whether this transition toward a private sector system has proven beneficial to taxpayers or to the private lending institutions, specifically highlighting the rise and dominance of Sallie Mae in the student loan business. The article explores the crucial question of which program better serves students and schools.

The recent health troubles of Fidel Castro have presented an opportunity for the United States to anticipate a post-Castro engagement with Cuba. Before such a sea change could occur, Congress would have to rewrite or repeal the two embargo statutes that have embodied U.S. policy toward Cuba for half a century. The third article in this section examines the prospects of Congress lifting its long-standing restrictions and President Bush's determination to veto any bill that would weaken that embargo.

Problems with runaway costs, the lagging pace of technological development and the diversion of resources to continuing operations in Iraq and Afghanistan have called into question the U.S. Army's ability to transform itself through use of increasingly high-tech, lighter-weight and more mobile weapons and vehicles. The first article in this section explores deficiencies in the army's Future Combat Systems program and critics' responses to the initiative.

Politicians on both sides of the stem cell research debate employ highly charged rhetoric pitched to their well-mobilized and sharply divided constituencies, but polls suggest that, for a majority of Americans, the issue is viewed in shades of gray. The fourth article in this section takes a look at this politically polarizing issue and contrasts it with other battles in the culture wars, such as abortion.

As Congress prepares to overhaul the 1996 Telecommunications Act, it confronts a dearth of competition in the high-speed Internet access market. The fifth article follows the development of the market, investigates new technologies that may bring it more competition and considers potential legislative and regulatory responses to potential antitrust problems.

The sixth article in this section examines the role race plays in the implementation of public policies and laws for combating drug epidemics. The growing scourge of methamphetamine abuse in rural white America has drawn the attention of lawmakers, who have chosen to focus largely on prevention and rehabilitation. This stands in contrast with the punitive congressional response to the crack epidemic that ravaged many inner-city African-American communities in the 1980s. The article goes on to examine possible reasons for this disparity.

FEELING THE PINCH:
Students protest this month at the Longworth Building office of House Majority Leader Boehner objecting that student loans are too expensive and that Congress has done little to make college affordable.

Molding the Loan Market

The federal government's 'direct loan' system of student aid is dying a slow death as its foes on the Hill carve off pieces and give them to private lenders

EARLIER THIS YEAR, President Bush signed into law a budget-cutting bill that was designed to save the government $39 billion over the next five years. Of that, $14 billion in savings came mostly from cutting the federal subsidies paid to banks that make college loans. In the same measure, Congress trimmed loan fees and increased the amounts that students could borrow.

"The students are getting the money, and we're making the program a lot more efficient for the taxpayers," Bush said at the Feb. 8 signing ceremony in the East Room with Republican leaders, including the author of the student loan provisions, John A. Boehner, by his side.

But even as Congress reduced the subsidies for banks, it gave them new advantages, too. Buried in the law's text were provisions that gave the private lenders a leg up, largely by restricting the business of their main competition in the student loan business: the federal government.

Boehner has made clear that he despises the Department of Education's "direct loan" program, which was expanded significantly during the Clinton administration but has experienced a gradual erosion since Republicans took control of Congress more than a decade ago.

The Ohio Republican, who now serves as majority leader but before that was chairman of the House Education and the Workforce Committee, has been a principal architect of a series of incremental changes over the past 10 years in the rules that govern federally financed student loans. Along the way, these changes have handed the banks an increasingly larger share of the $120 billion annual college loan market. That's meant that the 13-year-old system of direct loans has steadily lost ground to big banks such as Citicorp, Wachovia Corp.,

Wells Fargo & Co., and, most of all, the biggest player in the student loan business: SLM Corp., commonly known as Sallie Mae.

Boehner and the other proponents of this shift toward private lending say it is driven by the notion that a "market-based" system of loans is superior to one run by the government, just as they say is the case with health care, energy generation and other kinds of regulated industries.

"The idea that the government and the bureaucracy in the government could run a loan program more efficiently than the private sector just never made any sense to someone who came out of the private sector," Boehner told a conference of college lenders last December.

But with the student loan business, it is hard to say whether the advantages of the marketplace actually benefit the student or the taxpayer. Both the Congressional Budget Office and the White House Office of Management and Budget say that by their calculations, the government's direct lending program is cheaper for taxpayers than the guaranteed loan program run by banks.

In fact, experts say, the private lending system is hardly market-based at all. Private college loan providers don't compete on price because, except for some optional discounts, the government sets the terms for all student loans. And private lenders bear almost none of the risk usually associated with free-market business because federal law guarantees that as much as 100 percent of a student's loans will be repaid, and at the same time promises a minimum return on every dollar borrowed.

The upshot is that Congress has inexorably pushed both students, and the colleges that administer these loans, toward a private system that isn't proven to be better. The ability of the banks to gain market share, experts say, has had less to do with inherent advantages of a private system than with Congress' drive to get the government out of the loan business.

The Profits of Going Private

Sallie Mae's spokesman, Tom Joyce, tries to play down the company's size and influence: "I'm not sure I can agree with the word 'dominant,'" he says. But Sallie Mae itself isn't so shy. The company's 2005 annual report to investors is blunt: "We are the largest source of funding, delivery and servicing support for education loans in the United States."

Just how large? According to the government, about one of every five student loans made last year, whether a new loan or a consolidation of several old loans, was made by SLM Corp., as Sallie Mae is legally known. Only the government-run direct student loan program, with not quite a quarter of all loan originations, was bigger, and Sallie Mae is growing even as the government program shrinks.

"There's no question who's the big dog," says Tom Kelly, a spokesman for J.P. Morgan Chase & Co., which once made student

WORKING THE PHONES: Sallie Mae operates a customer service center in Killeen, Texas, to handle calls from borrowers.

loans in partnership with Sallie Mae. The bank ended the relationship in 2005 because Sallie Mae "was basically competing against their own partnership with us," Kelly says. The bank bought a smaller student lender in March to rebuild its student loan business on its own.

Other banks have long had a love-hate relationship with Sallie Mae. The company began life in 1972 as a so-called government-sponsored enterprise, a sort of quasi-governmental agency that bought student loans from banks, much the same way mortgage giants Fannie Mae and Freddie Mac buy home loans. The process puts cash back in the hands of banks and other loan originators, helping to create what's called a "secondary market" that benefits borrowers and lenders alike by increasing available capital.

But in 1993, banks banded together and persuaded Congress to slap a special fee against Sallie Mae's loan holdings. The banks argued that Sallie had an unfair edge in the secondary market because of its government ties.

At about the same time, Congress also had decided to expand the federally financed student loan business, and to emphasize the government-run direct loan program.

Sallie Mae's executives were already thinking that it might be a good idea to become a private company, says Larry Hough, who was the company's chief executive officer at the time. "You can't grow when you have a single-market, single-product business," he says. The holdings fee, as well as the advent of the direct loan program, pushed them to make the switch, beginning in 1997, after Congress passed a law allowing the company to go private.

The transition was supposed to take until 2008, at which time its government ties would end. But Sallie Mae didn't need that long, and went fully private in 2004.

"The industry basically had their way with Congress on making sure that the playing field tilts in their favor in every meaningful way," said Craig Munier, director of financial aid at the University of Nebraska-Lincoln and chairman of the National Direct Student Loan Coalition, which encourages colleges to use the government-run program.

If the trend continues, the number of students receiving government loans will continue to fall. The government's share of the student loan market has fallen to 23 percent from 34 percent in the past seven years; one banking insider calls it "a dead program walking."

THE GROWTH OF SALLIE

The growth of the student loan industry has corresponded with a surge in the price of a diploma. And not many students graduate

from college nowadays without some debt.

After adjusting for inflation, the combined cost of tuition, fees, and room and board has risen about 80 percent over the past two decades at four-year institutions, both public and private, according to The College Board. Moreover, in 1992, Congress decided to change the shape of aid to college students, focusing more on federally financed loans for everyone and less on outright gifts to poorer students. For example, while a Pell grant, the main federal grant program, covered more than half the cost of education at a public four-year school in 1986, it paid just 36 percent of the cost in 2005, College Board figures show.

College students and their parents now qualify for federally guaranteed borrowing regardless of need. And as a consequence of the availability of loans and rising costs, the num-

ber of graduates who have loans to repay has increased by more than 60 percent since 1993.

While many large banks have jumped into this business, the largest of the providers by far is Sallie Mae, whose own tale of success parallels and even exceeds that of other lenders.

Until 10 years ago, Sallie Mae was nothing more than a quasi-governmental agency whose job was to buy up loans created by banks and other lenders as a way to free up the cash for additional loans. But as lawmakers expanded the loan program, Sallie Mae got them to cast off its government reins in stages. A year and a half ago, it became a wholly private company. Its stockholders have seen shares increase fivefold in value since 2000. (*Sallie's growth*, p. 84)

Sallie Mae, which never made a student loan before 1996, now issues more than any other financial institution in the country — about 19

Decision to Sally Forth Makes Sallie First

Since starting to go private in 1997, Sallie Mae has rocketed to the top of the pack, leading in new private student loans issued last year. The company also holds a huge share of outstanding loans, outweighing its top 10 competitors combined.

Sallie Mae stock price, *weekly*

May 26 close: **$54.63**

Top private student loan issuers

	Fiscal 2005, *in millions*	
	Originations	**Total holdings**
Sallie Mae	$5,029.8	$102,334.1
Citibank	3,346.1	24,644.3
Bank One	3,197.6	1,305.6
Bank of America	2,862.1	3,803.1
Wells Fargo	2,344.5	9,646.6
J.P. Morgan Chase	2,160.8	721.0
Wachovia / First Union	2,141.9	10,734.4
College Loan Corp.	1,171.1	7,837.0
U.S. Bank	1,143.2	1,904.5
Access Group	1,074.8	3,818.0

SOURCE: Department of Education

It was a profitable move. In the last six years, Sallie Mae's stock price has risen to about $50 from below $10.

Sallie Mae still buys loans from other lenders — and still is the largest participant in the secondary market, holding about $100 billion in loans and other assets in its portfolio. But after it began its transformation to a private company, Sallie Mae began competing with banks to make loans, too. And many of the loans Sallie Mae now holds, it issued.

That's because in the student loan business, origination is where the money is. "A significant benefit of shedding our [government relationship]," the company says in its annual report, "is the ability to originate student loans directly." Loans the company makes itself, Sallie Mae says in its financial statements, are higher-yielding and lower-cost than those it buys from banks.

But loan origination also has brought Sallie closer in contact with borrowers, and some of them have become the company's enemies. Alan Collinge is a former Sallie Mae borrower who owes more than $100,000 in loans and interest that he didn't pay back to the company, a debt that has been assumed by the government. He now runs a Web site, studentloanjustice.org, where he argues that the company is a dangerous predatory lender. The site is full of stories from other borrowers — many of them anonymous — who claim to have been burned by the company.

"It's extremely unlikely — under current conditions, impossible — that any other student lender is going to be able to break the grip of Sallie Mae on the market," Collinge says.

Sallie Mae's investors certainly hope he's right.

MAKING ITS MARK: Sallie Mae runs its multibillion dollar business from its headquarters in a Washington suburb.

percent of all new borrowing. As the share of direct loans falls, Sallie Mae is poised to be the biggest loan originator of all.

Moreover, Sallie Mae holds $100 billion worth of loans in its portfolio, more than its 10 largest competitors combined, increasing its earnings potential in this market and its ability to dominate other lenders.

Company officials say Sallie Mae's growth and leadership have led to increased competition and improved business practices by all private lenders. That, in turn, benefits students and taxpayers, the company says.

"I think we have been an innovator when it comes to providing discounts — borrower benefits," said Tom Joyce, the company's spokesman. "I think we have certainly been an innovator when it comes to providing 24-by-7 service and leading technology to schools.

None of that would have been possible without the evolution we've undergone. Other banks, other lending institutions have invested more in this industry because of many of the moves we've made."

But the company's dominance in the marketplace has also made it a focal point for critics of the privately operated student lending program, including a recent unflattering segment on the CBS News show "60 Minutes" in which people who did not pay back their loans told stories of ballooning debt, damaged credit and an unforgiving attitude from Sallie Mae. The show contrasted that against the rise of the company's stock price and the financial success of its chairman, Albert L. Lord.

Because of Sallie's sheer size, the fight between private lenders and the direct loan program has almost come down to a fight

between Sallie Mae and the government.

In its 2005 annual report, Sallie Mae identifies the federal direct loan program as its most significant competition. Other private lenders come second and none are mentioned by name.

A THOUSAND CUTS

The system of private, federally guaranteed student loans actually predates the direct loan program by several decades. But for a brief time under President Bill Clinton, direct loans were on the ascendancy because they were seen as a cheaper and more efficient route to help college students finance their educations.

The first and last time that Congress gave its nod to the government-run system was in a 1993 deficit-reduction law that significantly strengthened a pilot direct loan program at the expense of private lenders.

Determining the Best Loan Deal

IT'S NOT A SIMPLE MATTER to determine which is cheaper of the two student loan programs that are financed by the federal government — direct loans managed by the Department of Education or guaranteed loans managed by private lenders such as Sallie Mae.

The White House Office of Management and Budget (OMB) and the Congressional Budget Office (CBO) estimate that the government-run program is less expensive for taxpayers. Private lenders say that's hogwash and have their own estimate that concludes the direct loan program is more expensive.

"I've been at it with, I thought, every expert imaginable over the last several years, trying to find a way to solve this problem, and we're not there yet," Ohio Republican John A. Boehner told a roomful of student lenders in December.

"What we need is, we need real numbers on direct lending, real numbers on [private lending]," said Boehner, who at the time was chairman of the House Education and the Workforce Committee and is now majority leader.

The OMB says the private loan program cost taxpayers about 17 cents for every dollar in loans in 2005 — more than five times as much as the government's direct loan program.

The CBO estimates the cost of loans made in the private program will be about 15 cents per dollar in 2006 — and by its measure the government-run program will return a 2 cent profit.

Under the government's accounting, the two programs differ so greatly in cost because they differ so greatly in the way cash flows through them.

With private loans, in many cases the government pays the lender interest while the student is in school, and then guarantees the lender a return on all loans while they are being repaid, regardless of the borrower's interest rate. Meanwhile, the government earns nothing from principal and interest payments.

But under the direct loan program, the government doesn't pay private lenders anything and reaps a return when the borrower repays.

THREE MAJOR DIFFERENCES

As straightforward as that seems, private lenders have a different view of the way the accounting should be done. America's Student Loan Providers, which represents lenders, released an analysis this month that concludes that private loans have been more than 2 cents less expensive, per dollar, than government loans from 1994 to 2002. "The truth is that guaranteed loans are a better deal for taxpayers," said Kevin Bruns, executive director of America's Student Loan Providers.

The disagreement centers on three things that private lenders say aren't properly accounted for by the OMB and the CBO.

First, the lenders use different figures for the so-called discount rate that accountants use to calculate the present value of all future revenue from a loan.

Government accountants use the rate the Treasury pays to borrow money — practically the lowest interest rate possible — to discount future revenue from loans. That's too low, private lenders say, and they're probably right, said former CBO director Douglas Holtz-Eakin.

The lenders prefer to use the Treasury rate plus a quarter percentage point, which they say better reflects the risk that borrowers will default on their loans.

Second, there are differences over how to account for the administrative costs paid by the Department of Education to manage both programs, which CBO mostly excluded in its cost estimates.

No one agrees on what those costs are exactly, but there is general agreement they are probably higher for the direct loan program. The debate is over how much higher.

The OMB estimates that administrative costs are about 1.5 cents per dollar of direct loans in 2005 — about twice as high as for private loans. The lenders say administrative costs are about 2.3 cents for direct loans — almost three times more than for private loans.

Third, lenders say the taxes they pay should be taken into account and used to offset what the government pays them. But neither the CBO or the OMB considers taxes in their estimates.

America's Student Loan Providers says the value of tax receipts from lenders is about 1.9 cents for every dollar in loans, and the group deducts that amount in their analysis of the cost of subsidizing private loans.

That might be going too far, Holtz-Eakin said. The lenders' analysis assumes that without student loans, the banks involved in the industry would be out of business, their workers unemployed. On the contrary, Holtz-Eakin said, "If they weren't in this business they'd be in another one, and you'd get the taxes anyway."

"I think it's a debatable point," said Bruns.

Ultimately, depending on economic circumstances, either loan program might be cheaper than the other in any given year, Holtz-Eakin said.

"As a result of the fact that the mix of loans changes over time, with the economic environment, the answer differs depending on which bundle of loans you look at," he said. "It's not a matter of firm science what the differences will look like."

Estimates of Federal Costs for Loans

White House and congressional budget offices both say the subsidy for private, federally guaranteed student loans exceeds that of the government-run direct loan program.

OMB

Private guaranteed: **17** cents per dollar cost

Direct loan: **3** cents per dollar cost

CBO

Private guaranteed: **15** cents per dollar cost

Direct loan: **2** cents per dollar profit

If Clinton had gotten his way, private loans would have been abandoned. Instead, the pendulum began to swing back in January 1995 when Republicans took over both chambers of Congress and brought along a decidedly antagonistic view of government-issued loans.

The shift didn't happen all at once. Congress has never voted outright to kill the direct loan program, and many lawmakers profess a desire to keep both systems.

Instead, advocates of the direct loan program describe what has happened as death by a thousand cuts. In repeated small steps over the past decade, GOP lawmakers chipped away at direct loans and gave advantage after advantage to private lenders. For instance, lawmakers imposed tighter caps on the market share permitted to direct loans, and they shielded private lenders from the risk inherent in borrowing at one rate and earning interest at a lower rate. In 1997, Congress took away a $10 per loan payment to colleges that participated in the direct loan program.

In the most recent budget law, Congress weakened two features unique to the government loan program that helped students manage their debts.

One change ended a process known as "in-school consolidation," which allowed borrowers to lump together multiple student loans from different lenders under a single direct loan while still in school. That prevents many borrowers from changing lenders by consolidation — a procedure akin to mortgage refinancing.

The other change limits the ability of borrowers with private loans from obtaining what is known as an "income-contingent repayment plan" from the direct loan program. Income-contingent repayment allows low-income borrowers to repay as they are able, forgiving any remaining debt after 25 years.

Costlier Colleges the Fuse for Student Loan Explosion

The inflation-adjusted cost of a college education has risen 41 percent at public schools and 35 percent at private schools since 1994. The higher price tag is a big reason for the past decade's growth in the student loan market.

Tuition, fees, room and board, *annually, in 2005 dollars*

1994: **$21,488**   Private   2005: **$29,026**

1994: **$8,622**   Public   2005: **$12,127**

In the last academic year for which complete records exist (2003-2004), only one in four students graduated without having borrowed to finance a college diploma.

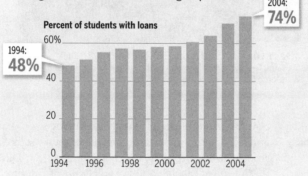

Percent of students with loans

1994: **48%**   2004: **74%**

Including consolidations (refinanced loans), Sallie Mae alone issued 19 percent of all loans for the current year, while government direct loans amounted to 23 percent.

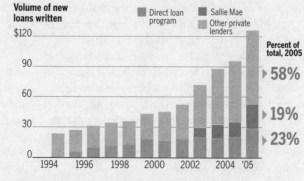

Volume of new loans written

Direct loan program — Sallie Mae — Other private lenders

Percent of total, 2005
▸ **58%**
▸ **19%**
▸ **23%**

SOURCES: College Board (top, middle); Department of Education (bottom). Tuition and total lending figures are shown for academic years; new loans are shown for fiscal years.

"That was a take-away from borrowers with, in my view, no policy basis," said Nancy Coolidge, an administrator at the University of California system who has advised Con-

gress to maintain both loan programs. She said the new law appears intended to make private lending look more attractive to colleges.

The new law also changed the way the Department of Education office that supervises student loan programs is financed. No longer will administrative costs be a mandatory expense, relatively immune from the congressional appropriations process. Instead, appropriators will be able — if they choose — to cut the budget.

That's more important for direct loans, because most administrative costs for private loans are borne by lenders. "It does open the door to political mischief by people who wish the direct loan program would go away," Munier said.

Boehner said the change, which was projected to save $2.2 billion over five years, made the student loan office "more accountable."

Supporters of the direct loan system say most of these changes were designed to make private loans more desirable to the people who decide which types of loans will be available to students: college administrators.

"It was one strategy after another to restrict the growth" of direct loans, said Frank Holleman, who was chief of staff at the Department of Education and later deputy Education secretary under Clinton.

One of the more esoteric changes was made in a 1999 law ostensibly aimed at expanding government health benefits for disabled working people. That law made it easier, analysts say, for lenders to hedge against the risk that the interest rate at which they borrow might exceed the yield guaranteed by the government.

Barmak Nassirian, an associate executive director of the American Association of College Registrars and Admissions Officers who is critical of private lenders, estimates their savings at between 2 cents and 4 cents on every $10 in loans.

Sallie Mae describes the change as a "win-win" for both lenders and the government. The company acknowledges that it saves money, but officials say they don't know how much. Citing Department of Education statistics, however, Sallie Mae says the change has saved taxpayers more than $500 million.

Nassirian argues, however, that the change cannot be good for taxpayers in the long run because the government now bears the risk of adverse interest-rate changes in the marketplace, which was once imposed on lenders.

"The party that has the risk of fluctuation between two rates is the party that is likely to lose over the long haul," he said. He describes the change as an example of financial illiteracy on the part of lawmakers and staff. "There's not a soul on the Hill that really grasps the underlying dynamics of the business this legislation has created."

TAXPAYER VIEW

Proponents of direct lending have long argued that the program's chief benefit is that it is cheaper for taxpayers than subsidizing private lenders. It's a claim supported by a variety of government accountants, though with caveats, and one that private lenders and their allies vehemently reject. (*Debate over accounting, p. 86*)

"There's significant savings in the direct loan program," said Munier from the University of Nebraska-Lincoln. "It's unequivocal. It's simply a matter of political choice that we're choosing not to share those significant savings back to students."

But Sallie Mae, other lenders and lawmakers such as Boehner contend that after years of improving their business, they are now more efficient than the government program and don't cost taxpayers more. Arguments to the contrary are based on improper accounting, they insist.

"We continue to see numbers come out of the direct lending folks that say over 10 years, if we went to direct lending, all across the board, we could save some $60 billion," Boehner told lenders in December. "Now, I know it's nonsense, you know it's nonsense; we can't get the scorekeepers to get the numbers right, and we've been at this for two or three years."

An analysis released this month by America's Student Loan Providers, which represents

DIRECT LOAN FOES: Boehner, left, and Howard P. "Buck" McKeon, R-Calif., now chairman of the House Education and the Workforce Committee, prefer subsidizing private lenders.

private lenders, concludes that private lending is in fact significantly cheaper than direct government lending, contrary to findings by both the Congressional Budget Office and Office of Management and Budget.

"If you had better ways to measure the program costs, [private lending] would be as expensive for taxpayers or cheaper than direct lending," said Kevin Bruns, executive director of America's Student Loan Providers.

Government accountants concede some of the criticism leveled by lenders, and say that direct lending may not be as cheap compared with private loans as their reports suggest. But at the same time they don't concede that private loans are cheaper for the taxpayer.

AND FOR STUDENTS?

A wholly different set of issues revolve around which program is better for students and schools.

Beginning with the fact that these two seemingly competitive college loan programs are both financed by the U.S. Treasury, they are far more alike than they are different. Loan eligibility, limits on amounts borrowed and even

interest rates are identical for the two programs.

The biggest difference for borrowers is the paperwork involved and to whom they apply. The direct loan program permits students and their parents to borrow right from the federal government through college financial aid offices, often with few forms to fill out. The private loan program requires borrowers to go through banks or other lenders, although school financial aid offices often steer students to particular institutions they prefer.

And the choice of which program a student uses is entirely up to the school.

That's where the private program has a significant advantage: While banks market themselves aggressively to colleges, the Department of Education stopped marketing the direct loan program about eight years ago.

George Mason University is a case study in how the two programs have evolved and how the private system has gained the upper hand.

Eleven years ago, the college was fed up with the tangle of paperwork it had to navigate to get private loans to its students. So when the direct loan program was begun in earnest, George Mason signed up.

Direct loans were quick and efficient, said Jevita deFreitas, director of financial aid at the Fairfax, Va., school. There was only one agency to deal with, as opposed to the multiple banks and loan guaranty agencies that the old system required. Much of the application and disbursement process was conducted electronically.

"We were quite happy," deFreitas said. "We were with direct loans forever."

But private lenders became more aggressive and more efficient, and forever didn't last long.

The government's share of the loan business peaked in the 1998-99 academic year at about 34 percent of the market, according to the Government Accountability Office (GAO). Almost 600 colleges have left direct lending and now work with private lenders instead, according to a count by Sallie Mae.

In 2004, George Mason abandoned direct loans. Today, students who apply for financial aid get a letter from deFreitas recommending Sallie Mae as their lender.

"There's an awful lot of government involved and not enough free markets, in my opinion."

— **Richard Vedder,** professor of economics at Ohio University

DeFreitas is aware there is a dispute about whether private lending is better for borrowers and taxpayers than direct lending and wrote testimony on the subject for her school president to deliver to Congress last year. She says she doesn't know who's right.

"I don't really care," she said. "All I really care about are that my students and parents get the funds they need as quickly as possible, as painlessly as possible, and get the best benefits at the end when they do make on-time payments."

Colleges, meanwhile, have found it increasingly difficult to administer direct loans. The GAO reported in 2003 that more than half of 61 schools it surveyed who had left the direct lending program said administrative tasks required by the Department of Education were "extremely or very important" in their decision.

SELLING COLLEGES AND CONGRESS

Banks and other lenders have lured colleges away from direct lending by offering discounts to borrowers that generally aren't available to the government-run program. These discounts include a reduction in the amount of the loan principal after a borrower has made several years of on-time payments.

Private lenders also have made their loans easier to administer than the government program. And they have sometimes formed partnerships that allow schools to earn money by making loans themselves to their graduate students.

At George Mason, for example, Sallie Mae offers borrowers a range of benefits that deFreitas says the direct loan program can't equal. Sallie will pay all borrowers' up-front loan fees. The company gives borrowers a credit of 2 percent of their principal balance when they begin repaying their loans, plus another 3.3 percent credit after 33 on-time payments. And it reduces the interest rate on loans by one-quarter percentage point when borrowers agree to an automatic payment plan.

The direct loan program is permitted to offer borrowers only the same quarter-point rate discount for automatic repayments and a small rebate for timely payments. When Education Department officials began waiving up-front fees for direct loans in 1999, private lenders sued, arguing that Congress hadn't authorized the decision. The case wasn't resolved before Congress passed this year's budget law, which limits fees on some loan programs to 1 percent. But the Education Department never cut its up-front fees as deeply as private lenders do.

Private lenders also sell themselves nonstop to college administrators. For instance, in July, Citicorp, Wells Fargo and Bank of America Corp. are hosting a party at the top of the Seattle Space Needle for members of the National Association of Student Financial Aid Administrators during the organization's annual conference, according to an invitation sent to the members.

"Every time you turn around, a friendly marketing rep is there if you need lunch," said Tom Butts, a former University of Michigan lobbyist who helped the Clinton administration develop the direct loan program. "At financial aid administrators' conferences, nothing is scheduled at night — lenders compete to have administrators come to dinner."

The student loan industry has worked to court members of Congress, whose decisions affect the competition between the private and government-run programs.

Six large college lenders, plus their trade association, spent $2.7 million lobbying Congress in 2004, according to the Center for Responsive Politics.

Sallie Mae alone spent $1.2 million, which Joyce, the company's spokesman, says is in line with other large financial institutions. In fact, MBNA Corp., which has large credit card operations and an interest in bankruptcy legislation, spent almost $5 million on lobbying in 2004, leading all financial services firms, according to the Center.

Sallie Mae was second to MBNA among all financial services firms in the amount of money it gave to congressional candidates in the 2004 election cycle: $1.4 million, both through its political action committee and individuals connected to the company, the Center reported. Boehner's campaign collected $10,250 from the company's PAC and its employees, the CRP reported — his fifth-most generous contributor.

The direct loan program itself, of course, can offer lawmakers nothing. As a consequence, the two programs "do not compete on a level playing field," said Tom Petri, a House Republican from Wisconsin and one of a handful of GOP lawmakers who favor the direct loan model over guaranteed private loans.

In 2004, Petri introduced legislation that would reward schools for choosing the direct lending program by using half the projected federal budget savings to increase spending on Pell grants at their campuses. His bill has never advanced in either chamber.

Munier's group, the National Direct Student Loan Coalition, calculates that if every school using private loans were to switch to direct loans, the government would save $4.5 billion annually. That money could then be used to increase the maximum Pell grant by $1,100 per student and to expand the grants to 400,000 additional students.

But that is unlikely to happen, given the clear preference in Congress for private lending. What bothers some experts, though, is that this trend continues based on the argument that there are "market forces" involved.

"There's an awful lot of government involved and not enough free markets, in my opinion," said Richard Vedder, a professor of economics at Ohio University.

Vedder, who serves as a member of the president's Commission on the Future of Higher Education, says the government should stop subsidizing student loans altogether and beef up grant programs for the poor instead.

In his view, the loan system has "had the effect of almost becoming . . . food stamps for banks."

In fact, says Douglas Holtz-Eakin, who was CBO director from 2003 to 2005 and now holds the Paul A. Volcker chair in international economics at the Council on Foreign Relations, the debate over which system is cheaper is not really the point. Congress, he says, ought to choose one program and work to make it as efficient as possible.

"The idea that we should somehow be able to say which one's cheaper and Congress should choose that one gets it backwards," he said. "Congress should choose which one they want to be cheaper." ■

Revolution vs. Evolution in Cuba

An ailing Castro has prompted new pushes for U.S. engagement, but the White House is standing pat

HOWEVER MUCH Fidel Castro wanted to create the impression that he would recover quickly from intestinal surgery, those waiting for the moment of profound change in Cuba champed loudly at the bit last week when Castro transferred power to his younger brother.

This was as true in Miami — and, presumably, parts of Cuba itself — as it was in official Washington, where the Bush administration and plenty of lawmakers of both parties have hopes of witnessing Cuba's transition toward democracy.

Christopher J. Dodd of Connecticut, the third-ranking Democrat on the Senate Foreign Relations Committee, described the elevation of Raúl Castro as a "tremendous opportunity" for hastening change there. He drafted a resolution declaring that "the transition to a post-Castro government has begun" and that the United States had best not "miss the opportunity to end the dictatorship."

For that to happen, the participation of Congress will be as necessary as that of the president. That is because the core of U.S. policy toward the island dictatorship is manifest in two embargo statutes that would need to be rewritten, if not repealed, if the United States decides to either reward or promote a new Cuban government by force-feeding it free-market economic principles and benefits.

The first law, enacted in 1961, two years after Castro's revolution, authorized President John F. Kennedy to impose a comprehensive trade embargo. The second, known as Helms-

Cuba's Campus Attrition

The U.S. trade embargo with Cuba loosened during the Clinton years, with ready travel visas for students, journalists, and religious and humanitarian groups serving as one sign of a thaw between the two nations. But since 2004, President Bush has tightened restrictions on those visas, to the point where religious and educational groups say they are unable to organize basic relief missions and study tours to the island.

So now a group of scholars is turning to the courts. Last month, the Emergency Coalition to Defend Educational Travel, a group of about 500 scholars, sued in federal court in Washington seeking to overturn the restrictions on academic travel.

The 2004 restrictions require that academic programs in Cuba last for at least 10 weeks, that only full-time faculty supply instruction, and that all student participants must be enrolled at the sponsoring institution. The new restrictions were aimed at limiting the access that Cuban dictator **Fidel Castro** has to U.S. dollars. But **Wayne Smith**, an adjunct professor at Johns Hopkins University who is spearheading the lawsuit, says they "violate academic freedom."

Smith was chief of mission at the State Department's U.S. Interests Section in Cuba in the early 1980s but is now barred from teaching in Cuba since he is not a full-time faculty member. "Academic institutions have the right to determine which courses will be taught, who will teach them and who can take them," he says, arguing that the new rules violate the First Amendment and the intent of Congress in approving the sanctions against the Castro regime.

Smith estimates that only a few American colleges are offering courses now, down from about 200 before the new rules went into place. Hopkins is among those suspending its Cuba program.

But **Molly Millerwise**, a spokeswoman for the Treasury Department, which administers the Cuba sanctions, defends the rule change. "The sanctions are in place to keep hard currency out of the hands of the Castro regime and hasten the day to a free and democratic Cuba," she says. And requiring courses to run longer ensures their academic seriousness, she adds.

Smith dismisses those arguments. Hopkins' program involved "serious course work," he says — and adds that tighter embargo restrictions actually contradict the main aim of U.S. policy: "The best way to get across the idea of American democracy is by having Americans travel abroad and have contact with people in the rest of the world."

Burton and enacted a decade ago, after Cuba shot down a pair of American civilian planes, put into law all the additional cultural, travel, educational and other sanctions that presidents had imposed in the intervening years — and said none of them could be lifted so long as either Fidel or Raúl Castro is in charge there.

Dodd said that, at a minimum, that law should be relaxed so that American business and government officials can get to know the people who might run Cuba once the Castro era is definitively over.

"We need to develop relations with people in the government who have no appetite for dictatorship," Dodd said. "We probably don't even know who the more moderate figures are."

PUSH FOR LIBERALIZATION

To that end, a few minutes before the Senate left for its summer recess Aug. 4, Majority Leader Bill Frist of Tennessee and fellow Republican Mel Martinez of Florida sought to pass a bill that would have promised aid to dissidents and non-governmental organizations in Cuba. But several Democrats objected, some saying they had not had time to consider the measure, and others saying it fell short of the more dramatic approach they would prefer.

Meanwhile in the House, Arizona Republican Jeff Flake, who has long been the most prominent congressional advocate of ending the economic embargo, said he would push legislation this fall to "give the president the flexibility that he needs to respond to changes in Cuba."

But Flake conceded that he could not accurately gauge congressional sentiment for an outright lifting of the embargo — even among the membership of the Cuba Working Group that he chairs with Massachusetts Democrat Bill Delahunt. President Bush's opposition to any relaxing of the embargo has been so emphatic since the day he took office — the White House has threatened to veto bills that it has otherwise liked until language opening relations was dropped — that in the past three years or so efforts in Congress to liberalize relations have disappeared almost entirely.

For his part, the president offered a subdued stance last week, saying the United States was "actively monitoring the situation" and repeating his call for "a free, independent, and democratic Cuba as a close friend and neighbor." But the administration signaled clearly that it was unwilling to go much further than that. "The fact that you have an autocrat handing power off to his brother does not mark an end to autocracy," said White House spokesman Tony Snow.

Those in Congress who advocate liberalization now — and their backers in the business community — say they are hopeful that Cuba under Raúl Castro, who has been the head of the armed forces, will soon seem different. Although there is no doubt he shares his broth-

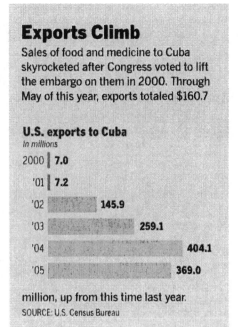

Exports Climb
Sales of food and medicine to Cuba skyrocketed after Congress voted to lift the embargo on them in 2000. Through May of this year, exports totaled $160.7

U.S. exports to Cuba
In millions

2000	7.0
'01	7.2
'02	145.9
'03	259.1
'04	404.1
'05	369.0

million, up from this time last year.
SOURCE: U.S. Census Bureau

er's ideology, he has none of Fidel's charisma and probably little of his unifying power, so this is the United States' big chance, they say.

And when Fidel dies, their thinking goes, the door to a transformation to democracy could swing wide open. Countries such as Venezuela, where Hugo Chavez has reveled at forming a bond with Fidel Castro as a means of antagonizing the United States, might find their options more limited. And the Cuban-American community, the embargo's fiercest defenders, might find their views complicated if the pragmatic glimmer that some see in Raúl's eyes turns out to be real.

John Price of InfoAmericas, a Miami-based business intelligence firm specializing in Latin America, acknowledged change may ensue under a weaker Castro, since "Raúl is not the kind of riveting historical figure that Fidel is." But he disputed the notion that this was a real opening.

SITTING TIGHT

But Rep. Mario Diaz-Balart, a Florida Republican whose family emigrated from Cuba in 1959, said there is no doubt but that the world was witnessing the final throes of the Castro regime. "If Cuba is a sugar cube, it is already in the water. It may not have disintegrated, but it's in the water," he said.

At the same time, he said, lifting the embargo now would be akin to "putting an IV into the corpse of the regime." Edward Gonzalez, professor emeritus of political science at UCLA and a member of the adjunct staff at the RAND Corp., also urges caution. "We have to be very, very careful that we don't ram something that

looks like it's made in America down their throats," he said. "Probably the best thing to do is just sit tight."

Pragmatists such as Dodd disagree. "I would hope the administration is not doing what it has been doing in the Middle East and just standing around," he said.

Democrats argue that the administration has failed to use its diplomatic muscle sufficiently in the Israeli-Palestinian conflict and also that it failed to boost the new government in Lebanon, whose powerlessness in the face of Hezbollah's popularity has become painfully clear with the bloodshed there.

Dodd suggested the administration was making the same mistake in Cuba by not being more proactive in response to the handover of power by Fidel Castro. "You can't just sit there and assume it will go smoothly," he said.

He revived the "soft landing" argument that Zbigniew Brzezinski made to the Clinton administration a decade ago in advocating negotiations with the Cuban government. Brzezinski's point was that a step-by-step path out of sanctions, if put on the table sooner rather than later, would be cheered by Europeans, Latin Americans and Cubans and weaken Castro.

WHITE HOUSE HOLDS FIRM

For all the bluff and bluster of embargo critics in Congress, one thing is clear: Diaz-Balart and others counseling confident patience with the status quo — most notably the Bush administration — are in control of the levers of power.

From day one of his presidency, Bush has promised a veto of any bill that would weaken the embargo, and he's backed it up by tightening rules governing travel to the island, as well as the limited U.S. exports that are allowed. So unless the president has a change of heart, the embargo stays.

That's a disappointment to business and farm groups, which figure they would reap a bonanza if the embargo were cut down. But it's one they've come to accept. The Bush administration's "foreign policy trumps everything else," says Tom Mouhsian, associate director for the Western Hemisphere at the U.S. Chamber of Commerce, the leading business group that before Bush took office in 2001 was a major embargo critic. "We have maintained our position, and we're looking for a more opportune time to play a more active role. But we have not had any lead role in Cuba policy for a few years."

When circumstances were different — in 2000, when Bill Clinton was president — a coalition of agricultural interests, business groups and religious leaders teamed up to lobby a majority in Congress to lift the embargo on food and medicine sales to the island. Clinton, by then a lame duck no longer courting Cuban-American voters, was a willing accomplice.

At that time, Thomas J. Donohue, president of the U.S. Chamber of Commerce, led a delegation to Havana. The American Farm Bureau, the most powerful agricultural lobbying group in Washington, guided the effort on Capitol Hill. A coalition called Americans for Humanitarian Trade with Cuba, whose members included such diverse luminaries as G. Allen Andreas of Archer Daniels Midland and former Treasury Secretary Lloyd Bentsen, joined the campaign.

Circumstances have clearly changed since then. Though the food and medicine exception has stayed on, essentially unchallenged, no further efforts to weaken the embargo have succeeded. The Farm Bureau says that it has continued to push Congress but admits that receptivity there has fallen off since Bush made his position clear. "This administration has been against any kind of further opening up of the Cuban market," says one of its lobbyists, Chris Garza.

The leading anti-embargo advocate in Washington is now Kirby Jones, a longtime adviser to the business community on Cuba who started the U.S.-Cuba Trade Association last year. But its membership list is something of a come-down when compared to the business tycoons that were involved back in 2000, Jones is the first to admit.

"Cuba's a tough issue," he says. "We're in a unique position of trying to establish a trade association whose objectives are not that of the current administration. But we have to start somewhere." Right now, he has about 50 members, among them the American Italian Pasta Co. in Missouri and the North Dakota Farm Bureau.

This year, the association is still holding out slight hope that conference negotiators will embrace two provisions in appropriations bills. One, in the House Treasury spending bill, would nullify the financing rules the Bush administration has imposed to limit the food and medicine sales. The other, in the Senate Agriculture bill, would permit easier travel for farmers and agricultural exporters.

George Nethercutt — who as a House Republican from Washington helped orchestrate the food and medicine shift — argues that the administration hasn't done itself any

Keeping Alive the Embargo

THERE WAS DANCING IN THE STREETS of Miami's Little Havana last week. Could the announcement that Fidel Castro was handing over power to his younger brother Raúl finally mark the end of the Cuban-American community's nearly 50-year exile?

Most Cuban-Americans have abandoned the notion that their homeland would be taken back by force, and their dreams of retiring in their home country. But they haven't stepped back an inch when it comes to their hard-line position on the U.S. embargo of Cuba, long the cornerstone of U.S. policy toward the island dictatorship. And their message on those Miami streets was clear: That policy is working.

In Washington, a new generation of Cuban-Americans has taken up the anti-Castro mantel and, just like their parents, are winning every policy battle. They believe fervently, just as their parents did, that an embargo is the best way to bring down the tyrant's regime.

Their face these days is Mauricio Claver-Carone, the 30-year-old executive director of the U.S.-Cuba Democracy PAC. Born of a Cuban-American mother and Spanish father, he went to Georgetown law school, did a stint at the Treasury and started the PAC in 2003 with the backing of some of Miami's most prominent Cuban-American business leaders. Through June, he'd raised more than $550,000 to support pro-embargo congressional candidates this year.

"The biggest worry in the exile community was that people would eventually forget," he says. "It never ceases to amaze me how the younger generation is even more outspoken and more energized."

For two decades, when members of Congress, or the president himself, had a question about Cuba policy, there was one person to turn to: Jorge Mas Canosa, the charismatic and zealously anti-Castro exile leader, and founder of the Cuban American National Foundation (CANF). But after he died in 1997, CANF slipped into infighting. Exploiting the weakness, business and farm groups in 2000 pushed Congress to allow some food and medicine sales to Cuba. That same year, Elián González, the marooned boy who lost his mother at sea, was seized by federal agents and put on a plane back to Cuba. Both of those defeats, many Cuban-Americans believe, would have been unthinkable if Mas had been alive.

Claver-Carone has helped restore their faith. Last year, he lobbied aggressively against several proposals to further relax the embargo and to allow more U.S. citizens to travel to Cuba. Congress rejected all of the initiatives. This year, he expects the same. The administration, meanwhile, has tightened rules governing food and medicine sales, as well as travel.

Part of the reason for the resurgent influence of hard-line Cuban-Americans, to be sure, was the election of George W. Bush, who defeated Al Gore by a ratio of 4-to-1 among Cuban-Americans in Florida in 2000 – and needed virtually every one of those votes. Bush quickly made it clear that he would veto any bill that weakened the embargo.

But business advocates and Cuban-American members of Congress say that Claver-Carone's lobby also has had something to do with it. "There was a moment of weakness," in 2000 says Kirby Jones, president of the U.S.-Cuba Trade Association, a business group that promotes enhanced commercial ties between the countries. "It continues to be a very effective lobby." And, Jones says, it's the PAC that is generating all the buzz.

"It's like if you asked me, 'Who's more important to the future of the Republican Party, John McCain or Tom Dewey?' " says Florida's Republican Rep. Lincoln Díaz-Balart, comparing the PAC to CANF.

With that kind of support, it's no wonder that Claver-Carone is speaking out in the same kind of bold tones that Mas was known for: "Our community was frustrated" in 2000, he says. "Jorge Mas Canosa's death had left a huge void. It created a division in the community. In 2003, with the PAC, the whole point was to bring the community together again, and it's amazing watching how it's come together."

favors in failing to follow his lead, especially if Castro leaves a power void.

"We've lost some momentum," he said. "Part of my motivation was that I knew he couldn't live forever, and I wanted to have a soft landing when he exited the scene. If there was no relationship, there would be nothing to follow up on." ■

Dream Army's
RUDE AWAKENING

The military envisioned a 'strategically responsive' Army. It would be expensive and time-consuming, but worth it. Six years later, it's becoming a headache.

WHEN THE Army launched its transformation program called Future Combat Systems six years ago, all things seemed possible. The Cold War was a memory, the peace dividend provided some financial breathing room, and the world was a quieter if not a safer place.

Deep thinkers at the Pentagon envisioned a future of low-intensity guerrilla conflicts, border clashes and peacekeeping, and the Army had responded with a plan to reorganize itself into mobile, self-contained combat units equipped with lighter-weight, high-tech weapons, vehicles and communications that could be airlifted anywhere on the globe in less than 96 hours.

The Army chief of staff at the time, Gen. Eric K. Shinseki, called it "a strategically responsive force that is dominant across the full spectrum of operations" — or an Army that could go anywhere and do anything.

It would be expensive — the initial estimates were in the neighborhood of $91.4 billion — and time-consuming. The first units would not be fielded until 2014, and the initial transformation, covering about one-fifth of the

CQ Weekly July 31, 2006

Army, would be completed by 2025. But the Army, Congress and the defense industry were enthusiastic.

Six years later, though, the Army's dream is in jeopardy. The projected cost of the Future Combat Systems has ballooned to $200 billion, even $300 billion by some estimates — at a time when the Army is cutting domestic travel and limiting credit cards in order to help pay for the wars in Iraq and Afghanistan. The Army also is five years behind in designing the Future Combat Systems, often called FCS.

The Government Accountability Office (GAO) and the Congressional Budget Office (CBO) have both harshly criticized the program for its runaway budget and the slow pace of its technology development. Some members of Defense committees in Congress worry that the Army simply cannot afford its visionary weapons program and should admit it.

Both the House and Senate Appropriations committees recommended slight reductions in the research and development funding for the program in fiscal 2007, an indication that they are worried. The House Armed Services Committee, meanwhile, in an unusually frank appraisal, wrote that it was concerned that "the Army may sacrifice the war-fighting capa-

bility of the current force" in order to pay for the FCS.

No one wants such a choice, of course, but as the war in Iraq drags on, hemorrhaging a billion-and-a-half dollars a week, and the cost of weapons systems such as the FCS continues to rise, members of Congress worry that the Army is being squeezed and that its readiness for combat is being compromised. The Army's long-term vision, in other words, is colliding with short-term realities.

To assess the FCS situation, the Senate Armed Services Committee has called for an independent cost estimate and a review of the management contract for the program by the GAO.

Cost is the biggest worry — but not the only one. Government auditors say the Army is pushing some weapons into advanced development even though their technologies have not been proved to work. Others haven't even been designed yet. At a technology demonstration last fall at the Aberdeen Proving Ground in Maryland, the Army showed off a black-painted "test bed" vehicle that quietly cruised the field with a diesel-electric hybrid engine. It turned out to be a leftover prototype of a vehicle that had previously been canceled.

Some defense experts question whether the weapons the Army is developing, with their heavy reliance on computer networks and lighter-weight materials, would be suitable for the kind of combat in which the Army is now engaged. Commanders in Iraq, beset by roadside bombs, want more steel protection rather than less.

The System

The Future Combat Systems consist of 18 new weapons and vehicles in categories spelled out on the following pages. Production is supposed to start in fiscal 2012, which leaves little time for research and development of some of the weapons.

Manned Ground Vehicles

The heart of the system are the eight vehicles that would carry soldiers — tank-like units of about 24 tons based on a common chassis and engine. They would replace many of the Army's vehicles, including today's tanks, personnel carriers and self-propelled artillery. The Army is proceeding with development though technology has lagged in some cases — as shown by the dates when prototype testing is supposed to begin.

TESTING BEGINS fiscal   2006   2007   2008   2009   2010   2011

Non-Line-of-Sight Cannon
A self-propelled 155 mm artillery piece will be the first of the new vehicles ready for testing. It is to have roughly the same weight and engine as other units.
Contractor:
BAE Systems   **2008**

Infantry Carrier Vehicle
An armored personnel carrier for a nine-member infantry squad. *BAE*   **2010**

Mounted Combat System
The replacement for the Abrams tank; it uses the same 120 mm cannon.
General Dynamics   **2011**

Non-Line-of-Sight Mortar
A 120 mm mortar carrier that could hit targets over the horizon and carry a mortar platoon. *BAE*   **2011**

Recovery and Maintenance Vehicle
Carrying a combat repair team, it could fix or tow damaged vehicles. *BAE*   **2010**

Command and Control Vehicle
An armored vehicle for a unit commander and staff. *General Dynamics*   **2011**

Reconnaissance and Surveillance Vehicle
This scout car and artillery spotter would carry four different, sophisticated sensors.
General Dynamics   **2011**

Medical Treatment and Evacuation Vehicle
An ambulance. *BAE*   **2011**

SOURCE: U.S. Army and GAO

> **"What this is going to allow the Army to do is to see first, to be able to act first and to be able to re-plan and react to the next situation even before the bad guy can do it."**
>
> — Army Maj. Gen. **Charles Cartwright**, Future Combat Systems program manager

CQ GRAPHIC / JAMIE BAYLIS: CQ / SCOTT J. FERRELL

the first place.

"A lot of people bought into this over-hyped image of a defense revolution that could radically change our fighting forces and make them much more deployable and lighter without any great downside in military effectiveness," said Michael O'Hanlon, a military analyst with the Brookings Institution. "It was always a pipe dream."

CRYSTAL BALL GAZING

The Army has always spent some of its time trying to look into the future. Before Future Combat was launched in 1999, the Pentagon had debated and experimented its way through "Army Vision 2010," "Force XXI" and "The Army After Next," even to the point of considering what kind of dental support such an Army would need.

The plan Shinseki outlined in late 1999 was based on Army strategists' belief that in the post-Cold War world the Army had to be able to move more quickly, but with the same overwhelming firepower, to quell conflicts. The NATO mission in Kosovo had been an embarrassing example of the Army's sluggishness: It had taken a solid month and the work of more than 5,000 people to move two dozen Apache attack helicopters from Germany to Albania and get them ready to fight. By then, they were no longer needed.

Shinseki's plan, later enthusiastically adopted by Defense Secretary Donald H. Rumsfeld, was to reorganize the Army from its current divisions of 10,000 to 15,000 soldiers into combat brigades — the Army's new term is "units of action" — of about 4,000 soldiers each. These brigades are essentially interchangeable so commanders can assemble however many they need for a particular mission. The plan is to equip each brigade with a new suite of weapons and vehicles from the FCS and link everything with a new communications and data network.

Rather than developing the weapons and vehicles from existing units, the Army has started fresh. The new tank, which the Army calls a "mounted combat system," would bear little resemblance to the current M1 Abrams main battle tank. In fact, the basic chassis of this mounted combat system would be used for

The low weight of the Army's new weapons may be a mirage anyway. The new Army vehicles have been putting on pounds during design and development. CBO auditors did some calculating and found that the Army wouldn't be able to transport them overseas much faster than the old vehicles, undercutting a main rationale for building FCS in

eight different vehicles, from an infantry carrier to an ambulance, theoretically saving on construction and maintenance costs.

The rest of the system consists of three kinds of robots, four varieties of aerial drones, two types of battlefield sensors, a remote-controlled missile launcher, and the most elaborate computer and radio network the Army has ever attempted.

Electronics are perhaps the most critical element of the FCS, enabling the crews of the lighter vehicles to avoid enemy fire or to destroy opponents over the horizon. What armor they carry would be stronger than today's steel. Individual soldiers would carry portable data units — something like super-Black Berries — that would enable them to communicate on a secure Internet while on the move in rugged terrain and during combat.

"What this is going to allow the Army to do is to see first, to be able to act first and to be able to re-plan and react to the next situation even before the bad guy can do it," said Maj. Gen. Charles Cartwright, who manages the program for the Army.

The initiative is so ambitious and multifaceted that the Army, which did not have the expertise to run the program by itself, hired the Boeing Co. and Science Applications International Corp. (SAIC) to manage it for $21 billion.

Despite the difficulty of designing weapons from scratch, the Army argues that its plan makes tactical and business sense: It's preferable to design, develop and build an entire brigade as one, rather than to evolve new weapons from old ones in piecemeal fashion and subsequently jury-rig the computer connections so the systems can work together. And the Army says it has reduced the risks in the program by stretching the schedule by four years and adding more testing, including a brigade dedicated to experimenting

with FCS systems.

"We are exactly on schedule with requirements and technological maturation," said Dennis Muilenburg, Boeing's FCS program manager.

Supporters of the program say that although the technology required for some of the weapons and vehicles is not yet ready, the Army and its contractors have six years to make it work before they start producing the first brigade's worth of equipment.

"Listen," said Army Secretary Francis Harvey, who was a government contractor himself during his years with Westinghouse Corp, "I have a Ph.D. in engineering, and I have run large engineering operations, and I have been involved in design and system development for 25 years, OK?"

"These guys have a solid plan."

WORRIES ON THE HILL

Harvey and the Army still have good support for their plan on Capitol Hill, though an increasing number of lawmakers are worried about the growing cost.

"It's a massive increase that's simply not acceptable with the budget pressures we're looking at," said Rep. Duncan Hunter, the California Republican who chairs House Armed Services. Spending on FCS, he said, "threatens to crowd out critical readiness funds."

As it is, both Hunter and the committee's ranking Democrat, Ike Skelton of Missouri, have asked President Bush to request an increase in the defense budget to cover the Army's shortfall in operating funds.

Defense leaders in the Senate are not critical of the Army's modernization even though they have asked for more cost projections and outside assessments. The seeming contradiction has led Democratic Rep. Neil Abercrombie of Hawaii to say that Congress is "schizophrenic" about the program.

Republican John W. Warner of Virginia, the

ARMOR DUEL: Controversy has followed the Army's plan to gradually replace the 70-ton Abrams main battle tank, with a 24-ton 'mounted combat system' that relies more on electronics than armor for survival. The new vehicles could be transported overseas by plane; the Abrams has to go by ship.

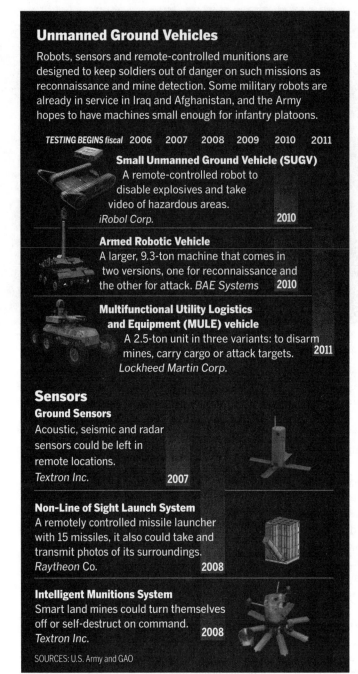

Unmanned Ground Vehicles

Robots, sensors and remote-controlled munitions are designed to keep soldiers out of danger on such missions as reconnaissance and mine detection. Some military robots are already in service in Iraq and Afghanistan, and the Army hopes to have machines small enough for infantry platoons.

TESTING BEGINS fiscal 2006 2007 2008 2009 2010 2011

Small Unmanned Ground Vehicle (SUGV)
A remote-controlled robot to disable explosives and take video of hazardous areas.
iRobol Corp. **2010**

Armed Robotic Vehicle
A larger, 9.3-ton machine that comes in two versions, one for reconnaissance and the other for attack. *BAE Systems* **2010**

Multifunctional Utility Logistics and Equipment (MULE) vehicle
A 2.5-ton unit in three variants: to disarm mines, carry cargo or attack targets. **2011**
Lockheed Martin Corp.

Sensors
Ground Sensors
Acoustic, seismic and radar sensors could be left in remote locations.
Textron Inc. **2007**

Non-Line of Sight Launch System
A remotely controlled missile launcher with 15 missiles, it also could take and transmit photos of its surroundings.
Raytheon Co. **2008**

Intelligent Munitions System
Smart land mines could turn themselves off or self-destruct on command. **2008**
Textron Inc.

SOURCES: U.S. Army and GAO

> **"A lot of people bought into this over-hyped image of a defense revolution. . . . It was always a pipe dream."**
>
> — Michael O'Hanlon,
> Brookings Institution

are bound to explode in terms of cost and deflate in terms of performance.

"The problem," he said, "is that nobody says no to these things. Because of the culture, in the Defense Department and in Congress, if you stand in the way of these things, then you're not a 'team player.'"

Though the Army has spent only about $8 billion on the FCS so far, all of it for research and development, the long-term cost estimates seem to increase by the month. Since the first cost projection in 2003 of $91.4 billion, the official estimates have grown 76 percent to $160.7 billion. When the cost of the communications network and other features are added, the price reaches $200 billion.

The Cost Analysis Improvement Group, an office within the Pentagon that makes cost estimates more impartially than those of the individual services, says the FCS could reach $300 billion when the cost of operating and supporting the brigades is figured in.

The Pentagon's decision to move beyond research and begin development of the weapons before some of the technologies were proven to work makes further cost hikes likely, according to many experts.

"There's been a lot of analytic work done to show that using immature technology ends up costing you more and taking longer," said Jacques S. Gansler, a former chief of Pentagon acquisition who is now vice president for research at the University of Maryland.

Even if the costs do not continue to spiral upward, they threaten other Army needs, devouring billions of its procurement budget. The Army projects that up to $12 billion, or up to 70 percent of its annual procurement budget from 2015 to 2022, will be used for the FCS. The CBO estimates that that figure could grow by about 60 percent, leaving little room for anything else. The wars in Iraq and Afghanistan will presumably be over by then, but the Army will still be replacing and refurbishing equipment worn down in the desert.

CBO auditors point out that the Army plans to equip only one out of every five of its brigades with the FCS in this project. That means it still will have to modernize and replace thousands of Abrams tanks, Bradley fighting vehicles and other gear in conventional units.

At a House Armed Services subcommittee hearing

chairman of Senate Armed Services, is unqualified in his praise of the Army's effort. "It's a bold initiative but it's the right way to move," he said last week. His tone then became almost confidential: "Old Army loves the past, which was tried, true, tested and worked. But this is a changing world, and we cannot be at a standstill. We've got to push the edge of technology."

At least part of the congressional support for the FCS is because it already employs at least 535 different contractors in 40 states and encompasses the districts of 220 House members — all of whom have an interest in keeping the project moving.

According to Winslow Wheeler, a former aide to senators of both parties and now an analyst with the Center for Defense Information, "The bigger part of the problem is not that somebody proposes ideas that

Broad Support: Contractors in 220 House Districts

Contractors and subcontractors for the Future Combat Systems are located in 40 states — and in 220 of the 435 House districts — giving most members of Congress a parochial incentive to sustain the program. The number continues to grow: a spokeswoman for project manager Boeing said subcontractors in two more states and a dozen districts have been added recently, but she declined to identify them.

SOURCE: U.S. Army

Number of contractors
46+   15-44   5-14   1-4   None

	HOUSE DISTRICTS WITH CONTRACTORS	TOTAL DISTRICTS
Alabama	2	(7)
Arizona	5	(8)
Arkansas	1	(4)
California	39	(53)
Colorado	5	(7)
Connecticut	2	(5)
Florida	12	(25)
Georgia	4	(13)
Idaho	1	(2)
Illinois	11	(19)
Indiana	4	(9)
Iowa	1	(5)
Kentucky	3	(6)
Louisiana	1	(7)
Maine	1	(2)
Maryland	6	(8)
Massachusetts	9	(10)
Michigan	12	(15)
Minnesota	5	(8)
Missouri	4	(9)
Nebraska	1	(3)
Nevada	1	(3)
New Hampshire	2	(2)
New Jersey	9	(13)
New Mexico	2	(3)
New York	9	(29)
North Carolina	3	(13)
North Dakota	1	(1)
Ohio	11	(18)
Oklahoma	2	(5)
Oregon	2	(5)
Pennsylvania	9	(19)
Rhode Island	1	(2)
South Carolina	3	(6)
Tennessee	1	(9)
Texas	17	(32)
Vermont	1	(1)
Virginia	10	(11)
Washington	5	(9)
Wisconsin	1	(8)

in April, chairman Curt Weldon, a Republican from Pennsylvania, bluntly complained to Army executives about the mounting costs.

"We do not have the money to buy the systems projected in the future," Weldon said. "You're asking us to make impossible decisions, which puts tremendous pressure on us."

PUSHING TECHNOLOGY

Even if Congress continues to pay for the FCS, there is no guarantee all of the weapons and vehicles will work as the Army intends. Right from the start, the director of the Defense Advanced Research Projects Agency at the time, Frank Fernandez, warned Army leaders that the program was "very, very, very risky" because of all of the new technology and complex computer software that would be required.

Each ground vehicle in the system is said to be as complex as a fighter jet. Software was among the factors that the Pentagon's Cost Analysis Improvement Group said created a "strong likelihood" that the new Army brigades would be fielded late and over budget. "The size and complexity of the FCS software development program is unprecedented in the Department's experience," said the report, which was not publicly released.

The Army has made several decisions that have exacerbated that technical challenge, according to defense experts. In 2003, for example, it approved the product development contract with Boeing and SAIC before any of the system's 49 most critical technologies had met the Pentagon's minimum standards for readiness.

Now, three years later, almost two-thirds of those vital technologies remain unproven by the Pentagon's standards and, according to the GAO, may still be so when production begins in 2012.

The combat computer networks also are a question mark. The tactical radio system could not meet range and security requirements within size and weight required by the Army. The Defense Department has acknowledged that it was trying to do too much too soon with the radios and in recent months adopted a more evolutionary approach.

The ground vehicles have their own problems. They will be protected from attack, officials say, by a kind of force field known as the "Active Protection System," which would automatically detect and intercept weapons in flight just before they hit the vehicles. Such systems are being developed by the Russian and Israeli militaries. But there are questions about whether such systems might also be dangerous to infantrymen or civilians who happen to be nearby.

A contractor who has studied the most advanced version, the Close-in Active Protection System, said it can intercept rocket-propelled grenades, or RPGs, but could kill anyone in the area because it intercepts the grenades by automatically scattering shell fragments in their direction. "The safest guy on the battlefield is the guy who fired the RPG," said the contractor, who agreed to be interviewed on the condition of anonymity.

If "our own troops are more afraid of the vehicle than the enemy, it's a problem," said John Pike, the director of GlobalSecurity.org, a nonpartisan think tank that studies defense and intelligence issues.

Other technologies that are crucial to soldiers' survival in the light vehicles are similarly not ready, according to an assessment last year by the office of the deputy assistant secretary of the Army for technology. These include new lightweight ceramic armor and protection on the vehicles' underbellies from the blast of some mines or improvised explosive devices.

Even technologies judged to be relatively mature are questionable. The Army plans to mount a modified version of the Abrams' powerful 120mm gun on the new tank, but it has never tested the weapon on such a lighter vehicle to see if it can withstand the recoil — it has only test-fired it from a hardstand.

"Firing it off the ground does not necessarily prove it can be fired off a vehicle successfully, even if you

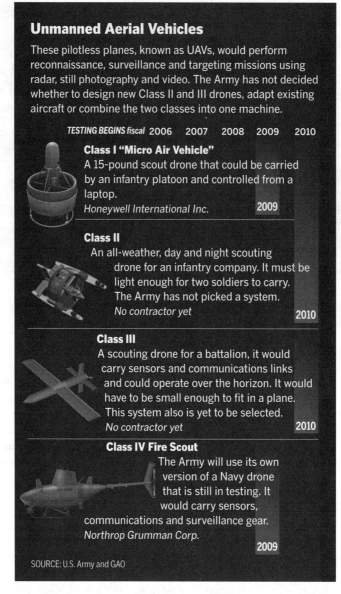

Unmanned Aerial Vehicles

These pilotless planes, known as UAVs, would perform reconnaissance, surveillance and targeting missions using radar, still photography and video. The Army has not decided whether to design new Class II and III drones, adapt existing aircraft or combine the two classes into one machine.

TESTING BEGINS fiscal 2006 2007 2008 2009 2010

Class I "Micro Air Vehicle"
A 15-pound scout drone that could be carried by an infantry platoon and controlled from a laptop.
Honeywell International Inc. 2009

Class II
An all-weather, day and night scouting drone for an infantry company. It must be light enough for two soldiers to carry. The Army has not picked a system.
No contractor yet 2010

Class III
A scouting drone for a battalion, it would carry sensors and communications links and could operate over the horizon. It would have to be small enough to fit in a plane. This system also is yet to be selected.
No contractor yet 2010

Class IV Fire Scout
The Army will use its own version of a Navy drone that is still in testing. It would carry sensors, communications and surveillance gear.
Northrop Grumman Corp. 2009

SOURCE: U.S. Army and GAO

believe you can measure all the forces," Paul L. Francis, a veteran analyst with GAO, said in an e-mail interview.

The Army has not finished writing the requirements setting forth how the weapons are supposed to perform, even though the papers were due in 2003. Because the weapons and vehicles are interdependent, a change in one might affect several others.

Some of the robots and drones haven't even been invented.

In an assessment in March, the GAO wrote that it was possible the Army's strategy for the FCS would succeed as planned, "but counting on it would require suspending credence in the lessons learned on other programs as well as the best practices of other programs."

PUTTING ON POUNDS

A big attraction of the FCS to Shinseki and other Army leaders was its portability. The idea was that everything could be airlifted, even the new tanks. At a planned weight of not more than 20 tons, the new ground vehicles would even fit inside a prop-driven C-130 Hercules transport, which could drop it off almost anywhere.

The plan has not worked out that way, though. Caught between the competing requirements of battlefield protection and intercontinental transportation, the vehicles have not met either one.

The vehicles, including the replacement for the Abrams tank, have grown during development. The Army realized that the C-130 requirement was unrealistic and now says three of the vehicles could fit on a larger transport, the C-17 Globemaster III. What's more, the Army has upped the assumed weight of the new vehicles, which is still being designed, to at least 24 tons.

The CBO did the math and found that airlifting an FCS brigade to Djibouti in Northeast Africa would take only four days less than a conventional brigade — 19 versus 23 days. The limiting factors are the finite number of transport planes and the paucity of paved runways around the world.

In fact, the Army rarely sends a brigade or two into battle alone anyway, but typically sends at least a division, or four brigades and support elements, the CBO and others say, and that would take even longer.

There is no reason to use planes to transport a division, CBO said, because the limited number of planes available means that airlifting a division takes as much as five times longer than sending it by sea.

What's more, on huge sealift ships, having a smaller vehicle is not an advantage.

But the design of the FCS vehicles has been tailored to the requirement that they fit aboard a C-130. Congressional aides who have reviewed the program but who asked not to be named said the Army had to shorten the length of an artillery piece to get it on the plane, which reduced the weapon's range and the number of shells it could fire.

More significant, a vehicle that weighs less than 30 tons is too light to survive attacks by weapons widely available to insurgents, according to an April 2005 study by the Institute for Defense Analyses for Rumsfeld's weapons analysis office.

The Network

The central nervous system of the Future Combat System is a computer network that would link combat units down to individual soldiers, enabling troops to share information about the battlefield. The system is designed to handle large amounts of video and voice data among multiple users who might be on the move in rugged conditions, and do so reliably and at broadband speed. The main elements:

System of Systems Common Operating Environment
Software that provides the operating system linking many applications and subsystems. First iterations in testing.
Boeing Co.

Joint Tactical Radio System
Software-based radios for vehicles, helicopters and soldiers that could be easily upgraded. Early models have been built but have failed to achieve requirements for range, weight and security. Officials are reappraising the program's objectives, including the schedule.
Boeing, General Dynamics Corp.

War Fighter Information Network-Tactical
A high-capacity satellite communications network for long-range contact with Army commanders. Early models have encountered problems, and a reappraisal is in progress.
General Dynamics

SOURCE: U.S. Army and GAO

"If a battle scenario is considered in which the attack can come from many directions (e.g., in an urban environment) increasing vehicle weight from 20 to 30 short tons has a significant effect on the vehicle survivability against easy-to-deploy-and-hide, medium-caliber weapons," the report said.

In fact, because of the threat to its heavier vehicles in Iraq, the Army is adding armor, not subtracting it, giving some lawmakers pause before they consider supporting a thin-skinned model.

"Every Army vehicle in Iraq today — Humvees, trucks, tanks, personnel carriers and Strykers — is heavier than they were three years ago," Abercrombie said during the April hearing in the House.

Army officials say that parts of the FCS such as robots and drones could help soldiers in urban combat — like that in Iraq's cities. But the surveillance technology of the robots and planes is not able to distinguish friend from foe in the crowded cities where adversaries, dressed the same as innocents, fade into the throng.

The threat in Iraq "is a human intelligence problem, not a technical intelligence problem," said Andrew F. Krepinevich Jr., executive director of the Center for Strategic and Budgetary Assessments, a defense think tank.

James A. Thomson, president and chief executive officer of RAND Corp., a research firm partly funded by the Pentagon, warned Rumsfeld in a letter more than a year ago that the first lesson of Iraq was: "Be cautious with respect to Army transformation plans that move to lightly armored vehicles and heavy reliance on networked information systems, given the difficulty in translating good sensor coverage of the battlefield into good situational awareness."

Having committed themselves to this transforma-tion plan, though, neither the Army nor Congress is likely to make major changes unless the problems continue to mount. The Pentagon says the program is on track. The Quadrennial Defense Review, a study of the military and its plans that was submitted to Congress in February, barely altered the program's proposed funding and confirmed the Army's course.

STAYING ON COURSE

Despite misgivings among some members, Congress has hardly touched the program, and those, like Warner, with the most influence over defense matters are unqualified in their support for it. In fiscal 2006, as many of the critical reports were coming to light, Congress provided about 93 percent of the president's $3.4 billion request for the program. For fiscal 2007, the president has sought another $3.7 billion, which Congress is still debating.

At the House Armed Services panel hearing in April, several lawmakers pressed Army officials to rank the importance of the 18 weapons and vehicles within the FCS, and the full committee subsequently required the Pentagon to decide by 2009 whether to continue with the program. A House-Senate conference will determine whether to keep that provision in the bill.

The Senate Armed Services Committee has increased oversight of the Army's contract but otherwise has done little to question the program's premises.

But that could change. If Arizona Republican John McCain becomes chairman of Armed Services next year, he is likely to be tougher on the program than he or the committee has been to date.

McCain said he is concerned about the vehicles' weights, the technologies, the costs and more.

"We have to have a complete review," he said. ■

Cost Estimates Balloon as Project Develops

As is often the case with new weapon systems, current cost estimates have far outpaced the original price tag. Projected procurement costs have gone up $58.4 billion while research and development costs are up $10.9 billion, for a total 76 percent increase in the cost of the system.

In billions

Research, development, testing and evaluation — ESTIMATED INCREASE
$19.6
$30.5 — **56%**

Procurement
$71.8
$130.2 — **81%**

Total
$91.4
$160.7 — **76%**

 2003   January 2006

SOURCE: Government Accountability Office

Stem Cell Politics: An Unsettled Issue

The rhetoric is fiery and the passions are deep, but public sentiment is more fluid than that of politicians

NOT SINCE LAST YEAR'S DEBATE over extending the life of Terri Schiavo has the Capitol been so caught up in the highly charged rhetoric of life and morality. In last week's showdown between President Bush and congressional advocates of embryonic stem cell research, medical science was once again put in direct conflict with social conservatives' views of what is right for humankind.

So deep were the convictions of each side that the Republican Congress publicly challenged the president of its own party on an issue they knew he cared deeply about, and then Bush reacted with the first veto of his presidency, rejecting legislation that would lift restrictions on federal funding for embryonic research. He imposed those restrictions in his first year in office.

The stem cell debate, like the Schiavo episode, took on many of the rhetorical and stage-managed trappings of the abortion debate. Both sides unabashedly brought real people in front of the cameras to make their case. Massachusetts Democratic Sen. John Kerry invited a 20-year-old, wheelchair-bound intern in his office to accompany him on the Senate floor during the debate to serve as "silent, powerful reminder of what is at stake here." Oregon Republican Sen. Gordon H. Smith, likewise, poignantly recalled his cousin, the late Rep. Morris K. Udall, who succumbed to Parkinson's disease in 1998.

EMOTIONAL APPEALS: Democrats accused Bush of stifling research to cure a host of afflictions. Spinal cord injury victim Jeff McCaffrey, right, appeared at a rally with Senate Minority Leader Harry Reid.

Bush announced his veto in a White House ceremony flanked by children produced from frozen embryos that their parents had adopted. "These boys and girls are not spare parts," the president said in a line that produced vigorous applause from his supporters.

And thereafter, both sides appeared primed to take their shows on the road, just in time for the fall campaigns. For the second week in a row, Democrats used Bush's opposition to the research as fodder for their weekly radio address.

But political scientists say it is not clear how much all of the speechifying will help either side on the stem cell issue. The ability to rally voters around the issue is complicated by the fact that public opinion on stem cell research is still fluid, partly because the science itself is still evolving and partly because people view the issue differently than they do other base-voter issues like abortion.

While polling suggests as many as 70 percent of Americans approve of the research, the support is very conditional. When pressed, many individuals reveal they are influenced by where the stem cells came from — for example, in vitro fertilization clinics versus cloning for the cells — and whether they were obtained through proper donor consent. A significant number would tolerate an indefinite delay in medical breakthroughs if a way could be found to extract stem cells without destroying embryos.

"I don't think there are many people who are undecided about stem cell research, but the opinion is kind of soft. The average American doesn't wake up and worry about this," said John C. Green, a senior fellow at the Pew Forum on Religion & Public Life. "The next few weeks will give us a sense of how intensely people feel about this research, especially if both sides use it as an issue in campaigns."

One reason for the public ambivalence may be that the still-nascent field of stem cell research has yet to produce a single proven cure. Scientists are only beginning to understand how these so-called master cells differentiate into body parts and, even under the most optimistic circumstances, are years away from harnessing them to produce clinical results, irrespective of how much federal funding they receive.

LIKE ABORTION, YET DIFFERENT

The politics of stem cells may be less settled than that of abortion because Americans perceive the two issues in a fundamentally different way, even though both processes involve the destruction of an embryo. Though social conservatives have devoted considerable energy to drawing linkages, some anti-abortion lawmakers such as Utah Republican Sen. Orrin G. Hatch have energetically supported lifting federal funding restrictions on the field.

Signs of similar sentiment exist among pockets of religious voters: When the Johns Hopkins University's Phoebe R. Berman Bioethics Institute surveyed 2,212 Americans about embryonic stem cell research last year, researchers found that one-third of respondents who believed an embryo in a Petri dish has elevated moral status — meaning akin to a human being — nonetheless support stem cell research.

The explanation may lie in the fact that the majority of Americans view access to abortion as a fundamental personal right, even though they personally abhor the procedure. The issue has long represented a moral riddle that Americans in the political center use to define such bedrock principles as privacy.

The stem cell debate resonates in a more personal way because many people have relatives or acquaintances with Parkinson's disease, Alzheimer's, spinal cord injuries or other afflictions scientists contend that the cells might cure. And with the baby boom generation nearing retirement age, experts say a significant segment of the aging electorate is likely to place a higher priority on medical research than on protecting embryos.

Research Dollars Keep Flowing

Last week's veto means that President Bush has succeeded in restricting federal funding for embryonic stem cell research. Nonetheless, the field continues to evolve, fueled by private support and financial commitments from a growing list of states. Legislatures increasingly are of the view that the research can generate huge economic benefits if the cells can be harnessed to cure afflictions such as juvenile diabetes and Parkinson's disease. But research opponents have mounted legal challenges to some of the efforts. Highlights of activity across the country:

CALIFORNIA made the most notable state expression of support for stem cell research two years ago, when 59 percent of voters approved an initiative to fund research at $300 million a year for 10 years. The funding is to be administered by the California Institute of Regenerative Medicine, which has planned to issue bonds and award grants. Taxpayer and religious groups, however, have mounted a series of challenges in state courts, charging that the money was being put in the hands of an agency that could operate free of meaningful state oversight. Opponents also maintain that institute members had conflicts of interest. A Superior Court judge in April ruled that the initiative complied with state law, but research opponents have vowed to appeal. GOP Gov. Arnold Schwarzenegger ordered a $150 million loan to the institute last week, one day after the Bush veto, saying research had to proceed immediately.

CONNECTICUT has committed to spending $100 million on stem cell research over 10 years. A state committee tasked with awarding $20 million this year has received more than 70 grant applications, which are to be ranked by a panel of scientists.

ILLINOIS, MARYLAND AND NEW JERSEY have approved initiatives similar to those in California and Connecticut, each pledging tens of millions of dollars in research funding. New Jersey legislators are considering a plan to spend $250 million to build three stem cell and biomedical research centers, but a deal has been stalled by disagreement over the allocation of the money. In Illinois, Democratic Gov. Rod Blagojevich signed an executive order to create a regenerative medicine institute and targeted $10 million in public health funds for the effort, which awarded its first grants this year.

NORTH CAROLINA is among the states weighing novel funding methods to fund stem cell initiatives. North Carolina legislators have taken up a proposal to use $10 million from the state's tobacco settlement money to bankroll research.

UNIVERSITIES have also moved to get a piece of the rapidly evolving field. Stanford University in 2002 established a stem cell research institute and set a goal of obtaining $120 million in funding. The effort was initially dogged by concerns that researchers were cloning embryos for the explicit purpose of extracting their stem cells. Johns Hopkins University received $58.5 million from an anonymous donor to establish a stem cell research center. The university received $23.8 million from Maryland to build a new research building for the center.

Yet public support for the science comes with significant caveats. Though most Americans disapprove of the current administration policy — which restricts federal funding for research to stem cell lines, or colonies, that existed in 2001 — they are uncomfortable with the prospect of destroying more embryos in order to further science. Many support narrow compromises, such as the one offered last week in the Senate, that would restrict research to stem cells derived from leftover embryos cultured in fertility clinics that often are discarded as medical waste.

"People are pragmatic at some level. They care about the embryos but also care about diseases and people who suffer and just generally tend to come down on the side of curing disease," said Josephine Johnston, a research associate at the Hastings Center, a bioethics research institute in New York's Hudson Valley.

"The public awareness is stunning when you consider this is a relatively new area of research," said Kathy L. Hudson, founder and director of the Genetics and Public Policy Center, noting that 81 percent of those polled said they knew about stem cell research. "People have sifted through what the issues are and have come to their own personal positions on research and policy. I think the scientific community has a growing appreciation of how important it is to communicate realistic expectations."

The field's elevated profile poses a big dilemma for GOP leaders, who have seen stem cell research create a rift between more moderate and pro-business Republicans and religious conservatives, who constitute an energetic and important part of the party's base. Many party moderates in Congress who represent swing districts fear Democrats in this fall's elections will use Bush's veto as an issue in local races, citing the decision as evidence that the Republican Party is out of touch with mainstream sentiment and beholden to religious conservatives.

CONTINUING THE FIGHT

In the meantime, both sides have employed every rhetorical device available to them, in some cases resorting to hyperbole to make their cases.

Most of the proponents who argued for lifting Bush's funding restrictions assumed that future medical breakthroughs are inevitable, ignoring the fact that other highly touted medical treatments such as gene therapy have not delivered on all their promises.

The other side ignored some realities, too.

Among the products of last week's deliberations was a new law making it illegal to perform research on embryos from "fetal farms," where human embryos could be created for the purpose of harvesting body parts. No one was against that measure — in either the House or Senate. But even its sponsors conceded that no such facilities actually exist.

The point, though, is less the law than the cause and using it to tap into a constituency of "values" voters who view the stem cell issue the same way they regard gay marriage and assisted suicide. They're seeking a way to halt what they see as a creeping secularization of society that cheapens life and threatens traditional values.

"They're unhappy with the direction of mainstream culture and looking for ways to make a stand and make their presence known," said Ronald M. Green, director of the ethics institute at Dartmouth College and an authority on the religious right. "In a way, it's not the individual issue that's prompting the controversy, but the reverse — a deeper controversy that's looking for issues."

Ronald Green says Bush's veto only strengthens his support with this minority of the electorate by convincing them that he is true to his convictions. Yet the strategy isn't risk-free. Last year's decision to intervene in the Schiavo case — which had become a cause célèbre with religious conservatives — prompted intense backlash from most Americans, including a majority of Republicans, who were

put off by federal intervention in what they viewed as a family matter.

Likewise, the veto ensures that research proponents will continue to press for a weakening of the federal restrictions, calculating that a new president or Congress will side with them. They are likely to be joined by a cadre of state and local officials, who want to attract high-

KEEPING HIS WORD: Bush announced his veto surrounded by children produced from frozen embryos, including one-year-old Jack Jones.

tech business and view the research as a promising economic tonic.

"They're going on faith as much as the people on the other side," said Dartmouth's Green. "For them, stem cells represent a very promising but long path that might not pan out, but they think they have to move in that direction, anyway. The majority of supporters see it as a victory of health over irrationality." ■

Searching for Competition.com

MOST AMERICANS' LIST OF BROADBAND OPTIONS IS SHORT: TELEPHONE OR CABLE. IS THE FREE MARKET WORKING?

BROADBAND DUOPOLY. The phrase has slipped into the Capitol Hill lexicon like pork into an omnibus spending bill. At virtually every telecommunications hearing in Congress — and there have been a lot of them lately — the expression rolls off the tongues of a bipartisan roster of lawmakers, consumer advocates and lobbyists.

The insinuation is clear: The powerful telephone and cable companies have almost complete control of the market for high-speed Internet access. Though consumers now have many choices when it comes to talking on the phone or watching television shows, when it comes to getting a fast Web connection, it's still only a two-wire world. And because most consumers lack much choice over who provides their high-speed ramp to the Net, many argue that the cable and phone giants who control that access can wield unfair power over how much to charge, where to make access available and even which Web sites to favor.

"In the face of the Bell-cable broadband duopoly, there is a need for equal-access protection — non-discriminatory rules so that the powerful incumbents can't put their thumb on the scale of competition," Chris Putala, executive vice president of Internet service provider Earthlink Inc., told the Senate Judiciary Committee on June 14.

Duopolies are markets limited or controlled by just two sellers — think Boeing and Airbus for large commercial airliners. The classic antitrust view is that such markets strangle innovation and lead to price gouging and diminishment of services. The government sometimes steps in if duopolies start engaging in anti-competitive behavior. In 2001, for example, a federal court sided with the Justice Department in its antitrust case against Visa and MasterCard, finding that they violated the Sherman Antitrust Act by barring their member banks from issuing other types of credit cards, such as American Express or Discover.

Whether cable and telephone companies represent a broadband duopoly, in that they wield too much control over the broadband market, is tough to answer. Much depends on how you define the market for Internet services. Government surveys of broadband subscribers indicate that more than 97 percent buy service from either their cable television company, which offers cable modem broadband over a hybrid fiber-coaxial network, or their local telephone company, which offers digital subscriber line (DSL) broadband over unused telephone network capacity. Yet a variety of cable and telephone companies have dominance in different geographical markets. Some experts say the more precise question is whether there are a series of regional broadband duopolies — and even monopolies — nationwide.

The question, in any case, is an important one as Congress considers broad new laws governing the regulation of phone, Internet and video communications. While the main thrust of the pending overhaul of the 1996 Telecommunications Act is to ease the regulatory hurdles for phone companies seeking to offer competing video service, the issue of "network neutrality" also is in play, amid fears that cable and phone company broadband providers have the market power to unfairly favor some Web sites over others in terms of speed and service quality.

"Most Americans are subject to a broadband duopoly, and some rural areas are subject to a broadband monopoly," said Republican F. James Sensenbrenner Jr. of Wisconsin, chairman of the House Judiciary Committee, on May 25. "These conditions have created a situation that is ripe for anti-competitive and discriminatory misconduct."

More competition in the broadband market would greatly ease concerns of potential abuses by cable and phone companies. But why hasn't more competition developed by now? What are the chances that new competitors will emerge, offering a broadband alternative to cable and phone companies? And, until they do, how should this not-quite-competitive market be regulated: using the old phone company method of "common carriage," which aims to ensure that the pipes remain open to all content providers, or the cable TV model of letting the owners of the pipes largely determine what content flows through them?

"There are two overwhelmingly compelling facts," said Blair Levin, managing director of the investment banking firm Stifel Nicolaus and a former Federal Communications Commission chief of staff from 1993 to 1997. "No. 1, in the broadband world as we know it, people get service from one or two providers. The second big factor is that it's a rapidly changing market."

The development of the Internet started in the 1960s, but it was only after the innovation of the World Wide Web and browser software that use of the Internet among the general public took off in the mid-

TRIPLE-PLAY: A Verizon lineman installs fiber optics in Fairfax County, Va., enabling the company to offer voice, video and data over one line.

1990s. Today, 73 percent of American adults use the Internet, according to a Pew Internet & American Life Project survey. By 2000, consumers started giving up dial-up service through some of the more than 4,000 competing Internet service providers (ISPs) that allowed them to surf the Internet over dial-up telephone lines. These consumers sought a faster way of connecting to the Internet. Broadband fit the bill.

Whereas dial-up connections offer transmission rates to the Internet of 56 kilobits per second (Kbps), the FCC defined high-speed lines as those with speeds starting at 200 Kbps in at least one direction — either upstream (from the consumer to the Internet) or downstream (from the Internet to the consumer). However, today consumers are often able to purchase broadband connections at speeds exceeding 1 million bits per second (Mbps). Greater speeds enable consumers to access data faster and use more complex applications or content — video or music files, for example — that are nearly impossible with a dial-up connection. Another appealing feature of broadband is that the connection is available around-the-clock: It's always on, not just when you dial in.

Broadband is not just about convenience. Spreading its availability from coast to coast has become national policy. Congress, in the 1996 law, instructed the FCC and state regulators to spur the deployment of broadband capacity. And in 2004, President Bush outlined a national goal to make affordable broadband access universal in the country by 2007 because of its promise for enhancing education, health care, the economy and entertainment. Lawmakers have been rankled by statistics from the Organization for Economic Co-operation and Development showing that the United States ranks 12th in broadband adoption among 30 nations surveyed, having dropped from 4th place in 2000.

As universal broadband became a national goal, the market responded to consumer demand. Cable companies already were upgrading their infrastructure in the late 1990s to offer digital video channels, in response to challenges from direct broadcast satellite providers such as DirecTV and Dish Network. At the same time, they built in two-way transmission capability so they could offer broadband Internet access to residential consumers. The National Cable and Telecommunications Association (NCTA) said the cable industry got its edge in broadband by investing $100 billion over 10 years to upgrade its fiber-optic network, a move that also allows cable to offer digital telephone service to consumers. Dan Brenner, senior vice president of the NCTA, dismisses the term "broadband duopoly" as simply "rhetoric."

"The idea that there is a duopoly seriously misstates the analysis that you need to undertake," Brenner said. "Our strong view is that markets should be allowed to work."

In the late 1990s, responding to the quick start of cable modem service, local telephone companies started to deploy DSL service over telephone networks on capacity that wasn't being used for traditional voice service. To ready their lines for DSL, telephone companies need to install equipment in their plants and remove other devices on phone lines to prevent interference. The United States Telecom Association, which represents 1,200 telecom providers, has said that member companies will spend $15 billion in 2006 alone building "next generation" broadband networks. At the same time, telecom companies such as Verizon Communications Inc. are developing video services to compete with cable so they can provide customers with a "triple play" bundle of communications services: voice, high-speed data and video.

"There is nothing to suggest that this market is going to develop into a duopoly market," said Walter McCormick Jr., president and chief executive officer of USTelecom. "In fact, everything suggests just the opposite."

The picture presented by the FCC's latest report on broadband Internet adoption in the United States is a rosy one, in which competition between providers is flourishing. In a report released in April, using survey data gathered from broadband providers as of June 2005, the FCC found that nearly 90 percent of the nation's ZIP codes were being served by two or more broadband providers — with 47 percent of ZIP codes enjoying competition between five or more providers. The FCC said its analysis indicates that 99 percent of Americans live in the 98 percent of ZIP codes where a provider reports having at least one high-speed service subscriber.

But immediately after that report was made public in April, a Government Accountability Office (GAO) report to Congress took the FCC to task. The FCC data was gathered not from broadband customers, but from companies reporting in which ZIP codes they provide any broadband service at all. The agency pointed out that if a broadband provider had only one subscriber (residential or business) in a ZIP code, that ZIP code was counted as having service from the provider. The implication was that service was available to everyone in the ZIP code, which is not necessarily true, particularly in rural areas.

Another problem with the data is that the FCC counted as competitors broadband resellers, who lease telecom lines and equipment but who mostly serve businesses (Earthlink and a small number of other companies also resell to residential subscribers). The GAO said including resellers might overstate the deployment of infrastructure.

After making what it called necessary adjustments to the FCC's calculations, the GAO reported "the median number of providers for the respondents fell to just two."

In other words, a cable-telecom duopoly.

The GAO recommended that the FCC identify strategies for improving its data collection to get a more accurate snapshot of residential broadband deployment throughout the country. But the FCC retorted that the commission has determined that it would be costly and impose large burdens on filers — particularly small entities — to require any more detailed filings on broadband deployment.

If the FCC were able to generate "honest numbers" it would most likely show that a "residential customer duopoly is a best-case scenario," said Harold Feld, senior vice president of the Media Access Project, a nonprofit public interest telecommunications law firm. Feld said the agency probably would find that, even within some urban and wealthy areas, there are inconsistencies in competition. For one thing, with DSL service, degradation can occur the farther away a house is from the neighborhood's central phone-switching facilities. "Even in areas we think are covered, we would find a Swiss cheese kind of thing, rather than a nice, uniform circle of who is covered where," Feld said.

But Alan Daley, director of security and infrastructure issues for Verizon, countered that the GAO report was based on a relatively small survey in contrast to the FCC material, which was based on nationwide data collected from all broadband providers. The company also criticized the GAO report for not including all forms of broadband in an area, such as DSL provided by competitors who lease phone lines and provide broadband to their own customers.

"In Manhattan's Upper East Side, there are 26 broadband providers," Daley said. "There are probably some parts of the ZIP code in the Upper East Side where one of the 26 providers won't offer service. That doesn't mean the observation is untrue."

A very different picture of the competitive landscape emerged when the FCC looked at where broadband Internet subscribers were getting

their service. The agency found that out of 42.9 million total high-speed lines that businesses and consumers had as of June 2005, 55.8 percent were cable modem, 39.8 percent were DSL, 2 percent consisted of fiber directly to the premises and 2.3 percent used other technologies. Since most households in the nation are served by no more than a single telephone wire and cable TV wire — and since neither cable nor telephone companies are required to share their broadband wires with competitors — that means a staggering 97.6 percent of the U.S. market for broadband Internet was through one of two platforms: cable or phone company.

How We Connect

Three-fifths of all U.S. households had computers with Internet access last spring — and their connections were split almost precisely between telephone dial-up modems and the two types of broadband service.

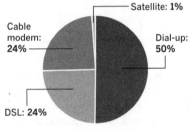

SOURCE: The Home Technology Monitor

ISP CASUALTIES

Technology has a way of changing a competitive landscape virtually overnight. There was plenty of competition for Internet access back in the days of slower dial-up connections, before faster broadband service became available. All an enterprising ISP had to do was buy a few computers, allow customers to dial into them with their low-speed modems, and pay the local phone company for a business data connection that linked the ISP's customers to the Web. But the arrival of broadband, with its "always on" feature and direct control by the local phone or cable company, knocked the ISPs out of the food chain.

"The first casualty of this duopoly was the ISPs," said Mark Cooper, director of research for the Consumer Federation of America. "There were thousands and thousands of ISPs that provided an important function." Cooper pointed out that the vigorous competition between ISPs kept prices low in the mid-to-late 1990s — $20 monthly for "all you can eat" service was a standard. The competition for dial-up customers also resulted in better service offerings, as ISPs were the first Internet providers to include e-mail as part of their service. Phone companies initially wanted to charge extra for e-mail. "By driving the ISPs out of the market," Cooper said, "you've moved out the people who were innovative."

Will another technology come along and bring real competition to the two-wire world? There are several contenders out there, but none appears to be a guaranteed mass-market contender.

"At the present time, for a very large number of households, they buy from one of two providers," said Robert Crandall, senior fellow in economic studies at the Brookings Institution and an expert in antitrust policy. "Any predictions about the market structure in the future would only be made by a fool. . . . The fact is that other technologies are looming and deploying, and the technology is changing for existing services."

Other broadband technologies — including satellite, terrestrial fixed wireless (licensed or unlicensed), terrestrial mobile wireless (licensed or unlicensed), and broadband over electric power lines — now account for only 2.3 percent of all broadband customers, according to the FCC. Some of these technologies haven't lived up to their promise, however, and have more reliability problems than cable or DSL broadband, which have connections over fixed lines to the home.

Satellite-based Internet access uses geosynchronous satellites orbiting above the equator, transmitting and receiving directly to or from subscribers. But subscribers need to have a clear view of the southern sky — eliminating those living in wooded areas or apartments with north-facing windows. Adoption of broadband over satellite has been hampered because initially subscribers could only receive Internet traffic from the satellite, while upstream traffic was relegated to slower, standard telephone connections. While satellite providers now offer transmission in both directions, the price is often higher than other broadband services.

Land-based, or terrestrial, wireless networks also hold promise. Using unlicensed bands of radio spectrum, some companies are working with municipal governments in such locations as Philadelphia and San Francisco to offer broadband wireless fidelity (WiFi) to businesses and residents. Cellular telephone carriers also have started offering mobile wireless broadband that allows subscribers to surf the Internet or send e-mail from mobile phones or laptop computers as they travel around the covered area. Unlicensed spectrum is also being used by a variety of businesses as a way to provide broadband access to customers, such as the WiFi networks now offered in many Starbucks, Kinko's, hotels and airports. One emerging technology, Worldwide Interoperability for Microwave Access — or WiMAX — is being designed to offer wireless broadband connections in either licensed or unlicensed bands that can reach as far as 30 miles, a much wider span than the coffee shop WiFi connections.

To the critics of broadband duopoly theory, the competition — or even potential competition — is enough of a check on market power. "That goes to the heart of the question about contestability," McCormick said. "The issue here is, are there insurmountable barriers to entry, or has technology brought us to a place where the market is contestable? There are many, many places in the country where individuals have a number of competitors. In many rural areas, there is only one gas station or one Wal-Mart store or one restaurant. Is the market contestable? Should that one provider of service start to raise its prices or should quality of service go down, that becomes a check on behavior."

DEFINING THE MARKET

To consider whether there is a duopoly among broadband Internet providers that could exert market power to harm consumers or businesses, antitrust experts say, the first step is to determine whether it's appropriate to even consider "broadband" as a market in its own right.

People who dismiss the notion of a "broadband duopoly" say the term too narrowly defines the market.

"You at least have to ask the question if the market is access to the Internet, or broadband access to the Internet," said David Cohen, executive vice president of Comcast Corp., one of the nation's largest cable companies. According to the GAO analysis, which was based on the FCC data and the Knowledge Networks/SRI's "The Home Technology Monitor" spring 2005 report, at least 50 percent of home Internet users still subscribe to dial-up service, while only 48 percent subscribe to a broadband service. If half of U.S. Internet users access the Internet through a dial-up service, and that number was more like 97 percent 10 years ago, there are clearly trends toward broadband as a growing route for Internet access. But the question remains, Cohen said, whether for a large number of people, who use their home computers to access e-mail and maybe do simple searches on the Internet, narrowband dial-up access is going to remain the preferred route to the Internet.

"I'm talking about people like my parents, who are never going to have any need for broadband," Cohen said. "They basically use the Internet for e-mail, and narrowband works well for them." Another factor is the people who have broadband access at work and manage to do most of their Internet activities there. Cohen questions whether many of those people ever will need broadband at home.

In Broadband, DSL Edges Ahead

In the contest to dominate the market in broadband, or high-speed, Internet service, all the momentum is with telephone companies' DSL, or digital subscriber lines. Their share of the broadband market edged ahead in the past year.

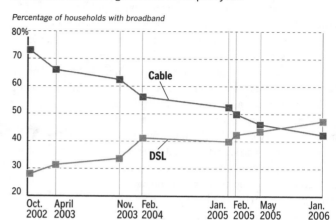

Percentage of households with broadband

SOURCE: Pew Internet & American Life Project

In studies of Internet migration to broadband technologies, the Pew Internet & American Life Project has found that "people make the switch from dial-up to broadband as their Internet usage deepens over time," according to John Horrigan, Pew's associate director for research. Pew's latest report, released in April, found that the overall number of Americans with broadband connections grew by 40 percent, from 60 million to 84 million, from March 2005 to March 2006. Only 42 percent of all Internet users had a high-speed connection in their home. When asked why they had upgraded to broadband, 57 percent of users said they wanted a faster connection. But when dial-up users were asked whether they wanted to migrate to broadband, 60 percent said they did not.

"People say they prefer to stick to their dial-up," Horrigan said. "Some of those people have high-speed connections at work. They may be content with doing their power surfing at work." The "dial-up die-hards" tend to be older on average than the rest of the Internet population, Horrigan said, and older people tend to have less active online profiles. They also tend to be at lower income levels than broadband users.

Another question that antitrust experts have about the broadband Internet "market" involves the tremendous disparities between the numbers of broadband Internet providers in different geographical locations. In rural or remote areas, residents are lucky to find one broadband provider — and if they do, they often pay higher prices for service. Yet in urban areas, such as New York City, there are so many broadband providers that some companies are advertising the going rate for a package of voice, video and high-speed Internet access at $99 per month.

Indeed, the most intense competition in broadband is between the cable and telephone company incumbents who are battling each other in established markets to offer broadband as part of a "bundle" that includes video, data and voice service. "Most people like the idea of getting everything on one bill," said David Farber, computer science professor at Carnegie Mellon University. "Video now captures the customer. Cable operators can offer everything. But telephone companies have only been able to offer two out of three of everything."

In the Washington, D.C., suburbs, Adam Thierer, a senior fellow at the conservative Progress and Freedom Foundation and the director of

PFF's Center for Digital Media Freedom, said he has living proof that the market for broadband Internet services is fiercely competitive. Thierer, who lives in McLean, Va., said he pitted his cable company, Cox Communications, against his telephone company, Verizon, which offers broadband Internet DSL service, and reduced his monthly bills for video, Internet and phone service by $100 per month. "I can go to either one and have service," Thierer said. "I bargained with them on the phone. Verizon got my monthly bill down by $30 and then I went back to Cox and said, 'Here is what Verizon is giving me.' Cox then said they had a $100 per month reduction they could offer him.

"It's marketplace arbitrage," Thierer said.

But in some upstate New York communities, there are no multiple broadband providers to play off one another. Andrea Nussinow, owner of a 40-acre horse farm, Blue Star Farms, had difficulty finding any broadband service in her ZIP code, 12583, that would extend to her home. Her community of Tivoli is located only 90 miles north of New York City, but she can't get broadband service from a cable company or a telephone provider. For a long time she was using a slower dial-up ISP over her local phone line, until the bills for calls to her local access number started running about $200 per month.

"I need the Internet for the horse farm," Nussinow said. "A lot of the buying and selling takes place on the Internet these days. It's an excellent way to advertise the horses. You put a photo online and get a lot of play." Earlier this year, Nussinow managed to upgrade to broadband with a wireless provider in the Hudson Valley called Webjogger, but she paid about $300 for installation, and her bills are running about $75 per month. "It's frustrating when I see advertisements for high speed Internet or DSL for something like $19.95 a month," she said.

REGIONAL MONOPOLIES

Competition for broadband Internet service seems to be robust in certain geographical markets and virtually non-existent in others. One reason is that both the cable and telephone industries have a history of regional monopolies and have been slow to challenge companies using the same platform in many of these regional markets.

Telephone service in the United States, the roots of which stretch back to Alexander Graham Bell and the 1876 invention of the telephone, evolved into a monopoly in the 20th century. The underlying principle was developed by Theodore Vail, president of AT&T and its Bell System, in 1907. He theorized that the industry would operate more efficiently as a monopoly providing service to all because of the nature of the technology, which needed to interconnect in order to complete calls. According to AT&T's Web site, Vail wrote in that year's AT&T Annual Report that government regulation, "provided it is independent, intelligent, considerate, thorough and just," was a fitting and suitable replacement for competition. The U.S. government agreed to this principle, as long as AT&T agreed to connect independent telephone companies to its network — and to provide "universal service" to all.

In this way, telephony in the United States was considered a "common carriage" service. Common carriage is a principle that extends back

Slow Speed in the Heartland

Three in 10 big-city and suburban homes accessed the Internet using broadband technology in the spring of 2005; the share of homes in rural areas with high-speed access was about one in six.

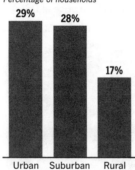

Percentage of households

- Urban 29%
- Suburban 28%
- Rural 17%

SOURCE: The Home Technology Monitor

to English common law in the Elizabethan period. It provides that businesses (and sometimes government agencies) should provide transportation of goods or people over defined routes according to predictable schedules and make those services available to anyone or any business. That's why industries such as airlines, railroads, trucking, natural gas and telecommunications have been subject to greater government regulation. The underlying principle kept the conduit of networks (roads, air routes, telephone service, etc.) separate from the content (shipments, passengers, telephone calls, etc.).

But when upstart MCI ushered in the era of long-distance telephone competition, starting in the 1960s, and the Bell system punished MCI by degrading their connections and requiring additional equipment to raise MCI's costs, Bell wound up saddled with an antitrust suit from the Justice Department in 1974. Under a settlement 10 years later, the system was broken up into seven regional "Baby Bells," which retained regional local phone monopolies but were barred from providing long-distance service, and AT&T, an equipment maker and long-distance provider in newly competitive markets.

While the 1996 telecommunications law was designed to bring about more competition in local markets, it instead opened the doors to mergers that brought the Bells' local, regional and long-distance networks back together: Bell Atlantic and Nynex (now Verizon), Pacific Bell and Southwestern Bell Corp. (SBC), SBC and Ameritech, and more recently SBC and AT&T (now AT&T). Regulators are still reviewing AT&T's requested acquisition of the last remaining independent regional Bell company, BellSouth.

The cable television industry, meanwhile, has its roots in providing competition to broadcast television. Developed as Community Antenna Television or CATV in the mountains of Pennsylvania in the late 1940s, the idea was to bring television to people who couldn't easily receive broadcast television signals. The era of pay television was ushered in when Home Box Office was offered over Service Electric's cable system in Wilkes-Barre, Pa., according to the Museum of Broadcasting. HBO has gone on to become the world's largest cable program provider, with more than 11 million viewers.

The rise of interest in cable, and concern from local broadcasters, led the FCC to regulate cable by imposing rules such as the "must carry" provision requiring cable services to carry local broadcast programming. Cable was also regulated at the local level, because cable providers need public rights of way to lay cable underground or string it along telephone or electric poles. As a result, cable operators had to negotiate franchise agreements with municipalities for these rights of way and, in exchange paid fees of about 5 percent of revenues to the municipal government. Through these agreements, cable systems were granted exclusive rights to serve local regions as long as they built out service to the entire community. Thus cable developed its own system of regional monopolies throughout the United States.

Cable and telephone companies evolved under very different regulatory regimes, and now Congress is working out ways to allow them to compete using the same rule book.

The main thrust of telecom legislation passed by the House last month, and pending in the Senate after its adoption in the Commerce Committee, is relief from local and state regulations in providing video services for both industries. The bills intend to make it easier for phone companies to offer TV service, creating a national franchise process that relieves them of the requirement to get approval from every community where they want to offer the service. Availability would be increased, proponents say, because phone companies would be able to package TV, phone and broadband Internet service in the same way that cable companies now can. The large cable providers have pressed for equal treatment under the legislation, giving them access to the same national franchises and relieving them of requirements to offer low-priced basic tier TV packages and build their service throughout an entire community once a phone company begins competing in a particular geographic area.

Critics of the broadband duopoly fear that cable and phone companies intend to treat their broadband Internet businesses like their video ventures, by carrying only select Web sites on higher-priced "tiers" of Internet access if those sites agree to pay them more than the usual access fees, while sticking those who don't on the bottom-tier slow lane.

Consumer groups, along with Web sites as wide-reaching as Google, Amazon and the Christian Coalition, advocate "network neutrality" language that would aim to ensure that neither phone nor cable operators could use their control of the nation's broadband networks to favor their own online traffic or discriminate against rivals.

Cable and phone companies say they have no intention of unfairly discriminating against any Web sites, but they fiercely defend their right to charge whatever they want for access to sites that, they say, place unusual demands on their network by dealing in large video and music files.

"Why should they be allowed to use my pipes?" said then-SBC CEO Edward Whitacre (now head of AT&T) in a now-infamous November 2005 interview with BusinessWeek. "The Internet can't be free in that sense, because we and the cable companies have made an investment, and for a Google or a Yahoo! or Vonage or anybody to expect to use these pipes [for] free is nuts!"

Vinton Cerf, chief Internet evangelist at Google and a pioneer in the development of the TCP/IP protocols underlying the Internet, said such ideas are tantamount to "building toll lanes" on the Internet. "They're basically saying to Google and others, 'We're not going to let your traffic on the pipes unless you pay extra for it.'"

Google and other Web sites already pay the telephone and cable companies for access to the Internet, like any other user, based on their usage, network neutrality advocates point out.

Right now Internet users expect to be able, for example, to shop for an iPod online and not worry about whether BestBuy.com has a business arrangement with its broadband provider giving it faster, more reliable service than Apple.com, which might not have such a deal.

The idea of preventing such content discrimination over communications lines dates back to the common-carriage principles codified in

the Communications Act of 1934, net neutrality supporters say. They cite the breakup of the AT&T monopoly, which imposed conditions of non-discriminatory access to the local telephone exchange market. Government regulators for years kept tabs on telephone companies to make sure they were not favoring one telemarketing company over another, for example, and for years they prevented them from entering the market for electronic "information services" such as online Yellow Pages out of concern that one company would own both the pipes and the content traveling over those pipes.

Consumer advocates argue that rules keeping the common carriers' hands off the content is behind the dynamic growth of the Internet. The telephone carriers that owned the underlying network were prohibited from discriminating against Web site owners and ISPs providing access to the Internet over those networks.

Telephone company representatives argue that the notion that conduit and content were always kept separate is a "misconception." McCormick, of USTelecom, said that telephone companies gradually had won the ability to control some content services over the network, such as retrieving voice mail off a cell phone or offering virtual private networks to corporate clients. Furthermore, he said, network providers already are allowed to manage their networks with regard to priority, and he cited as an example the Watts lines, toll-free lines that vendors could purchase for bulk service. "The concept of those who want to be able to buy capacity in bulk is not a new concept," McCormick said. "Today, there are volume purchases, those who buy in bulk, and enter into agreements with network providers. Today's telecom networks involved considerable private carriage."

A major step in defining the principle that broadband Internet providers were not providing a service that should be considered common carriage came at the hands of the U.S. Supreme Court, which ruled in *FCC v. Brand X Internet Services* in June 2005 that cable companies do not have to open their lines to competing ISPs. The cable industry argued that cable Internet access should be regarded as an information service, not a telecommunications service, because it offers features such as Web hosting and e-mail. It argued that competing services should do what it did: spend billions of dollars building an infrastructure.

After the ruling, the regional phone companies, including Verizon, SBC and BellSouth, pushed the FCC and Congress to release them from their obligations to make their DSL broadband lines similarly available to competitors. In August, the FCC eased requirements that phone companies lease their networks to rivals for selling high-speed Internet access. At the same time, the FCC voted — in principle — to support network neutrality so that subscribers should be able to access any Web site free from interference from the network provider.

So far, Congress has stopped short of putting any net neutrality protections into the pending telecom overhaul. Cable and telephone representatives argue that such measures amount to a solution in search of a problem. But Internet company representatives and public advocates now worry that the free and open Internet is going to be a casu-

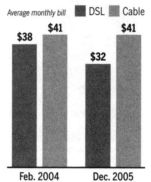

Price Differential

The overall price of broadband service dropped 8 percent in the 22 months ending in December. But while the typical cable modem bill did not change, the cost of a DSL line dropped almost 16 percent in that time. (Telephone dial-up service is still about half the price of DSL.)

Average monthly bill ■ DSL ■ Cable

Feb. 2004: DSL $38, Cable $41
Dec. 2005: DSL $32, Cable $41

SOURCE: Pew Internet & American Life Project

alty of broadband markets controlled by cable and telephone companies.

Lawmakers and regulators have "abandoned seven centuries of common practice that served us well" in the common-carriage rules, Cerf said. Those rules "allowed consumer choice and allowed carriers to escape responsibility for content." By doing away with the rules, Cerf said, the U.S. government might be effectively spelling the end of egalitarian access to the Internet.

There is speculation that Google may resort to becoming a third broadband provider, by joining with cities to provide municipal wireless access. But despite Google's participation in a project to create a municipal wireless network in San Francisco, Cerf said, "it's not in our business model to go spend huge sums of money on capital and equipment" around the country to create a new platform to rival cable and DSL. "We have no plans that I know of to exercise this design anywhere else."

Earthlink's Putala also said his company is working with several municipalities to develop wireless broadband service. But he said Earthlink has been unable to negotiate any deals with cable companies other than Time Warner for providing service over their lines. That deal was arranged, in part, due to conditions that regulators placed on the merger of AOL and Time Warner several years ago.

COLLUSION WATCH

Problems can arise in duopolistic markets when dominant players act in collusion to change prices or divide a market, instead of remaining competitive. In the late 1990s, U.S. antitrust regulators alleged that the two dominant art auction houses, Sotheby's and Christie's, were engaging in that type of collusive behavior to fix commission prices charged to buyers and sellers. Top officials of the companies were convicted of fixing prices, and the two companies wound up paying hundreds of millions of dollars in fines.

Regulators will often intervene if a proposed merger is likely to create a duopolistic market. In 2004, the Justice Department attempted to block software giant Oracle's acquisition of a rival, PeopleSoft, arguing that the pairing would narrow the high-end customer relations and financial management software market to just two players, Oracle and SAP. After a trial that included expert testimony that the market would be left a duopoly that would have the power to raise prices, a court found no proof of anti-competitive effects, and Oracle acquired PeopleSoft for almost $11 billion.

Currently, FCC and Justice Department officials are contemplating the impact of the proposed $67 billion merger of AT&T, BellSouth and their Cingular Wireless joint venture (60 percent owned by AT&T and 40 percent by BellSouth). In clearing a merger, regulators need to look at the current state of the market and decide whether the proposed merger will probably harm competition.

Jonathan Rubin, senior research fellow at the American Antitrust Institute, cited the broadband access market as of particular concern in testimony about the merger before a subcommittee of the Senate Judiciary Committee on June 22. "Soon that's going to be the only market of importance to consumers and most businesses," Rubin said in an interview. As voice communications increasingly are carried using the Internet, the phone companies themselves will rely less on traditional phone lines and more on their broadband service, he said.

In an effort to limit the consolidation of a broadband duopoly, some companies and public interest groups have asked the FCC to impose conditions that would free up unused wireless radio spectrum controlled by BellSouth and AT&T, out of concern that they will hoard the frequencies and stifle potential competition. The spectrum is ripe for using the WiMAX standard. Rubin said he supports limits on telephone or cable cross-ownership of WiMAX networks to clear the way for new entrants to develop a potential third broadband platform.

The essential antitrust problem is that common-carrier regulation was not intended for a competitive world. At the same time, many fear that the broadband market is not yet competitive enough to be unregulated.

Telephone and cable companies routinely point to existing antitrust statutes to police against any potential market abuses. Consumer advocates, however, point out that it took nearly 10 years for authorities to press and win an antitrust case against Microsoft Corp. for having a monopoly over the computer operating system software market.

Legislation is another way to lay down rules for this competitive landscape. But critics argue that the bills now under consideration in both chambers might even strengthen the so-called broadband duopoly rather than fostering new competition.

The main thrust of both bills is to make it easier for telephone companies to compete against cable by offering TV services and bundling video, data and voice. But consumer advocates say that to qualify for bundled discounts, the customer must take all of those services from a cable or phone company. "You really need to take cable television as well as cable modem service," said public interest lawyer Feld. "Broadband goes from being a $40-a-month decision to being an $80-a-month decision.... If my only choice is cable modem and I happen to be a DirecTV subscriber, I'm going to drop my DirecTV."

Verizon officials see bundling as one of the hallmarks of the competitive broadband market. "Bundling is a factor of competition in the marketplace today. It encourages the offering of more and better pricing options and more packages to meet an array of needs," said Link Hoewing, Verizon's vice president for Internet technology policy. In Keller, Texas, where Verizon is offering all services, customers are seeing discounts of 20 percent to 40 percent off what they would pay for each service individually.

But economists call that the "consumer lock-in" effect. Once a customer is locked in to buying video, voice and data from a cable or phone company, it is difficult for a competing broadband-only provider to pry him away. "We have the appearance of competition right now because we have a race" between cable and telephone companies, Feld said. "Five years from now, we need to think about whether that broadband duopoly is going to be serving our national needs. At that point, it may be too late to do anything about it." ∎

> **"In the face of the Bell-cable broadband duopoly, there is a need for equal-access protection — non-discriminatory rules so that the powerful incumbents can't put their thumb on the scale of competition."**
>
> — **Chris Patala**, Earthlink Inc.

White Powder

The meth menace has elicited all the sound and fury of the war on crack two decades ago. But this crisis has a new and paler face, and while race alone may not be steering lawmakers' response, their take on the drug's users has a sympathetic tone not heard before.

WHEN REP. Elijah E. Cummings visits rural communities in the Midwest that have been ravaged by methamphetamine use, he hears stories of despair and damage not unlike those he heard during the crack epidemic of the 1980s. His hometown of Baltimore includes some of the neighborhoods that were devastated the worst by crack, the last drug epidemic to draw an intense response from the federal government and local law enforcement.

The similarities exist despite fundamental differences between the populations affected by the two drugs. Meth is used mostly by white people in rural areas, while the epicenters of the crack epidemic were the African-American communities of the inner cities.

"If you were to close your eyes and listen to how they talk about the effect on communities, how it breaks up families and drives down property values, you would swear they were in any urban community" during crack's heyday, Cummings says.

What's different this time are the solutions that his congressional colleagues are promot-

"There seems to be more of an emphasis on shutting down these meth labs and trying to figure out ways to treat these addicts and then get them back into flow of society."

— Rep. Elijah E. Cummings,
a Maryland Democrat

ing. The first comprehensive federal anti-meth law, enacted this year, focuses on cutting off the supply of the chemical ingredients used to make the drug — not on toughening punishments for dealers or users.

"There seems to be more of an emphasis on shutting down these meth labs and trying to figure out ways to treat these addicts and then get them back into flow of society," says Cummings, a Maryland Democrat. "We don't get for crack or heroin that kind of support for prevention, treatment and rehabilitation."

Cummings is not alone in pointing out the apparent double standard, in both policy and rhetoric, that Congress is applying to the growing scourge of methamphetamine abuse. Lawmakers in both parties consistently characterize meth addicts in more sympathetic terms than they describe crack addicts, and they are showing far less enthusiasm for imprisoning users than at the height of the crack problem two decades ago.

It's not that meth is generating any less concern in affected areas today than crack did two decades ago. In both instances, members of Congress warned loudly that police in their communities were overwhelmed by a cheap, easy to obtain, highly addictive and almost untreatable menace.

Although lawmakers almost always rebut the notion, their own rhetoric suggests that race is an essential — albeit, perhaps subconscious — reason they are treating the two drug epidemics differently. Some sociologists and criminologists say the racial component is obvious.

"The difference is, meth is a white drug," says Daniel F. Wilhelm of the Vera Institute of Justice, a New York nonprofit organization that seeks to reduce racially disparate prosecutions.

"You don't see any pictures of young black men and women described as the face of meth," said Marc Mauer of the Sentencing Project, which advocates for overhauling sentencing law — a reference to the before-and-after mug shots that sheriffs' offices and lawmakers often display to highlight the physical toll of meth addiction.

Sixty percent of people sent to federal prison for meth crimes were white and just 2 percent were black in fiscal 2004, the last year with complete statistics reported by the U.S. Sentencing Commission. By contrast, 10 percent of the people convicted of crack crimes that year were white and 80 percent were black. (In both cases, Hispanics represent the bulk of the difference.)

Leaders in setting drug policy on Capitol Hill have three principal explanations for why Washington is approaching the meth problem differently from the crack problem. First, manufacturers of methamphetamines — also known as crank or speed — are uniquely dependent on a few commercially available chemical ingredients, so targeting them instead of the people involved is the more efficient way to limit the drug. Second, congressional enthusiasm for tough mandatory minimum prison sentences has waned recently among Republicans and Democrats alike. And, finally, the political benefits of waging a war on drugs has declined in recent years, especially as the nation's voters' attention has been shifted more to the war on terrorism since Sept. 11.

Still, listening to the way members of Congress talk about meth users and the images they invoke to portray the problem leaves observers such as Craig Reinarman, a sociology professor at the University of California Santa Cruz convinced that many lawmakers at least talk about drug users differently when they're "drawn from the good old boy segment of our society, the us rather than the them."

The 'Most Virulent' Drug

What hasn't changed is the level of alarm that members of Congress from both parties profess when they decide there's a drug crisis.

In 1986, they expressed anxiety over the emergence of crack, a cheap cocaine derivative that delivers a quick, powerful but relatively short-lived high when smoked. Then, too, there was a racial subtext to the rhetoric — particularly after the death of Len Bias, who had been picked first by the Boston Celtics in that year's NBA draft.

His high-profile death on the suburban University of Maryland campus exactly 20 years ago this month was initially attributed to an overdose of crack. Though an autopsy later showed cocaine rather than crack caused Bias' death, it nonetheless helped fuel a hysteria that summer about the drug, driven in part by fears that crack would jump "into the suburbs on both coasts," as a Newsweek cover story warned at the time.

In the succeeding months, lawmakers competed to describe crack in dire terms. Peter W. Rodino Jr., the New Jersey Democrat who then chaired the House Judiciary Committee, called it a "plague on our nation." Republican Sen. Paula Hawkins of Florida, warned that it turned people "into walking crime machines." That state's other senator at the time, Democrat Lawton Chiles, said it can

"make people into slaves."

Twenty years later, there is a new and bipartisan push to describe meth as an even worse drug plague. While it has been available much longer than crack, its use has grown — and spread geographically — much slower. Motorcycle gangs sold meth along the Pacific coast in the 1960s, but only in the last decade has its use spread widely throughout the West and into the Midwest. The drug's popularity has been principally in rural communities, which lack police forces and treatment centers to fight it.

The number of meth addicts more than doubled between 2002 and 2004, the year when the number of people who said they'd used meth in the previous year (1.4 million) for the first time exceeded the number who said they'd used crack (1.3 million), according to the Department of Health and Human Services. By 2005, a National Association of Counties survey of mostly rural and suburban jurisdictions found meth as the biggest drug problem for local law enforcement agencies.

Lawmakers argue that meth — which can be smoked, snorted, orally ingested or injected — is even cheaper to purchase, easier to find, more addictive and more harmful to the body than crack. Orrin G. Hatch, the No. 2 Republican on the Senate Judiciary Committee, calls it "the most virulent drug there is." Another Utah Republican, Rep. Chris Cannon, says that while "crack is associated with fast living," meth "is like crashing into a wall."

Rural and suburban lawmakers from the West and Midwest profess shock at the level of addiction that has reached into their parts of the country, which have never before been associated with widespread drug abuse.

Meth "is disturbing the quiet peaceful feelings in rural parts of the country," laments Republican Rep. Mark Kennedy of Minnesota,

who represents suburbs north and east of the Twin Cities. "Its use is now also transcending social classes and gender," says Rep. Raúl M. Grijalva, a Democrat whose Hispanic-majority district includes most of Arizona's border with Mexico. "There is no common denominator in categorizing a meth user. It could be your neighbor, a family member, a teenager, a mom."

Users as Victims

The lawmakers most vocally concerned about meth reject the notion that they're sympathetic to meth users because they tend to come from a higher-income, less urban and more white demographic than users of other narcotics.

In fact, Republican Mark Souder, who sponsored the House version of the anti-meth legislation enacted this year, says he and his northeastern Indiana constituents have less compassion for meth users than for other addicts. "When you come from areas where you see opportunities exist and you get whacked out on drugs, the sympathy is less than for in urban areas where they have no jobs or may not have fathers," he says.

But when many members talk about meth users, their sympathy often shines through.

"I view many of them as victims," says GOP Rep. Ken Calvert of Southern California.

Kennedy invoked "the tragic story of a young girl named Megan from a beautiful town" in his state when he appeared before a House Judiciary panel last fall to promote his own meth-fighting legislation. She got hooked on meth in seventh grade and turned to prostitution to pay for her habit, he said, and "In the face of so much suffering, we have an obligation to act."

Democrat Rick Larsen, who represents suburban territory north of Seattle, volunteers that he has no particular sympathy for meth

Who Gets Convicted

Those sent to federal prison for meth crimes are overwhelmingly white, those sentenced for crack cocaine offenses are disproportionately black, and an outsized share of marijuana convicts are Hispanic. The most recent data available is for the 14 weeks of fiscal 2004 after the Supreme Court, in *Blakely v. Washington,* first cast doubt on whether the mandatory minimum sentences enacted in the 1980s are binding on federal judges. But similar numbers are reflected in the data for previous years. In the weeks after the ruling, the average sentence for a crack convict was two years longer than for a meth convict.

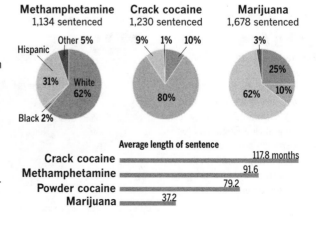

Methamphetamine
1,134 sentenced
Other 5%
Hispanic
31%
White 62%
Black 2%

Crack cocaine
1,230 sentenced
9%   1%   10%
80%

Marijuana
1,678 sentenced
3%
25%
10%
62%

Average length of sentence
Crack cocaine — 117.8 months
Methamphetamine — 91.6
Powder cocaine — 79.2
Marijuana — 37.2

users. But when talking about them, the constituent he first invokes by name is Ashley Kerwin, who became addicted at age 15 even though she is from "a good family, solid family" with a father who is "a successful commercial realtor."

And, at a Senate Finance Committee hearing in April on meth's effects on the welfare system, Republican Chairman Charles E. Grassley of Iowa and ranking Democrat Max Baucus of Montana clapped after a pair of recovering meth addicts from suburban St. Louis, Aaronette and Darren Noble, described their recovery. They applauded even though Darren, 34, had described how he served 46 months in prison for manufacturing meth. (Baucus also cooed over the "big blue eyes" of the couple's 15-month-old daughter, Summer, who sat on her mother's lap. The Nobles had only recently regained custody because she was born with meth in her system.)

In an interview later, Baucus said he was "quite certain" he would have reacted the same way to similar testimony by crack addicts. But, minutes later, he conceded that he feels more sympathy for meth users because "there are more kids involved, it's harder to solve, addictiveness is higher than crack or heroin."

The greater sympathy expressed by members of Congress, such as Baucus, is not much different than how African-American members responded to crack: Lawmakers are most concerned with problems that affect their constituents most directly. The problem is how little overlap there is between those two groups of lawmakers. Of the 138 members of the Congressional Meth Caucus, 127 are white.

Law enforcement officers on the front lines view the issue quite differently. Jim Tilley, who runs the Drug Enforcement Administration (DEA) field office in Baucus' home state and worked as an agent in New York City during the peak of the crack epidemic, rejects the idea that meth users are "just our neighbors or just people with some problems."

"The same people who use meth also sell meth, or cook it and sell it, and it ends up in our schools, your neighborhood," Tilley said. "Most people realize that, whether it's meth or crack, people have problems, but it doesn't get into our schools by itself."

Mark A.R. Kleiman, a UCLA public policy professor who studies drug addiction, says such lack of sympathy among law enforcement is typical: "If you talk to rural deputy sheriffs about meth users and urban cops about crackheads, you're going to hear exactly the same thing: These are bad scary people."

TOUGH ON CRACK

Concern about crack infused the writing of the anti-drug statutes of both 1986 and 1988 — the statutes that continue to dominate the way federal lawbooks address narcotics, and the baseline from which Congress starts in reshaping drug laws.

The 1980s laws did everything from mandating drug testing to funding domestic drug treatment and education and international interdiction. And buried in each were provisions subjecting people connected with crack to more stringent punishments than those connected to any other drug.

Without any legislative hearing and little controversy at the time, Congress in the 1986 law created the first mandatory minimum prison sentences for traffickers in different types of narcotics. For every drug except crack, the amount required to subject a person to the mandatory minimum appeared to approximate the quantity that a mid-level dealer might have in his possession for resale and was far above the amount someone would normally obtain for personal use.

For crack, however, the trigger was set much lower. And so there is a 100-to-1 differential between what subjects a powder cocaine dealer versus a crack cocaine dealer to a mandatory minimum stay in federal prison. Trafficking in 500 grams of powder — which can yield 10,000 or more "lines," or doses — draws the same five-year sentence as trafficking in five grams of crack, which yields no more than 50 "hits" off a pipe. Trafficking in 5,000 grams (or 11 pounds) of powder or 50 grams of crack triggers yields an identical a 10-year mandatory minimum.

The disparity was motivated partly by crack's perceived role at the time in spawning particularly violent crime and partly by the nature of the drug's distribution: Generally street dealers, not wholesaler "kingpins," put cocaine, baking powder and water in a microwave oven to create crack rocks for retail sale.

The 100-to-1 differential has contributed to the incarceration of huge numbers of African-Americans, who commit more than 80 percent of crack crimes. The average sentence for someone convicted of a crack crime in fiscal 2004 was 118 months, 38 months longer than for a cocaine crime and 26 months longer than for a meth crime.

The differential was determined not by any objective determinations of crack's more serious impact on society, said law professor David Alan Sklansky of the University of California at Berkeley, but instead was the result of a drive among lawmakers to come up with the toughest possible response. The differential "was driven by this hysteria about crack cocaine and by a lack of concern about who would be receiving these sentences," Sklansky said. "That lack of concern was related to the fact that everybody understood that crack dealers were black men."

That view is echoed by Eleanor Holmes Norton, Washington's non-voting Democratic delegate in the House: "Nobody in the African-American community will think it's not racially connected," she says of the differential. "It has to do with being unsympathetic towards drug dealers in the ghetto."

Those sentiments hardly surfaced in the congressional debate. In fact, such influential black lawmakers as Democrat Charles B. Rangel of New York, who at the time chaired a House Select Committee on Narcotics Abuse, initially supported the differential as a way to curb what that they viewed as a dangerous and potent drug devastating their constituents.

In 1988, Congress went on to create the

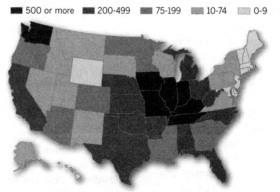

Where the Labs Are

Federal, state and local law enforcement agents seized 11,542 meth labs last year. One in five of them was in Missouri (2,151), compared with only 16 throughout New England. Most of these were small-volume "mom and pop" labs, which generally distribute the drugs they manufacture close by.

■ 500 or more ■ 200-499 ■ 75-199 ■ 10-74 □ 0-9

SOURCES: U.S. Sentencing Commission, Drug Enforcement Administration

first — and still only — mandatory minimum federal sentence for simple possession of a drug: Conviction for holding five grams of crack (three grams, if it's a second offense) draws a required five-year term. Simple possession of any amount of cocaine, by contrast, is a misdemeanor punishable by a year in jail.

> **"The same people who use meth also sell meth, or cook it and sell it, and it ends up in our schools, your neighborhood"**
>
> — Jim Tilley, Drug Enforcement Administraton

Crack possession is rarely prosecuted on its own and accounts for less than 1 percent of crack offenders sentenced in federal court. But former federal prosecutors say that having the option to prosecute such an offense can provide them leverage in obtaining plea agreements.

TARGETING THE LABS

While lawmakers of today describe meth as a scourge as severe as crack, if not worse, there has been no concerted legislative effort to create a mandatory minimum sentence for its possession. And this winter, congressional negotiators rejected an effort to make the mandatory minimum sentence for meth traffickers even stiffer than for crack traffickers — at least five years for peddling as few as three grams, and 10 years for selling as few as 30 grams.

With almost no notice, Congress, in the omnibus appropriations package of 1998, lowered the drug volume thresholds for applying the mandatory minimums to meth dealers to be the same as those for crack dealers. But the law continues to treat the two drugs unequally in this sense: Measure for measure, speed provides at least three times — and perhaps 10 times — as many "hits" as crack.

While the negotiators rebuffed proposals to make the sentences for meth traffickers the stiffest in the federal system, they did include some anti-meth measures in the extension of the 2001 law known as the Patriot Act that provides law enforcement with particularly broad powers to combat terrorism. Principally, the language focused on limiting backyard "mom and pop" meth production.

The DEA estimates the operators of such small-time meth labs produce about one-fifth of the drug distributed in the United States. But they are a disproportionately large concern to rural law enforcement agents because the highly flammable toxic stews used to make the drug can injure innocent bystanders and put police and firefighters at severe health risk.

Recipes for meth are readily available on the Internet, and the required equipment — coffee filters, a pressure cooker and gas cans — can be purchased at the hardware store for about $50. The key ingredient is pseudoephedrine, which is a principal ingredient of many cough and allergy medicines, such as Sudafed, on the shelves of pharmacies and convenience stores. The new law seeks to limit the supply of pseudoephedrine available to meth makers by limiting consumer purchases of medicines containing that chemical and requiring sales of those medicines from behind the counter as a means of curbing theft.

To address international production, the law authorizes funds to halt speed production in Mexico and requires major exporters and importers of drugs containing pseudoephedrine report their transactions. The rationale for focusing the campaign against meth on its ingredients is simple: It's much easier to enlist the corporate manufacturers and retailers of its precursor chemicals than to shut down the thousands of heroin poppy and coca fields spread all over the world.

BEYOND MANDATORY MINIMUMS

In the two decades since the crack epidemic peaked, much has changed in Congress' view of how best to fight drugs and punish those at the bottom of the supply chain.

In 1986, mandatory minimums and the entire federal sentencing guideline system were new innovations. "It was still a moment in time that sentences were still relatively low and there was a naïve belief that severe sentences

Race and Drugs In U.S History

THE FACT THAT the face of meth addiction is white is a marked departure from almost all the other drug epidemics in American history.

With the exception of the 1960s, when many hippies who dropped acid and ingested other mind-altering chemicals were white suburbanites, the drug crises that have drawn the most heated rhetoric have all had a strong racial or ethnic link, starting with the 19th century temperance movement that targeted drinking by Irish immigrants.

The surge in opium use in the 1880s was blamed on Chinese immigrants. The first federal law to restrict cocaine, enacted in 1914, was spurred by "the specter raised by the mass media of cocaine-crazed blacks committing heinous crimes," the National Institute on Drug Abuse said in a 1977 report, which cited press accounts about how the drug improved African-Americans' marksmanship and made them temporarily immune to gunshot wounds.

The federal ban on marijuana, enacted in 1937, was an outgrowth of public anger about its use among Mexican immigrants. And the selling and smoking of crack, the cocaine derivative that surged in popularity in the 1980s, was associated principally with young, inner-city black men.

could be the solution to this problem," said Douglas Berman, a criminal law professor at Ohio State University. "It's a radically different historical moment. We're at a time that we've got a greater realization that severe sentences cannot alone be the answer."

Souder says this year's anti-meth law reflects that lesson. "We're not abandoning possession, but we're being more sophisticated about the networks," he said. "Ultimately, we understand if we're going to beat meth, it's going to be international, it's got to be along the borders, it's got to be at the distribution systems. As long as they're there, you will have possession."

With the exception of child sex crimes, there is little enthusiasm in Congress for writing new mandatory minimum sentences. This winter, for example, the chairman of the House Judiciary Committee, Republican F. James Sensenbrenner Jr. of Wisconsin, stripped a collection of proposed mandatory minimum sentences from legislation aimed at curbing both street gangs and violence against judges. He did so, he said, to ease the bill's passage.

Rather than toughening punishment, Baucus says, "people are more concerned about prevention and rehabilitation and getting the bad actors." And such a sentiment comes not only from Democrats. "My focus has not been on punishing users," says Kennedy, who is the GOP candidate for the Senate in Minnesota this year. "I'm focused on those who are preying on those who may ultimately become meth users."

Souder, too, concluded that securing the new restrictions on pseudoephedrine was more important in the fight against meth than toughening the sentencing of the dealers — especially given the resistance from pharmaceutical companies and retailers to the notion of restricting access to cough syrup. In the end, Souder urged Sensenbrenner to drop the mandatory minimums in a bid to boost support for the restrictions on the medicines. "We decided moving ahead in a bipartisan way was more important than arguing over the minimums," he said. "For some Democrats, it was a non-starter. It was simply not the most important thing we wanted to do."

The broader political context of the fight against crime has also changed significantly in the last two decades. Polling during the 1986 and 1988 campaigns found that combating drugs was the nation's top priority. President Ronald Reagan and Democrats in Congress competed to come up with the most aggressive solutions.

"The Democrats were finally figuring out they couldn't afford to be portrayed as soft on crime, and Republicans figured out running on crime and justice issues served their interests very well," Berman said.

Now, crime and drugs have clearly become second-tier issues; in their nationwide polls during the past six weeks that sought to gauge which issues will matter the most to voters this fall, neither CNN, CBS, Harris, Fox or NBC even suggested those issues as an option. Instead, they have been supplanted as the principal political litmus test for judging lawmakers' toughness. "Terrorism has sort of superseded it," Hatch said. "People are more concerned

Who Takes Speed

Methamphetamine use in the United States has been going on since the 1960s on the Pacific Coast. In the past decade, use of the drug — also known as crank or speed — has grown steadily in the West and moved into the Midwest, where use has skyrocketed in rural communities.

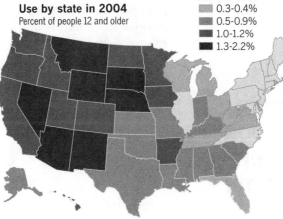

Use by state in 2004
Percent of people 12 and older

- 0.0-0.2%
- 0.3-0.4%
- 0.5-0.9%
- 1.0-1.2%
- 1.3-2.2%

Use by race in 2004
Percent of people 12 and older
(Figures in parenthesis are share of U.S. population; Hispanics may be of any race)

Native Hawaiian (0.1%)	2.2%
American Indian (0.7%)	1.7%
White (69.1%)	0.7%
Hispanic (12.5%)	0.5%
Asian (3.6%)	0.2%
Black (12.1%)	0.1%

SOURCE: Department of Health and Human Services, Census Bureau

about terrorism now."

SHIPS IN THE NIGHT

Another reason for the emerging double standard is that few lawmakers notice it. Those in Congress most engaged in the fight against meth are almost completely different from the set of lawmakers most concerned about crack. In general, members of each group focus on a drug problem that affects their own constituents and ignore the one that doesn't.

Only five of the 44 members of the Congressional Black Caucus, which has taken the unofficial lead at the Capitol on the crack issue, also belong to the Meth Caucus. Several members of the Black Caucus describe themselves as not paying any attention to the meth issue.

Cummings stands out as an exception. But his interest has little to do with parochial concerns. Instead, it has grown from his assignment as the top Democrat on a House Government Reform subcommittee assigned to oversee federal criminal justice and drug policy. Cummings has accompanied Souder, the panel's chairman, to field hearings on meth in

rural Ohio, Kentucky and Indiana.

With the area of intersection so small, few lawmakers are working to make federal policy treat crimes connected to the two drugs more consistently. That could most readily be accomplished by eliminating the unique mandatory minimum for crack possession and by increasing the quantity of crack required to draw a mandatory minimum for trafficking, as the U.S. Sentencing Commission recommended four years ago.

A bill by Roscoe G. Bartlett, a Maryland Republican, to narrow the sentencing differential has drawn just three cosponsors. There is no companion bill in the Senate, where Hatch last proposed similar legislation in 2001. Making punishments for crack crimes closer to that of other drug crimes is a matter of "decency and fairness," Hatch says, but there is minimal interest in the idea among his colleagues.

"Political realities make it too dangerous," Berman said, because advocates of lessening the crack penalties would inevitably be portrayed by their opponents as soft on crime. "Nobody sees the political benefits of this. It's very hard for anyone to see the political pros of this and extraordinarily easy to see the cons."

With the law to limit access to meth ingredients on the books, members of the House Meth Caucus and the Senate's leading voices against the drug, Democrat Dianne Feinstein of California and Republican Jim Talent of Missouri, say their top priority is providing more money for treatment.

Law-and-order Republicans' experience with meth may lead them to rethink harsh prison sentences for drug crimes across the board. Or they could buttress their contention that race plays no role in their policy making by instituting mandatory minimums that sweep in as many users and low-level dealers of meth as of crack.

Even supporters of this year's law acknowledge that, while putting cold medicines behind the counter may help curb local meth labs, it's unlikely to significantly reduce meth use.

If the focus on interdiction and treatment fails, Congress could turn to tougher criminal sentences as a way to show their constituents they are doing something about the problem. Or it might focus its ire on Mexico, the

If the focus on interdiction and treatment fails, Congress could turn to tougher criminal sentences as a way to show their constituents they are doing something about the problem. Or it might focus its ire on Mexico, the main location of the "super labs" that will supply almost all meth to the United States even if the mom and pop labs shut down.

main location of the "super labs" that will supply almost all meth to the United States even if the mom and pop labs shut down.

In the coming years, said Daniel Richman, a Fordham University law professor and former federal prosecutor, "I could imagine a legislative response to meth that wouldn't look much different than the legislative response to crack." ∎

Appendix

The Legislative Process in Brief

Note: Parliamentary terms used below are defined in the glossary.

INTRODUCTION OF BILLS

A House member (including the resident commissioner of Puerto Rico and nonvoting delegates of the District of Columbia, Guam, the Virgin Islands and American Samoa) may introduce any one of several types of bills and resolutions by handing it to the clerk of the House or placing it in a box called the hopper. A senator first gains recognition of the presiding officer to announce the introduction of a bill.

As the usual next step in either the House or Senate, the bill is numbered, referred to the appropriate committee, labeled with the sponsor's name and sent to the Government Printing Office so that copies can be made for subsequent study and action. House and Senate bills may be jointly sponsored and carry several senators' names. A bill written in the executive branch and proposed as an administration measure usually is introduced by the chairman of the congressional committee that has jurisdiction, as a courtesy to the White House.

Bills—Prefixed with HR in the House, S in the Senate, followed by a number. Used as the form for most legislation, whether general or special, public or private.

Joint Resolutions—Designated H J Res or S J Res. Subject to the same procedure as bills, with the exception of a joint resolution proposing an amendment to the Constitution. The latter must be approved by two-thirds of both houses and is then sent directly to the administrator of general services for submission to the states for ratification instead of being presented to the president for his approval.

Concurrent Resolutions—Designated H Con Res or S Con Res. Used for matters affecting the operations of both houses. These resolutions do not become law.

Resolutions—Designated H Res or S Res. Used for a matter concerning the operation of either house alone and adopted only by the chamber in which it originates.

COMMITTEE ACTION

With few exceptions, bills are referred to the appropriate standing committees. The job of referral formally is the responsibility of the Speaker of the House and the presiding officer of the Senate, but this task usually is carried out on their behalf by the parliamentarians of the House and Senate. Precedent, statute and the jurisdictional mandates of the committees as set forth in the rules of the House and Senate determine which committees receive what kinds of bills. Bills are technically considered "read for the first time" when referred to House committees.

When a bill reaches a committee it is placed on the committee's calendar. Failure of a committee to act on a bill is equivalent to killing it and most fall by the legislative roadside. The measure can be withdrawn from the committee's purview only by a discharge petition signed by a majority of the House membership on House bills, or by adoption of a special resolution in the Senate. Discharge attempts rarely succeed and the Senate procedure has not been used for decades.

The first committee action taken on a bill usually is a request for comment on it by interested agencies of the government. The committee chairman may assign the bill to a subcommittee for study and hearings, or it may be considered by the full committee. Hearings may be public, closed (executive session) or both. A subcommittee, after considering a bill, reports to the full committee its recommendations for action and any proposed amendments.

The full committee then votes on its recommendation to the House or Senate. This procedure is called "ordering a bill reported." Occasionally a committee may order a bill reported unfavorably; most of the time a report, submitted by the chairman of the committee to the House or Senate, calls for favorable action on the measure since the committee can effectively "kill" a bill by simply failing to take any action.

After the bill is reported, the committee chairman instructs the staff to prepare a written report. The report describes the purposes and scope of the bill, explains the committee revisions, notes proposed changes in existing law and, usually, includes the views of the executive branch agencies consulted. Often committee members opposing a measure issue dissenting minority statements that are included in the report.

Usually, the committee "marks up" or proposes amendments to the bill. If the amendments are substantial and the measure is complicated, the committee may order a "clean bill" introduced, which will embody the proposed amendments. The original bill then is put aside and the clean bill, with a new number, is reported to the floor.

The chamber must approve, alter or reject the committee amendments before the bill itself can be put to a vote.

FLOOR ACTION

After a bill is reported back to the house where it originated, it is placed on the calendar.

There are five legislative calendars in the House, issued in one cumulative calendar titled *Calendars of the United States House of Representatives and History of Legislation*. The House calendars are:

The Union Calendar to which are referred bills raising revenues, general appropriations bills and any measures directly or indirectly appropriating money or property. It is the Calendar of the Committee of the Whole House on the State of the Union.

The House Calendar to which are referred bills of public character not raising revenue or appropriating money.

The Corrections Calendar to which are referred bills to repeal rules and regulations deemed excessive or unnecessary when the Corrections Calendar is called the second and fourth Tuesday of each month. (Instituted in the 104th Congress to replace the seldom-used Consent Calendar.) A three-fifths majority is required for passage.

The Private Calendar to which are referred bills for relief in the nature of claims against the United States or private immigration bills that are passed without debate when the Private Calendar is called the first and third Tuesdays of each month.

The Discharge Calendar to which are referred motions to discharge committees when the necessary signatures are signed to a discharge petition.

There is only one legislative calendar in the Senate and one "executive calendar" for treaties and nominations submitted to the Senate.

Debate. A bill is brought to debate by varying procedures. In the Senate the majority leader, in consultation with the minority leader and others, schedules the bills that will be taken up for debate. If it is urgent or important it can be taken up in the Senate either by unanimous consent or by a majority vote.

In the House, precedence is granted if a special rule is obtained from the Rules Committee. A request for a special rule usually is made by the chairman of the committee that favorably reported the bill. The request is considered by the Rules Committee in the same fashion that other committees consider legislative measures. The committee proposes a resolution providing for immediate consideration of the bill. The Rules Committee reports the resolution to the House where it is debated and voted on in the same fashion as regular bills.

This graphic shows the most typical way in which proposed legislation is enacted into law. There are more complicated, as well as simpler, routes, and most bills never become law. The process is illustrated with two hypothetical bills, House bill No. 1 (HR 1) and

Senate bill No. 2 (S 2). Bills must be passed by both houses in identical form before they can be sent to the president. The path of HR 1 is traced by a gray line, that of S 2 by a black line. In practice, most bills begin as similar proposals in both houses.

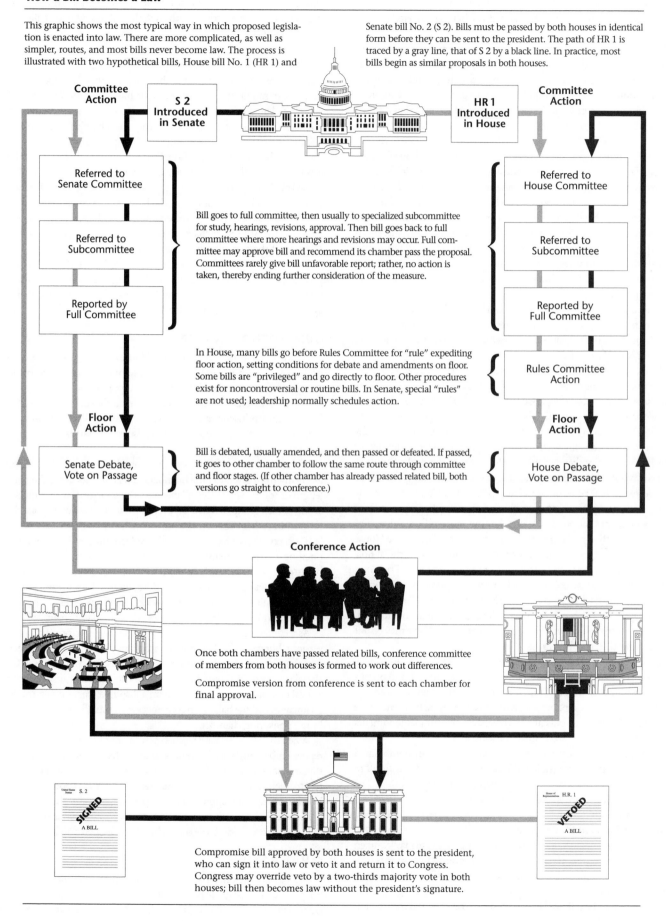

Committee Action

S 2 Introduced in Senate

HR 1 Introduced in House

Committee Action

Referred to Senate Committee

Referred to Subcommittee

Reported by Full Committee

Referred to House Committee

Referred to Subcommittee

Reported by Full Committee

Bill goes to full committee, then usually to specialized subcommittee for study, hearings, revisions, approval. Then bill goes back to full committee where more hearings and revisions may occur. Full committee may approve bill and recommend its chamber pass the proposal. Committees rarely give bill unfavorable report; rather, no action is taken, thereby ending further consideration of the measure.

In House, many bills go before Rules Committee for "rule" expediting floor action, setting conditions for debate and amendments on floor. Some bills are "privileged" and go directly to floor. Other procedures exist for noncontroversial or routine bills. In Senate, special "rules" are not used; leadership normally schedules action.

Rules Committee Action

Floor Action

Floor Action

Senate Debate, Vote on Passage

House Debate, Vote on Passage

Bill is debated, usually amended, and then passed or defeated. If passed, it goes to other chamber to follow the same route through committee and floor stages. (If other chamber has already passed related bill, both versions go straight to conference.)

Conference Action

Once both chambers have passed related bills, conference committee of members from both houses is formed to work out differences.

Compromise version from conference is sent to each chamber for final approval.

United States S. 2
SIGNED
A BILL

House of Representatives H.R. 1
VETOED
A BILL

Compromise bill approved by both houses is sent to the president, who can sign it into law or veto it and return it to Congress. Congress may override veto by a two-thirds majority vote in both houses; bill then becomes law without the president's signature.

APPENDIX

The resolutions providing special rules are important because they specify how long the bill may be debated and whether it may be amended from the floor. If floor amendments are banned, the bill is considered under a "closed rule."

When a bill is debated under an "open rule," amendments may be offered from the floor. Committee amendments always are taken up first but may be changed, as may all amendments up to the second degree; that is, an amendment to an amendment to an amendment is not in order.

Duration of debate in the House depends on whether the bill is under discussion by the House proper or before the House when it is sitting as the Committee of the Whole House on the State of the Union. In the former, the amount of time for debate is allocated with an hour for each member if the measure is under consideration without a rule. In the Committee of the Whole the amount of time agreed on for general debate is equally divided between proponents and opponents. At the end of general discussion, the bill is often read section by section for amendment. Debate on an amendment is limited to five minutes for each side; this is called the "five-minute rule." In practice, amendments regularly are debated more than ten minutes, with members gaining the floor by offering pro forma amendments or obtaining unanimous consent to speak longer than five minutes.

Senate debate usually is unlimited. It can be halted only by unanimous consent or by "cloture," which requires a three-fifths majority of the entire Senate except for proposed changes in the Senate rules. The latter requires a two-thirds vote.

The House considers almost all important bills within a parliamentary framework known as the Committee of the Whole. It is not a committee as the word usually is understood; it is the full House meeting under another name for the purpose of speeding action on legislation. Technically, the House sits as the Committee of the Whole when it considers any tax measure or bill dealing with public appropriations. Upon adoption of a special rule, the Speaker declares the House resolved into the Committee of the Whole and appoints a member of the majority party to serve as the chairman. The rules of the House permit the Committee of the Whole to meet when a quorum of 100 members is present on the floor and to amend and act on bills. When the Committee of the Whole has acted, it "rises," the Speaker returns as the presiding officer of the House and the member appointed chairman of the Committee of the Whole reports the action of the committee and its recommendations. The Committee of the Whole cannot pass a bill; instead it reports the measure to the full House with whatever changes it has approved. The full House then may pass or reject the bill — or, on occasion, recommit the bill to committee. Amendments adopted in the Committee of the Whole may be put to a second vote in the full House.

Votes. Voting on bills may occur repeatedly before they are finally approved or rejected. The House votes on the rule for the bill and on various amendments to the bill. Voting on amendments often is a more illuminating test of a bill's support than is the final tally. Sometimes members approve final passage of bills after vigorously supporting amendments that, if adopted, would have scuttled the legislation.

The Senate has three different methods of voting: an untabulated voice vote, a standing vote (called a division) and a recorded roll call to which members answer "yea" or "nay" when their names are called. The House also employs voice and standing votes, but since January 1973 yeas and nays have been recorded by an electronic voting device, eliminating the need for time-consuming roll calls.

After amendments to a bill have been voted upon, a vote may be taken on a motion to recommit the bill to committee. If carried, this vote is usually a death blow to the bill. If the motion is unsuccessful, the bill then is "read for the third time." After the third reading a vote on passage is taken. The final vote may be followed by a motion to reconsider, and this motion may be followed by a move to lay the motion on the table. Usually, those voting for the bill's passage vote for the tabling motion, thus safeguarding the final passage action. With that, the bill has been formally passed by the chamber.

ACTION IN SECOND CHAMBER

After a bill is passed it is sent to the other chamber. This body may then take one of several steps. It may pass the bill as is — accepting the other chamber's language. It may send the bill to committee for scrutiny or alteration, or reject the entire bill, advising the other chamber of its actions. Or it simply may ignore the bill submitted while it continues work on its own version of the proposed legislation. Frequently, one chamber may approve a version of a bill that is greatly at variance with the version already passed by the other chamber, and then substitute its contents for the language of the other, retaining only the latter's bill number.

Often the second chamber makes only minor changes. If these are readily agreed to by the other chamber, the bill then is routed to the president. However, if the opposite chamber significantly alters the bill submitted to it, the measure usually is "sent to conference." The chamber that has possession of the "papers" (engrossed bill, engrossed amendments, messages of transmittal) requests a conference and the other chamber may agree to it. If the second chamber does not agree, the bill dies.

CONFERENCE ACTION

A conference works out conflicting House and Senate versions of a legislative bill. The conferees usually are senior members from the committees that managed the legislation who are appointed by the presiding officers of the two houses. Under this arrangement the conferees of one house have the duty of trying to maintain their chamber's position in the face of amending actions by the conferees (also referred to as "managers") of the other house.

The number of conferees from each chamber may vary, the range usually being from seven to nine members in each group, depending on the length or complexity of the bill involved. But a majority vote controls the action of each group so that a large representation does not give one chamber a voting advantage over the other chamber's conferees.

Theoretically, conferees are not allowed to write new legislation in reconciling the two versions before them, but this curb sometimes is bypassed. Many bills have been put into acceptable compromise form only after new language was provided by the conferees. Frequently the ironing out of difficulties takes days or even weeks. Conferences on involved, complex and controversial bills sometimes are particularly drawn out.

As a conference proceeds, conferees reconcile differences between the versions, but generally they grant concessions only insofar as they remain sure that the chamber they represent will accept the compromises. Occasionally, uncertainty over how either house will react, or the positive refusal of a chamber to back down on a disputed amendment, results in an impasse, and the bills die in conference even though each was approved by its sponsoring chamber.

When the conferees have reached agreement, they prepare a conference report embodying their recommendations (compromises) and a joint explanatory statement. The report, in document form, must be submitted to each house. The conference report must be approved by each house. Consequently, approval of the report is approval of the compromise bill. In the order of voting on conference reports, the chamber that asked for a conference yields to the other chamber the opportunity to vote first.

FINAL ACTION

After a bill has been passed by both the House and Senate in identical form, all of the original papers are sent to the enrolling clerk of the chamber in which the bill originated. The clerk then prepares an enrolled bill, which is printed on parchment paper.

When this bill has been certified as correct by the secretary of the Senate or the clerk of the House, depending on which chamber originated the bill, it is signed first (no matter whether it originated in the Senate or House) by the Speaker of the House and then by the president of the Senate. It is next sent to the White House to await action.

If the president approves the bill, he signs it, dates it and usually writes the word "approved" on the document. If the president does not sign it within 10 days (Sundays excepted) and Congress is in session, the bill becomes law without his signature.

If Congress adjourns *sine die* at the end of the second session the president can pocket veto a bill and it dies without Congress having the opportunity to override.

A president vetoes a bill by refusing to sign it and, before the ten-day period expires, returning it to Congress with a message stating his reasons.

The message is sent to the chamber that originated the bill. If no action is taken on the message, the bill dies. Congress, however, can attempt to override the president's veto and enact the bill, "the objections of the president to the contrary notwithstanding." Overriding a veto requires a two-thirds vote of those present in each chamber, who must number a quorum and vote by roll call.

If the president's veto is overridden by a two-thirds vote in both houses, the bill becomes law. Otherwise it is dead.

When bills are passed finally and signed, or passed over a veto, they are given law numbers in numerical order as they become law. There are two series of numbers, one for public and one for private laws, starting at the number "1" for each two-year term of Congress. They are then identified by law number and by Congress — for example, Private Law 10, 105th Congress; Public Law 33, 106th Congress (or PL 106-33).

The Budget Process in Brief

Through the budget process, the president and Congress decide how much to spend and tax during the upcoming fiscal year. More specifically, they decide how much to spend on each activity, ensure that the government spends no more than that and spends it only for that activity and report on that spending at the end of each budget cycle.

THE PRESIDENT'S BUDGET

The law requires that, by the first Monday in February, the president submit to Congress his proposed federal budget for the next fiscal year, which begins on October 1. To accomplish this the president establishes general budget and fiscal policy guidelines. Based on these guidelines, executive branch agencies make requests for funds and submit them to the White House's Office of Management and Budget (OMB) nearly a year before the start of a new fiscal year. The OMB, receiving direction from the president and administration officials, reviews the agencies' requests and develops a detailed budget by December. From December to January the OMB prepares the budget documents, so that the president can deliver it to Congress in February.

The president's budget is the executive branch's plan for the next year — but it is just a proposal. After receiving it, Congress has its own budget process to follow from February to October. Only after Congress passes the required spending bills — and the president signs them — has the government created its actual budget.

ACTION IN CONGRESS

Congress first must pass a "budget resolution" — a framework within which the members of Congress will make their decisions about spending and taxes. It includes targets for total spending, total revenues and the deficit, and allocations within the spending target for the two types of spending — discretionary and mandatory.

Discretionary spending, which currently accounts for about 33 percent of all federal spending, is what the president and Congress must decide to spend for the next year through the thirteen annual appropriations bills. It includes money for such activities as the FBI and the Coast Guard, for housing and education, for NASA and highway and bridge construction and for defense and foreign aid.

Mandatory spending, which currently accounts for 67 percent of all spending, is authorized by laws that have already been passed. It includes entitlement spending — such as for Social Security, Medicare, veterans' benefits and food stamps — through which individuals receive benefits because they are eligible based on their age, income or other criteria. It also includes interest on the national debt, which the government pays to individuals and institutions that hold Treasury bonds and other government securities. The only way the president and Congress can change the spending on entitlement and other mandatory programs is if they change the laws that authorized the programs.

Currently, the law requires that legislation that would raise mandatory spending or lower revenues — compared to existing law — be offset by spending cuts or revenue increases. This requirement, called "pay-as-you-go" is designed to prevent new legislation from increasing the deficit.

Once Congress passes the budget resolution, legislators turn their attention to passing the 13 annual appropriations bills and, if they choose, "authorizing" bills to change the laws governing mandatory spending and revenues.

Congress begins by examining the president's budget in detail. Scores of committees and subcommittees hold hearings on proposals under their jurisdiction. The House and Senate Armed Services Authorizing Committees, and the Defense and Military Construction Subcommittees of the Appropriations Committees, for instance, hold hearings on the president's defense budget. The White House budget director, cabinet officers and other administration officials work with Congress as it accepts some of the president's proposals, rejects others and changes still others. Congress can change funding levels, eliminate programs or add programs not requested by the president. It can add or eliminate taxes and other sources of revenue, or make other changes that affect the amount of revenue collected. Congressional rules require that these committees and subcommittees take actions that reflect the congressional budget resolution.

The president's budget, the budget resolution and the appropriations or authorizing bills measure spending in two ways — "budget authority" and "outlays." Budget authority is what the law authorizes the federal government to spend for certain programs, projects or activities. What the government actually spends in a particular year, however, is an outlay. For example, when the government decides to build a space exploration system, the president and Congress may agree to appropriate $1 billion in budget authority. But the space system may take ten years to build. Thus, the government may spend $100 million in outlays in the first year to begin construction and the remaining $900 million during the next nine years as the construction continues.

Congress must provide budget authority before the federal agencies can obligate the government to make outlays. When Congress fails to complete action on one or more of the regular annual appropriations bills before the fiscal year begins on October 1, budget authority may be made on a temporary basis through continuing resolutions. Continuing resolutions make budget authority available for limited periods of time, generally at rates related through some formula to the rate provided in the previous year's appropriation.

MONITORING THE BUDGET

Once Congress passes and the president signs the federal appropriations bills or authorizing laws for the fiscal year, the government monitors the budget through (1) agency program managers and budget officials, including the Inspectors General, who report only to the agency head; (2) the Office of Management and Budget; (3) congressional committees; and (4) the Government Accountability Office, an auditing arm of Congress.

This oversight is designed to (1) ensure that agencies comply with legal limits on spending and that agencies use budget authority only for the purposes intended; (2) see that programs are operating consistently with legal requirements and existing policy; and (3) ensure that programs are well managed and achieving the intended results.

The president may withhold appropriated amounts from obligation only under certain limited circumstances — to provide for contingencies, to achieve savings made possible through changes in requirements or greater efficiency of operations or as otherwise provided by law. The Impoundment Control Act of 1974 specifies the procedures that must be followed if funds are withheld. Congress can also cancel previous authorized budget authority by passing a rescissions bill — but it also must be signed by the president.

Glossary of Congressional Terms

AA—(See Administrative Assistant.)

Absence of a Quorum—Absence of the required number of members to conduct business in a house or a committee. When a quorum call or roll-call vote in a house establishes that a quorum is not present, no debate or other business is permitted except a motion to adjourn or motions to request or compel the attendance of absent members, if necessary by arresting them.

Absolute Majority—A vote requiring approval by a majority of all members of a house rather than a majority of members present and voting. Also referred to as constitutional majority.

Account—Organizational units used in the federal budget primarily for recording spending and revenue transactions.

Act—(1) A bill passed in identical form by both houses of Congress and signed into law by the president or enacted over the president's veto. A bill also becomes an act without the president's signature if he does not return it to Congress within ten days (Sundays excepted) and if Congress has not adjourned within that period. (2) Also, the technical term for a bill passed by at least one house and engrossed.

Ad Hoc Select Committee—A temporary committee formed for a special purpose or to deal with a specific subject. Conference committees are ad hoc joint committees. A House rule adopted in 1975 authorizes the Speaker to refer measures to special ad hoc committees, appointed by the Speaker with the approval of the House.

Adjourn—A motion to adjourn is a formal motion to end a day's session or meeting of a house or a committee. A motion to adjourn usually has no conditions attached to it, but it sometimes may specify the day or time for reconvening or make reconvening subject to the call of the chamber's presiding officer or the committee's chairman. In both houses, a motion to adjourn is of the highest privilege, takes precedence over all other motions, is not debatable and must be put to an immediate vote. Adjournment of a house ends its legislative day. For this reason, the House or Senate sometimes adjourns for only one minute, or some other very brief period of time, during the course of a day's session. The House does not permit a motion to adjourn after it has resolved into Committee of the Whole or when the previous question has been ordered on a measure to final passage without an intervening motion.

Adjourn for More Than Three Days—Under Article I, Section 5 of the Constitution, neither house may adjourn for more than three days without the approval of the other. The necessary approval is given in a concurrent resolution to which both houses have agreed.

Adjournment *Sine Die*—Final adjournment of an annual or two-year session of Congress; literally, adjournment without a day. The two houses must agree to a privileged concurrent resolution for such an adjournment. A sine die adjournment precludes Congress from meeting again until the next constitutionally fixed date of a session (Jan. 3 of the following year) unless Congress determines otherwise by law or the president calls it into special session. Article II, Section 3 of the Constitution authorizes the president to adjourn both houses until such time as the president thinks proper when the two houses cannot agree to a time of adjournment. No president, however, has ever exercised this authority.

Adjournment to a Day (and Time) Certain—An adjournment that fixes the next date and time of meeting for one or both houses. It does not end an annual session of Congress.

Administration Bill—A bill drafted in the executive office of the president or in an executive department or agency to implement part of the president's program. An administration bill is introduced in Congress by a member who supports it or as a courtesy to the administration.

Administrative Assistant (AA)—The title usually given to a member's chief aide, political advisor and head of office staff. The administrative assistant often represents the member at meetings with visitors or officials when the member is unable (or unwilling) to attend.

Adoption—The usual parliamentary term for approval of a conference report. It is also commonly applied to amendments.

Advance Appropriation—In an appropriation act for a particular fiscal year, an appropriation that does not become available for spending or obligation until a subsequent fiscal year. The amount of the advance appropriation is counted as part of the budget for the fiscal year in which it becomes available for obligation.

Advance Funding—A mechanism whereby statutory language may allow budget authority for a fiscal year to be increased, and obligations to be incurred, with an offsetting decrease in the budget authority available in the succeeding fiscal year. If not used, the budget authority remains available for obligation in the succeeding fiscal year. Advance funding is sometimes used to provide contingency funding of a few benefit programs.

Adverse Report—A committee report recommending against approval of a measure or some other matter. Committees usually pigeonhole measures they oppose instead of reporting them adversely, but they may be required to report them by a statutory rule or an instruction from their parent body.

Advice and Consent—The Senate's constitutional role in consenting to or rejecting the president's nominations to executive branch and judicial offices and treaties with other nations. Confirmation of nominees requires a simple majority vote of senators present and voting. Treaties must be approved by a two-thirds majority of those present and voting.

Aisle—The center aisle of each chamber. When facing the presiding officer, Republicans usually sit to the right of the aisle, Democrats to the left. When members speak of "my side of the aisle" or "this side," they are referring to their party.

Amendment—A formal proposal to alter the text of a bill, resolution, amendment, motion, treaty or some other text. Technically, it is a motion. An amendment may strike out (eliminate) part of a text, insert new text or strike out and insert — that is, replace all or part of the text with new text. The texts of amendments considered on the floor are printed in full in the Congressional Record.

Amendment in the Nature of a Substitute—Usually, an amendment to replace the entire text of a measure. It strikes out everything after the enacting clause and inserts a version that may be somewhat, substantially or entirely different. When a committee adopts extensive amendments to a measure, it often incorporates them into such an amendment. Occasionally, the term is applied to an amendment that replaces a major portion of a measure's text.

Amendment Tree—A diagram showing the number and types of amendments that the rules and practices of a house permit to be offered to a measure before any of the amendments is voted on. It shows the relationship of one amendment to the others, and it may also indicate the degree of each amendment, whether it is a perfecting or substitute amendment, the order in which amendments may be offered and the order in which they are put to a vote. The same type of diagram can be used to display an actual amendment situation.

Annual Authorization—Legislation that authorizes appropriations for a single fiscal year and usually for a specific amount. Under the rules of the authorization-appropriation process, an annually authorized agency or program must be reauthorized each year if it is to receive appropriations for that year. Sometimes Congress fails to enact the reauthorization but nevertheless provides appropriations to continue the program, circumventing the rules by one means or another.

Appeal—A member's formal challenge of a ruling or decision by the presiding officer. On appeal, a house or a committee may overturn the ruling by majority vote. The right of appeal ensures the body against arbitrary control by the chair. Appeals are rarely made in the House and are even more rarely successful. Rulings are more frequently appealed in the Senate and occasionally overturned, in part because its presiding officer is not the majority party's leader, as in the House.

Apportionment—The action, after each decennial census, of allocating the number of members in the House of Representatives to each state. By law, the total number of House members (not counting delegates and a resident commissioner) is fixed at 435. The number allotted to each state is based approximately on its proportion of the nation's total population. Because the Constitution guarantees each state one representative no matter how small its population, exact proportional distribution is virtually impossible. The mathematical formula currently used to determine the apportionment is called the Method of Equal Proportions. (See Method of Equal Proportions.)

Appropriated Entitlement—An entitlement program, such as veterans' pensions, that is funded through annual appropriations rather than by a permanent appropriation. Because such an entitlement law requires the government to provide eligible recipients the benefits to which they are entitled, whatever the cost, Congress must appropriate the necessary funds.

Appropriation—(1) Legislative language that permits a federal agency to incur obligations and make payments from the Treasury for specified purposes, usually during a specified period of time. (2) The specific amount of money made available by such language. The Constitution prohibits payments from the Treasury except "in Consequence of Appropriations made by Law." With some exceptions, the rules of both houses forbid consideration of appropriations for purposes that are unauthorized in law or of appropriation amounts larger than those authorized in law. The House of Representatives claims the exclusive right to originate appropriation bills — a claim the Senate denies in theory but accepts in practice.

At-Large—Elected by and representing an entire state instead of a district within a state. The term usually refers to a representative rather than to a senator. (See Apportionment; Congressional District; Redistricting.)

August Adjournment—A congressional adjournment during the month of August in odd-numbered years, required by the Legislative Reorganization Act of 1970. The law instructs the two houses to adjourn for a period of at least thirty days before the second day after Labor Day, unless Congress provides otherwise or if, on July 31, a state of war exists by congressional declaration.

Authorization—(1) A statutory provision that establishes or continues a federal agency, activity or program for a fixed or indefinite period of time. It may also establish policies and restrictions and deal with organizational and administrative matters. (2) A statutory provision, as described in (1), may also, explicitly or implicitly, authorize congressional action to provide appropriations for an agency, activity or program. The

appropriations may be authorized for one year, several years or an indefinite period of time, and the authorization may be for a specific amount of money or an indefinite amount ("such sums as may be necessary"). Authorizations of specific amounts are construed as ceilings on the amounts that subsequently may be appropriated in an appropriation bill, but not as minimums; either house may appropriate lesser amounts or nothing at all.

Authorization-Appropriation Process—The two-stage procedural system that the rules of each house require for establishing and funding federal agencies and programs: first, enactment of authorizing legislation that creates or continues an agency or program; second, enactment of appropriations legislation that provides funds for the authorized agency or program.

Automatic Roll Call—Under a House rule, the automatic ordering of the yeas and nays when a quorum is not present on a voice or division vote and a member objects to the vote on that ground. It is not permitted in the Committee of the Whole.

Backdoor Spending Authority—Authority to incur obligations that evades the normal congressional appropriations process because it is provided in legislation other than appropriation acts. The most common forms are borrowing authority, contract authority and entitlement authority.

Baseline—A projection of the levels of federal spending, revenues and the resulting budgetary surpluses or deficits for the upcoming and subsequent fiscal years, taking into account laws enacted to date and assuming no new policy decisions. It provides a benchmark for measuring the budgetary effects of proposed changes in federal revenues or spending, assuming certain economic conditions.

Bells—A system of electric signals and lights that informs members of activities in each chamber. The type of activity taking place is indicated by the number of signals and the interval between them. When the signals are sounded, a corresponding number of lights are lit around the perimeter of many clocks in House or Senate offices.

Bicameral—Consisting of two houses or chambers. Congress is a bicameral legislature whose two houses have an equal role in enacting legislation. In most other national bicameral legislatures, one house is significantly more powerful than the other.

Bigger Bite Amendment—An amendment that substantively changes a portion of a text including language that had previously been amended. Normally, language that has been amended may not be amended again. However, a part of a sentence that has been changed by amendment, for example, may be changed again by an amendment that amends a "bigger bite" of the text — that is, by an amendment that also substantively changes the unamended parts of the sentence or the entire section or title in which the previously amended language appears. The biggest possible bite is an amendment in the nature of a substitute that amends the entire text of a measure. Once adopted, therefore, such an amendment ends the amending process.

Bill—The term for the chief vehicle Congress uses for enacting laws. Bills that originate in the House of Representatives are designated as HR, those in the Senate as S, followed by a number assigned in the order in which they are introduced during a two-year Congress. A bill becomes a law if passed in identical language by both houses and signed by the president, or passed over the president's veto, or if the president fails to sign it within ten days after receiving it while Congress is in session.

Bill of Attainder—An act of a legislature finding a person guilty of treason or a felony. The Constitution prohibits the passage of such a bill by the U.S. Congress or any state legislature.

Bills and Resolutions Introduced—Members formally present measures to their respective houses by delivering them to a clerk in the chamber when their house is in session. Both houses permit any number of members to join in introducing a bill or resolution. The first member listed on the measure is the sponsor; the other members listed are its cosponsors.

Bills and Resolutions Referred—After a bill or resolution is introduced, it is normally sent to one or more committees that have jurisdiction over its subject, as defined by House and Senate rules and precedents. A Senate measure is usually referred to the committee with jurisdiction over the predominant subject of its text, but it may be sent to two or more committees by unanimous consent or on a motion offered jointly by the majority and minority leaders. In the House, a rule requires the Speaker to refer a measure to the committee that has primary jurisdiction. The Speaker is also authorized to refer measures sequentially to additional committees and to impose time limits on such referrals.

Bipartisan Committee—A committee with an equal number of members from each political party. The House Committee on Standards of Official Conduct and the Senate Select Committee on Ethics are the only bipartisan, permanent full committees.

Borrowing Authority—Statutory authority permitting a federal agency, such as the Export-Import Bank, to borrow money from the public or the Treasury to finance its operations. It is a form of backdoor spending. To bring such spending under the control of the congressional appropriation process, the Congressional Budget Act requires that new borrowing authority shall be effective only to the extent and in such amounts as are provided in appropriations acts.

Budget—A detailed statement of actual or anticipated revenues and expenditures during an accounting period. For the national government, the period is the federal fiscal year (Oct. 1 to Sept. 30). The budget usually refers to the president's budget submission to Congress early each calendar year. The president's budget estimates federal government income and spending for the upcoming fiscal year and contains detailed recommendations for appropriation, revenue and other legislation. Congress is not required to accept or even vote directly on the president's proposals, and it often revises the president's budget extensively. (See Fiscal Year.)

Budget Act—Common name for the Congressional Budget and Impoundment Control Act of 1974, which established the basic procedures of the current congressional budget process; created the House and Senate Budget Committees; and enacted procedures for reconciliation, deferrals and rescissions. (See Budget Process; Deferral; Impoundment; Reconciliation; Rescission. See also Gramm-Rudman-Hollings Act of 1985.)

Budget and Accounting Act of 1921—The law that, for the first time, authorized the president to submit to Congress an annual budget for the entire federal government. Before passage of the act, most federal agencies sent their budget requests to the appropriate congressional committees without review by the president.

Budget Authority—Generally, the amount of money that may be spent or obligated by a government agency or for a government program or activity. Technically, it is statutory authority to enter into obligations that normally result in outlays. The main forms of budget authority are appropriations, borrowing authority and contract authority. It also includes authority to obligate and expend the proceeds of offsetting receipts and collections. Congress may make budget authority available for only one year, several years or an indefinite period, and it may specify definite or indefinite amounts.

Budget Enforcement Act of 1990—An act that revised the sequestration process established by the Gramm-Rudman-Hollings Act of 1985, replaced the earlier act's fixed deficit targets with adjustable ones, established discretionary spending limits for fiscal years 1991 through 1995, instituted pay-as-you-go rules to enforce deficit neutrality on revenue and mandatory spending legislation and reformed the budget and accounting rules for federal credit activities. Unlike the Gramm-Rudman-Hollings Act, the 1990 act emphasized restraints on legislated changes in taxes and spending instead of fixed deficit limits.

Budget Enforcement Act of 1997—An act that revised and updated the provisions of the Budget Enforcement Act of 1990, including by extending the discretionary spending caps and pay-as-you-go rules through 2002.

Budget Process—(1) In Congress, the procedural system it uses (a) to approve an annual concurrent resolution on the budget that sets goals for aggregate and functional categories of federal expenditures, revenues and the surplus or deficit for an upcoming fiscal year; and (b) to implement those goals in spending, revenue and, if necessary, reconciliation and debt-limit legislation. (2) In the executive branch, the process of formulating the president's annual budget, submitting it to Congress, defending it before congressional committees, implementing subsequent budget-related legislation, impounding or sequestering expenditures as permitted by law, auditing and evaluating programs and compiling final budget data. The Budget and Accounting Act of 1921 and the Congressional Budget and Impoundment Control Act of 1974 established the basic elements of the current budget process. Major revisions were enacted in the Gramm-Rudman-Hollings Act of 1985 and the Budget Enforcement Act of 1990.

Budget Resolution—A concurrent resolution in which Congress establishes or revises its version of the federal budget's broad financial features for the upcoming fiscal year and several additional fiscal years. Like other concurrent resolutions, it does not have the force of law, but it provides the framework within which Congress subsequently considers revenue, spending and other budget-implementing legislation. The framework consists of two basic elements: (1) aggregate budget amounts (total revenues, new budget authority, outlays, loan obligations and loan guarantee commitments, deficit or surplus and debt limit); and (2) subdivisions of the relevant aggregate amounts among the functional categories of the budget. Although it does not allocate funds to specific programs or accounts, the budget committees' reports accompanying the resolution often discuss the major program assumptions underlying its functional amounts. Unlike those amounts, however, the assumptions are not binding on Congress.

By Request—A designation indicating that a member has introduced a measure on behalf of the president, an executive agency or a private individual or organization. Members often introduce such measures as a courtesy because neither the president nor any person other than a member of Congress can do so. The term, which appears next to the sponsor's name, implies that the member who introduced the measure does not necessarily endorse it. A House rule dealing with by-request introductions dates from 1888, but the practice goes back to the earliest history of Congress.

Byrd Rule—The popular name of an amendment to the Congressional Budget Act that bars the inclusion of extraneous matter in any reconciliation legislation considered in the Senate. The ban is enforced by points of order that the presiding officer sustains. The provision defines different categories of extraneous matter, but it also permits certain exceptions. Its chief sponsor was Sen. Robert C. Byrd, D-W.Va.

Calendar—A list of measures or other matters (most of them favorably reported by committees) that are eligible for floor consideration. The House has five calendars; the Senate has two. A place on a calendar does not guarantee consideration. Each house decides which measures and matters it will take up, when and in what order, in accordance with its rules and practices.

Calendar Wednesday—A House procedure that on Wednesdays permits its committees to bring up for floor consideration nonprivileged measures they have reported. The procedure is so cumbersome and susceptible to dilatory tactics, however, that it is rarely used.

Call Up—To bring a measure or report to the floor for immediate consideration.

Casework—Assistance to constituents who seek assistance in dealing with federal and local government agencies. Constituent service is a high priority in most members' offices.

Caucus—(1) A common term for the official organization of each party in each house. (2) The official title of the organization of House Democrats. House and Senate Republicans and Senate Democrats call their organizations "conferences." (3) A term for an informal group of members who share legislative interests, such as the Black Caucus, Hispanic Caucus and Children's Caucus.

Censure—The strongest formal condemnation of a member for misconduct short of expulsion. A house usually adopts a resolution of censure to express its condemnation, after which the presiding officer reads its rebuke aloud to the member in the presence of his or her colleagues.

Chairman—The presiding officer of a committee, a subcommittee or a task force. At meetings, the chairman preserves order, enforces the rules, recognizes members to speak or offer motions and puts questions to a vote. The chairman of a committee or subcommittee usually appoints its staff and sets its agenda, subject to the panel's veto.

Chamber—The Capitol room in which a house of Congress normally holds its sessions. The chamber of the House of Representatives, officially called the Hall of the House, is considerably larger than that of the Senate because it must accommodate 435 representatives, four delegates and one resident commissioner. Unlike the Senate chamber, members have no desks or assigned seats. In both chambers, the floor slopes downward to the well in front of the presiding officer's raised desk. A chamber is often referred to as "the floor," as when members are said to be on or going to the floor. Those expressions usually imply that the member's house is in session.

Christmas Tree Bill—Jargon for a bill adorned with amendments, many of them unrelated to the bill's subject, that provide benefits for interest groups, specific states, congressional districts, companies and individuals.

Classes of Senators—A class consists of the thirty-three or thirty-four senators elected to a six-year term in the same general election. Because the terms of approximately one-third of the senators expire every two years, there are three classes.

Clean Bill—After a House committee extensively amends a bill, it often assembles its amendments and what is left of the bill into a new measure that one or more of its members introduces as a "clean bill." The revised measure is assigned a new number.

Clerk of the House—An officer of the House of Representatives responsible principally for administrative support of the legislative process in the House. The clerk is invariably the candidate of the majority party.

Cloakrooms—Two rooms with access to the rear of each chamber's floor, one for each party's members, where members may confer privately, sit quietly or have a snack. The presiding officer sometimes urges members who are conversing too loudly on the floor to retire to their cloakrooms.

Closed Hearing—A hearing closed to the public and the media. A House committee may close a hearing only if it determines that disclosure of the testimony to be taken would endanger national security, violate any law or tend to defame, degrade or incriminate any person. The Senate has a similar rule. Both houses require roll-call votes in open session to close a hearing.

Closed Rule—A special rule reported from the House Rules Committee that prohibits amendments to a measure or that only permits amendments offered by the reporting committee.

Cloture—A Senate procedure that limits further consideration of a pending proposal to thirty hours in order to end a filibuster. Sixteen senators must first sign and submit a cloture motion to the presiding officer. One hour after the Senate meets on the second calendar day thereafter, the chair puts the motion to a yea-and-nay vote following a live quorum call. If three-fifths of all senators (sixty if there are no vacancies) vote for the motion, the Senate must take final action on the cloture proposal by the end of the thirty hours of consideration and may consider no other business until it takes that action. Cloture on a proposal to amend the Senate's standing rules requires approval by two-thirds of the senators present and voting.

Code of Official Conduct—A House rule that bans certain actions by House members, officers and employees; requires them to conduct themselves in ways that "reflect creditably" on the House; and orders them to adhere to the spirit and the letter of House rules and those of its committees. The code's provisions govern the receipt of outside compensation, gifts and honoraria and the use of campaign funds; prohibit members from using their clerk-hire allowance to pay anyone who does not perform duties commensurate with that pay; forbids discrimination in members' hiring or treatment of employees on the grounds of race, color, religion, sex, handicap, age or national origin; orders members convicted of a crime who might be punished by imprisonment of two or more years not to participate in committee business or vote on the floor until exonerated or reelected; and restricts employees' contact with federal agencies on matters in which they have a significant financial interest. The Senate's rules contain some similar prohibitions.

College of Cardinals—A popular term for the subcommittee chairmen of the appropriations committees, reflecting their influence over appropriation measures. The chairmen of the full appropriations committees are sometimes referred to as popes.

Comity—The practice of maintaining mutual courtesy and civility between the two houses in their dealings with each other and in members' speeches on the floor. Although the practice is largely governed by long-established customs, a House rule explicitly cautions its members not to characterize any Senate action or inaction, refer to individual senators except under certain circumstances, or quote from Senate proceedings except to make legislative history on a measure. The Senate has no rule on the subject but references to the House have been held out of order on several occasions. Generally the houses do not interfere with each other's appropriations although minor conflicts sometimes occur. A refusal to receive a message from the other house has also been held to violate the practice of comity.

Committee—A panel of members elected or appointed to perform some service or function for its parent body. Congress has four types of committees: standing, special or select, joint, and, in the House, a Committee of the Whole. Committees conduct investigations, make studies, issue reports and recommendations and, in the case of standing committees, review and prepare measures on their assigned subjects for action by their respective houses. Most committees divide their work among several subcommittees. With rare exceptions, the majority party in a house holds a majority of the seats on its committees, and their chairmen are also from that party.

Committee Jurisdiction—The legislative subjects and other functions assigned to a committee by rule, precedent, resolution or statute. A committee's title usually indicates the general scope of its jurisdiction but often fails to mention other significant subjects assigned to it.

Committee of the Whole—Common name of the Committee of the Whole House on the State of the Union, a committee consisting of all members of the House of Representatives. Measures from the union calendar must be considered in the Committee of the Whole before the House officially completes action on them; the committee often considers other major bills as well. A quorum of the committee is 100, and it meets in the House chamber under a chairman appointed by the Speaker. Procedures in the Committee of the Whole expedite consideration of legislation because of its smaller quorum requirement, its ban on certain motions and its five-minute rule for debate on amendments. Those procedures usually permit more members to offer amendments and participate in the debate on a measure than is normally possible. The Senate no longer uses a Committee of the Whole.

Committee Ratios—The ratios of majority to minority party members on committees. By custom, the ratios of most committees reflect party strength in their respective houses as closely as possible.

Committee Report on a Measure—A document submitted by a committee to report a measure to its parent chamber. Customarily, the report explains the measure's purpose, describes provisions and any amendments recommended by the committee and presents arguments for its approval.

Committee Veto—A procedure that requires an executive department or agency to submit certain proposed policies, programs or action to designated committees for review before implementing them. Before 1983, when the Supreme Court declared that a legislative veto was unconstitutional, these provisions permitted committees to veto the proposals. Committees no longer conduct this type of policy review, and the term is now something of a misnomer. Nevertheless, agencies usually take the pragmatic approach of trying to reach a consensus with the committees before carrying out their proposals, especially when an appropriations committee is involved.

Concur—To agree to an amendment of the other house, either by adopting a motion to concur in that amendment or a motion to concur with an amendment to that amendment. After both houses have agreed to the same version of an amendment, neither house may amend it further, nor may any subsequent conference change it or delete it from the measure. Concurrence by one house in all amendments of the other house completes action on the measure; no vote is then necessary on the measure as a whole because both houses previously passed it.

Concurrent Resolution—A resolution that requires approval by both houses but does not need the president's signature and therefore cannot have the force of law. Concurrent resolutions deal with the prerogatives or internal affairs of Congress as a whole. Designated H. Con. Res. in the House and S. Con. Res. in the Senate, they are numbered consecutively in each house in their order of introduction during a two-year Congress.

Conferees—A common title for managers, the members from each house appointed to a conference committee. The Senate usually authorizes its presiding officer to appoint its conferees. The Speaker appoints House conferees, and under a rule adopted in 1993, can remove conferees "at any time after an original appointment" and also appoint additional conferees at any time. Conferees are expected to support the positions of their houses despite their personal views, but in practice this is not always the case. The party ratios of conferees generally reflect the ratios in their houses. Each house may appoint as many conferees as it pleases.

House conferees often outnumber their Senate colleagues; however, each house has only one vote in a conference, so the size of its delegation is immaterial.

Conference—(1) A formal meeting or series of meetings between members representing each house to reconcile House and Senate differences on a measure (occasionally several measures). Because one house cannot require the other to agree to its proposals, the conference usually reaches agreement by compromise. When a conference completes action on a measure, or as much action as appears possible, it sends its recommendations to both houses in the form of a conference report, accompanied by an explanatory statement. (2) The official title of the organization of all Democrats or Republicans in the Senate and of all Republicans in the House of Representatives. (See Party Caucus.)

Conference Committee—A temporary joint committee formed for the purpose of resolving differences between the houses on a measure. Major and controversial legislation usually requires conference committee action. Voting in a conference committee is not by individuals but within the House and Senate delegations. Consequently, a conference committee report requires the support of a majority of the conferees from each house. Both houses require that conference committees open their meetings to the public. The Senate's rule permits the committee to close its meetings if a majority of conferees in each delegation agree by a roll-call vote. The House rule permits closed meetings only if the House authorizes them to do so on a roll-call vote. Otherwise, there are no congressional rules governing the organization of, or procedure in, a conference committee. The committee chooses its chairman, but on measures that go to conference annually, such as general appropriation bills, the chairmanship traditionally rotates between the houses.

Conference Report—A document submitted to both houses that contains a conference committee's agreements for resolving their differences on a measure. It must be signed by a majority of the conferees from each house separately and must be accompanied by an explanatory statement. Both houses prohibit amendments to a conference report and require it to be accepted or rejected in its entirety.

Congress—(1) The national legislature of the United States, consisting of the House of Representatives and the Senate. (2) The national legislature in office during a two-year period. Congresses are numbered sequentially; thus, the 1st Congress of 1789-1791 and the 106th Congress of 1999-2001. Before 1935, the two-year period began on the first Monday in December of odd-numbered years. Since then it has extended from January of an odd-numbered year through noon on Jan. 3 of the next odd-numbered year. A Congress usually holds two annual sessions, but some have had three sessions and the 67th Congress had four. When a Congress expires, measures die if they have not yet been enacted.

Congressional Accountability Act of 1995 (CAA)—An act applying eleven labor, workplace and civil rights laws to the legislative branch and establishing procedures and remedies for legislative branch employees with grievances in violation of these laws. The following laws are covered by the CAA: the Fair Labor Standards Act of 1938; Title VII of the Civil Rights Act of 1964; Americans with Disabilities Act of 1990; Age Discrimination in Employment Act of 1967; Family and Medical Leave Act of 1993; Occupational Safety and Health Act of 1970; Chapter 71 of Title 5, U.S. Code (relating to federal service labor-management relations); Employee Polygraph Protection Act of 1988; Worker Adjustment and Retraining Notification Act; Rehabilitation Act of 1973; and Chapter 43 of Title 38, U.S. Code (relating to veterans' employment and reemployment).

Congressional Budget and Impoundment Control Act of 1974—The law that established the basic elements of the congressional budget process, the House and Senate Budget Committees, the Congressional

Budget Office and the procedures for congressional review of impoundments in the form of rescissions and deferrals proposed by the president. The budget process consists of procedures for coordinating congressional revenue and spending decisions made in separate tax, appropriations and legislative measures. The impoundment provisions were intended to give Congress greater control over executive branch actions that delay or prevent the spending of funds provided by Congress.

Congressional Budget Office (CBO)—A congressional support agency created by the Congressional Budget and Impoundment Control Act of 1974 to provide nonpartisan budgetary information and analysis to Congress and its committees. CBO acts as a scorekeeper when Congress is voting on the federal budget, tracking bills to ensure they comply with overall budget goals. The agency also estimates what proposed legislation would cost over a five-year period. CBO works most closely with the House and Senate Budget Committees.

Congressional Directory—The official who's who of Congress, usually published during the first session of a two-year Congress.

Congressional District—The geographical area represented by a single member of the House of Representatives. For states with only one representative, the entire state is a congressional district. As of 2001 seven states had only one representative each: Alaska, Delaware, Montana, North Dakota, South Dakota, Vermont and Wyoming.

Congressional Record—The daily, printed and substantially verbatim account of proceedings in both the House and Senate chambers. Extraneous materials submitted by members appear in a section titled "Extensions of Remarks." A "Daily Digest" appendix contains highlights of the day's floor and committee action plus a list of committee meetings and floor agendas for the next day's session.

Although the official reporters of each house take down every word spoken during the proceedings, members are permitted to edit and "revise and extend" their remarks before they are printed. In the Senate section, all speeches, articles and other material submitted by senators but not actually spoken or read on the floor are set off by large black dots, called bullets. However, bullets do not appear when a senator reads part of a speech and inserts the rest. In the House section, undelivered speeches and materials are printed in a distinctive typeface. The term "permanent Record" refers to the bound volumes of the daily Records of an entire session of Congress.

Congressional Research Service (CRS)—Established in 1917, a department of the Library of Congress whose staff provide nonpartisan, objective analysis and information on virtually any subject to committees, members and staff of Congress. Originally the Legislative Reference Service, it is the oldest congressional support agency.

Congressional Support Agencies—A term often applied to three agencies in the legislative branch that provide nonpartisan information and analysis to committees and members of Congress: the Congressional Budget Office, the Congressional Research Service of the Library of Congress and the General Accounting Office. A fourth support agency, the Office of Technology Assessment, formerly provided such support but was abolished in the 104th Congress.

Congressional Terms of Office—A term normally begins on Jan. 3 of the year following a general election and runs two years for representatives and six years for senators. A representative chosen in a special election to fill a vacancy is sworn in for the remainder of the predecessor's term. An individual appointed to fill a Senate vacancy usually serves until the next general election or until the end of the predecessor's term, whichever comes first. Some states, however, require their governors to call a special election to fill a Senate vacancy shortly after an appointment has been made.

Constitutional Rules—Constitutional provisions that prescribe procedures for Congress. In addition to certain types of votes required in particular situations, these provisions include the following: (1) the House chooses its Speaker, the Senate its president pro tempore and both houses their officers; (2) each house requires a majority quorum to conduct business; (3) less than a majority may adjourn from day to day and compel the attendance of absent members; (4) neither house may adjourn for more than three days without the consent of the other; (5) each house must keep a journal; (6) the yeas and nays are ordered when supported by one-fifth of the members present; (7) all revenue-raising bills must originate in the House, but the Senate may propose amendments to them. The Constitution also sets out the procedure in the House for electing a president, the procedure in the Senate for electing a vice president, the procedure for filling a vacancy in the office of vice president and the procedure for overriding a presidential veto.

Constitutional Votes—Constitutional provisions that require certain votes or voting methods in specific situations. They include (1) the yeas and nays at the desire of one-fifth of the members present; (2) a two-thirds vote by the yeas and nays to override a veto; (3) a two-thirds vote by one house to expel one of its members and by both houses to propose a constitutional amendment; (4) a two-thirds vote of senators present to convict someone whom the House has impeached and to consent to ratification of treaties; (5) a two-thirds vote in each house to remove political disabilities from persons who have engaged in insurrection or rebellion or given aid or comfort to the enemies of the United States; (6) a majority vote in each house to fill a vacancy in the office of vice president; (7) a majority vote of all states to elect a president in the House of Representatives when no candidate receives a majority of the electoral votes; (8) a majority vote of all senators when the Senate elects a vice president under the same circumstances; and (9) the casting vote of the vice president in case of tie votes in the Senate.

Contempt of Congress—Willful obstruction of the proper functions of Congress. Most frequently, it is a refusal to obey a subpoena to appear and testify before a committee or to produce documents demanded by it. Such obstruction is a misdemeanor and persons cited for contempt are subject to prosecution in federal courts. A house cites an individual for contempt by agreeing to a privileged resolution to that effect reported by a committee. The presiding officer then refers the matter to a U.S. attorney for prosecution.

Continuing Body—A characterization of the Senate on the theory that it continues from Congress to Congress and has existed continuously since it first convened in 1789. The rationale for the theory is that under the system of staggered six-year terms for senators, the terms of only about one-third of them expire after each Congress and, therefore, a quorum of the Senate is always in office. Consequently, under this theory, the Senate, unlike the House, does not have to adopt its rules at the beginning of each Congress because those rules continue from one Congress to the next. This makes it extremely difficult for the Senate to change its rules against the opposition of a determined minority because those rules require a two-thirds vote of the senators present and voting to invoke cloture on a proposed rules change.

Continuing Resolution (CR)—A joint resolution that provides funds to continue the operation of federal agencies and programs at the beginning of a new fiscal year if their annual appropriation bills have not yet been enacted; also called continuing appropriations. Continuing resolutions are enacted shortly before or after the new fiscal year begins and usually make funds available for a specified period. Additional resolutions are often needed after the first expires. Some continuing resolutions have provided appropriations for an entire fiscal year. Continuing resolutions for specific periods customarily fix a rate at which agencies may incur obligations based either on the previous year's appropriations, the president's budget request, or the amount as specified in the agency's regular annual appropriation bill if that bill has already been passed by one or both houses. In the House, continuing resolutions are privileged after Sept. 15.

Contract Authority—Statutory authority permitting an agency to enter into contracts or incur other obligations even though it has not received an appropriation to pay for them. Congress must eventually fund them because the government is legally liable for such payments. The Congressional Budget Act of 1974 requires that new contract authority may not be used unless provided for in advance by an appropriation act, but it permits a few exceptions.

Correcting Recorded Votes—The rules of both houses prohibit members from changing their votes after a vote result has been announced. Nevertheless, the Senate permits its members to withdraw or change their votes, by unanimous consent, immediately after the announcement. In rare instances, senators have been granted unanimous consent to change their votes several days or weeks after the announcement. Votes tallied by the electronic voting system in the House may not be changed. But when a vote actually given is not recorded during an oral call of the roll, a member may demand a correction as a matter of right. On all other alleged errors in a recorded vote, the Speaker determines whether the circumstances justify a change. Occasionally, members merely announce that they were incorrectly recorded; announcements can occur hours, days or even months after the vote and appear in the *Congressional Record*.

Cosponsor—A member who has joined one or more other members to sponsor a measure.

Credit Authority—Authority granted to an agency to incur direct loan obligations or to make loan guarantee commitments. The Congressional Budget Act of 1974 bans congressional consideration of credit authority legislation unless the extent of that authority is made subject to provisions in appropriation acts.

C-SPAN—Cable-Satellite Public Affairs Network, which provides live, gavel-to-gavel coverage of Senate floor proceedings on one cable television channel and coverage of House floor proceedings on another channel. C-SPAN also televises important committee hearings in both houses. Each house also transmits its televised proceedings directly to congressional offices.

Current Services Estimates—Executive branch estimates of the anticipated costs of federal programs and operations for the next and future fiscal years at existing levels of service and assuming no new initiatives or changes in existing law. The president submits these estimates to Congress with the annual budget and includes an explanation of the underlying economic and policy assumptions on which they are based, such as anticipated rates of inflation, real economic growth and unemployment, plus program caseloads and pay increases.

Custody of the Papers—Possession of an engrossed measure and certain related basic documents that the two houses produce as they try to resolve their differences over the measure.

Dance of the Swans and the Ducks—A whimsical description of the gestures some members use in connection with a request for a recorded vote, especially in the House. When members want their colleagues to stand in support of the request, they move their hands and arms in a gentle upward motion resembling the beginning flight of a graceful swan. When they want their colleagues to remain seated to avoid such a vote, they move their hands and arms in a vigorous downward motion resembling a diving duck.

Dean—Within a state's delegation in the House of Representatives, the member with the longest continuous service.

Debate—In congressional parlance, speeches delivered during consideration of a measure, motion or other matter, as distinguished from speeches in other parliamentary situations, such as one-minute and special order speeches when no business is pending. Virtually all debate in the House of Representatives is under some kind of time limitation. Most debate in the Senate is unlimited; that is, a senator, once recognized, may speak for as long as he or she chooses, unless the Senate invokes cloture.

Debt Limit—The maximum amount of outstanding federal public debt permitted by law. The limit (or ceiling) covers virtually all debt incurred by the government except agency debt. Each congressional budget resolution sets forth the new debt limit that may be required under its provisions.

Deferral—An impoundment of funds for a specific period of time that may not extend beyond the fiscal year in which it is proposed. Under the Impoundment Control Act of 1974, the president must notify Congress that he is deferring the spending or obligation of funds provided by law for a project or activity. Congress can disapprove the deferral by legislation.

Deficit—The amount by which the government's outlays exceed its budget receipts for a given fiscal year. Both the president's budget and the annual congressional budget resolution provide estimates of the deficit or surplus for the upcoming and several future fiscal years.

Degrees of Amendment—Designations that indicate the relationships of amendments to the text of a measure and to each other. In general, an amendment offered directly to the text of a measure is an amendment in the first degree, and an amendment to that amendment is an amendment in the second degree. Both houses normally prohibit amendments in the third degree — that is, an amendment to an amendment to an amendment.

Delegate—A nonvoting member of the House of Representatives elected to a two-year term from the District of Columbia, the territory of Guam, the territory of the Virgin Islands or the territory of American Samoa. By law, delegates may not vote in the full House but they may participate in debate, offer motions (except to reconsider) and serve and vote on standing and select committees. On their committees, delegates possess the same powers and privileges as other members and the Speaker may appoint them to appropriate conference committees and select committees.

Denounce—A formal action that condemns a member for misbehavior; considered by some experts to be equivalent to censure. (See Censure.)

Dilatory Tactics—Procedural actions intended to delay or prevent action by a house or a committee. They include, among others, offering numerous motions, demanding quorum calls and recorded votes at every opportunity, making numerous points of order and parliamentary inquiries and speaking as long as the applicable rules permit. The Senate rules permit a battery of dilatory tactics, especially lengthy speeches, except under cloture. In the House, possible dilatory tactics are more limited. Speeches are always subject to time limits and debate-ending motions. Moreover, a House rule instructs the Speaker not to entertain dilatory motions and lets the Speaker decide whether a motion is dilatory. However, the Speaker may not override the constitutional right of a member to demand the yeas and nays, and in practice usually waits for a point of order before exercising that authority. (See Cloture.)

Discharge a Committee—Remove a measure from a committee to which it has been referred in order to make it available for floor consideration. Noncontroversial measures are often discharged by unanimous consent. However, because congressional committees have no obligation to report measures referred to them, each house has procedures to extract controversial measures from recalcitrant committees. Six discharge procedures are available in the House of Representatives. The

Senate uses a motion to discharge, which is usually converted into a discharge resolution.

District Office—Representatives maintain one or more offices in their districts for the purpose of assisting and communicating with constituents. The costs of maintaining these offices are paid from members' official allowances. Senators can use the official expense allowance to rent offices in their home state, subject to a funding formula based on their state's population and other factors.

District Work Period—The House term for a scheduled congressional recess during which members may visit their districts and conduct constituency business.

Division Vote—A vote in which the chair first counts those in favor of a proposition and then those opposed to it, with no record made of how each member votes. In the Senate, the chair may count raised hands or ask senators to stand, whereas the House requires members to stand; hence, often called a standing vote. Committees in both houses ordinarily use a show of hands. A division usually occurs after a voice vote and may be demanded by any member or ordered by the chair if there is any doubt about the outcome of the voice vote. The demand for a division can also come before a voice vote. In the Senate, the demand must come before the result of a voice vote is announced. It may be made after a voice vote announcement in the House, but only if no intervening business has transpired and only if the member was standing and seeking recognition at the time of the announcement. A demand for the yeas and nays or, in the House, for a recorded vote, takes precedence over a division vote.

Doorkeeper of the House—A former officer of the House of Representatives who was responsible for enforcing the rules prohibiting unauthorized persons from entering the chamber when the House is in session. The doorkeeper was usually the candidate of the majority party. In 1995 the office was abolished and its functions transferred to the sergeant at arms.

Effective Dates—Provisions of an act that specify when the entire act or individual provisions in it become effective as law. Most acts become effective on the date of enactment, but it is sometimes necessary or prudent to delay the effective dates of some provisions.

Electronic Voting—Since 1973 the House has used an electronic voting system to record the yeas and nays and to conduct recorded votes. Members vote by inserting their voting cards in one of the boxes at several locations in the chamber. They are given at least fifteen minutes to vote. When several votes occur immediately after each other, the Speaker may reduce the voting time to five minutes on the second and subsequent votes. The Speaker may allow additional time on each vote but may also close a vote at any time after the minimum time has expired. Members can change their votes at any time before the Speaker announces the result. The House also uses the electronic system for quorum calls. While a vote is in progress, a large panel above the Speaker's desk displays how each member has voted. Smaller panels on either side of the chamber display running totals of the votes and the time remaining. The Senate does not have electronic voting.

Enacting Clause—The opening language of each bill, beginning "Be it enacted by the Senate and House of Representatives of the United States of America in Congress assembled..." This language gives legal force to measures approved by Congress and signed by the president or enacted over the president's veto. A successful motion to strike it from a bill kills the entire measure.

Engrossed Bill—The official copy of a bill or joint resolution as passed by one chamber, including the text as amended by floor action and certified by the clerk of the House or the secretary of the Senate (as appropriate). Amendments by one house to a measure or amendments of the other also are engrossed. House engrossed documents are printed on blue paper; the Senate's are printed on white paper.

Enrolled Bill—The final official copy of a bill or joint resolution passed in identical form by both houses. An enrolled bill is printed on parchment. After it is certified by the chief officer of the house in which it originated and signed by the House Speaker and the Senate president pro tempore, the measure is sent to the White House for the president's signature.

Entitlement Program—A federal program under which individuals, businesses or units of government that meet the requirements or qualifications established by law are entitled to receive certain payments if they seek such payments. Major examples include Social Security, Medicare, Medicaid, unemployment insurance and military and federal civilian pensions. Congress cannot control their expenditures by refusing to appropriate the sums necessary to fund them because the government is legally obligated to pay eligible recipients the amounts to which the law entitles them.

Equality of the Houses—A component of the Constitution's emphasis on checks and balances under which each house is given essentially equal status in the enactment of legislation and in the relations and negotiations between the two houses. Although the House of Representatives initiates revenue and appropriation measures, the Senate has the right to amend them. Either house may initiate any other type of legislation, and neither can force the other to agree to, or even act on, its measures. Moreover, each house has a potential veto over the other because legislation requires agreement by both. Similarly, in a conference to resolve their differences on a measure, each house casts one vote, as determined by a majority of its conferees. In most other national bicameral legislatures, the powers of one house are markedly greater than those of the other.

Ethics Rules—Several rules or standing orders in each house that mandate certain standards of conduct for members and congressional employees in finance, employment, franking and other areas. The Senate Permanent Select Committee on Ethics and the House Committee on Standards of Official Conduct investigate alleged violations of conduct and recommend appropriate actions to their respective houses.

Exclusive Committee—(1) Under the rules of the Republican Conference and House Democratic Caucus, a standing committee whose members usually cannot serve on any other standing committee. As of 2000 the Appropriations, Energy and Commerce (beginning in the 105th Congress), Ways and Means and Rules Committees were designated as exclusive committees. (2) Under the rules of the two party conferences in the Senate, a standing committee whose members may not simultaneously serve on any other exclusive committee.

Executive Calendar—The Senate's calendar for committee reports on its executive business, namely treaties and nominations. The calendar numbers indicate the order in which items were referred to the calendar but have no bearing on when or if the Senate will consider them. The Senate, by motion or unanimous consent, resolves itself into executive session to consider them.

Executive Document—A document, usually a treaty, sent by the president to the Senate for approval. It is referred to a committee in the same manner as other measures. Resolutions to ratify treaties have their own "treaty document" numbers. For example, the first treaty submitted in the 106th Congress would be "Treaty Doc 106-1."

Executive Order—A unilateral proclamation by the president that has a policy-making or legislative impact. Members of Congress have challenged some executive orders on the grounds that they usurped the authority of the legislative branch. Although the Supreme Court has ruled that a particular order exceeded the president's authority, it has upheld others as falling within the president's general constitutional powers.

Executive Privilege—The assertion that presidents have the right to withhold certain information from Congress. Presidents have based their claim on (1) the constitutional separation of powers; (2) the need for secrecy in military and diplomatic affairs; (3) the need to protect individuals from unfavorable publicity; (4) the need to safeguard the confidential exchange of ideas in the executive branch; and (5) the need to protect individuals who provide confidential advice to the president.

Executive Session—(1) A Senate meeting devoted to the consideration of treaties or nominations. Normally, the Senate meets in legislative session; it resolves itself into executive session, by motion or by unanimous consent, to deal with its executive business. It also keeps a separate Journal for executive sessions. Executive sessions are usually open to the public, but the Senate may choose to close them.

Expulsion—A member's removal from office by a two-thirds vote of his or her house; the supermajority is required by the Constitution. It is the most severe and most rarely used sanction a house can invoke against a member. Although the Constitution provides no explicit grounds for expulsion, the courts have ruled that it may be applied only for misconduct during a member's term of office, not for conduct before the member's election. Generally, neither house will consider expulsion of a member convicted of a crime until the judicial processes have been exhausted. At that stage, members sometimes resign rather than face expulsion. In 1977 the House adopted a rule urging members convicted of certain crimes to voluntarily abstain from voting or participating in other legislative business.

Extensions of Remarks—An appendix to the daily Congressional Record that consists primarily of miscellaneous extraneous material submitted by members. It often includes members' statements not delivered on the floor, newspaper articles and editorials, praise for a member's constituents and noteworthy letters received by a member, among other material. Representatives supply the bulk of this material; senators submit very little. "Extensions of Remarks" pages are separately numbered, and each number is preceded by the letter "E." Materials may be placed in the Extensions of Remarks section only by unanimous consent. Usually, one member of each party makes the request each day on behalf of his or her party colleagues after the House has completed its legislative business of the day.

Federal Debt—The total amount of monies borrowed and not yet repaid by the federal government. Federal debt consists of public debt and agency debt. Public debt is the portion of the federal debt borrowed by the Treasury or the Federal Financing Bank directly from the public or from another federal fund or account. For example, the Treasury regularly borrows money from the Social Security trust fund. Public debt accounts for about 99 percent of the federal debt. Agency debt refers to the debt incurred by federal agencies such as the Export-Import Bank but excluding the Treasury and the Federal Financing Bank, which are authorized by law to borrow funds from the public or from another government fund or account.

Filibuster—The use of obstructive and time-consuming parliamentary tactics by one member or a minority of members to delay, modify or defeat proposed legislation or rules changes. Filibusters are also sometimes used to delay urgently needed measures to force the body to accept other legislation. The Senate's rules permitting unlimited debate and the extraordinary majority it requires to impose cloture make filibustering particularly effective in that chamber. Under the stricter rules of the House, filibusters in that body are short-lived and therefore ineffective and rarely attempted.

Fiscal Year—The federal government's annual accounting period. It begins Oct. 1 and ends on the following Sept. 30. A fiscal year is designated by the calendar year in which it ends and is often referred to as FY. Thus, fiscal year 1998 began Oct. 1, 1997, ended Sept. 30, 1998, and is called FY98. In theory, Congress is supposed to complete action on all budgetary measures applying to a fiscal year before that year begins. It rarely does so.

Five-Minute Rule—A House rule that limits debate on an amendment offered in Committee of the Whole to five minutes for its sponsor and five minutes for an opponent. In practice, the committee routinely permits longer debate by two devices: the offering of pro forma amendments, each debatable for five minutes, and unanimous consent for a member to speak longer than five minutes. Consequently, debate on an amendment sometimes continues for hours. At any time after the first ten minutes, however, the committee may shut off debate immediately or by a specified time, either by unanimous consent or by majority vote on a nondebatable motion. The motion, which dates from 1847, is also used in the House as in Committee of the Whole, where debate also may be shut off by a motion for the previous question.

Floor—The ground level of the House or Senate chamber where members sit and the houses conduct their business. When members are attending a meeting of their house they are said to be on the floor. Floor action refers to the procedural actions taken during floor consideration such as deciding on motions, taking up measures, amending them and voting.

Floor Manager—A majority party member responsible for guiding a measure through its floor consideration in a house and for devising the political and procedural strategies that might be required to get it passed. The presiding officer gives the floor manager priority recognition to debate, offer amendments, oppose amendments and make crucial procedural motions.

Frank—Informally, members' legal right to send official mail postage free under their signatures; often called the franking privilege. Technically, it is the autographic or facsimile signature used on envelopes instead of stamps that permits members and certain congressional officers to send their official mail free of charge. The franking privilege has been authorized by law since the first Congress, except for a few months in 1873. Congress reimburses the U.S. Postal Service for the franked mail it handles.

Function or Functional Category—A broad category of national need and spending of budgetary significance. A category provides an accounting method for allocating and keeping track of budgetary resources and expenditures for that function because it includes all budget accounts related to the function's subject or purpose such as agriculture, administration of justice, commerce and housing and energy. Functions do not necessarily correspond with appropriations acts or with the budgets of individual agencies. As of 2000 there were twenty functional categories, each divided into a number of subfunctions.

Gag Rule—A pejorative term for any type of special rule reported by the House Rules Committee that proposes to prohibit amendments to a measure or only permits amendments offered by the reporting committee.

Galleries—The balconies overlooking each chamber from which the public, news media, staff and others may observe floor proceedings.

General Appropriation Bill—A term applied to each of the thirteen annual bills that provide funds for most federal agencies and programs and also to the supplemental appropriation bills that contain appropriations for more than one agency or program.

Germaneness—The requirement that an amendment be closely related — in terms of subject or purpose, for example — to the text it proposes to amend. A House rule requires that all amendments be germane. In the Senate, only amendments offered to general appropriation bills and budget measures or proposed under cloture must be germane.

Germaneness rules can be waived by suspension of the rules in both houses, by unanimous consent agreements in the Senate and by special rules from the Rules Committee in the House. Moreover, presiding officers usually do not enforce germaneness rules on their own initiative; therefore, a nongermane amendment can be adopted if no member raises a point of order against it. Under cloture in the Senate, however, the chair may take the initiative to rule amendments out of order as not being germane, without a point of order being made. All House debate must be germane except during general debate in the Committee of the Whole, but special rules invariably require that such debate be "confined to the bill." The Senate requires germane debate only during the first three hours of each daily session. Under the precedents of both houses, an amendment can be relevant but not necessarily germane. A crucial factor in determining germaneness in the House is how the subject of a measure or matter is defined. For example, the subject of a measure authorizing construction of a naval vessel is defined as being the construction of a single vessel; therefore, an amendment to authorize an additional vessel is not germane.

Gerrymandering—The manipulation of legislative district boundaries to benefit a particular party, politician or minority group. The term originated in 1812 when the Massachusetts legislature redrew the lines of state legislative districts to favor the party of Gov. Elbridge Gerry, and some critics said one district looked like a salamander. (See also Congressional District; Redistricting.)

Government Accountability Office (GAO)—A congressional support agency, often referred to as the investigative arm of Congress. It evaluates and audits federal agencies and programs in the United States and abroad on its initiative or at the request of congressional committees or members.

Gramm-Rudman-Hollings Act of 1985—Common name for the Balanced Budget and Emergency Deficit Control Act of 1985, which established new budget procedures intended to balance the federal budget by fiscal year 1991. (The timetable subsequently was extended and then deleted.) The act's chief sponsors were senators Phil Gramm (R-Texas), Warren Rudman (R-N.H.) Ernest Hollings (D-S.C.).

Grandfather Clause—A provision in a measure, law or rule that exempts an individual, entity or a defined category of individuals or entities from complying with a new policy or restriction. For example, a bill that would raise taxes on persons who reach the age of sixty-five after a certain date inherently grandfathers out those who are sixty-five before that date. Similarly, a Senate rule limiting senators to two major committee assignments also grandfathers some senators who were sitting on a third major committee before a specified date.

Grants-in-Aid—Payments by the federal government to state and local governments to help provide for assistance programs or public services.

Hearing—Committee or subcommittee meetings to receive testimony on proposed legislation during investigations or for oversight purposes. Relatively few bills are important enough to justify formal hearings. Witnesses often include experts, government officials, spokespersons for interested groups, officials of the Government Accountability Office and members of Congress.

Hold—A senator's request that his or her party leaders delay floor consideration of certain legislation or presidential nominations. The majority leader usually honors a hold for a reasonable period of time, especially if its purpose is to assure the senator that the matter will not be called up during his or her absence or to give the senator time to gather necessary information.

Hold (or Have) the Floor—A member's right to speak without interruption, unless he or she violates a rule, after recognition by the presiding officer. At the member's discretion, he or she may yield to another member for a question in the Senate or for a question or statement in the House, but may reclaim the floor at any time.

Hold-Harmless Clause—In legislation providing a new formula for allocating federal funds, a clause to ensure that recipients of those funds do not receive less in a future year than they did in the current year if the new formula would result in a reduction for them. Similar to a grandfather clause, it has been used most frequently to soften the impact of sudden reductions in federal grants. (See Grandfather Clause.)

Hopper—A box on the clerk's desk in the House chamber into which members deposit bills and resolutions to introduce them. In House jargon, to drop a bill in the hopper is to introduce it.

Hour Rule—A House rule that permits members, when recognized, to hold the floor in debate for no more than one hour each. The majority party member customarily yields one-half the time to a minority member. Although the hour rule applies to general debate in Committee of the Whole as well as in the House, special rules routinely vary the length of time for such debate and its control to fit the circumstances of particular measures.

House As In Committee of the Whole—A hybrid combination of procedures from the general rules of the House and from the rules of the Committee of the Whole, sometimes used to expedite consideration of a measure on the floor.

House Calendar—The calendar reserved for all public bills and resolutions that do not raise revenue or directly or indirectly appropriate money or property when they are favorably reported by House committees.

House Manual—A commonly used title for the handbook of the rules of the House of Representatives, published in each Congress. Its official title is Constitution, Jefferson's Manual and Rules of the House of Representatives.

House of Representatives—The house of Congress in which states are represented roughly in proportion to their populations, but every state is guaranteed at least one representative. By law, the number of voting representatives is fixed at 435. Four delegates and one resident commissioner also serve in the House; they may vote in their committees but not on the House floor. Although the House and Senate have equal legislative power, the Constitution gives the House sole authority to originate revenue measures. The House also claims the right to originate appropriation measures, a claim the Senate disputes in theory but concedes in practice. The House has the sole power to impeach, and it elects the president when no candidate has received a majority of the electoral votes. It is sometimes referred to as the lower body.

Immunity—(1) Members' constitutional protection from lawsuits and arrest in connection with their legislative duties. They may not be tried for libel or slander for anything they say on the floor of a house or in committee. Nor may they be arrested while attending sessions of their houses or when traveling to or from sessions of Congress, except when charged with treason, a felony or a breach of the peace. (2) In the case of a witness before a committee, a grant of protection from prosecution based on that person's testimony to the committee. It is used to compel witnesses to testify who would otherwise refuse to do so on the constitutional ground of possible selfincrimination. Under such a grant, none of a witness's testimony may be used against him or her in a court proceeding except in a prosecution for perjury or for giving a false statement to Congress. (See also Contempt of Congress.)

Impeachment—The first step to remove the president, vice president or other federal civil officers from office and to disqualify them from any future federal office "of honor, Trust or Profit." An impeachment is a formal charge of treason, bribery or "other high Crimes and Misdemeanors." The House has the sole power of impeachment and the Senate the sole power of trying the charges and convicting. The House impeaches by a simple majority vote; conviction requires a two-thirds vote of all senators present.

Impeachment Trial, Removal and Disqualification—The Senate conducts an impeachment trial under a separate set of twenty-six rules that appears in the *Senate Manual*. Under the Constitution, the chief justice of the United States presides over trials of the president, but the vice president, the president pro tempore or any other senator may preside over the impeachment trial of another official.

The Constitution requires senators to take an oath for an impeachment trial. During the trial, senators may not engage in colloquies or participate in arguments, but they may submit questions in writing to House managers or defense counsel. After the trial concludes, the Senate votes separately on each article of impeachment without debate unless the Senate orders the doors closed for private discussions. During deliberations senators may speak no more than once on a question, not for more than ten minutes on an interlocutory question and not more than fifteen minutes on the final question. These rules may be set aside by unanimous consent or suspended on motion by a two-thirds vote.

The Senate's impeachment trial of President Clinton in 1999 was only the second such trial involving a president. It continued for five weeks, with the Senate voting not to convict on the two impeachment articles.

Senate impeachment rules allow the Senate, at its own discretion, to name a committee to hear evidence and conduct the trial, with all senators thereafter voting on the charges. The impeachment trials of three federal judges were conducted this way, and the Supreme Court upheld the validity of these rules in *Nixon v. United States*, 506 U.S. 224, 1993.

An official convicted on impeachment charges is removed from office immediately. However, the convicted official is not barred from holding a federal office in the future unless the Senate, after its conviction vote, also approves a resolution disqualifying the convicted official from future office. For example, federal judge Alcee L. Hastings was impeached and convicted in 1989, but the Senate did not vote to bar him from office in the future. In 1992 Hastings was elected to the House of Representatives, and no challenge was raised against seating him when he took the oath of office in 1993.

Impoundment—An executive branch action or inaction that delays or withholds the expenditure or obligation of budget authority provided by law. The Impoundment Control Act of 1974 classifies impoundments as either deferrals or rescissions, requires the president to notify Congress about all such actions and gives Congress authority to approve or reject them.

Inspector General (IG) In the House of Representatives—A position established with the passage of the House Administrative Reform Resolution of 1992. The duties of the office have been revised several times and are now contained in House Rule II. The inspector general (IG), who is subject to the policy direction and oversight of the Committee on House Administration, is appointed for a Congress jointly by the Speaker and the majority and minority leaders of the House. The IG communicates the results of audits to the House officers or officials who were the subjects of the audits and suggests appropriate corrective measures. The IG submits a report of each audit to the Speaker, the majority and minority leaders and the chairman and ranking minority member of the House Administration Committee; notifies these five members in the case of any financial irregularity discovered; and reports to the Committee on Standards of Official Conduct on possible violations of House rules or any applicable law by any House member, officer or employee. The IG's office also has certain duties to audit various financial operations of the House that had previously been performed by the Government Accountability Office.

Instruct Conferees—A formal action by a house urging its conferees to uphold a particular position on a measure in conference. The instruc-

tion may be to insist on certain provisions in the measure as passed by that house or to accept a provision in the version passed by the other house. Instructions to conferees are not binding because the primary responsibility of conferees is to reach agreement on a measure and neither House can compel the other to accept particular provisions or positions.

Investigative Power—The authority of Congress and its committees to pursue investigations, upheld by the Supreme Court but limited to matters related to, and in furtherance of, a legitimate task of the Congress. Standing committees in both houses are permanently authorized to investigate matters within their jurisdictions. Major investigations are sometimes conducted by temporary select, special or joint committees established by resolutions for that purpose.

Some rules of the House provide certain safeguards for witnesses and others during investigative hearings. These permit counsel to accompany witnesses, require that each witness receive a copy of the committee's rules and order the committee to go into closed session if it believes the testimony to be heard might defame, degrade or incriminate any person. The committee may subsequently decide to hear such testimony in open session. The Senate has no rules of this kind.

Item Veto—Item veto authority, which is available to most state governors, allows governors to eliminate or reduce items in legislative measures presented for their signature without vetoing the entire measure and sign the rest into law. A similar authority was briefly granted to the U.S. president under the Line Item Veto Act of 1996. According to the majority opinion of the Supreme Court in its 1998 decision overturning that law, a constitutional amendment would be necessary to give the president such item veto authority.

Jefferson's Manual—Short title of *Jefferson's Manual of Parliamentary Practice,* prepared by Thomas Jefferson for his guidance when he was president of the Senate from 1797 to 1801. Although it reflects English parliamentary practice in his day, many procedures in both houses of Congress are still rooted in its basic precepts. Under a House rule adopted in 1837, the manual's provisions govern House procedures when applicable and when they are not inconsistent with its standing rules and orders. The Senate, however, has never officially acknowledged it as a direct authority for its legislative procedure.

Johnson Rule—A policy instituted in 1953 under which all Democratic senators are assigned to one major committee before any Democrat is assigned to two. The Johnson Rule is named after its author, Sen. Lyndon B. Johnson, D-Texas, then the Senate's Democratic leader. Senate Republicans adopted a similar policy soon thereafter.

Joint Committee—A committee composed of members selected from each house. The functions of most joint committees involve investigation, research or oversight of agencies closely related to Congress. Permanent joint committees, created by statute, are sometimes called standing joint committees. Once quite numerous, only four joint committees remained as of 2002: Joint Economic, Joint Taxation, Joint Library and Joint Printing. None has authority to report legislation.

Joint Resolution—A legislative measure that Congress uses for purposes other than general legislation. Similar to a bill, it has the force of law when passed by both houses and either approved by the president or passed over the president's veto. Unlike a bill, a joint resolution enacted into law is not called an act; it retains its original title. Most often, joint resolutions deal with such relatively limited matters as the correction of errors in existing law, continuing appropriations, a single appropriation or the establishment of permanent joint committees. Unlike bills, however, joint resolutions also are used to propose constitutional amendments; these do not require the president's signature and become effective only when ratified by three-fourths of the states. The House designates joint resolutions as H.J. Res., the Senate as S.J. Res. Each house numbers its joint resolutions consecutively in the order of introduction during a two-year Congress.

Joint Session—Informally, any combined meeting of the Senate and the House. Technically, a joint session is a combined meeting to count the electoral votes for president and vice president or to hear a presidential address, such as the State of the Union message; any other formal combined gathering of both houses is a joint meeting. Joint sessions are authorized by concurrent resolutions and are held in the House chamber, because of its larger seating capacity. Although the president of the Senate and the Speaker sit side by side at the Speaker's desk during combined meetings, the former presides over the electoral count and the latter presides on all other occasions and introduces the president or other guest speaker. The president and other guests may address a joint session or meeting only by invitation.

Joint Sponsorship—Two or more members sponsoring the same measure.

Journal—The official record of House or Senate actions, including every motion offered, every vote cast, amendments agreed to, quorum calls and so forth. Unlike the *Congressional Record*, it does not provide reports of speeches, debates, statements and the like. The Constitution requires each house to maintain a *Journal* and to publish it periodically.

Junket—A member's trip at government expense, especially abroad, ostensibly on official business but, it is often alleged, for pleasure.

Killer Amendment—An amendment that, if agreed to, might lead to the defeat of the measure it amends, either in the house in which the amendment is offered or at some later stage of the legislative process. Members sometimes deliberately offer or vote for such an amendment in the expectation that it will undermine support for the measure in Congress or increase the likelihood that the president will veto it.

King of the Mountain (or Hill) Rule—(See Queen of the Hill Rule.)

LA—(See Legislative Assistant.)

Lame Duck—Jargon for a member who has not been reelected, or did not seek reelection, and is serving the balance of his or her term.

Lame Duck Session—A session of a Congress held after the election for the succeeding Congress, so-called after the lame duck members still serving.

Last Train Out—Colloquial name for last must-pass bill of a session of Congress.

Law—An act of Congress that has been signed by the president, passed over the president's veto or allowed to become law without the president's signature.

Lay on the Table—A motion to dispose of a pending proposition immediately, finally and adversely; that is, to kill it without a direct vote on its substance. Often simply called a motion to table, it is not debatable and is adopted by majority vote or without objection. It is a highly privileged motion, taking precedence over all others except the motion to adjourn in the House and all but three additional motions in the Senate. It can kill a bill or resolution, an amendment, another motion, an appeal or virtually any other matter.

Tabling an amendment also tables the measure to which the amendment is pending in the House, but not in the Senate. The House does not allow the motion against the motion to recommit, in Committee of the Whole, and in some other situations. In the Senate it is the only permissible motion that immediately ends debate on a proposition, but only to kill it.

(The) Leadership—Usually, a reference to the majority and minority leaders of the Senate or to the Speaker and minority leader of the House.

The term sometimes includes the majority leader in the House and the majority and minority whips in each house and, at other times, other party officials as well.

Legislation—(1) A synonym for legislative measures: bills and joint resolutions. (2) Provisions in such measures or in substantive amendments offered to them. (3) In some contexts, provisions that change existing substantive or authorizing law, rather than provisions that make appropriations.

Legislation on an Appropriation Bill—A common reference to provisions changing existing law that appear in, or are offered as amendments to, a general appropriation bill. A House rule prohibits the inclusion of such provisions in general appropriation bills unless they retrench expenditures. An analogous Senate rule permits points of order against amendments to a general appropriation bill that propose general legislation.

Legislative Assistant (LA)—A member's staff person responsible for monitoring and preparing legislation on particular subjects and for advising the member on them; commonly referred to as an LA.

Legislative Day—The day that begins when a house meets after an adjournment and ends when it next adjourns. Because the House of Representatives normally adjourns at the end of a daily session, its legislative and calendar days usually coincide. The Senate, however, frequently recesses at the end of a daily session, and its legislative day may extend over several calendar days, weeks or months. Among other uses, this technicality permits the Senate to save time by circumventing its morning hour, a procedure required at the beginning of every legislative day.

Legislative History—(1) A chronological list of actions taken on a measure during its progress through the legislative process. (2) The official documents relating to a measure, the entries in the Journals of the two houses on that measure and the *Congressional Record* text of its consideration in both houses. The documents include all committee reports and the conference report and joint explanatory statement, if any. Courts and affected federal agencies study a measure's legislative history for congressional intent about its purpose and interpretation.

Legislative Process—(1) Narrowly, the stages in the enactment of a law from introduction to final disposition. An introduced measure that becomes law typically travels through reference to committee; committee and subcommittee consideration; report to the chamber; floor consideration; amendment; passage; engrossment; messaging to the other house; similar steps in that house, including floor amendment of the measure; return of the measure to the first house; consideration of amendments between the houses or a conference to resolve their differences; approval of the conference report by both houses; enrollment; approval by the president or override of the president's veto; and deposit with the Archivist of the United States. (2) Broadly, the political, lobbying and other factors that affect or influence the process of enacting laws.

Legislative Veto—A procedure, declared unconstitutional in 1983, that allowed Congress or one of its houses to nullify certain actions of the president, executive branch agencies or independent agencies. Sometimes called congressional vetoes or congressional disapprovals. Following the Supreme Court's 1983 decision, Congress amended several legislative veto statutes to require enactment of joint resolutions, which are subject to presidential veto, for nullifying executive branch actions.

Limitation on a General Appropriation Bill—Language that prohibits expenditures for part of an authorized purpose from funds provided in a general appropriation bill. Precedents require that the language be phrased in the negative: that none of the funds provided in a pending appropriation bill shall be used for a specified authorized activity. Limitations in general appropriation bills are permitted on the grounds that Congress can refuse to fund authorized programs and, therefore, can refuse to fund any part of them as long as the prohibition does not change existing law. House precedents have established that a limitation does not change existing law if it does not impose additional duties or burdens on executive branch officials, interfere with their discretionary authority or require them to make judgments or determinations not required by existing law. The proliferation of limitation amendments in the 1970s and early 1980s prompted the House to adopt a rule in 1983 making it more difficult for members to offer them. The rule bans such amendments during the reading of an appropriation bill for amendments, unless they are specifically authorized in existing law. Other limitations may be offered after the reading, but the Committee of the Whole can foreclose them by adopting a motion to rise and report the bill back to the House. In 1995 the rule was amended to allow the motion to rise and report to be made only by the majority leader or his or her designee. The House Appropriations Committee, however, can include limitation provisions in the bills it reports.

Line Item—An amount in an appropriation measure. It can refer to a single appropriation account or to separate amounts within the account. In the congressional budget process, the term usually refers to assumptions about the funding of particular programs or accounts that underlie the broad functional amounts in a budget resolution. These assumptions are discussed in the reports accompanying each resolution and are not binding.

Line-Item Veto—(See Item Veto.)

Line Item Veto Act of 1996—A law, in effect only from January 1997 until June 1998, that granted the president authority intended to be functionally equivalent to an item veto, by amending the Impoundment Control Act of 1974 to incorporate an approach known as enhanced rescission. Key provisions established a new procedure that permitted the president to cancel amounts of new discretionary appropriations (budget authority), new items of direct spending (entitlements) or certain limited tax benefits. It also required the president to notify Congress of the cancellation in a special message within five calendar days after signing the measure. The cancellation would become permanent unless legislation disapproving it was enacted within thirty days. On June 25, 1998, in *Clinton v. City of New York* the Supreme Court held the Line Item Veto Act unconstitutional, on the grounds that its cancellation provisions violated the presentment clause in Article I, clause 7, of the Constitution.

Live Pair—A voluntary and informal agreement between two members on opposite sides of an issue, one of whom is absent for a recorded vote, under which the member who is present withholds or withdraws his or her vote to offset the failure to vote by the member who is absent. Usually the member in attendance announces that he or she has a live pair, states how each would have voted and votes "present." In the House, under a rules change enacted in the 106th Congress, a live pair is only permitted on the rare occasions when electronic voting is not used.

Live Quorum—In the Senate, a quorum call to which senators are expected to respond. Senators usually suggest the absence of a quorum, not to force a quorum to appear, but to provide a pause in the proceedings during which senators can engage in private discussions or wait for a senator to come to the floor. A senator desiring a live quorum usually announces his or her intention, giving fair warning that there will be an objection to any unanimous consent request that the quorum call be dispensed with before it is completed.

Loan Guarantee—A statutory commitment by the federal government to pay part or all of a loan's principal and interest to a lender or the holder of a security in case the borrower defaults.

Lobby—To try to persuade members of Congress to propose, pass, modify or defeat proposed legislation or to change or repeal existing laws. Lobbyists attempt to promote their preferences or those of a group,

organization or industry. Originally the term referred to persons frequenting the lobbies or corridors of legislative chambers in order to speak to lawmakers. In a general sense, lobbying includes not only direct contact with members but also indirect attempts to influence them, such as writing to them or persuading others to write or visit them, attempting to mold public opinion toward a desired legislative goal by various means and contributing or arranging for contributions to members' election campaigns. The right to lobby stems from the First Amendment to the Constitution, which bans laws that abridge the right of the people to petition the government for a redress of grievances.

Lobbying Disclosure Act of 1995—The principal statute requiring disclosure of — and also, to a degree, circumscribing — the activities of lobbyists. In general, it requires lobbyists who spend more than 20 percent of their time on lobbying activities to register and make semiannual reports of their activities to the clerk of the House and the secretary of the Senate, although the law provides for a number of exemptions. Among the statute's prohibitions, lobbyists are not allowed to make contributions to the legal defense fund of a member or high government official or to reimburse for official travel. Civil penalties for failure to comply may include fines of up to $50,000. The act does not include grassroots lobbying in its definition of lobbying activities.

The act amends several other lobby laws, notably the Foreign Agents Registration Act (FARA), so that lobbyists can submit a single filing. Since the measure was enacted, the number of lobby registrations has risen from about 12,000 to more than 20,000. In 1998 expenditures on federal lobbying, as disclosed under the Lobbying Disclosure Act, totaled $1.42 billion. The 1995 act supersedes the 1946 Federal Regulation of Lobbying Act, which was repealed in Section 11 of the 1995 Act.

Logrolling—Jargon for a legislative tactic or bargaining strategy in which members try to build support for their legislation by promising to support legislation desired by other members or by accepting amendments they hope will induce their colleagues to vote for their bill.

Lower Body—A way to refer to the House of Representatives, which is considered pejorative by House members.

Mace—The symbol of the office of the House sergeant at arms. Under the direction of the Speaker, the sergeant at arms is responsible for preserving order on the House floor by holding up the mace in front of an unruly member, or by carrying the mace up and down the aisles to quell boisterous behavior. When the House is in session, the mace sits on a pedestal at the Speaker's right; when the House is in Committee of the Whole, it is moved to a lower pedestal. The mace is forty-six inches high and consists of thirteen ebony rods bound in silver and topped by a silver globe with a silver eagle, wings outstretched, perched on it.

Majority Leader—The majority party's chief floor spokesperson, elected by that party's caucus — sometimes called floor leader. In the Senate, the majority leader also develops the party's political and procedural strategy, usually in collaboration with other party officials and committee chairmen. The majority leader negotiates the Senate's agenda and committee ratios with the minority leader and usually calls up measures for floor action. The chamber traditionally concedes to the majority leader the right to determine the days on which it will meet and the hours at which it will convene and adjourn. In the House, the majority leader is the Speaker's deputy and heir apparent and helps plan the floor agenda and the party's legislative strategy and often speaks for the party leadership in debate.

Managers—(1) The official title of members appointed to a conference committee, commonly called conferees. The ranking majority and minority managers for each house also manage floor consideration of the committee's conference report. (2) The members who manage the initial floor consideration of a measure. (3) The official title of House members appointed to present impeachment articles to the Senate and to act as prosecutors on behalf of the House during the Senate trial of the impeached person.

Mandatory Appropriations—Amounts that Congress must appropriate annually because it has no discretion over them unless it first amends existing substantive law. Certain entitlement programs, for example, require annual appropriations.

Markup—A meeting or series of meetings by a committee or subcommittee during which members mark up a measure by offering, debating and voting on amendments to it.

Means-Tested Programs—Programs that provide benefits or services to low-income individuals who meet a test of need. Most are entitlement programs, such as Medicaid, food stamps and Supplementary Security Income. A few—for example, subsidized housing and various social services—are funded through discretionary appropriations.

Members' Allowances—Official expenses that are paid for or for which members are reimbursed by their houses. Among these are the costs of office space in congressional buildings and in their home states or districts; office equipment and supplies; postage-free mailings (the franking privilege); a set number of trips to and from home states or districts, as well as travel elsewhere on official business; telephone and other telecommunications services; and staff salaries.

Member's Staff—The personal staff to which a member is entitled. The House sets a maximum number of staff and a monetary allowance for each member. The Senate does not set a maximum staff level, but it does set a monetary allowance for each member. In each house, the staff allowance is included with office expenses allowances and official mail allowances in a consolidated allowance. Representatives and senators can spend as much money in their consolidated allowances for staff, office expenses or official mail, as long as they do not exceed the monetary value of the three allowances combined. This provides members with flexibility in operating their offices.

Method of Equal Proportions—The mathematical formula used since 1950 to determine how the 435 seats in the House of Representatives should be distributed among the fifty states in the apportionment following each decennial census. It minimizes as much as possible the proportional difference between the average district population in any two states. Because the Constitution guarantees each state at least one representative, fifty seats are automatically apportioned. The formula calculates priority numbers for each state, assigns the first of the 385 remaining seats to the state with the highest priority number, the second to the state with the next highest number and so on until all seats are distributed. (See Apportionment.)

Midterm Election—The general election for members of Congress that occurs in November of the second year in a presidential term.

Minority Leader—The minority party's leader and chief floor spokesman, elected by the party caucus; sometimes called minority floor leader. With the assistance of other party officials and the ranking minority members of committees, the minority leader devises the party's political and procedural strategy.

Minority Staff—Employees who assist the minority party members of a committee. Most committees hire separate majority and minority party staffs but they also may hire nonpartisan staff. Senate rules state that a committee's staff must reflect the relative number of its majority and minority party committee members, and the rules guarantee the minority at least one-third of the funds available for hiring partisan staff. In the House, each committee is authorized thirty professional staff, and the minority members of most committees may select up to ten of these staff

(subject to full committee approval). Under House rules, the minority party is to be "treated fairly" in the apportionment of additional staff resources. Each House committee determines the portion of its additional staff it allocates to the minority; some committees allocate one-third; and others allot less.

Modified Rule—A special rule from the House Rules Committee that permits only certain amendments to be offered to a measure during its floor consideration or that bans certain specified amendments or amendments on certain subjects.

Morning Business—In the Senate, routine business that is to be transacted at the beginning of the morning hour. The business consists, first, of laying before the Senate, and referring to committees, matters such as messages from the president and the House, federal agency reports and unreferred petitions, memorials, bills and joint resolutions. Next, senators may present additional petitions and memorials. Then committees may present their reports, after which senators may introduce bills and resolutions. Finally, resolutions coming over from a previous day are taken up for consideration. In practice, the Senate adopts standing orders that permit senators to introduce measures and file reports at any time, but only if there has been a morning business period on that day. Because the Senate often remains in the same legislative day for several days, weeks or months at a time, it orders a morning business period almost every calendar day for the convenience of senators who wish to introduce measures or make reports.

Morning Hour—A two-hour period at the beginning of a new legislative day during which the Senate is supposed to conduct routine business, call the calendar on Mondays and deal with other matters described in a Senate rule. In practice, the morning hour very rarely, if ever, occurs, in part because the Senate frequently recesses, rather than adjourns, at the end of a daily session. Therefore the rule does not apply when the senate next meets. The Senate's rules reserve the first hour of the morning for morning business. After the completion of morning business, or at the end of the first hour, the rules permit a motion to proceed to the consideration of a measure on the calendar out of its regular order (except on Mondays). Because that normally debatable motion is not debatable if offered during the morning hour, the majority leader may, but rarely does, use this procedure in anticipating a filibuster on the motion to proceed. If the Senate agrees to the motion, it can consider the measure until the end of the morning hour, and if there is no unfinished business from the previous day it can continue considering it after the morning hour. But if there is unfinished business, a motion to continue consideration is necessary, and that motion is debatable.

Motion—A formal proposal for a procedural action, such as to consider, to amend, to lay on the table, to reconsider, to recess or to adjourn. It has been estimated that at least eighty-five motions are possible under various circumstances in the House of Representatives, somewhat fewer in the Senate. Not all motions are created equal; some are privileged or preferential and enjoy priority over others. Some motions are debatable, amendable or divisible, while others are not.

Multiple and Sequential Referrals—The practice of referring a measure to two or more committees for concurrent consideration (multiple referral) or successively to several committees in sequence (sequential referral). A measure may also be divided into several parts, with each referred to a different committee or to several committees sequentially (split referral). In theory this gives all committees that have jurisdiction over parts of a measure the opportunity to consider and report on them.

Before 1975, House precedents banned such referrals. A 1975 rule required the Speaker to make concurrent and sequential referrals "to the maximum extent feasible." On sequential referrals, the Speaker could set deadlines for reporting the measure. The Speaker ruled that this provision authorized him to discharge a committee from further consideration of a measure and place it on the appropriate calendar of the House if the committee fails to meet the Speaker's deadline. The Speaker also used combinations of concurrent and sequential referrals. In 1995 joint referrals were prohibited. Now each measure is referred to a primary committee and also may be referred, either concurrently or sequentially, to one or more other committees, but usually only for consideration of portions of the measure that fall within the jurisdiction of each of those other committees.

In the Senate, before 1977 concurrent and sequential referrals were permitted only by unanimous consent. In that year, a rule authorized a privileged motion for such a referral if offered jointly by the majority and minority leaders. Debate on the motion and all amendments to it is limited to two hours. The motion may set deadlines for reporting and provide for discharging the committees involved if they fail to meet the deadlines. To date, this procedure has never been invoked; multiple referrals in the Senate continue to be made by unanimous consent.

Multiyear Appropriation—An appropriation that remains available for spending or obligation for more than one fiscal year; the exact period of time is specified in the act making the appropriation.

Multiyear Authorization—(1) Legislation that authorizes the existence or continuation of an agency, program or activity for more than one fiscal year. (2) Legislation that authorizes appropriations for an agency, program or activity for more than one fiscal year.

Nomination—A proposed presidential appointment to a federal office submitted to the Senate for confirmation. Approval is by majority vote. The Constitution explicitly requires confirmation for ambassadors, consuls, "public Ministers" (department heads) and Supreme Court justices. By law, other federal judges, all military promotions of officers and many high-level civilian officials must be confirmed.

Oath of Office—Upon taking office, members of Congress must swear or affirm that they will "support and defend the Constitution...against all enemies, foreign and domestic," that they will "bear true faith and allegiance" to the Constitution, that they take the obligation "freely, without any mental reservation or purpose of evasion," and that they will "well and faithfully discharge the duties" of their office. The oath is required by the Constitution, and the wording is prescribed by a statute. All House members must take the oath at the beginning of each new Congress. Usually, the member with the longest continuous service in the House swears in the Speaker, who then swears in the other members. The president of the Senate or a surrogate administers the oath to newly elected or reelected senators.

Obligation—A binding agreement by a government agency to pay for goods, products, services, studies and the like, either immediately or in the future. When an agency enters into such an agreement, it incurs an obligation. As the agency makes the required payments, it liquidates the obligation. Appropriation laws usually make funds available for obligation for one or more fiscal years but do not require agencies to spend their funds during those specific years. The actual outlays can occur years after the appropriation is obligated, as with a contract for construction of a submarine that may provide for payment to be made when it is delivered in the future. Such obligated funds are often said to be "in the pipeline." Under these circumstances, an agency's outlays in a particular year can come from appropriations obligated in previous years as well as from its current-year appropriation. Consequently, the money Congress appropriates for a fiscal year does not equal the total amount of appropriated money the government will actually spend in that year.

Off-Budget Entities—Specific federal entities whose budget authority, outlays and receipts are excluded by law from the calculation of budg-

et totals, although they are part of government spending and income. As of early 2001, these included the Social Security trust funds (Federal Old-Age and Survivors Insurance Fund and the Federal Disability Insurance Trust Fund) and the Postal Service. Government-sponsored enterprises are also excluded from the budget because they are considered private rather than public organizations.

Office of Management and Budget (OMB)—A unit in the Executive Office of the President, reconstituted in 1970 from the former Bureau of the Budget. The Office of Management and Budget (OMB) assists the president in preparing the budget and in formulating the government's fiscal program. The OMB also plays a central role in supervising and controlling implementation of the budget, pursuant to provisions in appropriations laws, the Budget Enforcement Act and other statutes. In addition to these budgetary functions, the OMB has various management duties, including those performed through its three statutory offices: Federal Financial Management, Federal Procurement Policy and Information and Regulatory Affairs.

Officers of Congress—The Constitution refers to the Speaker of the House and the president of the Senate as officers and declares that each house "shall chuse" its "other Officers," but it does not name them or indicate how they should be selected. A House rule refers to its clerk, sergeant at arms and chaplain as officers. Officers are not named in the Senate's rules, but Riddick's Senate Procedure lists the president pro tempore, secretary of the Senate, sergeant at arms, chaplain and the secretaries for the majority and minority parties as officers. A few appointed officials are sometimes referred to as officers, including the parliamentarians and the legislative counsels. The House elects its officers by resolution at the beginning of each Congress. The Senate also elects its officers, but once elected Senate officers serve from Congress to Congress until their successors are chosen.

Omnibus Bill—A measure that combines the provisions of several disparate subjects into a single and often lengthy bill.

One-Minute Speeches—Addresses by House members that can be on any subject but are limited to one minute. They are usually permitted at the beginning of a daily session after the chaplain's prayer, the pledge of allegiance and approval of the *Journal*. They are a customary practice, not a right granted by rule. Consequently, recognition for one-minute speeches requires unanimous consent and is entirely within the Speaker's discretion. The Speaker sometimes refuses to permit them when the House has a heavy legislative schedule or limits or postpones them until a later time of the day.

Open Rule—A special rule from the House Rules Committee that permits members to offer as many floor amendments as they wish as long as the amendments are germane and do not violate other House rules.

Order of Business (House)—The sequence of events prescribed by a House rule during the meeting of the House on a new legislative day that is supposed to take place, also called the general order of business. The sequence consists of (1) the chaplain's prayer; (2) reading and approval of the Journal; (3) the pledge of allegiance; (4) correction of the reference of public bills to committee; (5) disposal of business on the Speaker's table; (6) unfinished business; (7) the morning hour call of committees and consideration of their bills; (8) motions to go into Committee of the Whole; and (9) orders of the day. In practice, the House never fully complies with this rule. Instead, the items of business that follow the pledge of allegiance are supplanted by any special orders of business that are in order on that day (for example, conference reports; the corrections, discharge or private calendars; or motions to suspend the rules) and by other privileged business (for example, general appropriation bills and special rules) or measures made in order by special rules or unanimous consent. The regular order of business is also modified by unanimous consent practices and orders that govern recognition for one-minute speeches (which date from 1937) and for morning-hour debates, begun in 1994. By this combination of an order of business with privileged interruptions, the House gives precedence to certain categories of important legislation, brings to the floor other major legislation from its calendars in any order it chooses and provides expeditious processing for minor and noncontroversial measures.

Order of Business (Senate)—The sequence of events at the beginning of a new legislative day, as prescribed by Senate rules and standing orders. The sequence consists of (1) the chaplain's prayer; (2) the pledge of allegiance; (3) the designation of a temporary presiding officer if any; (4) Journal reading and approval; (5) recognition of the majority and minority leaders or their designees under the standing order; (6) morning business in the morning hour; (7) call of the calendar during the morning hour (largely obsolete); and (8) unfinished business from the previous session day.

Organization of Congress—The actions each house takes at the beginning of a Congress that are necessary to its operations. These include swearing in newly elected members, notifying the president that a quorum of each house is present, making committee assignments and fixing the hour for daily meetings. Because the House of Representatives is not a continuing body, it must also elect its Speaker and other officers and adopt its rules.

Original Bill—(1) A measure drafted by a committee and introduced by its chairman or another designated member when the committee reports the measure to its house. Unlike a clean bill, it is not referred back to the committee after introduction. The Senate permits all its legislative committees to report original bills. In the House, this authority is referred to in the rules as the "right to report at any time," and five committees (Appropriations, Budget, House Administration, Rules and Standards of Official Conduct) have such authority under circumstances specified in House Rule XIII, clause 5.

(2) In the House, special rules reported by the Rules Committee often propose that an amendment in the nature of a substitute be considered as an original bill for purposes of amendment, meaning that the substitute, as with a bill, may be amended in two degrees. Without that requirement, the substitute may only be amended in one further degree. In the Senate, an amendment in the nature of a substitute automatically is open to two degrees of amendment, as is the original text of the bill, if the substitute is offered when no other amendment is pending.

Original Jurisdiction—The authority of certain committees to originate a measure and report it to the chamber. For example, general appropriation bills reported by the House Appropriations Committee are original bills, and special rules reported by the House Rules Committee are original resolutions.

Other Body—A commonly used reference to a house by a member of the other house. Congressional comity discourages members from directly naming the other house during debate.

Outlays—Amounts of government spending. They consist of payments, usually by check or in cash, to liquidate obligations incurred in prior fiscal years as well as in the current year, including the net lending of funds under budget authority. In federal budget accounting, net outlays are calculated by subtracting the amounts of refunds and various kinds of reimbursements to the government from actual spending.

Override a Veto—Congressional enactment of a measure over the president's veto. A veto override requires a recorded two-thirds vote of those voting in each house, a quorum being present. Because the president must return the vetoed measure to its house of origin, that house votes first, but neither house is required to attempt an override, whether immediately or at all. If an override attempt fails in the house of origin, the veto stands and the measure dies.

Oversight—Congressional review of the way in which federal agencies implement laws to ensure that they are carrying out the intent of Congress and to inquire into the efficiency of the implementation and the effectiveness of the law. The Legislative Reorganization Act of 1946 defined oversight as the function of exercising continuous watchfulness over the execution of the laws by the executive branch.

Oxford-Style Debate—The House held three Oxford-style debates in 1994, modeled after the famous debating format favored by the Oxford Union in Great Britain. Neither chamber has held Oxford-style debates since then. The Oxford-style debates aired nationally over C-SPAN television and National Public Radio. The organized event featured eight participants divided evenly into two teams, one team representing the Democrats (then holding the majority in the chamber) and the other the Republicans. Both teams argued a single question chosen well ahead of the event. A moderator regulated the debate, and began it by stating the resolution at issue. The order of the speakers alternated by team, with a debater for the affirmative speaking first and a debater for the opposing team offering a rebuttal. The rest of the speakers alternated in kind until all gained the chance to speak.

Parliamentarian—The official advisor to the presiding officer in each house on questions of procedure. The parliamentarian and his or her assistants also answer procedural questions from members and congressional staff, refer measures to committees on behalf of the presiding officer and maintain compilations of the precedents. The House parliamentarian revises the *House Manual* at the beginning of every Congress and usually reviews special rules before the Rules Committee reports them to the House. Either a parliamentarian or an assistant is always present and near the podium during sessions of each house.

Party Caucus—Generic term for each party's official organization in each house. Only House Democrats officially call their organization a caucus. House and Senate Republicans and Senate Democrats call their organizations conferences. The party caucuses elect their leaders, approve committee assignments and chairmanships (or ranking minority members, if the party is in the minority), establish party committees and study groups and discuss party and legislative policies. On rare occasions, they have stripped members of committee seniority or expelled them from the caucus for party disloyalty.

Pay-as-You-Go (PAYGO)—A provision first instituted under the Budget Enforcement Act of 1990 that applies to legislation enacted before Oct. 1, 2002. It requires that the cumulative effect of legislation concerning either revenues or direct spending should not result in a net negative impact on the budget. If legislation does provide for an increase in spending or decrease in revenues, that effect is supposed to be offset by legislated spending reductions or revenue increases. If Congress fails to enact the appropriate offsets, the act requires presidential sequestration of sufficient offsetting amounts in specific direct spending accounts. Congress and the president can circumvent this requirement if both agree that an emergency requires a particular action or if a law is enacted declaring that deteriorated economic circumstances make it necessary to suspend the requirement.

Permanent Appropriation—An appropriation that remains continuously available, without current action or renewal by Congress, under the terms of a previously enacted authorization or appropriation law. One such appropriation provides for payment of interest on the public debt and another the salaries of members of Congress.

Permanent Authorization—An authorization without a time limit. It usually does not specify any limit on the funds that may be appropriated for the agency, program or activity that it authorizes, leaving such amounts to the discretion of the appropriations committees and the two houses.

Permanent Staff—Term used formerly for committee staff authorized by law, who were funded through a permanent authorization and also called statutory staff. Most committees were authorized thirty permanent staff members. Most committees also were permitted additional staff, often called investigative staff, who were authorized by annual or biennial funding resolutions. The Senate eliminated the primary distinction between statutory and investigative staff in 1981. The House eliminated the distinction in 1995 by requiring that funding resolutions authorize money to hire both types of staff.

Personally Obnoxious (or Objectionable)—A characterization a senator sometimes applies to a president's nominee for a federal office in that senator's state to justify his or her opposition to the nomination.

Pocket Veto—The indirect veto of a bill as a result of the president withholding approval of it until after Congress has adjourned *sine die*. A bill the president does not sign but does not formally veto while Congress is in session automatically becomes a law ten days (excluding Sundays) after it is received. But if Congress adjourns its annual session during that ten-day period the measure dies even if the president does not formally veto it.

Point of Order—A parliamentary term used in committee and on the floor to object to an alleged violation of a rule and to demand that the chair enforce the rule. The point of order immediately halts the proceedings until the chair decides whether the contention is valid.

Pork or Pork Barrel Legislation—Pejorative terms for federal appropriations, bills or policies that provide funds to benefit a legislator's district or state, with the implication that the legislator presses for enactment of such benefits to ingratiate himself or herself with constituents rather than on the basis of an impartial, objective assessment of need or merit. The terms are often applied to such benefits as new parks, post offices, dams, canals, bridges, roads, water projects, sewage treatment plants and public works of any kind, as well as demonstration projects, research grants and relocation of government facilities. Funds released by the president for various kinds of benefits or government contracts approved by him allegedly for political purposes are also sometimes referred to as pork.

Postcloture Filibuster—A filibuster conducted after the Senate invokes cloture. It employs an array of procedural tactics rather than lengthy speeches to delay final action. The Senate curtailed the postcloture filibuster's effectiveness by closing a variety of loopholes in the cloture rule in 1979 and 1986.

Power of the Purse—A reference to the constitutional power Congress has over legislation to raise revenue and appropriate monies from the Treasury. Article I, Section 8 states that Congress "shall have Power To lay and collect Taxes, Duties, Imposts and Excises, [and] to pay the Debts." Section 9 declares: "No Money shall be drawn from the Treasury, but in Consequence of Appropriations made by Law."

Preamble—Introductory language describing the reasons for and intent of a measure, sometimes called a whereas clause. It occasionally appears in joint, concurrent and simple resolutions but rarely in bills.

Precedent—A previous ruling on a parliamentary matter or a long-standing practice or custom of a house. Precedents serve to control arbitrary rulings and serve as the common law of a house.

President of the Senate—One constitutional role of the vice president is serving as the presiding officer of the Senate, or president of the Senate. The Constitution permits the vice president to cast a vote in the Senate only to break a tie, but the vice president is not required to do so.

President Pro Tempore—Under the Constitution, an officer elected by the Senate to preside over it during the absence of the vice president of the United States. Often referred to as the "pro tem," this senator is usually a member of the majority party with the longest continuous service in the chamber and also, by virtue of seniority, a committee chairman. When attending to committee and other duties the president pro tempore appoints other senators to preside.

Presiding Officer—In a formal meeting, the individual authorized to maintain order and decorum, recognize members to speak or offer motions and apply and interpret the chamber's rules, precedents and practices. The Speaker of the House and the president of the Senate are the chief presiding officers in their respective houses.

Previous Question—A nondebatable motion which, when agreed to by majority vote, usually cuts off further debate, prevents the offering of additional amendments and brings the pending matter to an immediate vote. It is a major debate-limiting device in the House; it is not permitted in Committee of the Whole in the House or in the Senate.

Private Bill—A bill that applies to one or more specified persons, corporations, institutions or other entities, usually to grant relief when no other legal remedy is available to them. Many private bills deal with claims against the federal government, immigration and naturalization cases and land titles.

Private Calendar—Commonly used title for a calendar in the House reserved for private bills and resolutions favorably reported by committees. The private calendar is officially called the Calendar of the Committee of the Whole House.

Private Law—A private bill enacted into law. Private laws are numbered in the same fashion as public laws.

Privilege—An attribute of a motion, measure, report, question or proposition that gives it priority status for consideration. Privileged motions and motions to bring up privileged questions are not debatable.

Privilege of the Floor—In addition to the members of a house, certain individuals are admitted to its floor while it is in session. The rules of the two houses differ somewhat but both extend the privilege to the president and vice president, Supreme Court justices, cabinet members, state governors, former members of that house, members of the other house, certain officers and officials of Congress, certain staff of that house in the discharge of official duties and the chamber's former parliamentarians. They also allow access to a limited number of committee and members' staff when their presence is necessary.

Pro Forma Amendment—In the House, an amendment that ostensibly proposes to change a measure or another amendment by moving "to strike the last word" or "to strike the requisite number of words." A member offers it not to make any actual change in the measure or amendment but only to obtain time for debate.

Pro Tem—A common reference to the president pro tempore of the Senate or, occasionally, to a Speaker pro tempore. (See President Pro Tempore; Speaker Pro Tempore.)

Procedures—The methods of conducting business in a deliberative body. The procedures of each house are governed first by applicable provisions of the Constitution, and then by its standing rules and orders, precedents, traditional practices and any statutory rules that apply to it. The authority of the houses to adopt rules in addition to those specified in the Constitution is derived from Article I, Section 5, clause 2, of the Constitution, which states: "Each House may determine the Rules of its Proceedings...." By rule, the House of Representatives also follows the procedures in Jefferson's Manual that are not inconsistent with its standing rules and orders. Many Senate procedures also conform with Jefferson's provisions, but by practice rather than by rule. At the beginning of each Congress, the House uses procedures in general parliamentary law until it adopts its standing rules.

Proxy Voting—The practice of permitting a member to cast the vote of an absent colleague in addition to his or her own vote. Proxy voting is prohibited on the floors of the House and Senate, but the Senate permits its committees to authorize proxy voting, and most do. In 1995, House rules were changed to prohibit proxy voting in committee.

Public Bill—A bill dealing with general legislative matters having national applicability or applying to the federal government or to a class of persons, groups or organizations.

Public Debt—Federal government debt incurred by the Treasury or the Federal Financing Bank by the sale of securities to the public or borrowings from a federal fund or account.

Public Law—A public bill or joint resolution enacted into law. It is cited by the letters "PL" followed by a hyphenated number. The digits before the hyphen indicate the number of the Congress in which it was enacted; the digits after the hyphen indicate its position in the numerical sequence of public measures that became law during that Congress. For example, the Budget Enforcement Act of 1990 became PL 101-508 because it was the 508th measure in that sequence for the 101st Congress. (See also Private Law.)

Qualification (of Members)—The Constitution requires members of the House of Representatives to be twenty-five years of age at the time their terms begin. They must have been citizens of the United States for seven years before that date and, when elected, must be "Inhabitant[s]" of the state from which they were elected. There is no constitutional requirement that they reside in the districts they represent. Senators are required to be thirty years of age at the time their terms begin. They must have been citizens of the United States for nine years before that date and, when elected, must be "Inhabitant[s]" of the states in which they were elected. The "Inhabitant" qualification is broadly interpreted, and in modern times a candidate's declaration of state residence has generally been accepted as meeting the constitutional requirement.

Queen of the Hill Rule—A special rule from the House Rules Committee that permits votes on a series of amendments, especially complete substitutes for a measure, in a specified order, but directs that the amendment receiving the greatest number of votes shall be the winning one. This kind of rule permits the House to vote directly on a variety of alternatives to a measure. In doing so, it sets aside the precedent that once an amendment has been adopted, no further amendments may be offered to the text it has amended. Under an earlier practice, the Rules Committee reported "king of the hill" rules under which there also could be votes on a series of amendments, again in a specified order. If more than one of the amendments was adopted under this kind of rule, it was the last amendment to receive a majority vote that was considered as having been finally adopted, whether or not it had received the greatest number of votes.

Quorum—The minimum number of members required to be present for the transaction of business. Under the Constitution, a quorum in each house is a majority of its members: 218 in the House and 51 in the Senate when there are no vacancies. By House rule, a quorum in Committee of the Whole is 100. In practice, both houses usually assume a quorum is present even if it is not, unless a member makes a point of no quorum in the House or suggests the absence of a quorum in the Senate. Consequently, each house transacts much of its business, and even passes bills, when only a few members are present. For House and Senate committees, chamber rules allow a minimum quorum of one-third of a committee's members to conduct most types of business.

Quorum Call—A procedure for determining whether a quorum is present in a chamber. In the Senate, a clerk calls the roll (roster) of senators. The House usually employs its electronic voting system.

Ramseyer Rule—A House rule that requires a committee's report on a bill or joint resolution to show the changes the measure, and any committee amendments to it, would make in existing law. The rule requires the report to present the text of any statutory provision that would be repealed and a comparative print showing, through typographical devices such as stricken-through type or italics, other changes that would be made in existing law. The rule, adopted in 1929, is named after its sponsor, Rep. Christian W. Ramseyer, R-Iowa. The Senate's analogous rule is called the Cordon Rule.

Rank or Ranking—A member's position on the list of his or her party's members on a committee or subcommittee. When first assigned to a committee, a member is usually placed at the bottom of the list, then moves up as those above leave the committee. On subcommittees, however, a member's rank may not have anything to do with the length of his or her service on it.

Ranking Member—(1) Most often a reference to the minority member with the highest ranking on a committee or subcommittee. (2) A reference to the majority member next in rank to the chairman or to the highest ranking majority member present at a committee or subcommittee meeting.

Ratification—(1) The president's formal act of promulgating a treaty after the Senate has approved it. The resolution of ratification agreed to by the Senate is the procedural vehicle by which the Senate gives its consent to ratification. (2) A state legislature's act in approving a proposed constitutional amendment. Such an amendment becomes effective when ratified by three-fourths of the states.

Reapportionment—(See Apportionment.)

Recess—(1) A temporary interruption or suspension of a meeting of a chamber or committee. Unlike an adjournment, a recess does not end a legislative day. Because the Senate often recesses from one calendar day to another, its legislative day may extend over several calendar days, weeks or even months. (2) A period of adjournment for more than three days to a day certain, especially over a holiday or in August during odd-numbered years.

Recess Appointment—A presidential appointment to a vacant federal position made after the Senate has adjourned *sine die* or has adjourned or recessed for more than thirty days. If the president submits the recess appointee's nomination during the next session of the Senate, that individual can continue to serve until the end of the session even though the Senate might have rejected the nomination. When appointed to a vacancy that existed thirty days before the end of the last Senate session, a recess appointee is not paid until confirmed.

Recommit—To send a measure back to the committee that reported it; sometimes called a straight motion to recommit to distinguish it from a motion to recommit with instructions. A successful motion to recommit kills the measure unless it is accompanied by instructions.

Recommit a Conference Report—To return a conference report to the conference committee for renegotiation of some or all of its agreements. A motion to recommit may be offered with or without instructions.

Recommit with Instructions—To send a measure back to a committee with instructions to take some action on it. Invariably in the House and often in the Senate, when the motion recommits to a standing committee, the instructions require the committee to report the measure "forthwith" with specified amendments.

Reconciliation—A procedure for changing existing revenue and spending laws to bring total federal revenues and spending within the limits established in a budget resolution. Congress has applied reconciliation chiefly to revenues and mandatory spending programs, especially entitlements. Discretionary spending is controlled through annual appropriation bills.

Recorded Vote—(1) Generally, any vote in which members are recorded by name for or against a measure; also called a record vote or roll-call vote. The only recorded vote in the Senate is a vote by the yeas and nays and is commonly called a roll-call vote. (2) Technically, a recorded vote is one demanded in the House of Representatives and supported by at least one-fifth of a quorum (forty-four members) in the House sitting as the House or at least twenty-five members in Committee of the Whole.

Recorded Vote by Clerks—A voting procedure in the House where members pass through the appropriate "aye" or "no" aisle in the chamber and cast their votes by depositing a signed green (yea) or red (no) card in a ballot box. These votes are tabulated by clerks and reported to the chair. The electronic voting system is much more convenient and has largely supplanted this procedure. (See Committee of the Whole; Recorded Vote; Teller Vote.)

Redistricting—The redrawing of congressional district boundaries within a state after a decennial census. Redistricting may be required to equalize district populations or to accommodate an increase or decrease in the number of a state's House seats that might have resulted from the decennial apportionment. The state governments determine the district lines. (See Apportionment; Congressional District; Gerrymandering.)

Referral—The assignment of a measure to committee for consideration. Under a House rule, the Speaker can refuse to refer a measure if the Speaker believes it is "of an obscene or insulting character."

Report—(1) As a verb, a committee is said to report when it submits a measure or other document to its parent chamber. (2) A clerk is said to report when he or she reads a measure's title, text or the text of an amendment to the body at the direction of the chair. (3) As a noun, a committee document that accompanies a reported measure. It describes the measure, the committee's views on it, its costs and the changes it proposes to make in existing law; it also includes certain impact statements. (4) A committee document submitted to its parent chamber that describes the results of an investigation or other study or provides information it is required to provide by rule or law.

Representative—An elected and duly sworn member of the House of Representatives who is entitled to vote in the chamber. The Constitution requires that a representative be at least twenty-five years old, a citizen of the United States for at least seven years and an inhabitant of the state from which he or she is elected. Customarily, the member resides in the district he or she represents. Representatives are elected in even-numbered years to two-year terms that begin the following January.

Reprimand—A formal condemnation of a member for misbehavior, considered a milder reproof than censure. The House of Representatives first used it in 1976. The Senate first used it in 1991. (See also Censure; Code of Official Conduct; Denounce; Ethics Rules; Expulsion; Seniority Loss.)

Rescission—A provision of law that repeals previously enacted budget authority in whole or in part. Under the Impoundment Control Act of 1974, the president can impound such funds by sending a message to Congress requesting one or more rescissions and the reasons for doing so. If Congress does not pass a rescission bill for the programs requested by the president within forty-five days of continuous session after receiving the message, the president must make the funds available for obligation and expenditure. If the president does not, the comptroller general of the United States is authorized to bring suit to compel the release of those funds. A rescission bill may rescind all, part or none of an amount proposed by the president, and may rescind funds the president has not impounded.

Reserving the Right To Object—Members' declaration that at some indefinite future time they may object to a unanimous consent request. It is an attempt to circumvent the requirement that members may prevent such an action only by objecting immediately after it is proposed.

Resident Commissioner from Puerto Rico—A nonvoting member of the House of Representatives, elected to a four-year term. The resident commissioner has the same status and privileges as delegates. Like the delegates, the resident commissioner may not vote in the House or Committee of the Whole.

Resolution—(1) A simple resolution; that is, a nonlegislative measure effective only in the house in which it is proposed and not requiring concurrence by the other chamber or approval by the president. Simple resolutions are designated H. Res. in the House and S. Res. in the Senate. Simple resolutions express nonbinding opinions on policies or issues or deal with the internal affairs or prerogatives of a house. (2) Any type of resolution: simple, concurrent or joint. (See Concurrent Resolution; Joint Resolution.)

Resolution of Inquiry—A resolution usually simple rather than concurrent calling on the president or the head of an executive agency to provide specific information or papers to one or both houses.

Resolution of Ratification—The Senate vehicle for agreeing to a treaty. The constitutionally mandated vote of two-thirds of the senators present and voting applies to the adoption of this resolution. However, it may also contain amendments, reservations, declarations or understandings that the Senate had previously added to it by majority vote.

Revenue Legislation—Measures that levy new taxes or tariffs or change existing ones. Under Article I, Section 7, clause 1 of the Constitution, the House of Representatives originates federal revenue measures, but the Senate can propose amendments to them. The House Ways and Means Committee and the Senate Finance Committee have jurisdiction over such measures, with a few minor exceptions.

Revise and Extend One's Remarks—A unanimous consent request to publish in the Congressional Record a statement a member did not deliver on the floor, a longer statement than the one made on the floor or miscellaneous extraneous material.

Revolving Fund—A trust fund or account whose income remains available to finance its continuing operations without any fiscal year limitation.

Rider—Congressional slang for an amendment unrelated or extraneous to the subject matter of the measure to which it is attached. Riders often contain proposals that are less likely to become law on their own merits as separate bills, either because of opposition in the committee of jurisdiction, resistance in the other house or the probability of a presidential veto. Riders are more common in the Senate.

Roll Call—A call of the roll to determine whether a quorum is present, to establish a quorum or to vote on a question. Usually, the House uses its electronic voting system for a roll call. The Senate does not have an electronic voting system; its roll is always called by a clerk.

Rule—(1) A permanent regulation that a house adopts to govern its conduct of business, its procedures, its internal organization, behavior of its members, regulation of its facilities, duties of an officer or some other subject it chooses to govern in that form. (2) In the House, a privileged simple resolution reported by the Rules Committee that provides methods and conditions for floor consideration of a measure or, rarely, several measures.

Rule Twenty-Two—A common reference to the Senate's cloture rule. (See Cloture)

Second-Degree Amendment—An amendment to an amendment in the first degree. It is usually a perfecting amendment.

Secretary of the Senate—The chief financial, administrative and legislative officer of the Senate. Elected by resolution or order of the Senate, the secretary is invariably the candidate of the majority party and usually chosen by the majority leader. In the absence of the vice president and pending the election of a president pro tempore, the secretary presides over the Senate. The secretary is subject to policy direction and oversight by the Senate Committee on Rules and Administration. The secretary manages a wide range of functions that support the administrative operations of the Senate as an organization as well as those functions necessary to its legislative process, including record keeping, document management, certifications, housekeeping services, administration of oaths and lobbyist registrations. The secretary is responsible for accounting for all funds appropriated to the Senate and conducts audits of Senate financial activities. On a semiannual basis the secretary issues the Report of the Secretary of the Senate, a compilation of Senate expenditures.

Section—A subdivision of a bill or statute. By law, a section must be numbered and, as nearly as possible, contain "a single proposition of enactment."

Select or Special Committee—A committee established by a resolution in either house for a special purpose and, usually, for a limited time. Most select and special committees are assigned specific investigations or studies but are not authorized to report measures to their chambers. However, both houses have created several permanent select and special committees and have given legislative reporting authority to a few of them: the Ethics Committee in the Senate and the Intelligence Committees in both houses. There is no substantive difference between a select and a special committee; they are so called depending simply on whether the resolution creating the committee calls it one or the other.

Senate—The house of Congress in which each state is represented by two senators; each senator has one vote. Article V of the Constitution declares that "No State, without its Consent, shall be deprived of its equal Suffrage in the Senate." The Constitution also gives the Senate equal legislative power with the House of Representatives. Although the Senate is prohibited from originating revenue measures, and as a matter of practice it does not originate appropriation measures, it can amend both. Only the Senate can give or withhold consent to treaties and nominations from the president. It also acts as a court to try impeachments by the House and elects the vice president when no candidate receives a majority of the electoral votes. It is often referred to as "the upper body," but not by members of the House.

Senate Manual—The handbook of the Senate's standing rules and orders and the laws and other regulations that apply to the Senate, usually published once each Congress.

Senator—A duly sworn elected or appointed member of the Senate. The Constitution requires that a senator be at least thirty years old, a citizen of the United States for at least nine years and an inhabitant of the state from which he or she is elected. Senators are usually elected in even-numbered years to six-year terms that begin the following January. When a vacancy occurs before the end of a term, the state governor can appoint a replacement to fill the position until a successor is chosen at the state's next general election or, if specified under state law, the next feasible date for such an election, to serve the remainder of the term. Until the Seventeenth Amendment was ratified in 1913, senators were chosen by their state legislatures.

Senatorial Courtesy—The Senate's practice of declining to confirm a presidential nominee for an office in the state of a senator of the president's party unless that senator approves.

Seniority—The priority, precedence or status accorded members according to the length of their continuous service in a house or on a committee.

Seniority Loss—A type of punishment that reduces a member's seniority on his or her committees, including the loss of chairmanships. Party caucuses in both houses have occasionally imposed such punishment on their members, for example, for publicly supporting candidates of the other party.

Seniority Rule—The customary practice, rather than a rule, of assigning the chairmanship of a committee to the majority party member who has served on the committee for the longest continuous period of time.

Seniority System—A collection of long-standing customary practices under which members with longer continuous service than their colleagues in their house or on their committees receive various kinds of preferential treatment. Although some of the practices are no longer as rigidly observed as in the past, they still pervade the organization and procedures of Congress.

Sequestration—A procedure for canceling budgetary resources — that is, money available for obligation or spending — to enforce budget limitations established in law. Sequestered funds are no longer available for obligation or expenditure.

Sergeant at Arms—The officer in each house responsible for maintaining order, security and decorum in its wing of the Capitol, including the chamber and its galleries. Although elected by their respective houses, both sergeants at arms are invariably the candidates of the majority party.

Session—(1) The annual series of meetings of a Congress. Under the Constitution, Congress must assemble at least once a year at noon on Jan. 3 unless it appoints a different day by law. (2) The special meetings of Congress or of one house convened by the president, called a special session. (3) A house is said to be in session during the period of a day when it is meeting.

Severability (or Separability) Clause—Language stating that if any particular provisions of a measure are declared invalid by the courts the remaining provisions shall remain in effect.

Sine Die—Without fixing a day for a future meeting. An adjournment *sine die* signifies the end of an annual or special session of Congress.

Slip Law—The first official publication of a measure that has become law. It is published separately in unbound, single-sheet form or pamphlet form. A slip law usually is available two or three days after the date of the law's enactment.

Speaker—The presiding officer of the House of Representatives and the leader of its majority party. The Speaker is selected by the majority party and formally elected by the House at the beginning of each Congress. Although the Constitution does not require the Speaker to be a member of the House, in fact, all Speakers have been members.

Speaker Pro Tempore—A member of the House who is designated as the temporary presiding officer by the Speaker or elected by the House to that position during the Speaker's absence.

Speaker's Vote—The Speaker is not required to vote, and the Speaker's name is not called on a roll-call vote unless so requested. Usually, the Speaker votes either to create a tie vote, and thereby defeat a proposal or to break a tie in favor of a proposal. Occasionally, the Speaker also votes to emphasize the importance of a matter.

Special Session—A session of Congress convened by the president, under his constitutional authority, after Congress has adjourned sine die at the end of a regular session. (See Adjournment *Sine Die*; Session.)

Spending Authority—The technical term for backdoor spending. The Congressional Budget Act of 1974 defines it as borrowing authority, contract authority and entitlement authority for which appropriation acts do not provide budget authority in advance. Under the Budget Act, legislation that provides new spending authority may not be considered unless it provides that the authority shall be effective only to the extent or in such amounts as provided in an appropriation act.

Spending Cap—The statutory limit for a fiscal year on the amount of new budget authority and outlays allowed for discretionary spending. The Budget Enforcement Act of 1997 requires a sequester if the cap is exceeded.

Split Referral—A measure divided into two or more parts, with each part referred to a different committee.

Sponsor—The principal proponent and introducer of a measure or an amendment.

Staff Director—The most frequently used title for the head of staff of a committee or subcommittee. On some committees, that person is called chief of staff, clerk, chief clerk, chief counsel, general counsel or executive director. The head of a committee's minority staff is usually called minority staff director.

Standing Committee—A permanent committee established by a House or Senate standing rule or standing order. The rule also describes the subject areas on which the committee may report bills and resolutions and conduct oversight. Most introduced measures must be referred to one or more standing committees according to their jurisdictions.

Standing Order—A continuing regulation or directive that has the force and effect of a rule, but is not incorporated into the standing rules. The Senate's numerous standing orders, like its standing rules, continue from Congress to Congress unless changed or the order states otherwise. The House uses relatively few standing orders, and those it adopts expire at the end of a session of Congress.

Standing Rules—The rules of the Senate that continue from one Congress to the next and the rules of the House of Representatives that it adopts at the beginning of each new Congress.

Standing Vote—An alternative and informal term for a division vote, during which members in favor of a proposal and then members opposed stand and are counted by the chair.

Star Print—A reprint of a bill, resolution, amendment or committee report correcting technical or substantive errors in a previous printing; so called because of the small black star that appears on the front page or cover.

State of the Union Message—A presidential message to Congress under the constitutional directive that the president shall "from time to time give to the Congress Information of the State of the Union, and recommend to their Consideration such Measures as he shall judge necessary and expedient." Customarily, the president sends an annual State of the Union message to Congress, usually late in January.

Statutes at Large—A chronological arrangement of the laws enacted in each session of Congress. Though indexed, the laws are not arranged by subject matter nor is there an indication of how they affect or change previously enacted laws. The volumes are numbered by Congress, and the laws are cited by their volume and page number. The Gramm-Rudman-Hollings Act, for example, appears as 99 Stat. 1037.

Straw Vote Prohibition—Under a House precedent, a member who has the floor during debate may not conduct a straw vote or otherwise ask for a show of support for a proposition. Only the chair may put a question to a vote.

Strike From the *Record*—Expunge objectionable remarks from the *Congressional Record*, after a member's words have been taken down on a point of order.

Subcommittee—A panel of committee members assigned a portion of the committee's jurisdiction or other functions. On legislative committees, subcommittees hold hearings, mark up legislation and report measures to their full committee for further action; they cannot report directly to the chamber. A subcommittee's party composition usually reflects the ratio on its parent committee.

Subpoena Power—The authority granted to committees by the rules of their respective houses to issue legal orders requiring individuals to appear and testify, or to produce documents pertinent to the committee's functions, or both. Persons who do not comply with subpoenas can be cited for contempt of Congress and prosecuted.

Subsidy—Generally, a payment or benefit made by the federal government for which no current repayment is required. Subsidy payments may be designed to support the conduct of an economic enterprise or activity, such as ship operations, or to support certain market prices, as in the case of farm subsidies.

Sunset Legislation—A term sometimes applied to laws authorizing the existence of agencies or programs that expire annually or at the end of some other specified period of time. One of the purposes of setting specific expiration dates for agencies and programs is to encourage the committees with jurisdiction over them to determine whether they should be continued or terminated.

Sunshine Rules—Rules requiring open committee hearings and business meetings, including markup sessions, in both houses, and also open conference committee meetings. However, all may be closed under certain circumstances and using certain procedures required by the rules.

Supermajority—A term sometimes used for a vote on a matter that requires approval by more than a simple majority of those members present and voting; also referred to as extraordinary majority.

Supplemental Appropriation Bill—A measure providing appropriations for use in the current fiscal year, in addition to those already provided in annual general appropriation bills. Supplemental appropriations are often for unforeseen emergencies.

Suspension of the Rules (House)—An expeditious procedure for passing relatively noncontroversial or emergency measures by a two-thirds vote of those members voting, a quorum being present.

Suspension of the Rules (Senate)—A procedure to set aside one or more of the Senate's rules; it is used infrequently, and then most often to suspend the rule banning legislative amendments to appropriation bills.

Task Force—A title sometimes given to a panel of members assigned to a special project, study or investigation. Ordinarily, these groups do not have authority to report measures to their respective houses.

Tax Expenditure—Loosely, a tax exemption or advantage, sometimes called an incentive or loophole; technically, a loss of governmental tax revenue attributable to some provision of federal tax laws that allows a special exclusion, exemption or deduction from gross income or that provides a special credit, preferential tax rate or deferral of tax liability.

Televised Proceedings—Television and radio coverage of the floor proceedings of the House of Representatives has been available since 1979 and of the Senate since 1986. They are broadcast over a coaxial cable system to all congressional offices and to some congressional agencies on channels reserved for that purpose. Coverage is also available free of charge to commercial and public television and radio broadcasters. The Cable-Satellite Public Affairs Network (C-SPAN) carries gavel-to-gavel coverage of both houses.

Teller Vote—A voting procedure, formerly used in the House, in which members cast their votes by passing through the center aisle to be counted, but not recorded by name, by a member from each party appointed by the chair. The House deleted the procedure from its rules in 1993, but during floor discussion of the deletion a leading member stated that a teller vote would still be available in the event of a breakdown of the electronic voting system.

Third-Degree Amendment—An amendment to a second-degree amendment. Both houses prohibit such amendments.

Third Reading—A required reading to a chamber of a bill or joint resolution by title only before the vote on passage. In modern practice, it has merely become a pro forma step.

Three-Day Rule—(1) In the House, a measure cannot be considered until the third calendar day on which the committee report has been available. (2) In the House, a conference report cannot be considered until the third calendar day on which its text has been available in the *Congressional Record*. (3) In the House, a general appropriation bill cannot be considered until the third calendar day on which printed hearings on the bill have been available. (4) In the Senate, when a committee votes to report a measure, a committee member is entitled to three calendar days within which to submit separate views for inclusion in the committee report. (In House committees, a member is entitled to two calendar days for this purpose, after the day on which the committee votes to report.) (5) In both houses, a majority of a committee's members may call a special meeting of the committee if its chairman fails to do so within three calendar days after three or more of the members, acting jointly, formally request such a meeting.

In calculating such periods, the House omits holiday and weekend days on which it does not meet. The Senate makes no such exclusion.

Tie Vote—When the votes for and against a proposition are equal, it loses. The president of the Senate may cast a vote only to break a tie. Because the Speaker is invariably a member of the House, the Speaker is entitled to vote but usually does not. The Speaker may choose to do so to break, or create, a tie vote.

Title—(1) A major subdivision of a bill or act, designated by a roman numeral and usually containing legislative provisions on the same general subject. Titles are sometimes divided into subtitles as well as sections. (2) The official name of a bill or act, also called a caption or long title. (3) Some bills also have short titles that appear in the sentence immediately following the enacting clause. (4) Popular titles are the unofficial names given to some bills or acts by common usage. For example, the Balanced Budget and Emergency Deficit Control Act of 1985 (short title) is almost invariably referred to as Gramm-Rudman (popular title). In other cases, significant legislation is popularly referred to by its title number (see definition (1) above). For example, the federal legislation that requires equality of funding for women's and men's sports in educational institutions that receive federal funds is popularly called Title IX.

Track System—An occasional Senate practice that expedites legislation by dividing a day's session into two or more specific time periods, commonly called tracks, each reserved for consideration of a different measure.

Transfer Payment—A federal government payment to which individuals or organizations are entitled under law and for which no goods or services are required in return. Payments include welfare and Social Security benefits, unemployment insurance, government pensions and veterans benefits.

Treaty—A formal document containing an agreement between two or more sovereign nations. The Constitution authorizes the president to make treaties, but the president must submit them to the Senate for its approval by a two-thirds vote of the senators present. Under the Senate's rules, that vote actually occurs on a resolution of ratification. Although the Constitution does not give the House a direct role in approving treaties, that body has sometimes insisted that a revenue treaty is an invasion of its prerogatives. In any case, the House may significantly affect the application of a treaty by its equal role in enacting legislation to implement the treaty.

Trust Funds—Special accounts in the Treasury that receive earmarked taxes or other kinds of revenue collections, such as user fees, and from which payments are made for special purposes or to recipients who meet the requirements of the trust funds as established by law. Of the more than 150 federal government trust funds, several finance major entitlement programs, such as Social Security, Medicare and retired federal employees' pensions. Others fund infrastructure construction and improvements, such as highways and airports.

Unanimous Consent—Without an objection by any member. A unanimous consent request asks permission, explicitly or implicitly, to set aside one or more rules. Both houses and their committees frequently use such requests to expedite their proceedings.

Uncontrollable Expenditures—A frequently used term for federal expenditures that are mandatory under existing law and therefore cannot be controlled by the president or Congress without a change in the existing law. Uncontrollable expenditures include spending required under entitlement programs and also fixed costs, such as interest on the public debt and outlays to pay for prior-year obligations. In recent years, uncontrollables have accounted for approximately three-quarters of federal spending in each fiscal year.

Unfunded Mandate—Generally, any provision in federal law or regulation that imposes a duty or obligation on a state or local government or private sector entity without providing the necessary funds to comply. The Unfunded Mandates Reform Act of 1995 amended the Congressional Budget Act of 1974 to provide a mechanism for the control of new unfunded mandates.

Union Calendar—A calendar of the House of Representatives for bills and resolutions favorably reported by committees that raise revenue or directly or indirectly appropriate money or property. In addition to appropriation bills, measures that authorize expenditures are also placed on this calendar. The calendar's full title is the Calendar of the Committee of the Whole House on the State of the Union.

Upper Body—A common reference to the Senate, but not used by members of the House.

U.S. Code—Popular title for the United States Code: Containing the General and Permanent Laws of the United States in Force on.... It is a consolidation and partial codification of the general and permanent laws of the United States arranged by subject under 50 titles. The first six titles deal with general or political subjects, the other forty-four with subjects ranging from agriculture to war, alphabetically arranged. A supplement is published after each session of Congress, and the entire Code is revised every six years.

User Fee—A fee charged to users of goods or services provided by the federal government. When Congress levies or authorizes such fees, it determines whether the revenues should go into the general collections of the Treasury or be available for expenditure by the agency that provides the goods or services.

Veto—The president's disapproval of a legislative measure passed by Congress. The president returns the measure to the house in which it originated without his signature but with a veto message stating his objections to it. When Congress is in session, the president must veto a bill within ten days, excluding Sundays, after the president has received it; otherwise it becomes law without his signature. The ten-day clock begins to run at midnight following his receipt of the bill. (See also Committee Veto; Item Veto; Line Item Veto Act of 1996; Override a Veto; Pocket Veto.)

Voice Vote—A method of voting in which members who favor a question answer aye in chorus, after which those opposed answer no in chorus, and the chair decides which position prevails.

Voting—Members vote in three ways on the floor: (1) by shouting "aye" or "no" on voice votes; (2) by standing for or against on division votes; and (3) on recorded votes (including the yeas and nays), by answering "aye" or "no" when their names are called or, in the House, by recording their votes through the electronic voting system.

War Powers Resolution of 1973—An act that requires the president "in every possible instance" to consult Congress before committing U.S. forces to ongoing or imminent hostilities. If the president commits them to a combat situation without congressional consultation, the president must notify Congress within forty-eight hours. Unless Congress declares war or otherwise authorizes the operation to continue, the forces must be withdrawn within sixty or ninety days, depending on certain conditions. No president has ever acknowledged the constitutionality of the resolution.

Well—The sunken, level, open space between members' seats and the podium at the front of each chamber. House members usually address their chamber from their party's lectern in the well on its side of the aisle. Senators usually speak at their assigned desks.

Whip—The majority or minority party member in each house who acts as assistant leader, helps plan and marshal support for party strategies, encourages party discipline and advises his or her leader on how colleagues intend to vote on the floor. In the Senate, the Republican whip's official title is assistant leader.

Yeas and Nays—A vote in which members usually respond "aye" or "no" (despite the official title of the vote) on a question when their names are called in alphabetical order. The Constitution requires the yeas and nays when a demand for it is supported by one-fifth of the members present, and it also requires an automatic yea-and-nay vote on overriding a veto. Senate precedents require the support of at least one-fifth of a quorum, a minimum of eleven members with the present membership of 100.

Congressional Information on the Internet

A huge array of congressional information is available for free at Internet sites operated by the federal government, colleges and universities and commercial firms. The sites offer the full text of bills introduced in the House and Senate, voting records, campaign finance information, transcripts of selected congressional hearings, investigative reports and much more.

THOMAS

The most important site for congressional information is THOMAS (*http://thomas.loc.gov*), which is named for Thomas Jefferson and operated by the Library of Congress. THOMAS' highlight is its databases containing the full text of all bills introduced in Congress since 1989, the full text of the *Congressional Record* since 1989 and the status and summary information for all bills introduced since 1973.

THOMAS also offers special links to bills that have received or are expected to receive floor action during the current week and newsworthy bills that are pending or that have recently been approved. Finally, THOMAS has selected committee reports, answers to frequently asked questions about accessing congressional information, publications titled *How Our Laws Are Made* and *Enactment of a Law* and links to lots of other congressional Web sites.

House of Representatives

The U.S. House of Representatives site (*http://www.house. gov*) offers the schedule of bills, resolutions and other legislative issues the House will consider in the current week. It also has updates about current proceedings on the House floor and a list of the next day's meeting of House committees. Other highlights include a database that helps users identify their representative, a directory of House members and committees, the House ethics manual, links to Web pages maintained by House members and committees, a calendar of congressional primary dates and candidate-filing deadlines for ballot access, the full text of all amendments to the Constitution that have been ratified and those that have been proposed but not ratified and lots of information about Washington, D.C., for visitors.

Another key House site is The Office of the Clerk On-line Information Center (*http://clerk.house.gov*), which has records of all roll-call votes taken since 1990. The votes are recorded by bill, so it is a lengthy process to compile a particular representative's voting record. The site also has lists of committee assignments, a telephone directory for members and committees, mailing label templates for members and committees, rules of the current Congress, election statistics from 1920 to the present, biographies of Speakers of the House, biographies of women who have served since 1917 and a virtual tour of the House Chamber.

One of the more interesting House sites is operated by the Subcommittee on Rules and Organization of the House Committee on Rules (*http://www.house.gov/rules/crs_reports. htm*). Its highlight is dozens of Congressional Research Service reports about the legislative process. Some of the available titles include *Legislative Research in Congressional Offices: A Primer, How to Follow Current Federal Legislation and Regulations; Investigative Oversight: An Introduction to the Law, Practice and Procedure of Congressional Inquiry;* and *Presidential Vetoes 1789 – Present: A Summary Overview.*

Senate

At least in the Internet world, the Senate is not as active as the House. Its main Web site (*http://www.senate.gov*) has records of all roll-call votes taken since 1989 (arranged by bill), brief descriptions of all bills and joint resolutions introduced in the Senate during the past week and a calendar of upcoming committee hearings. The site also provides the standing rules of the Senate, a directory of senators and their committee assignments, lists of nominations that the president has submitted to the Senate for approval, links to Web pages operated by senators and committees and a virtual tour of the Senate.

Information about the membership, jurisdiction and rules of each congressional committee is available at the U.S. Government Printing Office site (*http://www.access.gpo.gov/congress/ index.html*). It also has transcripts of selected congressional hearings, the full text of selected House and Senate reports and the House and Senate rules manuals.

General Reference

The Government Accountability Office, the investigative arm of Congress, operates a site (*http://www.gao.gov*) that provides the full text of its reports from 1975 to the present. The reports cover a wide range of topics: aviation safety, combating terrorism, counternarcotics efforts in Mexico, defense contracting, electronic warfare, food assistance programs, Gulf War illness, health insurance, illegal aliens, information technology, long-term care, mass transit, Medicare, military readiness, money laundering, national parks, nuclear waste, organ donation and student loan defaults, among others.

The GAO Daybook is an excellent current awareness tool. This electronic mailing list distributes a daily list of reports and testimony released by the GAO. Subscriptions are available by sending an e-mail message to *majordomo@www.gao.gov*, and in the message area typing "subscribe daybook" (without the quotation marks).

Current budget and economic projections are provided at the Congressional Budget Office Web site (*http://www.cbo.gov*). The site also has reports about the economic and budget outlook for the next decade, the president's budget proposals, federal civilian employment, Social Security privatization, tax reform, water use conflicts in the West, marriage and the federal income tax and the role of foreign aid in development, among other topics. Other highlights include monthly budget updates, historical budget data, cost estimates for bills reported by congressional committees and transcripts of congressional testimony by CBO officials.

Campaign Finance

Several Internet sites provide detailed campaign finance data for congressional elections. The official site is operated by the Federal Election Commission (*http://www.fec.gov*), which regulates political spending. The site's highlight is its database of campaign reports filed from May 1996 to the present by House and presidential candidates, political action committees and political party committees. Senate reports are not included because they are filed with the Secretary of the Senate. The reports in the FEC's database are scanned images of paper reports filed with the commission.

The FEC site also has summary financial data for House and Senate candidates in the current election cycle, abstracts of court decisions pertaining to federal election law from 1976 to 1997, a graph showing the number of political action committees in existence each year from 1974 to the present and a directory of national and state agencies that are responsible for releasing information about campaign financing, candidates on the ballot, election results, lobbying and other issues. Another useful feature is a collection of brochures about federal election law, public funding of presidential elections, the ban on contributions by foreign nationals, independent expenditures supporting or opposing a candidate for federal office, contribution limits, filing a complaint, researching public records at the FEC and other topics. Finally, the site provides the FEC's legislative recommendations, its annual report, a report about its first twenty years in existence, the FEC's monthly newsletter, several reports about voter registration, election results for the most recent presidential and congressional elections and campaign guides for corporations and labor organizations, congressional candidates and committees, political party committees and nonconnected committees.

The best online source for campaign finance data is Political Money Line (*http://www.tray.com*). The site's searchable databases provide extensive itemized information about receipts and expenditures by federal candidates and political action committees from 1980 to the present. The data, which are obtained from the FEC, are quite detailed. For example, for candidates contribu-

tions can be searched by Zip Code. The site also has lists of the top political action committees in various categories, lists of the top contributors from each state and much more.

Another interesting site is the American University Campaign Finance Web site (*http://www1.soc.american.edu/campfin/index.cfm*), which is operated by the American University School of Communication. It provides electronic files from the FEC that have been reformatted in .dbf format so they can be used in database programs such as Paradox, Access and FoxPro. The files contain data on PAC, committee and individual contributions to individual congressional candidates.

More campaign finance data is available from the Center for Responsive Politics (*http://www.opensecrets.org*), a public interest organization. The center provides a list of all "soft money" donations to political parties of $100,000 or more in the current election cycle and data about "leadership" political action committees associated with individual politicians. Other databases at the site provide information about travel expenses that House members received from private sources for attending meetings and other events, activities of registered federal lobbyists and activities of foreign agents who are registered in the United States.

Index